COUNTDOWN AND COUNT UP DEVOTIONAL CALENDAR YEAR 2019

A DAILY DEVOTIONAL TO HELP YOU:
- GROW IN GOD & GRACE DAILY
- CALL ON GOD TO CARRY YOU THROUGH THE YEAR
- COUNTING DOWN YOUR GOD-GIVEN DAYS
- COUNT UP YOUR GOD-GIVEN BLESSINGS

Pastor Zacch Olorunnipa, PhD.

VOLUME 1, Year 2019

Countdown and Count up Devotional Calendar Year 2019

Copyright © 2019 by Pastor Zacch Olorunnipa, PhD.

All rights reserved. No part of this book may be reproduced or transmitted in any form or by any means without written permission of the author.

Scriptures marked KJV are taken from the KING JAMES VERSION (KJV): KING JAMES VERSION, public domain.

Scriptures marked NAS are taken from the NEW AMERICAN STANDARD (NAS): Scripture taken from the NEW AMERICAN STANDARD BIBLE®, copyright© 1960, 1962, 1963, 1968, 1971, 1972, 1973, 1975, 1977, 1995 by The Lockman Foundation. Used by permission.

Scriptures marked NIV are taken from the NEW INTERNATIONAL VERSION (NIV): Scripture taken from THE HOLY BIBLE, NEW INTERNATIONAL VERSION ®. Copyright© 1973, 1978, 1984, 2011 by Biblica, Inc.™. Used by permission of Zondervan Scriptures marked ERV are taken from the HOLY BIBLE: EASY-TO-READ VERSION © 2001 by World Bible Translation Center, Inc. and used by permission.

GOD'S WORD is a copyrighted work of God's Word to the Nations. Quotations are used by permission. Copyright 1995 by God's Word to the Nations. All rights reserved.

The ESV Global Study Bible is based on the ESV Student Study Bible, copyright © 2011 Crossway, and on the ESV Study Bible, copyright © 2008 Crossway.

Scripture taken from The Message. Copyright Â© 1993, 1994, 1995, 1996, 2000, 2001, 2002. Used by permission of NavPress Publishing Group.

The Holy Bible, English Standard Version (ESV) is adapted from the Revised Standard Version of the Bible, copyright Division of Christian Education of the National Council of the Churches of Christ in the U.S.A. All rights reserved.

Scripture quotations marked (NLT) are taken from the Holy Bible, New Living Translation, copyright ©1996, 2004, 2015 by Tyndale House Foundation. Used by permission of Tyndale House Publishers, Inc., Carol Stream, Illinois 60188. All rights reserved.

Published by:
Eleviv Publishing Group
Houston, TX 77082
www.elevivpublishing.com

2019 Calendar

January 2019
S	M	T	W	T	F	S
		1	2	3	4	5
6	7	8	9	10	11	12
13	14	15	16	17	18	19
20	21	22	23	24	25	26
27	28	29	30	31		

February 2019
S	M	T	W	T	F	S
					1	2
3	4	5	6	7	8	9
10	11	12	13	14	15	16
17	18	19	20	21	22	23
24	25	26	27	28		

March 2019
S	M	T	W	T	F	S
					1	2
3	4	5	6	7	8	9
10	11	12	13	14	15	16
17	18	19	20	21	22	23
24	25	26	27	28	29	30
31						

April 2019
S	M	T	W	T	F	S
	1	2	3	4	5	6
7	8	9	10	11	12	13
14	15	16	17	18	19	20
21	22	23	24	25	26	27
28	29	30				

May 2019
S	M	T	W	T	F	S
			1	2	3	4
5	6	7	8	9	10	11
12	13	14	15	16	17	18
19	20	21	22	23	24	25
26	27	28	29	30	31	

June 2019
S	M	T	W	T	F	S
						1
2	3	4	5	6	7	8
9	10	11	12	13	14	15
16	17	18	19	20	21	22
23	24	25	26	27	28	29
30						

July 2019
S	M	T	W	T	F	S
	1	2	3	4	5	6
7	8	9	10	11	12	13
14	15	16	17	18	19	20
21	22	23	24	25	26	27
28	29	30	31			

August 2019
S	M	T	W	T	F	S
				1	2	3
4	5	6	7	8	9	10
11	12	13	14	15	16	17
18	19	20	21	22	23	24
25	26	27	28	29	30	31

September 2019
S	M	T	W	T	F	S
1	2	3	4	5	6	7
8	9	10	11	12	13	14
15	16	17	18	19	20	21
22	23	24	25	26	27	28
29	30					

October 2019
S	M	T	W	T	F	S
		1	2	3	4	5
6	7	8	9	10	11	12
13	14	15	16	17	18	19
20	21	22	23	24	25	26
27	28	29	30	31		

November 2019
S	M	T	W	T	F	S
					1	2
3	4	5	6	7	8	9
10	11	12	13	14	15	16
17	18	19	20	21	22	23
24	25	26	27	28	29	30

December 2019
S	M	T	W	T	F	S
1	2	3	4	5	6	7
8	9	10	11	12	13	14
15	16	17	18	19	20	21
22	23	24	25	26	27	28
29	30	31				

Foreword

I give all glory, honor and thanks to the Almighty God for making possible the publication of this maiden issue of the Countdown and Count up Daily Devotional (edition 2019). May you be richly blessed as you prayerfully use the devotional in Jesus name.

God wants us and enjoins us "to number our days, that we may apply our hearts unto wisdom"(Psalm 90:12). The Countdown and Count up Devotional is written to help us do exactly what this scripture says, using the platform of God's word which undergirds our existence and everything about us including our days and our activities. Jesus Christ is the power and wisdom of God (1 Cor. 1:24). The more we can apply our heart to love Him and do His will the more He will bless us and ensure all is well with us (Exo. 23:25). This devotional provides the opportunity to note, keep track and give thanks to God for His blessings that are loaded into our lives daily (Psalm 68:19; Ps.103:1-5).

The Bible tells us that, "To everything there is a season, and a time to every purpose under the heaven" (Eccl. 31:1). This scripture and several others, as well as the leading of the Holy Spirit enabled the author to prayerfully bring each day of the year under Biblical lens to find out what significant events, personalities, principles, prophesies, landmarks, miracles, blessings, warnings, counsels, injunctions etc. are there to glean that can provide worthy lessons to learn to help believers in Jesus Christ and others to achieve many purposes of life including the following: (1) Receiving salvation by faith in Jesus Christ (2) Strengthened in the faith and growing "- - in grace, and in the knowledge of our Lord and Saviour Jesus Christ --" (2 Pet. 3:18). (3) Adequately equipped and armed with wisdom and strategies that can help one anticipate and successfully manage issues that may occur each day. (4) Harnessing opportunities to be blessed and be a blessing anywhere any time. (5) etc. The devotional is definitely a work in progress and I pray that the Holy Spirit will continue to be our teacher, in Jesus mighty name. Amen.

Everything that has a beginning must definitely also have an end. As year 2019 begins on January 1, this devotional will help you not only to countdown the year, but also to count upward on God's daily innumerable blessings including power in God's words, prayers, miracles, breakthroughs, successes, fruitfulness, joy, peace, etc.

I am highly indebted to God for bringing this work into fruition. My beloved wife, Pastor (Mrs.) Florence Olorunnipa deserve commendation for her unflinching love, support, understanding and suggestions while I was working on this project. I also acknowledge the support and encouragement of my children (Biological and spiritual) and many other persons too many to mention names. I have deep appreciation for insights I received from reading various Bible commentaries by Scholars like Adam Clarke, John Calvin, John Gill, John Trapp, Matthew Henry, Dr. Jeremiah, etc. I am grateful to my publisher, Mrs. Vivian Okojie, for doing an excellent job of exercising patience and professionalism in producing a quality product. For all my helpers and supporters, I pray your rewards from God will count upwards astronomically, in Jesus mighty name.

Pastor Zacch I. Olorunnipa,
Zacch51@yahoo.com

Prayer for Salvation (Romans 10:13)

Lord Jesus, thank You for dying for sinners like me. Today, I confess and repent of my sins and plead for Your mercy to forgive me. I surrender/rededicate my life to You, please be my Lord and Savior forever

Tuesday January 1, 2019
Topic: BRIGHT AND JOYFUL BEGINNING

Scripture: "*And it came to pass in the six hundredth and first year, in the first month, the first day of the month, the waters were dried up from off the earth: and Noah removed the covering of the ark, and looked, and, behold, the face of the ground was dry" (Genesis 8:13).*

Praise the Lord and welcome to the New Year's Day! Today is January 1st and is day #1 in year 2019. The number of days remaining to end this year is 364. You will end this year alive, safe and sound with God in Jesus name.

Happy New Year! The countdown of days as well as the count up of God's blessings for 2019 has begun today. Given that God loads us with benefits every day, (Ps. 68:19) it is obvious that our blessings will always count upward each day though no attempt will be made to assign any numerical figure to these blessings simply because they are too many to number. Just imagine the number of breaths you have taken (through the blessings of God) since year 2019 began! The song writer says "Count your blessings, name them one by one; it will surprise you what the LORD has done". Plenty of pleasant surprises shall manifest for you this year, IJN.

As indicated in today's opening scripture above, it was on the first day of the first month (New Year Day) that Noah looked and saw that the flood waters were dried up and the face of the ground was dry. In other words, it was the first time in about 10 months, that Noah saw bright and dried ground, no longer soaked and saggy capable of sinking him. I am sure Noah was full of joy, hope and expectation that very soon he would be able to walk on dry ground. God is telling us to look and begin to see a bright and joyful year 2019 free of messy and muddy circumstances. With your spiritual eyes backed. By faith and prayer look and start seeing glory, honor, favor, miracles, freedom from sins and sickness, peace, prosperity, open heaven, and many other blessings in year 2019. Note, you can't possess what you can't see. (spiritually and/or physically). Instead of sinking, you will soar higher this year, in Jesus mighty name.

Prayer: Father, the Alpha and Omega, as I start this year with brightness and joy, give me eyes to see all my blessings and the grace to shine and rejoice throughout the year in Jesus name.

Wednesday January 2, 2019
Topic: FAITHFUL FRIEND

Scripture: "And it came to pass on the morrow, which was the second day of the month, that David's place was empty: and Saul said unto Jonathan his son, Wherefore cometh not the son of Jesse to meat, neither yesterday, nor to day" (1 Sam. 20:27).

Praise the Lord. Today is January 2nd and is day #2 in year 2019. The number of days remaining to end this year is 363. Your enemy's trap for you shall fail today and forever in Jesus name.

One of the daily benefits of God to His followers is deliverance from the weapons formed against them by the enemy (Isa. 54:17; 45:24). After David was anointed King of Israel to replace Saul who has lost his position due to disobedience, Saul became a staunch enemy of David. Saul was looking for every opportunity to kill David. By divine arrangement, Jonathan (son of Saul) and David became intimate and faithful covenant friends (1 Sam. 20:17).

David received divine revelation that Saul has planned to kill him on a new moon day on the 2nd of the month at a dinner table. David shared this revelation with Jonathan his intimate friend (1 Sam. 20:17). The 2 friends agreed that David would be in hiding and be absent from the dinner appointment with Saul. On the 'death dinner appointment day', Saul found David's place empty on the table. He realized Jonathan had approved an absentee excuse for David. Saul became violently furious and attempted to kill Jonathan for conspiring to save the life of David. Jonathan escaped the attack angrily and tried to dissuade his father from killing his intimate and innocent friend, David.

David and Jonathan were loyal and faithful friends of each other to the extent Jonathan secretly defended David from been killed by Saul his father. The Bible says "- - there is a friend that sticketh closer than a brother" (Pro. 18:24). That friend is Jesus Christ. He is the most faithful friend any one can have. If you, by faith, believe in Him and accept Him as your Lord and Savior, He can do much more than defend and protect you physically; He can also defend you spiritually and save you. empowering you to live holy, make you fruitful, supply all your needs according to his riches in glory by Christ Jesus, etc. *Prayer: Father, as I abide in You throughout this year, send me destiny helpers and relocate me from any place harboring a death trap prepared for me, IJN.*

Thursday January 3, 2019
Topic: BRINGING FORTH

Scripture: "And God said, Let the earth bring forth grass, the herb yielding seed, and the fruit tree yielding fruit after his kind, whose seed is in itself, upon the earth: and it was so. And the earth brought forth grass, and herb yielding seed after his kind- - - And the evening and the morning were the third day" (Gen 1: 11-13).

Praise the Lord. Today is January 3rd and is day #3 in year 2019. The number of days remaining to end this year is 362. May good things come forth from you today and forever in Jesus name.

God is a God of addition and multiplication as reflected in His record of creation in Genesis Chapter one. Initially, the heaven and earth God created was empty and full of darkness (Gen. 1:1). Then He began to add good stuffs like light, Day, Night, etc. It was not until the third day that He added other things that were empowered to reproduce themselves. For example, on the 3rd day he commanded the earth to bring forth grass, herb and fruit tree, each with seed capable of reproducing itself. God even declared. "While the earth remained, seedtime and harvest, - - shall not cease" (Gen. 8:22). When later on in the sixth day God created man in His own image (male and female) he blessed them with the "bring forth" decree, saying, "- -Be fruitful, and multiply, and replenish the earth, and subdue it: and have dominion- -"(Gen 1:28).

In this new year we must think of what we can "bring forth" to enhance God's kingdom agenda and make our world a better place. We must not just be consumers only, we must exercise God-endowed creative power to add good things (physical, biological and spiritual) to our world. Why is there so much poverty and hunger in the world today? What are we doing with the seed of creativity, love, mercy, business ideas, witnessing, sharing, etc. in us? Plant these seeds and bring forth to make the world a better place. That is one way you can let your blessings count upwards. Remember apostle Paul said "I have planted, Apollos watered; but God gave the increase" (1 Cor. 3:6). Your season of increase has come, in Jesus mighty name.

Prayer: Father, give me ideas that will help me bring forth, so as to add value to my life, my family and to my generation in Jesus mighty name.

Friday January 4, 2019
Topic: BE A LIGHT TO THE WORLD

Scripture: "And God made two great lights; the greater light to rule the day, and the lesser light to rule the night: he made the stars also. And the evening and the morning were the fourth day" (Gen 1:16,19)"

Praise the Lord. Today is January 4th and is day #4 in year 2019. The number of days remaining to end this year is 361. By God's grace, you will shine brighter this year and you shall see the end of 2019 and beyond, IJN.

Considering God's work of creation, we can count up 3 main things (sun, moon, and stars) that were added to the universe on the fourth day. The primary function common to these 3 entities is to provide light. Jesus Christ declares "As long as I am in the world, I am the light of the world" (Jn 9:6). Jesus also describes those who believe in Him as, "- - the light of the world--" (Jn. 5:14). Some of the functions of light include provision of visibility, reflection, and energy for food production through photosynthesis. If you are in Christ you are very important in that you have many value-adding attributes in you. In particular, you are the light to your environment and you are expected to reflect Christly virtues to attract people into the kingdom of God.

If you are not born again, (that is, you have not given your life to Jesus Christ as your Lord and Savior) you are groping in darkness, awaiting God's judgment. Without Christ you cannot be the light of the world because you cannot give what you don't have. Accept Jesus Christ today and start enjoying being the light of the world. As the light you are to illuminate your community (home, job, ministry, etc.) with love, kindness, positive activities etc. Let your light dispel the darkness in unbelievers often manifesting in unbecoming behaviors such as stealing, drug addiction, violence, disobedience, pride, lusts, etc. Obey the Biblical injunction that says "Be ye not unequally yoked together with unbelievers: for what fellowship hath righteousness with unrighteousness? and what communion hath light with darkness?' (2 Cor. 6:14) You can make a difference, go for it.

Prayer: Father as I abide in Christ, let me arise and shine, in Jesus mighty name.

Saturday January 5, 2019
Topic: DIVINE INCREASE

Scripture: "Though thy beginning was small, yet thy latter end should greatly increase."(Job 8:7)

Praise the Lord. Today is January 5th and is day #5 in year 2019. The number of days remaining to end this year is 360. By God's grace, your life shall be better this year and you shall see the end of 2019 and beyond, IJN.

God is a methodological and progressive worker. During the creation of the world God was gradually adding specific things each day to what He had already created. On the 5th day He added birds, fishes and other moving creatures. He blessed them and commanded them to be fruitful and multiply (Gen. 1: 20-23). As this year progresses you too must plan and pray to increase in various beneficial dimensions.

As long as you are alive, you have the seed of increase in you. This seed may be in form of God's word which is quick and powerful (Heb. 4:12). Sharing the word of God with others can bring increase and multiplication as it did for the disciples at the beginning of the New Testament Church: "And the word of God increased; and the number of the disciples multiplied in Jerusalem greatly; and a great company of the priests were obedient to the faith" (Acts 6:7). Seed may also be in the form of what you give to God, His servants and others for the word of God declares, "There is that scattereth, and yet increaseth- -" (Pro. 11:24). The first time the words "blessed", "fruitful" and "multiply" are used in the Bible is on the 5th day of creation (Gen 1:22). As you have seen this 5th day of year 2019, I decree and declare that throughout this year, you shall be blessed, you shall be fruitful and you shall multiply, and you shall increase positively by the day, in the mighty name of Jesus

Action: Name 5 blessings God has bestowed on you and your family this year. Give thanks to God for each one of these blessings.

Prayer: Father, shower me with supernatural increases in favor, mercy, divine revelation, wisdom, soul winning, finances, etc. in Jesus name.

Sunday January 6, 2019
Topic: MADE IN GOD'S IMAGE

Scripture: "So God created man in his own image, in the image of God created he him; male and female created he them. 31 And God saw everything that he had made, and, behold, it was very good. And the evening and the morning were the sixth day". (Gen.1: 27, 31).

Praise the Lord. Today is January 6th and is day #6 in year 2019. The number of days remaining to end this year is 359. Surely, goodness and mercy shall follow you forever, and you shall see the end of 2019 and beyond, IJN.

The number 6 in the Bible symbolizes man, mainly because man was created on the 6th day. We should be extremely thankful to God and proud of the unique way God created us: He made us in His own image, He made us in the company of His Son and the Holy Spirit (notice "Let us make - -" in Gen 1:26), He breathed the breath of life in us (Gen 2:7).

God created man to be uniquely superior to any other creature. In addition to the factors aforementioned about man's creation above, the following 6 additional unique attributes reflected in Genesis chapter one, verse twenty-eight are noteworthy. God, (1) blessed man, (2) commanded man to be fruitful, and (3) to multiply, and (4) to replenish the earth, and (5) to subdue the earth, and (6) to have dominion. Attributes 5 and 6 are exclusive to man.

Are you conscious and appreciative of who you are, how you are made and what you are made to be? The Bible says you are fearfully and wonderfully made (Ps. 139:14), you are made a little lower than angels and crowned with glory and honor (Ps. 8:4-6), you are a god and the child of the most High God (Ps. 82:6). Additionally, you are created to praise God and give Him pleasure (Ps.150:6, 1 Pet 2:9, Rev. 4:11), you "- - are a chosen generation, a royal priesthood, an holy nation, a peculiar people- -" (1 Pet 2:9). In essence you are very important to God. That is why He had invested in you considerably and He wants to be your God and you to belong to Him (Exo. 6:7). If you fail to give your life to Jesus Christ, you will fail to be everything God made you to be. *Prayer: Father, thank You for making me in Your own image, let me remain Yours's, and to be very good, free from sins, sickness, sorrow and satanic activities all the days of my life, IJN.*

Monday January 7, 2019
Topic: SACREDNESS OF THE NUMBER SEVEN

Scripture: "And God blessed the seventh day and sanctified it: because that in it he had rested from all his work which God created and made" (Gen 2:3).

Praise the Lord. Today is January 7th and is day #7 in year 2019. The number of days remaining to end this year is 358. Each of the remaining days of this year shall be perfected for you in Jesus name.

Welcome to a unique day, the 7th day. The number 7 is the number of completeness and perfection, physical and spiritual. In terms of spiritual perspective, the Bible talks about the seven Spirits of God (Rev. 3:1, 4:5, and 5:6). Furthermore, God rested, blessed and sanctified the 7th day after completing the creation of heaven and earth with spoken word (Gen 2: 1-3). The physical signification of completeness of the number 7 is also evident in the cleansing of Naaman's leprosy which was completed only after he had bathed 7 times in River Jordan as commanded by prophet Elisha (2 Kings 5:10). Another example in this regard is the collapse of the wall of Jericho after Joshua and the Israelites, at God's command, marched round Jericho for seven days. Also, on the seventh day, seven circuits were made round the walls by seven priests who blew seven trumpets outside the city walls (Joshua 6:3–4). Whatever projects and other activities you embark upon this year shall be completed successfully at record time in the name of Jesus.

The seven-day week observed around the world today is largely modelled after the fact that God rested on the seventh day. Appropriate resting is crucial for healthy living and effectiveness. Believers must take a cue from God and respond positively to His invitation that says "Come unto me, all ye that labour and are heavy laden, and I will give you rest" (Mt. 28:11).

Are you overwhelmed and/or burdened with the pressure of work, marital and family demands, debts, delays, disappointments, etc.? Take time out to commune regularly with God in prayer for relief and rest (2 Sam 7:1, 1Kgs 5:4). Make room for rest, relaxation and appropriate exercise. To every storm of unrest in your life I decree "Peace be still" in the mighty name of Jesus.

Prayer: Father, please terminate all unrest in my life; keep me in perfect peace and let my mind be stayed on You, IJN.

Tuesday January 8, 2019
Topic: CIRCUMCISION AND NAMING OF JESUS CHRIST

Scripture: "And when eight days were accomplished for the circumcising of the child, his name was called Jesus, which was so named of the angel before he was conceived in the womb" (Lk 2:21).

Praise the Lord. Today is January 8th and is day #8 in year 2019. The number of days remaining to end this year is 357. By God's grace, you shall see the end of 2019 and beyond, IJN.

The number 8 is important for various reasons. Both John the Baptist and Jesus Christ were circumcised and officially given their names independently on the 8th day of their births (Luke 1:59 & 2:21). Circumcision (for male) is the removal of the foreskin from the human penis. God gave Abraham the mandate to circumcise every male child on the 8th day as a token of an everlasting covenant He made with Abraham. The all-encompassing covenant (see Gen 17) also came with many promises of blessings for Abraham and his descendants (exceeding multiplication, becoming father of many nations and possessing the land wherein they sojourned). If you are born again you are a descendent of Abraham and your blessings should count upward, in the mighty name of Jesus.

There are several lessons to learn from the circumcision and naming of Jesus Christ on the 8th day. First, it demonstrates His humanity and humility and confirms His claim that He has not come to destroy the law, or the prophets but to fulfil them (Matt 15: 17-18). Secondly, the blood shed during circumcision of Jesus marked the beginning of his redemption of sinners (1 John 1:7). Thirdly, it is shows that it is Biblical to conduct "naming ceremony" on the 8th day of birth for a newly born baby. Prior to the birth of Jesus his name was given by God and revealed to the parents. However, it was during his circumcision on the 8th day that he was officially named Jesus. The Hebrew name of Jesus is Joshua, pronounced Yeshua, which means 'The Lord saves' or simply 'Saviour'. Subsequently, Jesus had an added name 'Christ', which is a Greek translation of the Hebrew word, 'Mashiakh', which means 'Anointed One' or 'Messiah'.

Prayer: Father thank You for the gift Jesus Christ and the power that His name carries

Wednesday January 9, 2019
Topic: GIVING GRATITUDE TO GOD

Scripture: "And Jesus answering said, Were there not ten cleansed? but where are the nine?" (Lk 17:17).

Praise the Lord. Today is January 9th and is day #9 in year 2019. The number of days remaining to end this year is 356. By God's grace, you shall be sickness free this year and you shall see the end of 2019 and beyond, IJN.

Giving gratitude to God is the gateway to getting more of His daily blessings to us. The Bible is replete with commands to give thanks to God (Ps.106:1; 107: 1; 118:1, 29; 1 Chron. 16:34; 1 Thes.5:18, etc.). Dietrich Bonhoeffer said, "It is only with gratitude that life becomes rich!". The Lord will give you the grace to give more gratitude so that you can be enriched the more in Jesus name. Out of 10 lepers healed by Jesus, the only one that returned to give thanks is the only one that got his life enriched in terms of permanent and wholesome healing. The remaining 9 who failed to return to give thanks also failed to maximize their blessing (Lk 17: 1-20). Whatever you do that stands out can make you outstanding.

Perhaps the most outstanding miracles of Jesus Christ (raising Lazarus back to life after he was 4 days dead in the grave), was predicated on intensive thanksgiving and homage from Jesus to His father God. At Lazarus grave, Jesus lifted up his eyes and said "--Father, I thank thee that thou hast heard me. And I knew that thou hearest me always- -" (Jn 11: 41-42). Thereafter, "- -he cried with a loud voice, Lazarus, come forth" (v. 43). Miraculously, Lazarus obeyed the command and came forth and Jesus said, "- -, Loose him, and let him go" (v. 44). On this 9th day, and henceforth keep your life's tanks full of thanksgiving so that you can be enriched the more. Give thanks to God for everything (good or bad) for only God can make all things work together for your goodness and your peace (Rm. 8:28, Phil 4: 6-7). Have a blessed day.

Prayer: Father, let ceaseless thanksgiving transform my life for Your pleasure, IJN.

Thursday January 10, 2019
Topic: YOU SHALL BE FREE INDEED

Scripture: "Speak ye unto all the congregation of Israel, saying, In the tenth day of this month they shall take to them every man a lamb, according to the house of their fathers, a lamb for an house:" (Exodus 12:3).

Praise the Lord. Today is January 10th and is day #10 in year 2019. The number of days remaining to end this year is 355. By God's grace, you shall see the end of 2019 and beyond, IJN

As part of the preparation for their freedom from bondage, God told the Israelites to select an unblemished lamb in each house on the 10th day of the month. The blood of the lamb without blemish (typifying Jesus Christ), was to be used to mark the door post of the houses of the Israelites. The houses of the Egyptians were not marked in this way. At night on the eve of the exodus of the Israelites from Egypt, God's destroyer went through the houses to strike down the firstborn of the Egyptians in houses without the blood mark. Wherever the destroyer saw the blood mark, he passed over to spare the Israeli firstborn.

It was this last plague of killing all Egyptian firstborn male child that forced Pharaoh to let the Israelites go (Exo. 12: 1-36). Pharaoh was under so much divine pressure to release the people of God that he virtually came to them on bended knees saying "-- go, serve the Lord, as ye have said. Also take your flocks and your herds, as ye have said, and be gone; and bless me also" (Exo. 12: 31-32). God gave the Israelites favor in the sight of the Egyptians and they gave the Israelites whatever they asked for. As they were departing the Israelites "stripped the Egyptians of their wealth" (Exo. 12:36b, NLT). Henceforth, you shall be totally free from anything that has held you bound and you shall enjoy divine restoration, IJN.

Failure to confess and repent of your sins is tantamount to being in bondage of Satan. The blood of Jesus that cleanses all sins, (1 John 1:7) can set you free today if you will surrender your life to Him. It does not matter how weighty your sins can be or how long you have been sinning. The God that forgave the robber on the cross can forgive you if you cry to him for mercy.

Prayer: *Father as Your child, cover me with the blood of Jesus and let sin and death pass over me, IJN. Have a blessed day.*

Friday January 11, 2019
Topic: BLESSING OR BANE?

Scripture: "Blessed is the man that walketh not in the counsel of the ungodly, nor standeth in the way of sinners, nor sitteth in the seat of the scornful." (Psalm 1:1).

Praise the Lord. Today is January 11th and is day #11 in year 2019. The number of days remaining to end this year is 354. By God's grace, you shall be blessed and you shall see the end of 2019 and beyond, IJN

Blessing can be defined as a special favor, mercy or benefit while bane is anything that ruins or spoils. Bane can also simply mean death, destruction or ruin. Suppose you are asked to choose between blessing and bane, which one will you choose? I suppose blessing will be the choice of most people. Blessing produces happiness and inward joy while bane produces misery and destruction. You shall be blessed, IJN.

The opening scripture today provides us with the conditions or requirements that must be met in order to be blessed. These are (a) not to walk in the counsel of the ungodly, (b) not to stand in the way of sinners and (c) not to sit in the seat of the scornful. Essentially, these conditions are the basic elements of salvation based on faith in Jesus Christ. Any one genuinely born again will not pitch his/her camp with the one who is without God since such one automatically is a sinner and a scorner or mocker of God.

The entire Psalm chapter 1 with its 6 verses compare the godly and the ungodly. The godly is likened to a tree planted by the rivers of water. Such a tree, supplied with adequate nutrients will be fruitful, fresh and flourishing all the time (Ps. 1:2-3). Such will be the life of anyone who has accepted Jesus Christ as Lord and Savior. Such a person is nourished regularly by delighting and meditating in God's word. The ungodly are the unbelievers whose lot will be bane instead of blessing. Therefore, the ungodly will be fruitless, dry and perishing as they are blown away by wind or burnt off by fire. That will not be your lot, IJN. To attract blessings instead of bane, accept Jesus Christ as your Lord.

Prayer: Father, separate me from any ungodly thing that can rob me of my blessings, IJN.

Saturday January 12, 2019
Topic: I SHALL FINISH WELL

Scripture: "Then we departed from the river of Ahava on the twelfth day of the first month, to go unto Jerusalem: and the hand of our God was upon us, and he delivered us from the hand of the enemy, and of such as lay in wait by the way" (Ezra 8:31).

Praise the Lord. Today is January 12th and is day #12 in year 2019. The number of days remaining to end this year is 353. By God's grace, the hand of God shall be upon you throughout this year and you shall see the end of 2019 and beyond, IJN

According to the opening scripture above, it was on a day like today (12th day of the first month) that Prophet Ezra and a group of Israeli exiles set out on a journey from the river of Ahava to go to Jerusalem. Their mission was to deliver precious and costly gifts (gold, silver, etc.) to the Temple in Jerusalem (Ezra 8). Being conscious of the precarious and dangerous nature of their journey amidst enemies, bandits, natural hazards, etc., Prophet Ezra declared a period of prayer and fasting for their journey. God was entreated and His hand was upon the travelers and they made it safely to Jerusalem to accomplish their mission.

Life is a conglomeration of many journeys. Apart from physical journey of moving from one geographical location to another there are other types of journeys such as that of faith, love, academics, etc.). Whatever journey you have embarked / will embark on this year 2019, it shall end up successfully and safely, IJN. In all your journeys throughout this year, the powerful hand of God shall be upon you. God will give you treasures and riches embedded in this year. Any enemy waiting along your path to kill you shall die in your place, IJN. By God's grace, you will reach all your targeted "Jerusalem" this year safely, IJN. You must pray seriously before embarking on any journey this year.

Prayer: Father, let Your hand of help be upon me to ensure I succeed profitably in anything I embark on doing this year IJN.

Sunday January 13, 2019
Topic: REVERSING THE IRRIVERSIBLE

Scripture: "On the thirteenth day of the month Adar; and on the fourteenth day of the same rested they and made it a day of feasting and gladness" (Esther 9:2).

Praise the Lord. Today is January 13th and is day #13 in year 2019. The number of days remaining to end this year is 352. By God's grace, you shall celebrate throughout this year and you shall see the end of 2019 and beyond, IJN.

We serve a God who can reverse the irreversible. Due to the evil plot of Haman, 13th day of a particular month was to be the day of execution and extermination of Mordecai, Esther and all other Jews who were captives in Persia under king Ahasuerus (Est. 3:13). The king had signed this death decree which under the Persian and Medes' law was ordinarily irreversible. However, after 3 days of praying and fasting, the divine intervention and favor of God made it possible for Esther (who has become the Queen instead of Vasti) to persuade king Ahasuerus to reverse the death decree (Est. 8: 3-17). Consequently, instead of perishing on the 13th of the month the Jews celebrated with pomp and pageantry and prevailed over their enemies (Est. 8:17; 9:1-6).

God has promised that "No weapon that is formed against thee shall prosper ---" (Isaiah 54:17). Every evil plan against you in this year and henceforth shall be overturned, IJN. As it happened for Joseph (Gen 50:20) evil agenda of people for you shall be turned by God to be an advantage for you, IJN. Why don't you pause and give thanks to God for the numerous ways He had turned evil plans against you to good, both the ones you know and those you don't know.

Prayer: Father, hang and hammer every Haman after my life and cancel every plan to kill me and any member of my family this year, IJN.

Monday January 14, 2019
Topic: PROBLEMS SHALL PASS ME OVER

Scripture: "And in the fourteenth day of the first month is the Passover of the Lord." (Number 28:16).

Praise the Lord. Today is January 14th and is day #14 in year 2019. The number of days remaining to end this year is 351. By God's grace, evil will passover you this year and you shall see the end of 2019 and beyond, IJN

The Passover is one of the annual Israelites feasts known as the "Feasts of the LORD" (Lev. 23). The Passover is celebrated annually on the 14th day of the first month to commemorate the liberation of the Israelites by God from slavery in Egypt and their freedom as a nation (Ex. 12:14). During His earthly ministry, Jesus Christ observed the Passover regularly. In fact, it was during one of the Passover feasts that He had the last meal with his disciples (called the Last Super). It was during the Last Super that Jesus Christ was betrayed, arrested and crucified (Luke 22 & 23). Today, Christians commemorate the Last Super and the events surrounding it by partaking in a meal known as "Holy Communion" which Jesus Christ commanded His followers to do in remembrance of Him (1 Cor. 11: 23 -34).

The Holy Communion is a miracle meal that reminds us of many things including release of the Israelites form slavery, salvation and freedom from sins and sickness, etc. Of particular interest is that the Passover points to the fact that riches and lost glories can be restored to the believer. All the riches and treasures lost by the Israelites in 430 years were recovered in a day because God gave them favor before the Egyptians (Ex. 12: 35-36). Anywhere you and/or your blessings have been held up, I command an immediate release and restoration now, IJN. Consider making a vow in this regard; you will testify to God's glory.

Prayer: Father, as I remember The Lord's Passover, liberate me from all problems and let me recover everything I have ever lost (blessings, riches, honors, opportunities, etc.), IJN.

Tuesday January 15, 2019
Topic: THANKSGIVING IN FEAST OF TABERNACLES

Scripture: "Speak unto the children of Israel, saying, The fifteenth day of this seventh month shall be the feast of tabernacles for seven days unto the Lord" (Leviticus 23:34).

Praise the Lord. Today is January 15th and is day #15 in year 2019. The number of days remaining to end this year is 350. By God's grace, your place of habitation shall be safe throughout this year and you shall see the end of 2019 and beyond, IJN.

The Feast of Tabernacles (called variously as 'Sukkot', 'Feast of Booths', or 'Feast of the Ingathering') takes place on the 15th of the Hebrew month Tishrei (the 7th month on the Hebrew Calendar). It was a time of joyous celebration as the Israelites celebrated: (a) God's continued provision for them in the current harvest (see Exo 34:22) and (b) the remembrance of God's provisions and protection during the 40 years in the wilderness when they dwelled majorly in booths (Leviticus 23: 42-43).

In remembrance of all God's blessings to us, it is pertinent to give thanks to Him every day and also pause to celebrate from time to time. God is called the "EL Shaddai" meaning the Almighty, All-Sufficient One who provides and protects (Gen 17:1). He is called Jehovah-jireh meaning the great provider (Gen 17:1; 22:14). He has promised to supply all your need (Phil 4:19). On this 15th day of the month, remember the feast of the Tabernacles and count your blessings, name them one by one. You will be surprised what the LORD has done already in the new year 2019! Let us cultivate the attitude to constantly thank God, praise Him, worship Him and serve Him. He will definitely bless us and satisfy us with the goodness of His house (Ps. 23:6; 65:4; 67: 5-7).

Prayer: Father, thank You for providing all my needs, I shall never lack in Jesus name.

Wednesday January 16, 2019
Topic: REFORMING TO RESTORE

Scripture: "Now they began on the first day of the first month to sanctify- -- - - so they sanctified the house of the lord in eight days; and in the sixteenth day of the first month they made an end" (2 Chronicles 29:17).

Praise the Lord. Today is January 16th and is day #16 in year 2019. The number of days remaining to end this year is 349. By God's grace, you shall see the end of 2019 and beyond, IJN.

Immediately Hezekiah became king of the nation of Judah the Bible says, "And he did that which was right in the sight of the Lord, according to all that David his father had done" (2 Chron. 29:2). He began a reform process that involved cleaning and repairing the house of God that had been abandoned for a long time. He also restored people's attention to the God of Israel that they had forsaken. He gathered all the priests together and ordered them to sanctify themselves and the Temple. They did, and the work was finished in the 16th day of the month as indicated in today's opening scripture.

As you proceed with this year 2019 think of what reforms are needed to restore and/or improve your relationship with God, relationships in your family, in the church of God to which you belong, in your community, in your nation, etc.? Let God use you in building His Church, build people's lives for better, build the nation. Whatever project you begin this season shall not be aborted, it shall be finished successfully, IJN.

Prayer: Father let everything evil come to an end in my life and give me the grace to do what is right in Your sight, IJN. Have a blessed day.

Thursday January 17, 2019
Topic: ARK'S ARRIVAL AT MOUNT ARARAT

Scripture: "And the ark rested in the seventh month, on the seventeenth day of the month, upon the mountains of Ararat." (Gen 8:4).

Praise the Lord. Today is January 17th and is day #17 in year 2019. The number of days remaining to end this year is 348. By God's grace, you will not have any reason to run helter-skelter this year and you shall see the end of 2019 and beyond, IJN.

As indicated in today's opening scripture above, it was on the 17th day of the month that the Noah's Ark came to a rest on the mountain of Ararat after 150 days of roaming about on the flood. Inside the Ark were Noah and his family, the only family that survived the flood that destroyed the rest of the world! Noah and his family escaped destruction by flood primarily because of God's grace (Gen 6:8). Of course, the Bible also noted that God invited Noah and his house to come into the ark saying, "-- for thee have I seen righteous before me in this generation" (Gen 7:1). By His righteousness you and your household shall be preserved from all disasters, IJN.

The Ark symbolizes Jesus Christ. Those who come to Jesus, repenting of their sins and asking for forgiveness will be made righteous and admitted into His Ark of salvation by grace (Eph. 2:8). If you have not, do so today and find rest in the LORD (Mt. 11:28). What aspect of your life has been "roaming" and can't settle? conflicts in marriage? financial disarray? inability to find or keep a job? afflictions from sickness? etc. Come and cry to Jesus, to settle and put all matters concerning you to rest, IJN.

Prayer: Father thank You for saving my soul, please let me find permanent rest in You, IJN.

Friday January 18, 2019

Topic: BREAKING BOND OF BONDAGE

Scripture: "And ought not this woman, being a daughter of Abraham, whom Satan hath bound, lo, these eighteen years, be loosed from this bond on the Sabbath day?" (Lk. 13:18).

Praise the Lord. Today is January 18th and is day #18 in year 2019. The number of days remaining to end this year is 347. By God's grace, you shall no longer be held bound in any way by Satan, and you shall see the end of 2019 and beyond safely, IJN.

The number 18 in the Bible is symbolic of bondage (spiritual and physical). Bondage is anything exercising suppressive power or control over somebody. An example of spiritual bondage is the woman referred to in today's opening scripture above. For 18 years, she was bound by Satan via spirit of infirmity. She was kept perpetually bowed down, unable to stand up until Jesus saw her in the synagogue on a Sabbath and set her loose (Lk. 13:10-13). Example of physical bondage is the oppression of the Israelites by several nations including Moab and the Philistines who oppressed the Israelites for 18 years (Judges 3:12, 14; 10:7-8).

Through Satanic influences today, many people are under the bondage of sickness, bareness, joblessness, untimely death, business failure, curses, etc. Anyone who has not accepted Jesus Christ as his/her Lord and savior is perpetually under the bondage of sin and Satan. Give your life to Jesus Christ today and be free indeed (John 8:6). In Jesus name I break any form of bondage imposed on you, IJN.

Prayer: Father, set me loose completely and permanently from physical and spiritual bondage, IJN. Have a blessed day.

Saturday January 19, 2019
Topic: SAVED BY GRACE AND MERCY

Scripture: "Behold now, thy servant hath found grace in thy sight, and thou hast magnified thy mercy, which thou hast shewed unto me in saving my life; and I cannot escape to the mountain, lest some evil take me, and I die" (Gen 19:19).

Praise the Lord. Today is January 19th and is day #19 in year 2019. The number of days remaining to end this year is 346. By God's grace, you shall live and not die this year, and you shall see the end of 2019 and beyond, IJN.

On this 19th day let us be reminded that grace and mercy are two of the blessings of God that are added to the life of the believer every day. In other word, you are counting upwards on the benefits of mercy and grace every day. (Ps. 68:19). Mercy and grace are two terms that have similar meanings but are not the same. What then is the difference? Someone put it this way: "Mercy is God not punishing us as our sins deserve, and grace is God blessing us despite the fact that we do not deserve it, Mercy is deliverance from judgment (e.g. forgiveness instead of penalty of death for our sins). Grace is extending kindness (e.g. salvation) to the unworthy.

Aren't you glad your salvation is by grace! (Eph. 2:8). In today's opening scripture, Lot said he was saved from the destruction of Sodom and Gomorrah only because of the grace and mercy of God (Gen 19:19). Lot and his household were not only saved by grace from the destruction of Sodom, Lot was, because of grace, able to negotiate with God to escape to the nearby city of Zoar instead of escaping to the more distant mountains initially intended by God (Gen. 19: 20-22). I pray that God's grace in your life will position you for favorable and successful negotiations of your wishes with Him in the mighty name of Jesus. Given that "- -safety is of the Lord" (Pro. 21:31), I decree that none of the calamities associated with this year 2019 will come near you, in Jesus mighty name.

Prayer: Father, Let the Blood of Jesus, Grace and Mercy cover me and my entire household to protect us against evil occurrences this year and forever more, IJN.

Sunday January 20, 2019
Topic: SAVED BY GRACE AND MERCY

Scripture: "And it came to pass on the twentieth day- - -- -that the cloud was taken up from off the tabernacle of the testimony. And the children of Israel took their journeys out of the wilderness of Sinai; and the cloud rested in the wilderness of Paran" (Num 10:11-12).

Praise the Lord. Today is January 20th and is day #20 in year 2019. The number of days remaining to end this year is 345. By God's grace, all your journeys this year shall be safe, and you shall see the end of 2019 and beyond, IJN.

After about a year of departing from Egypt on their way to the promised land, the Israelites arrived and settled on Mt Sinai. Mt. Sinai occupies an important place in human history, as well as in the history of God's people. Most significantly, it was the place where God appeared in person to Moses and gave him the law and the instruction for constructing the Tabernacle (Ex. 19-31). As they were getting too comfortable to continue their journey God told the Israelites they have dwelt long enough on the mountain and it was time to move forward (Dt. 1:6).

Therefore, on the 20th day of a month, the cloud was taken off the tabernacle of the testimony signifying it was time to move on. Lessons: As we journey through our lives in general, and through year 2019 in particular, it's important that, (a) we depend on God and must not forsake Him (Ps. 32:8, Pro 3: 5-6; Heb. 12:2), (b) we set measurable goals and targets for ourselves in terms of what to accomplish during the year (Hab. 2: 2-3; Ps. 37:4), and (c) we don't get too comfortable and complacent at anytime (Phil. 3:13-14, 1 Cor. 9:26-27).

Prayer: Father, let me live, move and have my being in You, in Jesus mighty name. Have a blessed day.

Sunday January 21, 2019
Topic: PARALYZING HIJACKERS OF PRAYERS

Scripture: "Then he said, "Don't be frightened, Daniel, for your request has been heard in heaven and was answered the very first day you began to fast before the Lord and pray for understanding; that very day I was sent here to meet you. But for twenty-one days the mighty Evil Spirit who overrules the kingdom of Persia blocked my way. Then Michael, one of the top officers of the heavenly army, came to help me, so that I was able to break through these spirit rulers of Persia" (Dan 10:13, TLB).

Praise the Lord. Today is January 21st and is day #21 in year 2019. The number of days remaining to end this year is 344. By God's grace, no power shall be able to block answers to your prayers this year, and you shall see the end of 2019 and beyond, IJN. Do you wonder why sometimes answers to your prayers are delayed or fail to manifest? This could be due to the wicked work of prayer blockers or prayer hijackers. Daniel was a powerful prayer champion who embarked on a long fast to avert imminent wars and sorrows revealed to him in a vision. As today's opening scripture indicates, Evil Spirit withheld answers to Daniel's prayer for 21 days even though answers were released from heaven the first day Daniel began his prayer. Had God not sent Angel Michael to help Daniel, answer would not have come.

Henceforth, include as part of your regular prayer points that blockers and hijackers of prayers shall become paralyzed and powerless in your prayer life, IJN. Instead of delay there shall be express answers to all your prayers, IJN. Furthermore, the God of restoration shall release answers to your past prayers and blessings that might have been hijacked, IJN.

Prayer: Father, henceforth I bind the activities of prayer blockers and hijackers of my prayers, IJMN.

Monday January 22, 2019
Topic: WORTH OF GOD'S WORD

Scripture: "Thy word is a lamp unto my feet, and a light unto my path" (Psalm 119:105).

Praise the Lord. Today is January 22nd and is day #22 in year 2019. The number of days remaining to end this year is 343. By God's grace, you will enjoy divine guidance in all things throughout this year, and you shall see the end of 2019 and beyond, IJN.

There is an important connection between the number 22 and the word of God. The Hebrew alphabet has 22 letters which were used to compose the Holy Bible. The word of God is called the lamp and /or light (Ps. 119:105; Pro. 6:22); it is the light by which we are to live to please God. Therefore, by implication 22 represents light or word of God.

Shortly, before dying for the sins of all mankind Jesus Christ quoted from Ps. 22:1 - "My God, my God, why hast thou forsaken me? - - - "(Mk. 15:34). Knowing that 22 represents the word of God, begin today (the 22nd day) to ascribe greater importance to the word of God. It was by His word that God created the entire universe (Gen 1). The word of God is of tremendous power which can do many things for you: it can save you (Rm. 10: 8-9), keep sin away from you (Ps. 119:11), bring you good success and prosperity (Jos. 1:8), heal you and deliver you from destruction (Ps. 107:20), show you the way to go (Isa. 30:21), help you overcome temptations (Lk. 4:4, 8, 10), keep you alive (John 6:63, 68), etc.

Prayer: Father let Your word dwell richly in me and work for my advantage, IJN (Col. 3:16).

Tuesday January 23, 2019
Topic: POSSESSING GOD'S GOODNESS AND MERCY

Scripture: "Surely goodness and mercy shall follow me all the days of my life: and I will dwell in the house of the Lord forever." (Psalm 23:6).

Praise the Lord. Today is January 23nd and is day #23 in year 2019. The number of days remaining to end this year is 342. By God's grace, nothing will separate you from the house of God this year, and you shall see the end of 2019 and beyond, IJN.

While counting down the number of days to end this year, the goodness and mercy of God are among the things we can also count upwards on as more days are added to our lives. The Bible declares that, "- - It is of the Lord's mercies that we are not consumed, because his compassions fail not. They are new every morning: great is thy faithfulness" (Lam. 3:22-23). In addition, the Bible says the LORD loads us with benefits daily (Ps. 68:19). This implies that each additional day we live adds more compassions, mercies and benefits to our lives.

David's positive confession regarding how goodness and mercy will follow him all the days of his life should be instructive to us as believers because what we confess can determine what we possess. This is especially so because the LORD says "- - as ye have spoken in mine ears, so will I do to you:" (Num. 14:28). Do like David and prayerfully tell God what you desire from Him (Matt 7:7).

Prayer: Father, let goodness and mercy and other blessings of Your house follow me all the days of my life, IJN.

Wednesday January 24, 2019
Topic: COUNT UP ON "SPIRITUAL VICTORY VITAMINS"

Scripture: "Now on the twenty-fourth day of this month the children of Israel were assembled with fasting- -,and confessed their sins and the iniquities of their fathers, - - and read from the Book of the Law of the Lord their God for one–fourth of the day; and for another fourth they confessed and worshiped the Lord their God" (Nehemiah 9: 1-3, NKJV).

Praise the Lord. Today is January 24th and is day #24 in year 2019. The number of days remaining to end this year is 341. By God's grace, you shall be rewarded exceedingly for interceding for your family and others this year, and you shall see the end of 2019 and beyond, IJN.

As we count down this year, it is important that we also invest in and count up on many of the things God has given us to help us live victorious life, pleasing unto Him. Among these things are what I call " spiritual victory vitamins". They include prayers, praise, worship and the word of God. The Bible admonishes us to pray without ceasing (1 Thess. 5:17), to praise and worship God continually (Ps. 34:1), and to study and meditate on the word of God daily (Josh. 1:9, 1 Tim 2:15).

The opening scripture for today describes a revival that was set in motion by the Israelites during Nehemiah time (Neh. Chaps. 8-10). Realizing that Israel had become engulfed with sins and had abandoned God and His word, the 24th day of a month was declared a day of fasting and praying. During the program individuals and the entire nation engaged in intercession, confession, reading of God's word and intensive worship.

The world today needs revival as during Nehemiah times, for, as the Bible says, perilous times has come and the world is laden with multitude of sins (2 Tim 3: 1-8). Believers must step up the propagation of the gospel, praise and worship of God, and confession of our sins and that of nations if we want God to bless us and heal our land (Ps. 67: 1-7; 2 Chron. 7:14). Evaluate and step up your prayer, praise, worship and studying and sharing the word of God. You will be victorious and mightily blessed, IJN.

Prayer: Father, by your mercy restore revival and righteousness into this world in Jesus name.

Friday January 25, 2019
Topic: FANTABULOUS FINISHING

Scripture: "So the wall was finished in the twenty and fifth day - " (Neh. 6:15)

Praise the Lord. Today is January 25th and is day #25 in year 2019. The number of days remaining to end this year is 340. By God's grace, you will achieve great things this year, and you shall see the end of 2019 and beyond, IJN.

Aside from counting down the number of days to end this year, I am sure many of you have other things on which you are counting down. Your expectation shall not be cut off, IJN. On a day like today (25th of a particular month) Nehemiah and his workers didn't have to countdown any further; they finished building the wall of Jerusalem in 52 days!

Whatever you have embarked upon or looking forward to accomplish - school, training, degree, wedding, pregnancy, healing, building project, immigration matters, business, etc. you shall finish successfully as Nehemiah and his workers did. It has been said that the number 25 in the Bible symbolizes 'grace upon grace' as it is composed of 20 (meaning redemption) and five (grace) or grace multiplied (i.e. 5 x 5). The Bible says it is from His (Jesus Christ) fullness we have all received, grace upon grace. (John 1:16, ESV). The most important role of grace in one's life is to make salvation possible through faith in Jesus Christ (Eph. 2:8).

Aside from salvation through Jesus Christ, grace can add numerous other blessings to believer's life. Examples include: protection as in the case of Noah who found grace and was saved along with his family from flood destruction (Gen. 6:8), divine promotion as in the case of Esther who by grace was promoted from being a maid to become a Queen in a foreign land (Esther 2:17), and Joseph who, because of grace, was promoted from prison to the palace as prime minister of Egypt (Gen 39:21), etc. In this year 2019, and forever, the grace of God will cause you to be protected, promoted and celebrated, IJN.

Prayer: Father, let Your grace be sufficient for me to finish this year well and strong, IJN.

Saturday January 26, 2019
Topic: MAN CREATED AS GOD'S MODEL

Scripture: "And God said, Let us make man in our image, after our likeness-" (Gen. 1: 26).

Praise the Lord. Today is January 26th and is day #26 in year 2019. The number of days remaining to end this year is 339. By God's grace, every one that sees you this year will see the favor and glory of God in your life and you shall see the end of 2019 and beyond, IJN.

On this 26th day, let us reflect on GOD and how the number 26 relates to Him and man as well as the expected relationship between God and man. The 26th verse in the first chapter of the Bible (Gen. 1:26) speaks of the image of God to which man was privileged to be modeled after. One of the ways we as humans identify ourselves with God is to bear names that have meaning implying God or His attributes. For example, with El representing the Hebrew Name of God, the name Daniel is same as 'El Is My Judge', Nathanael is stands for 'Gift of El, Samuel connotes 'Heard by El, Elijah implies 'El Is Yahweh' and Elizabeth indicates 'El is an oath or El is abundance'.

God who created man in His image expects man to remain His forever (Isa. 43:1; Heb. 13:5). After creation, Satan crept into the world and caused man to sin against God. Sin separated man from God (Isa 55: 1-2) and man was heading for eternal damnation and death, for "the soul that sinneth, it shall die" (Ezek. 18:4). God sent His son to redeem man back to Him and Jesus Christ had to pay for man's sins with His own life sacrificed on the Cross. Jesus Christ died and resurrected thereby paving the way for man to be restored back to God.

Although you were made in God's image, Satan will continue to lay claim on you until you confess your sins, ask for forgiveness and receive Jesus Christ by faith as your Lord and Savior. This will afford you to be a beneficiary of the redemption work completed by Jesus Christ so that you can become a child of God and not that of Satan any more. Let your life model that of God who created you.

Prayer: Father thank you for making me in your own image, please let me fulfill destiny and remain yours forever, IJN.

Sunday January 27, 2019
Topic: FAITH THAT DRIVES AWAY FEAR

Scripture: " The Lord is my light and my salvation; whom shall I fear? the Lord is the strength of my life; of whom shall I be afraid?" (Psalm. 27:1)

Praise the Lord. Today is January 27th and is day #27 in year 2019. The number of days remaining to end this year is 338. By God's grace, fear shall be far from you throughout this year, and you shall see the end of 2019 and beyond, IJN.

How wonderful it is to know God so much to be able to make a boast in Him as David did (Ps. 27: 1 & Ps. 34:2). After identifying 3 things that the LORD is to him (Light, Salvation and Strength) David's trust in God served as shields for him against fear.

As the Bible says fear is a tormentor (1 John 4:18) and is one of the worst enemies of man. The word phobia refers to persistent, irrational fear of a specific object, activity or situation that leads to a compelling desire to avoid it. After the fall of man in the garden of Eden, the first thing that happened to him was that he was gripped by fear: "And he (Adam) said, I heard thy voice in the garden, and I was afraid, - -"(Gen 3:10). There are gazillions of types of phobia tied to the letters of the alphabet, from, Ablutophobia- Fear of washing or bathing to Zeusophobia or fear of God or gods.

For all who are fearful or afraid of one thing or the other God's solution for you is "fear not"; instead have perfect love which 'casteth out fear' (Mt. 10:28, 1 Jn. 4:18, 1 Tim 1:7). The only fear that is profitable is the reverential fear of God (Pro. 9:10). A strong faith in God will drive away non-godly reverential fears.

Prayer: Father, I shall not fear, for I have faith in You as my Light, Salvation and Strength, IJN. I command fear to be far from me in the mighty name of Jesus.

Monday January 28, 2019
Topic: GOD's MOST IMPORTANT CREATURE

Scripture: "And God blessed them. And God said to them, "Be fruitful and multiply and fill the earth and subdue it and have dominion over the fish of the sea and over the birds of the heavens and over every living thing that moves on the earth." (Gen 1:28, KJV).

Praise the Lord. Today is January 28th and is day #28 in year 2019. The number of days remaining to end this year is 337. By God's grace, you will dominate your enemies this year, and you shall see the end of 2019 and beyond, IJN.

Although man was the last creation of God before He finished His work in Genesis 1, it turned out that, for various reasons, the same man is the most unique and most important in God's creative work Reasons while man has this unique position include: #1, Man is the only one created in God's image (Gen 1:26), # 2, Man is the only one whose creation involved the "US" entities entailing the unity of triune Godhead (Father, Son, and the Holy Spirit), #3, man is the only one whose creation was evaluated as very good, others were described only as "good" (Gen 1:31); #4, Man is the only one God breathed in to his nostrils (Gen 2:7). #5, Man is the only one "blessed" by God (Gen. 1:28), etc.

After God created man, He added some notable value to him as can be seen in today's opening scripture. For instance, God (a) blessed man, (b) commanded him to be fruitful, (c) multiply, (d) replenish the earth, (e) subdue the earth, and (6) have dominion. These are part and parcel of the "abundant life" promised by Christ to his followers (Jn 10:10). Therefore, as a redeemed child of God you have been given the divine favor to 'count upwards' on these value-added virtues of humanity and many more. That is your bona fide right in the Lord.

Prayer: Father by Your divine power I claim all things that pertain unto life and godliness, through the knowledge of him that hath called us to glory and virtue (2 Pet. 1:3).

Tuesday January 29, 2019
Topic: EXPECTED JOYFUL END

Scripture: "For I know the thoughts that I think toward you, saith the LORD, thoughts of peace, and not of evil, to give you an expected end" (Jeremiah 29:11).

Praise the Lord. Today is January 29th and is day #29 in year 2019. The number of days remaining to end this year is 336. By God's grace, you shall not be disappointed concerning your expectations this year, and you shall see the end of 2019 and beyond in Jesus name.

On this 29th day of the year, the word of God in Jeremiah in 29:11 should encourage somebody reading this note who is facing a discouraging situation. God says don't give up, don't throw in the towel, just trust in God for things are about to turn around for good for you according to the good plans God has for you. Your breakthroughs are about to manifest, IJN.

The Israelites were in captivity when the words in today's opening scripture (above) were sent to them through prophet Jeremiah. Whatever situation you are facing now (uncertainty, hardship, sickness, marital problems, children's disobedience, etc.) shall become your ride to victory and joy in the mighty name of Jesus. You shall weep no more, IJN.

Remember, God is with you (Isaiah 43:2-4, Heb. 13:5) and that the end of a thing is better than the beginning thereof (Ecl. 7:8). Determine to end every situation of your life with Jesus Christ, (the Alpha and Omega) and you shall rejoice, IJN.

Prayer: Father, thank You for all your good plans for me; let every situation of my life end well and joyfully with You, IJN.

Wednesday January 30, 2019
Topic: BETRAYAL OF JESUS A BLESSING?

Scripture: "Then Judas, who had betrayed Jesus, regretted what had happened when he saw that Jesus was condemned. He brought the 30 silver coins back to the chief priests and leaders." (Matthew 27:3, GW).

Praise the Lord. Today is January 30th and is day #30in year 2019. The number of days remaining to end this year is 335. By God's grace, you shall not regret any action you take this year and you shall see the end of 2019 and beyond in Jesus name.

One of the ways God manifests His love and omnipotence is in the conversion of a bad or evil plan or action against an innocent person or a group of persons to a blessing or an advantage for that person and / or other persons. In this regard, Joseph's experience and testimony about how he was treated by his brothers speaks volume: "But as for you, ye thought evil against me; but God meant it unto good, to bring to pass, as it is this day, to save much people alive" (Gen. 50:20). Another example is the wicked betrayal of Jesus Christ by Judas Iscariot for 30 pieces of silver as indicated in today's scripture. While Judas lost his life and lost the 30 pieces of silver (Mt 27: 3-8), his action paved the way for redemption and salvation of countless number of sinners.

The betrayal of Jesus by Judas was a fulfillment of prophecy (Zech. 11:12-13). Judas' action led to the ultimate sacrifice of the Lamb of God. It is the blood of Jesus Christ shed on the cross that has made it possible for the forgiveness and redemption of all sinners who will confess and repent of their sins (1 Jn 1:7). The betrayal of Jesus Christ is therefore, a blessing. Do you want to benefit from Judas' betrayal of Jesus? Then repent of your sins today and ask Jesus to wash away your sins with his blood and save your soul from perishing (John 3:16).

Has someone betrayed you, disappointed you, let you down or hurt you? Forgive and do your best to resolve the matter in love. Above all, prayerfully let God handle it and know that, for a bona fide believer and lover of God, "that all things work together for good" (Rom. 8:28). You will laugh last in the mighty name of Jesus.

Prayer: Father, let the blood of Jesus that saved my soul save many souls today and let every bad action planned against me become a blessing, IJN.

Thursday January 31, 2019
Topic: CONQUERING BEFORE POSSESSING

Scripture: "And these are the kings of the country which Joshua and the children of Israel conquered on this side of the Jordan, - - -, all the kings, thirty-one." (Josh. 12:7-24, NKJV)

Praise the Lord. Today is January 31st and is day #31 in year 2019. The number of days remaining to end this year is 334. By God's grace, you shall see the end of 2019 and beyond in Jesus name.

There are 31 countries and their kings that are listed in (Josh 12: 7,24, NKJV). God enabled Joshua and the Israelites to defeat and to possess the land belonging to these countries according to His promise to Joshua (Jos 1:2-4). Before you can possess anything, you must 'conquer' that thing. Power to conquer and possess anything belongs to God (Ps. 62:11). God gave David power to defeat Goliath and to possess his armor (1 Sam. 17:54). After God empowered Jehoshaphat and Judah to conquer the armies of 3 nations that attacked them, they spent 3 days possessing the goods, clothes and valuables of the dead enemies (2 Chron. 20: 21-25)

What are those things (doubts, procrastination, fears, greed, laziness, lying, indecision, lack of information, angers, evil forces, etc.) standing between you and your potential possessions? The land of 2019 you have set your feet on is full of many possessions God has prepared for you. However, you must identity the "kings" that are occupying your possessions and seek divine help to get rid of them before you can possess your bona fide domain.

Action / Prayer: In addition to being alive for the first 31 days of this year take stock of other positive things that have taken place in your life this year and give thanks to God. Then pray: Oh Lord of hosts empower me to conquer, defeat, dethrone and destroy any enemy debarring me from possessing what rightly belong to me, IJN.

Friday February 1, 2019.
Topic: GIVING TRIBUTE TO GOD

Scripture: "And the persons were sixteen thousand; of which the Lord's tribute was thirty and two persons." (Number 32:40).

Praise the Lord. Today is February 1st and is day #32 in year 2019. The number of days remaining to end this year is 333. By God's grace, you shall not lack throughout this year and you shall see the end of 2019 and beyond in Jesus name.

Giving is an important injunction from God that believers must obey (Lk 6:38, Mal. 3:10-22). Everything we own comes from God (James 1:17) and it is a privilege and a great blessing to give to God (Acts 20:35). In today's opening scripture above, God, through Moses, told the Israelites to give a tribute to Him from the booty they gathered from war against the Medianites who polluted the Israelites. Part of the tributes included 32 virgins (read Num. Chap. 31 for detail).

There are many reasons Christians must give to God: (i). it is a command (Mal. 3:10-13; Lk 6:38), (ii). It is an act of loyalty and honor to God (Pro 3:9-10), (iii). It is an opportunity to be blessed (Pro 11:25, Gal 6:7). (iv). You usually get more than you give (Lk 6:38), (v). It is a sign of love (Jn 3:16), (vi). God owns everything (Ps. 24:1, James 1:17), (vii). It is a way of helping the poor and getting blessed and getting rewarded by God (Deut. 15:10, Pro 19:17), etc.

Prayer: (1) Father thank You for the gift of new month of February; please give me the grace to give unto You befitting tributes that will provoke my blessings, IJN.

(2) Father, please defeat and destroy all 'Medianites' enemies attempting to pollute my life in the mighty name of Jesus.

Saturday February 2, 2019
Topic: PERFECT PURIFICATION

Scripture: "After waiting thirty-three days, she will be purified from the bleeding of childbirth. During this time of purification, she must not touch anything that is set apart as holy. And she must not enter the sanctuary until her time of purification is over" (Lev. 12:4, NLT)

Praise the Lord. Today is February 2nd and is day #33 in year 2019. The number of days remaining to end this year is 332. By God's grace, you shall be free from spiritual and physical pollution forever and you shall see the end of 2019 and beyond, IJN.

Let us focus briefly on purification as this is an important requirement for counting upwards on the blessings of God (Mt. 5:8, Pro 22:11). To help elucidate this point, it is helpful to consider one major similarity and one major difference between the Old Covenant (OC) under Mosaic Law and the New Covenant (NC) under Jesus Christ. In terms of similarity God is the center stage in both cases and He does not change (Mal.3:6). In terms of major difference, the OC could not free a person from sin (Heb. 10:4) while those under the NC can be made free from sin (Jn. 8:36).

Regulations regarding uncleanness and purification under OC were very stringent and were given to keep the Israelites in constant need of doing physical things to try to maintain their privileged status as God's chosen people. For example, under OC, normal sexual intercourse rendered both husband and wife unclean (Lev.15:18). Furthermore, childbirth made women unclean and purification process (in terms of length of days required) depended on baby's gender (Lev. 12: 1-5). In both cases, her purification ceremony involved a burnt offering and staying away from the sanctuary for about 40 days.

Since Jesus Christ is the end of the Law (Rm 10:4), He has satisfied all the requirements of the laws (OC &NC). Therefore, Jesus Christ is the perfect purifier and a bona fide believer and follower of Jesus Christ only need to love Jesus and his/her neighbors to meet the OC and NC requirements. There is no need for legalistic and dogmatic obligation to the OC laws such as staying away from Church for 40 days after childbirth as some believer still do blindly. You have been redeemed from the curse of the law.

Prayer: Father, let my sanctification and purification be complete in You in Jesus Name.

Sunday February 3, 2019
Topic: FRUITFULNESS AND LONG LIFE

Scripture: "Eber was 34 years old when he became the father of Peleg. 17 After he became the father of Peleg, Eber lived 430 years and had other sons and daughters" (Gen 11:16-17)

Praise the Lord. Today is February 3rd and is day #34 in year 2019. The number of days remaining to end this year is 331. By God's grace, you shall be hail and healthy throughout this year and you shall see the end of 2019 and beyond, IJN.

The command to be "fruitful and multiply" handed down to married man and woman by God at creation entails having children and manifesting productivity in other areas. However, some married couples who desire to have children, for diabolical and other reasons do find it difficult to have this need met. It is my prayer that families having problems in bearing children in their marriage will soon overcome the problem of barrenness.

As indicated in today's opening scripture child bearing was not a problem for Eber. He was from the genealogy of Shem and the 5th generation descendant of Noah (Gen. 11:10-17). At age 34, Eber had his first son called Peleg and thereafter he lived for 430 years 'and begot sons and daughters' (Gen 11:16). Eber fulfilled his destiny regarding fruitfulness and longevity. You too shall be fruitful and live your full age, IJN. Jesus Christ said "--I am come that they might have life, and that they might have it more abundantly" (Jn. 10:10). Get connected with Jesus Christ and do His will and all the reasons for which you were created shall be achieved.

Prayer: Father, thank You for my life, please let me be fruitful and fulfill destiny in all areas that will bring glory unto You, IJN.

Monday February 4, 2019
Topic: SELF DESTROYING ENEMIES

Scripture: "Jehoshaphat was 35 years old when he began to rule, and he ruled for 25 years in Jerusalem. His mother's name was Azubah, daughter of Shilhi." (1 Kings 22:42, GW)

Praise the Lord. Today is February 4th and is day #35 in year 2019. The number of days remaining to end this year is 330. By God's grace, you shall be highly honored this year and you will see the end of 2019 and beyond in Jesus name.

During his 25 years of reign, things were not always easy for Jehoshaphat but one thing that helped him tremendously was that he was accustomed to "- - doing that which was right in the eyes of the LORD- - " (1 KGS 22: 43). For example, Jehoshaphat led Judah to seek help from God when on one occasion three countries (Moab, Ammon and Mount Seir) banded together with their large armies to attack him and Judah. God arose and fought for them.

All Jehoshaphat and Judah had to do at the war front was sing praises to God. As they did so, their enemies turned their weapons against themselves until all the attackers of Judah were completely destroyed (2 Chron. 20). Jehoshaphat and Judah spent three days to carry precious jewels and other resources left behind by the defeated and destroyed enemies (2 Chron 20:25).

You may or may not be an earthly king like Jehoshaphat, but if you are a believer and follower of Jesus Christ, the Bible says He has made you a king and a priest unto God (Rev 1:6). You will reign with Jesus Christ, not for 25 years, but for eternity. Shout, Hallelujah! Anyone or anything or conspirators attacking you and your domain shall be utterly destroyed, IJN.

Prayer: Father, let all my attackers destroy themselves in Jesus mighty name.

Tuesday February 5, 2019
Topic: CONSEQUENCES OF ACCURSED THINGS

Scripture: "The men of Ai chased the Israelites from the town gate as far as the quarries, and they killed about thirty-six who were retreating down the slope. The Israelites were paralyzed with fear at this turn of events, and their courage melted away." (Josh 7:5)

Praise the Lord. Today is February 5th and is day #36 in year 2019. The number of days remaining to end this year is 329. By God's grace, you shall see the end of 2019 and beyond in Jesus name.

On this 36th day of the year, let me bring to your attention important lessons to learn from the killing of 36 of Israeli soldiers and the embarrassing defeat of the Israeli army by a very tiny nation called Ai. The shameful and embarrassing defeat was due to the sin of one individual in Israelite army. When Joshua cried to God why the shameful defeat, God told him it was because of sin in the camp and gave him specific instruction how to identify the culprit (read Josh chap 7). Although Achan alone committed the sin of taking accursed things (forbidden by God), Achan and his entire family were burnt to death, 36 Israeli soldiers lost their lives, the whole nation was woefully defeated and Israel's morale hit bottom rock.

There are several lessons to learn but I will just mention 2 for brevity. (1) The wages of sin is death (Rm 3:23), (2) At all levels (individual, family, Church, etc.,) it is imperative that all hands be on deck in fighting against sins, crimes, terrorists, etc. It is necessary to ensure comprehensive obedience to the ordinances of God. Otherwise, the innocent will continue to be a partaker in the grievous casualties that may attend to the sins or violation of God's ordinances by an individual. The whole nation of Israel was put to shame, flight and embarrassment, discouragement, etc. simply because of the sin of only one person in the camp of Israel.

Things to consider: Let us think of any "accursed thing" we might have knowingly or by ignorance taken and restitute them. Examples: tithes, stolen things, lies, unforgiveness, etc.

Prayer: Father, deliver me from the consequences of accursed things at all levels.

Wednesday, February 6, 2019
Topic: ABROGATION OF AFFLICTIONS

Scriptures: "And the Lord said, I have surely seen the affliction of my people which are in Egypt and have heard their cry by reason of their taskmasters; for I know their sorrows;" (Exo. 3:7).

Praise the Lord. Today is February 6th and is day #37 in year 2019. The number of days remaining to end this year is 328. By God's grace, all your prayers shall be favorably answered this year and you shall see the end of 2019 and beyond in Jesus name.

While Moses was tending the flock of Jethro (his father in law), God appeared to him in angelic form at the backside of the desert on mount Horeb. The LORD had a dialogue with Moses introducing Himself as the God of his father, the God of Abraham, the God of Isaac, and the God of Jacob (Exo 3:1-6). In this season may you enjoy an encouraging divine visitation from the Almighty God.

Today's opening scripture is part of God's dialogue with Moses. Don't you ever think that God is ignorant about what goes on in your life. God is omniscient, meaning He knows all things including past, present and future situations and circumstances of everybody. God is also omnipotent meaning He is full of power (Psalm 62:11). With His divine knowledge and power, God is able to provide solution to any problem faced by His children.

Having seen your afflictions, heard your cry and known your sorrows, as He did for the Israelites, I pray God will readily deliver you out of every problem. Afflictions are over in your life and you shall not have any reason to sorrow, IJN. In this year 2019, you shall enter into a good and a large land flowing with milk and honey in the mighty name of Jesus Christ.

Prayer: Father, visit me and terminate all afflictions from my life and that of my family, IJN

Thursday February 7, 2019
Topic: HELP FOR THE HELPLESS

Scripture: "One man, who had been sick for 38 years, was lying there. Jesus told the man, "Get up, pick up your cot, and walk." The man immediately became well, picked up his cot, and walked. That happened on a day of worship." (John 5:5,8,9, GW)

Praise the Lord. Today is February 7th and is day #38 in year 2019. The number of days remaining to end this year is 327. By God's grace, every problem that has lingered long in your life shall end this year, and you shall see the end of 2019 and beyond in Jesus name.

Just imagine how devastating the condition of the man in today's opening scripture above must have been for having an infirmity for 38 years (at least 13,870 days)! That is about half of his life! His problem was exacerbated because he was down trodden and pushed aside every time he made an attempt to be the first to jump into the water to get healed as an angel came to stir the water. He must have suffered pain, rejection, low esteem, shame, hunger, discouragement, frustration, helplessness, hopelessness, etc.

Fortunately, this crippled man's problem came to an end when Jesus saw him and had compassion on him amidst so many invalids at the pool waiting to get healed. Jesus asked him if he wanted to be healed. He told Jesus more of his frustration of not getting any help that could get him into the water. The man did not know he was talking to The Very Present Help (Ps. 46:2). He needed only a few words from the great physicians: "Rise, take up your bed and walk". Immediately, he was made well.

Some of the lessons to learn from this man's ordeals and the ultimate breakthrough include persistence, patience, faith, keeping hope alive and courage. Whatever "infirmity" or problem(s) have lingered long and caused you anguish, pain, frustration, shame, limitation, shall be terminated by Jesus Christ.

Prayer: Father, let my destiny helpers locate me and let me arise and walk away totally free from all limitations (spiritual, physical, financial, etc.), IJN. Have a blessed day.

Friday, February 8, 2019
Topic: SUFFERING WHILE SERVING

Scripture: "Five times the Jewish leaders had me beaten with 39 lashes". (2 Cor. 11:24).

Praise the Lord. Today is February 8th and is day #39 in year 2019. The number of days remaining to end this year is 326. By God's grace, nothing will torture you this year, and you shall see the end of 2019 and beyond in Jesus name.

Excruciating 39 lashes repeated 5 times were part of the torture inflicted on Apostle Paul simply because of his faith in Jesus Christ. Apart from various beatings, Paul was subjected to a litany of sufferings including pains, hunger, nakedness, bondage, stoned, devoured, smitten, reproached, imprisoned, shipwrecked multiple times, numerous perils, died several times and finally beheaded, most likely (2 Cor.11: 19-27). No doubt he experienced exactly what Jesus told him at the point of his conversion: "For I will shew him how great things he must suffer for my name's sake" (Acts 9:16).

Today, Christians still suffer many vicissitudes including sickness, bareness, failure, discrimination, imprisonment, beheadings, beatings, ridicule, etc. The question is, why do Christians suffer? and what should be our reaction to suffering? Christian suffering may arise due to many reasons such as living in a sinful world and facing persecution (Jer. 17:9, 2 Tim 3:12).

Christian reaction to sufferings should include holy living (as Job did), prayer for deliverance from sufferings, perseverance, and rejoicing if the suffering is because of Christ and His gospel (Mt.5:11-12). Note that not all sufferings are necessarily the result of sins; some may be designed for your promotion so long you pass the test embedded in the suffering as in the case of Job (Job 1:8, 2:3 & 42:10). Any suffering for Christ and the gospel is actually a blessing in disguise because it is written "- - the sufferings of this present time are not worthy to be compared with the glory which shall be revealed in us" (Rm. 8:18, 2 Cor. 4:17).

Prayer: Father let the cups of sufferings and afflictions escape my mouth but give me the grace to drink any one meant to prepare me for Your glorious kingdom, IJN.

Saturday February 9, 2019
Topic: GETTING RID OF 'GOLIATH'

Scripture: "Each morning and evening for 40 days, the Philistine came forward and made his challenge". (1 Sam 17:16, GW).

Praise the Lord. Today is February 9th and is day #40 in year 2019. The number of days remaining to end this year is 325. By God's grace, anything challenging your life shall suffer sudden defeat this year, and you shall see the end of 2019 and beyond in Jesus name.

From Biblical, historical and foundational perspectives, the number 40 is of great significance to the world, human race and particularly, to believers in Jesus Christ. A few examples will illustrate the point. The Holy Bible is written by 40 different authors under God's inspiration. The first time the number 40 occurred in the Bible is in regards to when God said He would destroy the sinful world with flood and that the flood would result from 40 days and 40 nights of rain (Gen 7:4). Only Noah and his family and selected living things survived the flood, having been preserved safely in an ark for 40 days (Gen. chap. 8). God fed the Israelites with manna from heaven for 40 years in the wilderness (Exo. 16:35). Jesus Christ fasted 40 days at the end of which He was victorious of Satan who tempted Him 3 times (Mt. 4: 1-11).

Another noteworthy incidence regarding the number 40 pertains to the Goliath, the giant Philistine who taunted and threatened the army of Israel for 40 days, every morning and evening as indicated in today's opening scripture. When David learnt of Goliath's reproach to the army of God, he confronted the heavily armed giant boldly in the name of the LORD (1 Sam 17:45). With only a sling shot carrying a stone David brought down the giant Goliath shamefully and cut of his head (I Sam 17: 50-52).

On this 40th day of year 2019, I decree that you will be a partaker of the blessings associated with the number 40 as pointed out above. The holy word of God shall quicken and empower you, you shall be preserved from all floods, fire and other hazards, God will supply all your needs and you shall suffer no hunger, IJN. Additionally, you shall be victorious over temptations and every Goliath challenging your health, job, mirage, business, academic, ministry, peace, etc. shall be defeated shamefully, IJN.

Prayer: Father, contend against my enemies and give total victory over them, IJN.

Sunday February 10, 2019
Topic: STARTING AND FINISHING WELL

Scripture: "In Jeroboam's twentieth year as king of Israel, Asa began to rule as king of Judah. 10 He ruled 41 years in Jerusalem- - - 11 Asa did what the Lord considered right, as his ancestor David had done" (1 kgs. 15: 9-11, GW).

Praise the Lord. Today is February 10th and is day #41 in year 2019. The number of days remaining to end this year is 324. By God's grace, you will act right before the Lord throughout this year, and you shall see the end of 2019 and beyond in Jesus name.

On this 41st day of year 2019, let us look briefly at the life of King Asa who reigned in Jerusalem for 41 years. Asa started well but finished bad. During the first 10 years of his reign he obeyed God and carried out a partially successful effort to abolish idolatry including deposing his idolatrous grandmother Maacah (1 Kgs 15: 9-15; 2 Chron. 14 & 16). When attacked by the vast army of Cushites, Asa cried to God for help and God gave him victory over the Cushites from whom Asa also carried off a large plunder (2 Chron. 14: 9-15). Regrettably, towards the end of his reign Asa relied more on himself and unholy human alliance than on God. When Hanani, a seer, warned king Asa against his backsliding attitude and his unholy alliance with Benhadad, king of Aram, Asa got upset and put Hanani in prison.

You cannot go unpunished when you violate God's injunction of "Touch not mine anointed, and do my prophets no harm" (Ps.105:15). Because Asa "touched" Hanani with imprisonment, God avenged for Hanan and Asa was afflicted with a disease on his feet that killed him (2 Kgs. 16: 7-14). It is not how you start, but how you finish that will matter most. Apostle Paul started as an assassin but ended as the greatest Apostle. Rahab started as a harlot and ended up as a helper of God's people and she is listed in the Faith Hall of Fame (Heb. 11: 3-31). Whatever you are now - a saint, sinner, drug addict, an alcoholic, homosexual, atheist, Moslem, etc. Jesus Christ is expecting and waiting for you to remain connected / connect with Him for a journey that will end well with Him in eternity. Cry to Him now to have mercy on you, and save you. **Prayer: Father, let my heart be fully committed to You and let me finish well and strong at Your kingdom, IJN.**

Monday February 11, 2019
Topic: COMMITTING CHILDREN TO CHRIST

Scripture: "Elisha turned, took one look at them, and cursed them in the name of God. Two bears charged out of the underbrush and knocked them about, ripping them limb from limb—forty-two children in all (2 Kgs 2:24, MSG).

Praise the Lord. Today is February 11th and is day #42 in year 2019. The number of days remaining to end this year is 323. By God's grace, you shall see the end of 2019 and beyond in Jesus name.

As part of the measures to protect our children against sudden destruction we must pray over them regularly and train them (right from birth) how to honor and respect God as well as the elders, particularly, the men and women of God (Lev.19:32, Pro 22:6, 1 Pet 5:5, Eph. 5: 1-3).

According to our lead scripture above, 42 children were violently torn apart and completely destroyed by 2 she bears. Why? Because Elisha cursed them for mocking him and calling him bald head after he has just received double portion of Elijah's spirit (2 Kgs 2). Imagine the destinies terminated and sorrows inflicted upon the families of those 42 children. May no one reading this piece lose any child, IJN.

Prayer: Father, teach my family to honor You and respect the elderly; forever let us be blessed and immunized against all curses, IJN.

Tuesday February 12, 2019
Topic: THE PRESENT HELP

Scripture: "When thou passest through the waters, I will be with thee; and through the rivers, they shall not overflow thee: when thou walkest through the fire, thou shalt not be burned; neither shall the flame kindle upon thee (Isaiah 43:2).

Praise the Lord. Today is February 12th and is day #43 in year 2019. The number of days remaining to end this year is 322. By God's grace, you shall enjoy divine protection every day of this year, and you shall see the end of 2019 and beyond in Jesus name.

God is not a man that he should lie (Num 19:23). With the kind of promise in Isaiah 43:2 coming from God, every believer can confidently count upward on the blessings and security of God as the days of the year count down.

Beloved, when God is with you, you enjoy divine security and you are free from troubles (Psalms 16:11, 48:2). You can cross every "Red sea" dry without drowning, and every "fiery furnace" becomes a funfair. I decree that for the rest of year 2019 God shall be with you and He will give you "power to tread on serpents and scorpions, and over all the power of the enemy: and nothing shall by any means hurt you" (Lk. 10:19), IJN.

Prayer: *O LORD GOD, Emmanuel, please let Your presence go with me wherever I go this year, IJN.*

Wednesday February 13, 2019
Topic: ADVANTAGE OF CHRIST'S ASCENSION

Scripture: " - -Christ died for our sins according to the scriptures; And that he was buried, and that he rose again the third day according to the scriptures" (1 Cor. 15: 3-4).

Praise the Lord. Today is February 13th and is day #44 in year 2019. The number of days remaining to end this year is 321. By God's grace, you shall enjoy restoration of lost glories this year, and you shall see the end of 2019 and beyond in Jesus name.

Biblical history has it that 44 is the number of days between Jesus' crucifixion and His ascension to heaven from Mount Olive. Many notable events took place during the last 44 days of Jesus' earthly ministry. These include His miraculous resurrection from the dead and His 8 appearances to different sets of people (Matt 28:6-10, Acts 1:3, 1 Cor 15:6).

The resurrection of Jesus Christ is vital to the believer because it demonstrates the power of God over death and life and guarantees that the bodies of those who believe in Christ will not remain dead but will be resurrected unto eternal life. Jesus declares to Martha, "- - I am the resurrection, and the life: he that believeth in me, though he were dead, yet shall he live" (Jn. 11:25).

Complete account of Jesus' ascension to heaven can be found in Lk 24:50-51 & Acts 1:9-11. Christ's ascension is significant for the believer because it signifies success of His earthly ministry, it allowed Him to prepare a place for us (Jn 14:2), it enabled him to make intercession for us (Rom 8:34), it sets a pattern for His return to take us (Acts 1:11), etc.

Do you have this hope of eternal life? If No, repent of your sins today and ask Jesus Christ to forgive you and be your Lord and Savior. Then you will live because Jesus lives (Jn. 14:19).

Prayer: Father, thank You for the life, resurrection and ascension of Jesus Christ, please let me be ready to go with Him when He comes back to take His own.

Thursday February 14, 2019
Topic: RARITY OF RIGHTEOUSNESS

Scripture: "Abraham asked, "Consider now, if I may be so bold as to ask you, although I'm only dust and ashes, what if there are 45 innocent people? Will you destroy the whole city because of 5 fewer people?" The Lord answered, "I will not destroy it if I find 45 there...." (Genesis 18: 27-28, GW).

Praise the Lord. Today is February 14th and is day #45 in year 2019. The number of days remaining to end this year is 320. By God's grace, many calamities shall be averted because of you this year, and you shall see the end of 2019 and beyond in Jesus name

God is the best Negotiator and Bargainer any one can ever deal with. Intercessory prayer is a powerful tool for negotiating or bargaining with God. Moses successfully negotiated with God to reverse His plan to completely destroy the Israelites in the wilderness at least on 2 occasions (Num. 14: 11-24, Ex. 32: 9-14). Hezekiah also negotiated with God and got 15 years added to his life beyond the time he was initially scheduled to die (2 Kgs 20: 1-11).

As indicated today's opening scripture Abraham asked if God would spare Sodom and Gomorrah (S&G) from destruction if He found 45 righteous people there and God said He would. In His bargaining request Abraham actually counted down the number of righteous people required to spare S & G successively from 50 to 45, to 40, to 30, to 20, and to 10. At each level of Abraham's request, God consented. Abraham stopped his demand at 10 probably not to abuse the grace and generosity of God. Ultimately, God destroyed S & G with brimstone and fire apparently because He couldn't find 10 righteous people in the place. Only Lot's family was spared with the exception of his wife who looked back and became a pillar of salt (Gen 19:24-26).

Are you born again and made righteous by Jesus Christ? If Jesus returns now to take righteous people, are you ready? To avoid S&G experience repent and receive Jesus Christ today if you are not yet born again. He will impute righteousness to you.

Prayer: Father, anytime you are looking for righteous people, let me be in the number, IJN.

Friday February 15, 2019
Topic: HONORING GOD'S HOUSE

Scripture: "Are you going to build it again in three days?" they asked him. "It has taken 46 years to build this Temple!" (John 2:20, GNB).

Praise the Lord. Today is February 15th and is day #46 in year 2019. The number of days remaining to end this year is 319. By God's grace, God will facilitate things for you this year, and you shall see the end of 2019 and beyond in Jesus name.

The house of God or any place He is worshipped is a place of honor and should be treated so. One day when Jesus entered the temple in Jerusalem and met people trading animals, other goods and exchanging money, He got angry, overturned their trading tables and drove them out of the place with serious beating. He rebuked them for turning His Father's house into a place of merchandise. God backed Jesus up by silencing the merchandisers who quickly obeyed Jesus and left the Temple as commanded. The Jews who were amazed at His display of power and authority asked Him for sign by which Jesus did "all these things?". Jesus responded (apparently pointing to Himself) and said, "Destroy this temple, and in three days I will raise it up" (John 2:19).

The Jews, wondered how Jesus would raise up, in 3 days, the temple that took them 46 years to build. They did not know that Jesus was talking about His own resurrection that would take place 3 days after His crucifixion. On this 46th day of year 2019, let us be reminded that the Temple (or place where God is worshipped) is sacred and must be honored, respected, kept clean and orderly. It should not be a place to come to with lackadaisical attitude, lateness and absenteeism. God is looking for co-laborers with Him in the building of His Church (1 Cor. 3:9). Can God count on you? Are you zealous about God's house /work like Jesus was? (Ps. 69:9). Note that your body is also the Temple of God and should not be a laboratory for sins and sickness (1 Cor. 6:19-20).

Prayer: Father, as I help build your Church, build my life and let not the enemy prevail against me, IJN.

Saturday February 16, 2019
Topic: HEADING FOR GOSHEN?

Scripture: "So Israel dwelt in the land of Egypt, in the country of Goshen; and they had possessions there and grew and multiplied exceedingly". (Gen 47:27).

Praise the Lord. Today is February 16th and is day #47 in year 2019. The number of days remaining to end this year is 318. By God's grace, you shall enjoy the best of things this year, and you shall see the end of 2019 and beyond in Jesus name

One characteristic of God is that He can turn what was meant for evil to good from which other blessings can flow. This is what He did for Joseph, Jabez, Jesus, Daniel, etc. Take the case of Joseph for instance. He was sold as a slave into Egypt by his own brothers. There, he found favor in the sight of God and man and became the second in command to Pharaoh the king of Egypt. Joseph arranged for his people, Israel to join him in Egypt. On arrival, Pharaoh gave them Goshen as the place to settle as indicated in today's opening scripture. Goshen is described as the best land in Egypt, suitable for both crops and livestock (Gen. 47:6).

As you are reading this piece, I decree to you that God is about to settle you in a 'comfort zone - your own 'Goshen' in Jesus mighty name. Look beyond the situation you are going through right now; focus on the better future God has planned for you (Jer. 29:11). Put your trust in God and depend on Him for your transformation. The favor of God will usher you into your "Goshen" where you will have possessions, grow and multiply exceedingly, IJN. Jesus Christ has gone to prepare a place far better than Goshen for all that put their faith in Him. Accept Him today and make your own reservation for your 'divine Goshen" (Jn. 14: 1-3).

Prayer: Father, turn the tide in my favor and let my enemy become my enabler, hinderers to become helpers, adversity to become advantage, IJN.

Sunday February 17, 2019
Topic: GOD CATERS FOR HIS OWN

Scripture: "Within the territory owned by the Israelites there were 48 cities in all for Levi's descendants". (Joshua 21:41).

Praise the Lord. Today is February 17th and is day #48 in year 2019. The number of days remaining to end this year is 317. By God's grace, you will not miss any of your blessings for this year, and you shall see the end of 2019 and beyond in Jesus name.

God is a wonderful, incomparable promise keeper. In Genesis 12, God made many promises to Abraham including the fact that he would bless him, make his name great, he would be a blessing and in him will all the families of the earth be blessed. Abraham acted in obedience and when he got to the land of Canaan and Shechem the Lord appeared to him and said, "- - To your descendants I will give this land." (Gen 12:7).

It is evident that all God's promises to Abraham were fulfilled. For example, as regards land, Joshua 21:43 declares "So the Lord gave to Israel all the land of which He had sworn to give to their fathers, and they took possession of it and dwelt in it". According to God's instruction to Moses, Joshua ensured that the Levites, who were ministers of God, were adequately catered for. From the tithes paid by the Israelites on their allocated land and the proceeds thereof, the Levites were given 48 cities as indicated in today's opening scripture.

Every believer in God is a descendant of Abraham and qualifies to partake in the blessings God promised to Abraham. If you know and serve God, you shall be blessed, you shall be great, you shall be fruitful, you shall have dominion and you shall not lack any good thing.

Prayer: Father, thank You for Your plan for me not to lack any good thing, IJN.

Monday February 18, 2019
Topic: FREE INDEED?

Scripture: "And you shall count seven sabbaths of years for yourself, seven times seven years; and the time of the seven sabbaths of years shall be to you forty-nine years" (Lev. 25:8, NKJV)

Praise the Lord. Today is February 18th and is day #49 in year 2019. The number of days remaining to end this year is 316. By God's grace, you shall be free from debts this year, and you shall see the end of 2019 and beyond in Jesus name.

The number 49 reminds us of the 49 Sabbath years indicated today's opening scripture. God told the Israelites that when they arrived in the Promised Land, they should observe the sabbath year similar to the sabbath day. The sabbath year was the 7th year when the land was left fallow (uncultivated) after 6 consecutive years of producing on the land. Seven of such 7 sabbath years (7 x7) constituted the 49th sabbath year which was very significant being the penultimate (preceding) year for the jubilee year (Lev.25: 1-12).

The jubilee (50th year) was a celebrative year expected to be marked by many things including cancellation of debts, freeing all slaves, and returning to its original owners all land that had been sold. In essence, preparation for the jubilee begins in the 49th year. The most reliable, peaceful and enjoyable freedom is the one provided by Jesus Christ (John 8:36). Have you accepted Him as your Lord and Savior and are you serving Him diligently? If Yes, praise the Lord. If No, do it today and be free from the bondage of sins. I pray that your seasons of total freedom from sins, sickness, debts, poverty, failure, disappointment, etc. has begun.

Prayer: Father, give me rest from all troubles, IJN.

Tuesday February 19, 2019
Topic: GREATER GRATITUDE

Scripture: "Count fifty days to the day after the seventh Sabbath; then you shall offer a new grain offering to the Lord" (Lev. 23:16, NKJV).

Praise the Lord. Today is February 19th and is day #50 in year 2019. The number of days remaining to end this year is 315. By God's grace, you shall have many things to thank God for this year, and you shall see the end of 2019 and beyond in Jesus name

There are 7 celebrative feasts and holy convocations listed in the Bible that are known as the "Feasts of the LORD" (Lev. 23:2). One of these feasts, called the Feast of Weeks or Pentecost, takes place 50 days after another feast called the Feast of Firstfruits. The Feast of Firstfruits involved bringing first harvest to God as an expression of thanksgiving for successful season of production.

The Feast of Weeks, or Pentecost (from the Greek term pentekostos, or fiftieth), was the grand celebration at the end of the grain harvest. The occasion involved lavish offerings of food and animals to the Lord to thank Him for the tremendous bounty He had provided (Lev. 23:15-22). How thankful are you to the LORD for what He has enabled you to do in your career? academics? business? etc. God is the one who can give power to get wealth (Deut. 8:18). He promised that when we praise Him, He will cause the earth to yield increase (Ps. 67: 5-6). This year, let your praises to God count up the more and you shall be productive and have bountiful harvest, IJN.

Prayer: Father, thank You for Your past blessings of my efforts; please empower me to show greater gratitude to You in Jesus mighty name.

Wednesday February 20, 2019
Topic: ETERNAL LIFE OR ETERNAL DEATH?

Scripture: "Have mercy upon me, O God, according to thy loving-kindness: according unto the multitude of thy tender mercies blot out my transgressions. Wash me thoroughly from mine iniquity and cleanse me from my sin" (Psalm 51:1-2).

Praise the Lord. Today is February 20th and is day #51 in year 2019. The number of days remaining to end this year is 314. By God's grace, sins shall not have dominion over you this year, and you shall see the end of 2019 and beyond in Jesus name.

The scripture today comes from Psalm 51 which is known as Psalm of Repentance. David who composed this Psalm was truly sorry for his adultery with Bathsheba and for murdering her husband to cover up the wickedness. God accepted David's repentance and cry for mercy and forgave him. Other than the sin against the Holy Spirit (Mt. 31:22) no sin is too great to be forgiven. Every human being is a sinner and needs repentance and forgiveness (Rm 3:23, 1 John 1: 8-9). The ultimate consequence of un-repented and un-forgiven sin(s) is eternal death and eternity in hell fire (Rm. 6:23; Rev 20:15; 21:8).

Jesus Christ who came into this world to seek and to save sinners has made provision (through His death and resurrection) for the salvation of everyone who will by faith, receive Him as his/her Lord and Savior (John 3:16; Eph. 2:8-9). The ultimate countdown destination of every human being will be to either 'Eternal Life' or to 'Eternal Death'. Your choice will depend on your acceptance or rejection of Jesus Christ as your Lord and Savior (John 3:18). Receive Him today and begin your journey to eternal life.

Prayer: Father, please wash me thoroughly clean from all sins and let me qualify to spend eternity with Jesus Christ in Your Kingdom, IJN.

Thursday February 21, 2019
Topic: SPEEDY SUCCESS

Scripture: "The wall was finished on the twenty-fifth day of the month of Elul. The wall took 52 days to finish" (Neh. 6:15, GW).

Praise the Lord. Today is February 21st and is day #52 in year 2019. The number of days remaining to end this year is 313. By God's grace, all your projects scheduled for completion this year shall be accomplished, and you shall see the end of 2019 and beyond in Jesus name.

It took Nehemiah and his team only 52 days to rebuild the wall of Jerusalem! This great accomplishment happened in the face of serious opposition, discouragement and skepticism from enemies such as Sanballat and Tobias. They said it couldn't be done, the job was too big and the problems were too great. But, "With God, nothing shall be impossible" (Lk. 1:37). Among other things, Nehemiah engaged prayer, power of God, persistence, determination, passion, and people's togetherness in getting his assignment done in record time.

Do you want speedy success in all your undertakings? Then, adopt Nehemiah's approach as described above and watch God swinging into action to help you as He has promised (Isa. 41:10). Not only can God help you finish quickly He has the power to remove hindrances and detractors as He did for Nehemiah. In this season I pray that God will accelerate the countdown of the time required for completing all the projects you may be involved in, IJN.

Prayer: Father, grand me speedy success in all my endeavors that will shame my mockers and adversaries, IJN.

Friday February 22, 2019
Topic: SOLUTION TO SINS AND SICKNESS

Scripture: "But he was wounded for our transgressions, he was bruised for our iniquities: the chastisement of our peace was upon him; and with his stripes we are healed" (Isaiah 53:5).

Praise the Lord. Today is February 22nd and is day #53 in year 2019. The number of days remaining to end this year is 312. By God's grace, you shall enjoy divine healing throughout this year, and you shall see the end of 2019 and beyond in Jesus name.

Isaiah 53 is the most vivid prophecy of the sufferings and death of the Lord Jesus Christ. By His sufferings and subsequent death and resurrection, the LORD Jesus Christ has brought many advantages to mankind. These advantages include salvation and total healing (spiritual, physical, emotional, etc.). By His sufferings and stripes Jesus has paid for our sins and sickness. Claim your rights in Jesus Christ by believing in Him and accepting Him as your Lord and Savior. The Bible declares, "But as many as received him, to them gave he power to become the sons of God, even to them that believe on his name" (John 1:12). Once you are His, He becomes your insurance against sins and sicknesses.

Prayer: Father thank You for the price you paid for my salvation; I declare that with your stripes I am totally and completely healed, IJN.

Saturday February 23, 2019
Topic: DIVINE DEFENSE

Scripture: "No weapon that is formed against thee shall prosper; and every tongue that shall rise against thee in judgment thou shalt condemn. This is the heritage of the servants of the Lord, and their righteousness is of me, saith the Lord" (Isaiah 54:17).

Praise the Lord. Today is February 23rd and is day #54 in year 2019. The number of days remaining to end this year is 311. By God's grace, every weapon of the enemy aimed at you this year shall backfire, and you shall see the end of 2019 and beyond in Jesus name.

The best security any one can have is that of God and His allies such as Jesus Christ, Holy Spirit, innumerable angels, etc.). When you are on the side of God and He is on your side, Isaiah 54:17 says no weapon can be used by anyone to truncate your countdown to your targeted goal. Part of the heritage of those who belong to God is to enjoy sacred security or divine defense.

To enjoy divine defense just do your part by giving your life to Jesus Christ, live holy, be obedient, and serve Him prayerfully and faithfully. He will do anything necessary to guarantee your safety. In this regard, His promises are yea and Amen and His track records are impeccable (2 Cor. 1:20'; LK 10:19; Isa. 43: 1-3; Gen 7:1 & 8: 1-20; Dan. Chps3 & 6).

Two examples of God's divine defense are (a) defense of Elijah against an arrest order from king Ahaziah of Samaria by sending fire from heaven to consume the arresters (2 kings 2: 1-16), (b) God defended Paul and Silas and released them from prison using "earthquake" as an ally (Acts 16: 25 - 34). All your arresters shall suffer destructive defeat, IJN.

Prayer: Father, fight all my battles and let nothing stop me from fulfilling my destiny, IJN.

Sunday February 24, 2019
Topic: GOD OF SECOND CHANCE

Scripture: "Manasseh was 12 years old when he began to rule, and he ruled for 55 years in Jerusalem" (2 Chron 33:1, GW).

Praise the Lord. Today is February 24th and is day #55 in year 2019. The number of days remaining to end this year is 310. By God's grace, you will do that which is right in the sight of God throughout this year, and you shall see the end of 2019 and beyond in Jesus name.

Anyone who finds himself/herself in a leadership position including the President of a nation must know that "--there is no authority except from God, and the authorities that exist are appointed by God" (Rm 13: 1-2). Therefore, any misuse of authoritative power in an ungodly manner may provoke the anger of God. Such was the case of Manasseh who ruled in Judah for 55 years. For most of his tenure, Manasseh did what was evil in the eyes of the LORD, committing detestable sins of shedding blood of the innocent, idol worshipping, occultism, sorcery, consulting mediums, sacrificing his own sons in the fire, etc. (2 Kgs 21: 2- 16).

Regrettably, many people today are still being led astray, turning to forbidden sins such as palm reading, occultism, mediums, witchcraft, divination, etc. (Deut. 18: 9-13). Be warned and don't be like Manasseh who, together with his people, failed to heed God's warning. God therefore brought the army commanders of king Assyria against Manasseh. He was taken as a prisoner to Babylon with hook in his nose and bound with bronze hackles. What a shame!

In his distress, Manasseh sought the favor of God, humbled himself greatly and prayed, pleading his case with God. God had mercy on him and gave him a second chance. Manasseh was restored back to Jerusalem and to his Kingdom (2 Chron. 33:13). He embarked on religious reformation to undo the evils he did before. Second chance is not guaranteed to everybody. Now is the time to turn away from evil ways and do what is right in the sight of God. Tomorrow may be too late. Repent, restitute, return to God and be restored. Otherwise, Satan will rule your life.

Prayer: Father, guide our leaders and forbid them from pursuing evil agendas, IJN.

Monday February 25, 2019
Topic: EXIT FROM EXILE I

Scripture: "*Here is the list of the Jewish exiles of the provinces who returned from their captivity. King Nebuchadnezzar had deported them to Babylon, but now they returned to Jerusalem and the other towns in Judah where they originally lived. The people of Netophah, 56" (Ezra 2: 1,22, NLT).*

Praise the Lord. Today is February 25th and is day #56 in year 2019. The number of days remaining to end this year is 309. By God's grace, nothing will hold you in captivity this year, and you shall see the end of 2019 and beyond in Jesus name.

It is a terrible thing to be held in hostage and/or carried into captivity. After 70 years in exile the captives from Judah were allowed to return to their homeland. Nearly 50,000 made the journey. Among the 2,172 listed in Ezra chapter 2 as descendants of Parosh, are the 56 men of Netophah family mentioned in the scripture above. Thank God, majority of people are not in exile today, and our prayer goes forth for those who are.

Are you physically away from your homeland and desire to return home one day on your own? I decree that at the appointed time you will make it home joyfully alive, IJN.

It is sad that in the present world 'satanic Nebuchadnezzar' has exiled many people (willingly or unwillingly) into Babylonian enclave of sin, corruption, bribery, kidnapping, alcoholism, homosexualism, transgenderism, drugs, atheism, ungodliness, poverty, stagnation, delay, retrogression, pride, etc. God is calling you to come out of exile and be free, IJN.

Prayer: Father, visit those in exile with Your power and meet each one at the point of his/her need, IJN

Tuesday February 26, 2019
Topic: DELIVERANCE FROM 'DDD' SYNDROME

Scripture: "Be merciful unto me, O God, be merciful unto me: for my soul trusteth in thee: yea, in the shadow of thy wings will I make my refuge, until these calamities be overpast. I will cry unto God most high; unto God that performeth all things for me." (Psalm 57: 1-2).

Praise the Lord. Today is February 26th and is day #57 in year 2019. The number of days remaining to end this year is 308. By God's grace, you will see the helping hands of God in all your performances this year, and you shall see the end of 2019 and beyond in Jesus name.

Psalm 57 is said to be written by David when he was hiding in cave Adullam from Saul for his life (1 Sam 22-24). Aside from his own troubles, David had to carry the problems of about 400 brethren from his father's house who came to him for help. The men were suffering from "DDD syndrome" - Distress, Debt and Discontentment. David, who by this time, should have been counting upwards his time on the throne as king of Israel, was engulfed in being pursued, persecution and problems. David cried to God for mercy knowing that God is 'a very present help in trouble' (Ps. 46:1).

Every believer needs to borrow a leaf from David. He did not result into complaining, blaming, retaliating, cursing, idling, doing nothing. Instead, David cried to God for mercy and sang praises unto Him (read all Ps. 57). God heard His cry and delivered him and all who ran to him for refuge. No matter what you are going through or what is going through you now and any time, cry to God for mercy. God who is plenteous in mercy (Ps. 86:15), will perform and perfect all things for you as He did for David, IJN.

Prayer: Father, please continue to perform Your goodness to me including liberating me from debt, depression and discontentment, IJN.

Wednesday February 27, 2019
Topic: PLEASING GOD ATTRACTS PROTECTION

Scripture: "And in the second month, on the twenty-seventh day of the month, the earth was dried." (Gen. 8:14).

Praise the Lord. Today is February 27th and is day #58 in year 2019. The number of days remaining to end this year is 307. By God's grace, no disaster shall come near you this year, and you shall see the end of 2019 and beyond in Jesus name.

In Biblical times, it was a day like today (the 27th day of the second month) that God dried up the flood from the earth. The same flood that destroyed the rest of the world was also the one God used to carry Noah and his household into safety in an ark that floated around and around for 150 days before settling down on the mountains of Ararat (Gen 6: 1-8; 7:1-24; 8: 1-19).

While others were cast down Noah was lifted up together with his household. This is God's promise for the believer who will separate himself/herself from sins and serve God obediently (Job 22: 29). How Noah got his breakthrough is instructive. The Bible declares, "But Noah found grace in the eyes of the Lord.- Noah was a just man and perfect in his generations, and Noah walked with God" (Gen 6: 8-9). Simply put, in a perverse world, Noah pleased God with his life and God protected and preserved him and his household. In this perverse world may you find grace that will let you separate yourself from sins, serve God obediently and faithfully. Then your life's ark shall not drown nor drift aimlessly, IJN.

Prayer: Father dry up all problematic floods in my life - sickness, famine, recession, delays, fruitlessness, demonic attacks, etc., IJN.

Thursday February 28, 2019
Topic: DELIVERANCE FROM AGENTS OF DESTRUCTION

Scripture: "Deliver me from mine enemies, O my God: defend me from them that rise up against me" (Psalm 59:1).

Praise the Lord. Today is February 28th and is day #59 in year 2019. The number of days remaining to end this year is 306. By God's grace, you shall see the end of 2019 and beyond in Jesus name.

Psalm 59 was penned by David when Saul sent messengers unto David's house to watch him and to slay him. God delivered David from this plot through the clever move of his wife (Michal). She warned David of the imminent death plan of her father and quickly let David down to escape through a window (1 Sam. 19: 9-18). Thank God for good wives like mine. It is heartbreaking to hear awful stories of how spouses today are killing each other. That will not be your portion, IJN. Spouses must prayerfully seek God's help to defend their marriages against devil's plan for destruction.

The Bible warns us against the devil, our greatest enemy whose primary assignment is to kill, to steal and to destroy (John 10:10). The good news for the believer is that God has better plan to defend and deliver His own (54: 15, 17; Ex. 14:14). He did it for Jesus Christ and will do it for all followers of Jesus Christ.

Prayer: Father, fight all my battles and deliver me from all my enemies, IJN.

Friday March 1, 2019
Topic: DECLARING ENEMY'S DEMISE

Scripture: "And it came to pass in the eleventh year, in the third month, in the first day of the month, that the word of the Lord came unto me, saying, Son of man, speak unto Pharaoh king of Egypt, and to his multitude; - -thou be brought down with the trees of Eden unto the nether parts of the earth: thou shalt lie in the midst of the uncircumcised with them that be slain by the sword. This is Pharaoh and all his multitude, saith the Lord God" (Ezek. 31: 1-2; 18).

Praise the Lord. Today is March 1st and is day #60 in year 2019. The number of days remaining to end this year is 305. By God's grace, the Pharaoh and his multitude after your life shall perish this year, and you shall see the end of 2019 and beyond in Jesus name.

Welcome to the first day of March. We give thanks to the Almighty God who has brought us safely out of February into March. According to the scripture above, it was on a day like today that the word of the LORD came unto Ezekiel commanding him to prophesy the doom and demise of the enemy of Israel, the king of Egypt called Pharaoh.

Today and henceforth you must speak the word of God unto your "Pharaoh", your enemies. God says "-- as ye have spoken in mine ears, so will I do to you" (Num 14:28). For example, tell your unrelenting enemies to die like Goliath (1 Sam 17:51,54), to be roasted by fire from heaven (2 kgs 1:10), to be smitten with blindness (2 Kgs 6:18), to eat their own flesh and drink their own blood (Isa. 49:26), etc.

Prayer: Father, let your word come to me this month to heal me, prosper me and save me from all destruction plans of my enemies, IJN.

Saturday March 2, 2019
Topic: RESTORED AND TRANSFORMED LIFE

Scripture: "Instead of shame and dishonor, you will enjoy a double share of honor. You will possess a double portion of prosperity in your land, and everlasting joy will be yours" (Isaiah 61:7, NLT).

Praise the Lord. Today is March 2nd and is day #61 in year 2019. The number of days remaining to end this year is 304. By God's grace, double honor shall be part of your blessings this year, you shall see the end of 2019 and beyond in Jesus name.

Restoration and transformation of lives was / is the primary focus of Christ's mission in to the world. Isaiah chapter 61: 1-9 and Luke 4:18-19) contain a long list of types of restoration and transformation available to followers of Jesus Christ. Based on the authority of the word of God, I decree to you that, as you countdown the days of year 2019, positive transformations will count upwards for you, IJN. Adversity shall turn to advantage, shame shall be replaced with double honor, poverty shall be wiped away by prosperity, sorrow shall turn to everlasting joy, rejection shall suddenly become acceptance, scarcity shall disappear in the presence of surplus, etc.

Prayer: Father, renew, restore and transform my life to conform to your perfect will, IJN.

Sunday March 3, 2019
Topic: POWER TO PROSPER

Scripture: "God hath spoken once; twice have I heard this; that power belongeth unto God" (Psalm 62:11).

Praise the Lord. Today is March 3rd and is day #62 in year 2019. The number of days remaining to end this year is 303. By God's grace, you witness the manifestation of God's power in your life every day of this year, and you shall see the end of 2019 and beyond in Jesus name.

God's power is far beyond human comprehension and description. Due to His power God only needs speak once and it stands, it is irreversible, immutable, firm, unalterable, trustworthy, undeniable and cannot return to Him void (Isa. 55:11). With His power what God has done /can do for us are innumerable. To mention just a few, God's power enables us to: have salvation /redemption (Rm 1:16, Jn. 1:12, Neh. 1:10), to be more than conquerors (Rom 8:37), tread on serpents, scorpions and over all the power of the enemy without been hurt (Lk 10:19), to witness (Acts 1:8) etc.

Has the Lord done anything for you lately with His power? Count up on them and give Him praise. Personally, one important thing I want you to join me in thanking God for is for sparing my life to see this day that marks my birthday anniversary. Glory be to God.

Action/Prayer: Thank God on behalf of all whose birthday is today. Pray that God will empower them to prosper spiritually and otherwise and be in good health in Jesus name, (Dt 8:18); get help (2 Chron 25:8); not fear, but love and have sound mind (2 Tim 1:7); have all things that pertain unto life and godliness (2 Pet 1:3), etc.

Monday March 4, 2019
Topic: POWERFUL TOOL OF PRAISE

Scripture: "Thus will I bless thee while I live: I will lift up my hands in thy name. - - 7 Because thou hast been my help, therefore in the shadow of thy wings will I rejoice." (Ps. 63:4, 7).

Praise the Lord. Today is March 4th and is day #63 in year 2019. The number of days remaining to end this year is 302. By God's grace, your constant praise of God will bring you all the help you need this year, and you shall see the end of 2019 and beyond in Jesus name.

Praising, worshipping and giving thanks to God has numerous benefits. David the writer of Psalm 63, and many other servants of God knew this secret and have engaged it to achieve many benefits including answer to prayer, victory, provisions, protection, etc.

The primary reason God created us is for us to praise Him and give him pleasure (1 Pet. 2:9, Rev. 4:11). Beloved, one of the secrets of praising, worshipping and giving thanks to God is long life. No wonder Psalm 150:6 says "Let everything that hath breath praise the Lord. Praise ye the Lord" and Isaiah 38:19a declares, "The living, the living, he shall praise thee, as I do this day" (Isa 38:19). If you want to live long, live a life of praise, worship and giving of thanks to God.

Prayer: Father, let not the enemy silence my voice of praise, worship and thanksgiving; give me the grace to praise You the more from now till eternity, IJN

Tuesday March 5, 2019
Topic: LOOSED BY THE LORD

Scripture: "And he was teaching in one of the synagogues on the sabbath. And, behold, there was a woman which had a spirit of infirmity eighteen years, and was bowed together, and could in no wise lift up herself. And when Jesus saw her, he called her to him, and said unto her, Woman, thou art loosed from thine infirmity. And he laid his hands on her: and immediately she was made straight, and glorified Go" (Lk 13: 10-13).

Praise the Lord. Today is March 5th and is day #64 in year 2019. The number of days remaining to end this year is 301. By God's grace, your miracles will locate you this year, and you shall see the end of 2019 and beyond in Jesus name.

The woman described in the scripture above must have been counting upwards the number of years she has been suffering from the infirmity that kept her bound for 18 years. Thank God she went to Church on a particular Sabbath day (what we will call Sunday today). Jesus "saw her" and terminated that infirmity. Suddenly, the counting upwards of years of infirmity came to ZERO. She would have missed her miracle had she not gone to Church on that particular day. Go to Church regularly to worship God and fellowship with the brethren (Heb. 10:25). Jesus Christ will see you, give you joy and loose you from whatever He has not planted in your life.

Prayer: Father, give me the grace to worship You regularly and please separate me from all forms of infirmities in Jesus mighty name.

Wednesday March 6, 2019
Topic: WALKING CLOSER WITH GOD

Scripture: " When Enoch was 65 years old, he became the father of Methuselah. After he became the father of Methuselah, Enoch walked with God for 300 years ……. Enoch lived a total of 365 years. Enoch walked with God; then he was gone because God took him." (Gen. 5:21-24, GW).

Praise the Lord. Today is March 6th and is day #65 in year 2019. The number of days remaining to end this year is 300. By God's grace, you shall be positively notable in your family, and you shall see the end of 2019 and beyond in Jesus name.

Enoch was a great man of faith whose name is listed in the faith hall of fame (Heb. 11:5). Part of his family tree is as follows, number in parenthesis indicating years lived by each predecessor before him: Adam (930), Seth (912), Enosh (905), Kenan (910), Mahalalel (895), Jared (962), Enoch (365 +), Methuselah (969), Lamech (777), Noah (950).

There are several notable points about Enoch: (a) like his grandfather (Mahalalel), Enoch had his first son, Methuselah at age 65 (Gen 5: 15, 21). (b) Longevity characterized Enoch's family - his son Methuselah is the oldest human being who ever lived on this earth, (c) Enoch himself did not taste death. (d) For 300 years, Enoch "walked with God" before God took him (Gen. 5: 22-24). As the Lord lives you too shall live long, IJN

I challenge myself (and you too) to determine to walk closer with God in the remaining 300 days of 2019. This will call for greater faith, greater trust in God, greater obedience, greater service, etc. It is a tall order, but is doable (Lk. 1:37). If Noah and others could do it (Gen 6:9) we can do it.

Prayer: Father, for the rest of this year and my life give me the grace to walk closer with You, IJN.

Thursday March 7, 2019
Topic: TRIALS TURNED TO TESTIMONIES

Scripture: "Thou hast caused men to ride over our heads; we went through fire and through water: but thou broughtest us out into a wealthy place" (Psalm 66:12).

Praise the Lord. Today is March 7th and is day #66 in year 2019. The number of days remaining to end this year is 299. By God's grace, you shall not be downtrodden, you shall brought into wealthy place this year, and shall see the end of 2019 and beyond in Jesus name.

A bona fide follower of Jesus Christ (i.e. a Christian) must be aware that life in this present world is not going to be all rosy all the time. It wasn't for Jesus Christ or any of the Apostles. Occasionally, there will be bumps on the road to victory. The good news is that God has promised to be with us, no matter what we are going through - fire, water, etc. (Isa. 43: 1-3). He has promised to help us and as long as we stay loyal and obedient to Him, all things will work together for our good (Rm 8:28).

Are you facing some challenges right now - health, bills, relationships, business, education, immigration, etc.; prayerfully look up to Jesus for solutions. Don't panic and don't fear.

Keep hope alive, be positive, strong, and courageous. Study about each situation and seek counsel/help when possible. It is possible that the challenges you are facing now are part of the divine plan of God to get you to your wealthy place as it was for Joseph, Daniel and some others. Claim what God's word says - "weeping may endure for a night but joy cometh in the morning" (Ps. 30:5). Trust in the LORD and know that 'with God all things are possible' (Lk. 1:37). God can turn your trials to testimonies.

Prayer: Father, please turn my adversity into advantage in Jesus mighty name.

Friday March 8, 2019
Topic: POWER OF PRAISE

Scripture: "Let the people praise thee, O God; let all the people praise thee. Then shall the earth yield her increase; and God, even our own God, shall bless us. 7 God shall bless us; and all the ends of the earth shall fear him." (Psalm 67:4-7).

Praise the Lord. Today is March 8th and is day #67 in year 2019. The number of days remaining to end this year is 298. By God's grace, you shall experience divines increases this year, and you shall see the end of 2019 and beyond in Jesus name.

Praise is one thing that God cherishes so much because it is central to the reason why He created us (Isa 43:21, Ps. 22:3,1 Pet. 2:9, Rev 4:11). The quality and quantity of your praise will determine the number of blessings you will get from God (Gal. 6: 6-7; 2 Cor. 9:6). No wonder it is repeated twice in Psalm 67 that ALL the people should praise God (Ps 67: 3,5).

King Jehoshaphat and the nation of Judah can testify to the potency of praise in provoking God's blessings. All they had to do to defeat and destroy their enemies and inherit treasures that took them three days to gather was just to sing praises to God in the beauty of His holiness (2 Chron 20). If you want a count upward of more blessings, not only must you step up your personal praise, you must get ALL your family members, all your Church members, etc. to praise God passionately abundantly.

Prayer: Father, please empower me to praise You the more and let the earth yield her increase to me, IJN.

Saturday March 9, 2019
Topic: BLESSED BOUNTIFULLY

Scripture: "Blessed be the Lord, who daily loadeth us with benefits, even the God of our salvation. Selah" (Psalm 68:19).

Praise the Lord. Today is March 9th and is day #68 in year 2019. The number of days remaining to end this year is 297. By God's grace, you shall be loaded with benefits daily this year, and you shall see the end of 2019 and beyond in Jesus name

Each day we count into our life is a gift from God loaded with innumerable benefits. A song writer says "Count your blessings name them one by one and it will surprise you what the Lord has done" (Oatman Jr, 1897). One of my favorite choruses says "When I think of the goodness of Jesus, and all He has done for me, my very soul shall shout Halleluiah, praise God for saving me". The Bible says God, by His divine power, "- -hath given unto us all things that pertain unto life and godliness- -" (2 Pet. 1:3). Anybody that has Jesus as his/her Lord and Savior is rich and secured, for Christ's riches are unsearchable (Eph. 3:8)

The best riches/treasures to have are those towards God that will not block our way to heaven (Lk.12:15 -21; Mk 8: 35-36). We should have an attitude of gratitude to God every day for the benefits life, faith in him, our family, our friends, fellowship, hope for better future, etc. We should continue to work hard and trust God to supply all our needs according to His promise (Phil. 4:19). May your benefits today include divine peace, protection, favor, miracles, etc.

Prayer: Father, thank You for your daily benefits into my life, let me stay in Your will, IJN.

Sunday March 10, 2019
Topic: LONGEVITY OF LIFE

Scripture: "Altogether, Methuselah lived a total of 969 years, and then he died." (Gen 5: 27, NIV).

Praise the Lord. Today is March 10th and is day #69 in year 2019. The number of days remaining to end this year is 296. By God's grace, the spirit of untimely death shall not have room in your family this year, and you shall see the end of 2019 and beyond in Jesus name.

Methuselah is the oldest human being known to have lived in the earth and he lived for 969 years! Of course, life expectancy (LE) today is dismally shorter than in Methuselah's era. Opinions for this difference are many including the result of multiplication of sins, differences in measurement of "years", in genetic makeup, climatic changes, etc.

The current average worldwide LE is about 71.0 years, with women living longer (73.5 years) than men (68.5 years). This LE is generally consistent with what the Psalmist says: "Our days may come to seventy years, or eighty, if our strength endures--" (Psalm 90:10, NIV).

As of January 2018, the world oldest person living was Nabi Tajima, a Japanese female born August 4, 1900 and has lived for 117 years and 171 days. Available information indicates that 60 percent of the oldest women in the world were of Japanese origin. Some experts credit their relative longer life to their food diet. However, as believers we must remember that ultimately our times are in the hands of God (Ps. 31:15; Dan 2:21). He has promised to satisfy His own with long life (Ps. 91:16) and fulfill the number of our days (Ex. 23:26). He is the only one who can multiply our days and add years to our lives (Pro. 9:11). Glory be to God!

Prayer: Father, let me fulfill my destiny and live my full age, all to Your glory, IJN.

Monday March 11, 2019
Topic: COMMITTED TO THE GREAT COMMISSION?

Scripture: "After this, the Lord appointed 70 other disciples to go ahead of him to every city and place that he intended to go. They were to travel in pairs" (Luke 10:1, GW)

Praise the Lord. Today is March 11th and is day #70 in year 2019. The number of days remaining to end this year is 295. By God's grace, you shall continually be a forerunner for Jesus Christ, and you shall see the end of 2019 and beyond in Jesus name

What is called "The Great Commission" is the instruction of the resurrected Jesus Christ (shortly before His ascension) to his disciples to spread His teachings to all the nations of the world (Mt.28: 16-20). Jesus Christ had earlier introduced this concept of evangelism to his disciples during his ministry. He sent 70 of them out in pairs ahead of him into town and villages where he was going to minister. Among other things they were to disseminate peace into each house they entered, heal the sick and tell people about the nearness of God's kingdom (Lk. 10: 1-17). The 70 disciples carried out the assignment and returned with joy and testifying that, "- - even the demons are subject to us in Your name". (Lk. 10:17).

Spreading the good news of salvation by faith in Jesus Christ to others is what Jesus Christ expects all His followers to do. Doing this obediently and faithfully can attract many blessings including joy, victory over demons, provoking God's favor, laying treasures in heaven, etc.

On this 70th day of 2019, let us all do some form of evangelism - pray for souls, distribute tracts, encourage a backslider / somebody's faith, use social media (text, email, Facebook, WhatsApp, etc.) to minister to somebody), sow a seed of evangelism. Once you start today, don't let the fire go out. How committed are you to the Great Commission?

Prayer: Father, help me to be more passionate and more effective in witnessing for You, IJN.

Tuesday March 12, 2019
Topic: DEFLECTING FROM DISGRACE

Scripture: "O Lord, I have come to you for protection; don't let me be disgraced" (Psalm 71:1)

Praise the Lord. Today is March 12th and is day #71 in year 2019. The number of days remaining to end this year is 294. By God's grace, you will receive grace upon grace this year, and you shall see the end of 2019 and beyond in Jesus name

Some Bible scholars say that Psalm 71 was written by King David when his son Absalom conspired against him attempting to dethrone him as king of Israel. The situation turned David's family to a dysfunctional one and caused him tremendous distress, dilemma, sorrow, shame etc. David even had to vacate his throne in Jerusalem in order to save lives (2 Sam chaps. 15-18).

The terrible political and spiritual upheaval in David's life could be attributed to several factors including evil outcomes of his earlier adulterous and polygamous life, bad counsel from Ahithophel and failure to deal promptly with lusts and disputes among his children. Whenever Satan smells success, he wastes no time to try to soil it. To avert the shame been perpetrated by Satan on his personality and dynasty, David cried to God for protection as indicated in today's opening scripture. God answered him and quelled the violent attack of Absalom and his supporters. They suffered sudden and disgraceful death while pursuing after David and Israel ((2 Sam. 18:6-15).

Prayer: Father protect me and my family against turmoil and disgrace, let Your peace reign in our lives, IJN.

Wednesday March 13, 2019
Topic: GOD'S OWN CATTLE GIFT

Scripture: "The cattle were 36,000, of which the Lord's tribute was 72" (Numbers 31:38)

Praise the Lord. Today is March 13th and is day #72 in year 2019. The number of days remaining to end this year is 293. By God's grace, your tribute to God shall increase this year, and you shall see the end of 2019 and beyond in Jesus name.

The God who made us in His own image has always wanted us to maintain fellowship with Him. One of the ways to maintain fellowship and devotion to God is by giving to Him different things such as "thanks" (1 Chron 16: 34, 41, Ps. 92:1; Eph. 5:18), "praise" (Ps. 108:1), "glory" (Isa. 42:12) and even "tribute of cattle" as indicated in today's opening scripture.

The LORD spoke to Moses saying "Avenge the children of Israel of the Midianites." (Num. 31:2). The vengeance is with respect to how the Midianites sent their daughters among them, who enticed them to commit sexual impurity and idol worshipping which brought the wrath of God upon them, and for which 24,000 persons were killed (Num. 25: 1-9). Following Moses detailed instruction, the Israelite army, led by Phinehas, son of Eleazar, went to battle and killed all the Midianite men. They captured the Midianite women and children and seized their cattle and flocks and all their wealth as plunder (Num 31:7-9).

God through Moses and Eleaza the priest, gave specific instruction as to how the battle plunder was to be shared equally, half to the men who fought the battle and the other half to the rest of the people. From the army's portion, they were to first give the Lord his share of the plunder—one of every 500 of the prisoners and of the cattle, donkeys, sheep, and goats. Based on this distribution formula, God's own tribute was 72 cattle. What have you given to the LORD this year in appreciation of His innumerable blessings to you. Remember, it is more blessed to give than to receive (Acts 20:38).

Prayer: Father, give me the grace to give You tribute from the benefits You bestow unto me daily.

Thursday March 14, 2019
Topic: GETTING CLOSER TO GOD

Scripture: "But it is good for me to draw near to God: I have put my trust in the Lord God, that I may declare all thy works" (Psalm 73:28).

Praise the Lord. Today is March 14th and is day #73 in year 2019. The number of days remaining to end this year is 292. By God's grace, you will not waiver in trusting God this year, and you shall see the end of 2019 and beyond in Jesus name.

Getting closer to God everyday should be the desire and goal of every believer because God has promised to draw near to those who draw near unto Him (James 4:8; Heb 13:5). God is our greatest ally and when He is for us no one can be against us (Rom. 8:31). God has everything we need so we stand to enjoy many blessings from Him by getting close to Him. Some of the ways of drawing close to God include giving our lives to Him, engaging in regular prayer, praise, worship, reading, hearing and meditating on His words, fellowshipping with other believers, serving in God's house, witnessing, etc.

The blessings obtainable from drawing close to God are numerous and include love, joy, peace, longsuffering, gentleness, goodness, faith, meekness, temperance, (Gal 5: 16-22, Ps. 16:11), freedom from problems (Matt 11:28), safety (Ps. 119:117), provisions, (Phil 4:19), divine protection (Isa. 43: 2-3), etc. The closer you are to God; the farther away Satan will be from you.

Prayer: Father, please let nothing separate me from You and Your ceaseless flow of ceaseless blessings into my life, IJN.

Friday March 15, 2019
Topic: EXIT FROM EXILE II

Scripture: "Here is the list of the Jewish exiles of the provinces who returned from their captivity - - These are the Levites who returned from exile: The families of Jeshua and Kadmiel (descendants of Hodaviah)", 74" (Ezra, 2: 1, 40).

Praise the Lord. Today is March 15th and is day #74 in year 2019. The number of days remaining to end this year is 291. By God's grace, you shall not embark on journey of no return this year, and you shall see the end of 2019 and beyond in Jesus name.

From his invasion of Jerusalem and Judah, Nebuchadnezzar had carried many Jews into captivity in Babylon. At the intervention of God, these exiles began to return to Judah and Jerusalem, every one unto his city (Ezra 2:1). A detailed listing of the 42,360 returnees by categories (such as priests, singers, porters, etc.) and their livestock is provided in Ezra chapter 2. In an earlier devotional material (Feb. 25th) we saw that 56 exiled men of Netophah family of the descendant of Parosh had successfully returned to Jerusalem.

Today's ministration also involves another set of returning exiles. These are unique group called Levites. While other Israelites were worshipping the golden calf at Mt. Horeb, the Levites remained faithful to Yahweh. They were rewarded with the right to special service in and around the Tabernacle (Gen 32) and later in the Temple. As noted in today's opening scripture, 74 of these Levites also returned successfully from exile to Jerusalem. When God set them free, nobody could stop them from escaping bondage.

Many people today are unable to enjoy freedom because the enemy has kept them bound in captivity of sins, sickness, stagnation, sorrows, joblessness, marital problems, fruitlessness, failures, rejection, etc. If this describes you, cry to Jesus Christ and claim the word of God in Isaiah 49:2. that says "- Even the captives of the most mighty and most terrible shall all be freed; for I will fight those who fight you, and I will save your children." In Isaiah 49:25. , TLB). Any one Jesus Christ sets free shall be free indeed (John 8:36). In this season, your countdown on freedom from captivity shall clock zero, IJN.

Prayer: Father, set me and my family completely free from anything that has held us captive, in Jesus mighty name.

Saturday March 16, 2019
Topic: HEARING FROM GOD

Scripture: "So Abram departed, as the Lord had spoken unto him; and Lot went with him: and Abram was seventy and five years old when he departed out of Haran." (Gen 12:4).

Praise the Lord. Today is March 16th and is day #75 in year 2019. The number of days remaining to end this year is 290. By God's grace, you will be divinely ordered this year to towards fulfilling your destiny, and you shall see the end of 2019 and beyond in Jesus name.

At age 75, an important turning point took place in the life of Abraham, simply because he heard from God and obeyed God completely. God had told Abraham to depart from his country, out of his father's house to go to a land that God would show him. God promised to make Abraham great and to bless him in other ways (Gen 12: 2-3). Without argument, delay or doubt, Abraham did exactly what God told him and today we are still counting upwards the blessings accruing to his obedience.

Aside from terminating barrenness and fulfilling all His promises to Abraham, God honored Abraham in so many other ways including calling Abraham "my friend" (Isa. 41:8; James 2:23). The God that spoke to Abraham is still speaking today. What has He said/been saying to you regarding yourself, your family, other people, forgiveness, tithing, serving in the Church, witnessing, that immoral relationship, drug, alcoholism, etc? On this 75th day of year 2017 and henceforth, may the grace to hear, obey God and receive the blessings appertaining multiply in our lives, IJN.

Action/Prayer: Find and prayerfully sing the Hymn "Master Speak thy Servant Heareth- "

Friday March 17, 2019
Topic: CREATED IN IMAGE OF CHRIST

Scripture: "So God created man in his own image, in the image of God created he him; male and female created he them." (Gen 1:27).

Praise the Lord. Today is March 17th and is day #76 in year 2019. The number of days remaining to end this year is 289. By God's grace, your life and activities this year shall testify that you are truly the child of God,, and you shall see the end of 2019 and beyond in Jesus name.

We can gain some meaningful insights by looking at the numerical digits that make up the number 76 - i.e. #7 and #6. The number 7 connotes perfection and completeness (Gen 2: 1-3) while the number 6 is the number of man (Gen 1: 27-31). Putting the 2 numbers together in the context of the opening scripture above we can say that the perfect God made man in His own image on the sixth day of creation. Therefore, when we think of the number 76 and what the digits represent, we must be grateful to God for making us to be partakers of His divine nature (2 Pet. 1:4).

While this divine nature attribute we have is a blessing, it also exposes us to attack by the enemy who is constantly seeking who to kill, still or destroy (John 10:10). That is why we must pray like David: "Arise, O Lord, in thine anger, lift up thyself because of the rage of mine enemies: and awake for me to the judgment that thou hast commanded" (Psalm 7:6)

Prayer: Father, because You created me, and I carry Your divine nature, arise and let the enemy lose his battle against me, IJN.

Monday March 18, 2019
Topic: CANCELING GENERATIONAL CURSES

Scripture: "Lamech said to his wives, "Adah and Zillah, listen to me! Wives of Lamech, hear what I say! I killed a man for bruising me, a young man for wounding me. If Cain is avenged 7 times, then Lamech, 77 times." (Gen 4: 23-24, GW).

Praise the Lord. Today is March 18th and is day #77 in year 2019. The number of days remaining to end this year is 288. By God's grace, no evil pattern shall characterize you this year, and you shall see the end of 2019 and beyond in Jesus name.

Sometimes certain evil traits can run in the family that can bring untold hardship to generations to come if not prayerfully dealt with. A case in point is Cain who killed his brother Abel because of envy. Lamech, who was about the 5th generation descendant of Cain was also a murderer, much worse than Cain. He killed 2 people and boasted of his action to his 2 wives. What made the sin of Lamech (the first recorded polygamist in the Bible) more heinous than that of Cain is the mockery of God he made of it. Lamech said if Cain is avenged 7 times, he (Lamech) should be avenged 77 times.

Essentially, Lamech was implying that if God allowed Cain who killed one person (his blood brother) to go unpunished, how much more he (Lamech) who killed 2 non-relatives should be exonerated from any punishment. Lamech has forgotten that God is a just God and His ways and thoughts are far superior to that of man. (Isa 55:8-9). Food for thought: What is the role (physical, spiritual and emotional) of the mark God put on Cain for killing Abel? (Gen 4:15).

Prayer: Father, please break and terminate all generational evil traits and curses in my family, IJN.

Tuesday March 19, 2019
Topic: ENDING EXCELLENTLY

Scripture: "Better is the end of a thing than the beginning thereof: and the patient in spirit is better than the proud in spirit" (Eccl. 7:8).

Praise the Lord. Today is March 19th and is day #78 in year 2019. The number of days remaining to end this year is 287. By God's grace, you shall see the end of 2019 and beyond in Jesus name.

True believers and followers of Jesus Christ must always have a positive outlook. In particular we must believe in God's word and put faith to work in all that we do. The scripture above must be prayerfully applied to any activity we engage in and counting down on. Obedience to God and optimism are critical elements among factors that can influence positively the outcome of believer's activities. Jesus Christ adopted this strategy and He gloriously finished his mission of coming to save the world (Heb 12:2).

Whatever good thing you have started or plan to start - journey to heaven, academic programs, business activity, job, relationship, etc. don't give up. Work patiently and consistently on your activity; trust, obey, pray and serve God and He will ensure that you finish well, IJN.

Prayer: Father, give me the grace to embark on noble tasks and to finish them successfully, strongly and excellently, IJN.

Wednesday March 20, 2019
Topic: READY FOR GOD'S KINGDOM?

Scripture: "After this I beheld, and, lo, a great multitude, which no man could number, of all nations, and kindreds, and people, and tongues, stood before the throne, and before the Lamb, clothed with white robes, and palms in their hands;" (Rev. 7:9).

Praise the Lord. Today is March 20th and is day #79 in year 2019. The number of days remaining to end this year is 286. By God's grace, you not stand before mean men this year, and you shall see the end of 2019 and beyond in Jesus name.

Among the vision of heaven given to John is the multitude of victorious people that will stand before the throne of God. I pray you and I will make it to God's kingdom. While there will be plenty of room in God's kingdom, not everyone born into this world will make it there because not everyone will meet the criteria for admission into God's kingdom (Mt. 7:21, Rev 21:8). The only way to get to heaven is through Jesus Christ: "Jesus saith unto him, I am the way, the truth, and the life: no man cometh unto the Father, but by me" (John 14:6).

Accept the salvation offered by Jesus Christ today by asking Him to forgive you your sins and be your Lord and Savior. Then you will be enlisted as one of the multitudes that will stand before the throne of God. Anyone not listed in the multitude to be in heaven is already listed in the multitude that will be in hell where they will burn forever in the lake of fire (Rev 20:15). Hellfire is not your portion, IJN.

Prayer: Father, deny me of anything that will deny me of standing before your throne, IJN.

Thursday March 21, 2019
Topic: FREEDOM BY DIVINE FORCE

Scripture: "And the Lord said to Moses, 'See, I have made you like God to Pharaoh, - - You shall speak all that I command you, and your brother Aaron shall tell Pharaoh to let the people of Israel go out of his land. - -' Moses and Aaron did so; they did just as the Lord commanded them. Now Moses was eighty years old, - -when they spoke to Pharaoh." (Exodus 7: 1-2 & 6-7, ESV).

Praise the Lord. Today is March 21st and is day #80 in year 2019. The number of days remaining to end this year is 285. By God's grace, you shall be used to make the lives of many people better this year, and you shall see the end of 2019 and beyond in Jesus name.

At the age of 80, God sent Moses and Aaron to go tell Pharaoh to let the Israelites go free after about 430 years of slavery and servitude in the land of Egypt. They went with the boldness of God to deliver the message. Despite 9 terrible plagues that brought untold sufferings to him and his people, the stubborn Pharaoh resisted the order to let the people of God go. However, at God's appointed time when the 10th plague (the slaying of the first born male child and animals) of the Egyptians was introduced, Pharaoh knew that power pass power and he begged the Israelites to leave in a haste (Exo. 12:33).

The Israelites did not leave empty; they carried as much wealth of the Egyptians as they could (Exo. 12). Irrespective of your age, tap into the anointing of Moses and Aaron and speak to the enemy / "Pharaoh" to set you free from whatever amounts to slavery and servitude - serving Satan instead of God, sickness, "not enough syndrome", delay, stagnation, marital problems, working like elephants and eating like rats, etc. As you countdown on your time to freedom you shall not go empty in Jesus name.

Prayer: Father, by fire by force, liberate me from all demonic embargoes and restore unto me everything I have ever lost in Jesus mighty name.

Friday March 22, 2019
Topic: GOD DOES'NT FORGET, HE REMEMBERS

Scripture: "And God remembered Noah, and every living thing, and all the cattle that was with him in the ark: and God made a wind to pass over the earth, and the water assuaged." (Genesis 8:1).

Praise the Lord. Today is March 22nd and is day #81 in year 2019. The number of days remaining to end this year is 284. By God's grace, the book of remembrance linked with your accelerated promotions hall be opened and read this year, and you shall see the end of 2019 and beyond in Jesus name.

God is omniscient, meaning He knows all things perfectly well and can never forget as humans do. When the Bible says God 'remembered' it means He brings His attention to that person especially as regards His promise to that person. When God remembers somebody for good, He brings an end to the problem(s) in the life of that person. God remembered Noah and caused his ark to come to a rest on Mount Ararat after 150 days of roaming aimlessly about on rising waters. God remembered Rachel and terminated her bareness (Gen. 30:22). God remembered Abraham and, "sent Lot out of the midst of the overthrow, when He overthrew the cities in which Lot dwelt" (Gen 19:29). God remembered His covenant with Abraham and freed the Israelites from bondage (Exo. 2:24, 6:5, 12:31-32).

In this season may God remember you and put an end to any problem that has lingered on concerning your health, finances, family, business, etc. The Ark of safety in which Noah and his family were kept during the flood that destroyed everyone else typifies the salvation and security available in Jesus Christ. As Bible says, whosoever believes in Jesus Christ shall not perish, but have everlasting life (John 3:16). Get on board today and be saved.

Prayer: Father, remember me and my family and terminate all our problems, IJN.

Saturday March 23, 2019
Topic: WORSHIP AS A WEAPON

Scripture: "And, behold, there came a leper and worshipped him, saying, Lord, if thou wilt, thou canst make me clean" (Matthew 8:2).

Praise the Lord. Today is March 23rd and is day #82 in year 2019. The number of days remaining to end this year is 283. By God's grace, no evil shall taint your life this year, and you shall see the end of 2019 and beyond in Jesus name.

Worship refers to reverent honor and homage paid to God. Worship can be a powerful weapon in the hand of a believer for dealing with many problems of life. Worship is very important to God that He will not trade it for anything. In one of his temptations of Jesus Christ, Satan told Jesus to worship him in exchange for receiving all the power and glory of all the kingdoms of the world. Jesus refused the offer and lectured Satan that it is written that only God is to be worshipped and served (Lk. 4: 5-8). The Bible makes it clear that God is constantly seeking for people who will worship Him in spirit and in truth (John 4: 23).

Holy worshipping is unsurpassable in terms of how to get God's attention. Paul and Silas were in the prison worshipping God when He sent an earthquake to erupt in the prison to free them and other prisoners (Acts 16: 25- 34). As instructed by God, Jehoshaphat organized a praise and worship ensemble as the only weapon needed for defeating armies of three nations that attacked him and the people of Judah (2 Chron 20: 21-23).

As indicated in the opening scripture for today, a leper who apparently was desperate for healing broke protocol rule and came to Jesus worshipping Him. When Jesus saw the faith and determination of the leper, He did not hesitate in healing him. "And Jesus put forth his hand, and touched him, saying, I will; be thou clean. And immediately, his leprosy was cleansed" (Matt 8:3). Are you a victim of "leprosy" of sins, sickness, poverty, joblessness, bareness, etc? Jesus Christ is able to heal them all. Bring them all to Him today and be healed, IJN.

Prayer: *Father, please let the blood of Jesus clear away whatever constitutes "leprosy" in my life in Jesus name.*

Sunday March 24, 2019
Topic: THE WORD OF LIFE AND POWER

Scripture: "And he humbled thee, and suffered thee to hunger, and fed thee with manna, which thou knewest not, neither did thy fathers know; that he might make thee know that man doth not live by bread only, but by every word that proceedeth out of the mouth of the Lord doth man live" (Deut. 8:3).

Praise the Lord. Today is March 24th and is day #83 in year 2019. The number of days remaining to end this year is 282. By God's grace, you shall enjoy divine provisions this year, and you shall see the end of 2019 and beyond in Jesus name.

Everything God does or permits to happen in man's life has a purpose. He allowed the Israelites to suffer thirst and hunger in the wilderness to test their trust and dependency on Him. Unfortunately, they failed both tests and they displayed their ingratitude to God by murmuring against Moses (Exodus 15:23-24 & 16:2-3). When Moses cried to God concerning the complaints of the Israelites, God miraculously provided drinkable water and rained down manna from heaven for the people.

By these miraculous provisions God intended to teach us many lessons including (a) God is able to supply all needs (b) We should know that both physical food and spiritual food (word of God) are needed for healthy life (c) Instead of murmuring we should be thankful to God for His past blessings and prayerfully trust Him for subsequent needs. In the remaining days of this year 2019, you shall not lack, IJN.

Prayer: Father, let the power of Your word work to my advantage in all areas of my life

Monday March 25, 2019
Topic: CONSTANT COMMITMENT TO CHRIST

Scripture: "Anna, a prophet, was also there. …. She was now very old. Her husband had died seven years after they were married, 37 and she had been a widow for 84 years. Anna never left the temple courtyard but worshiped day and night by fasting and praying". (Luke 2: 36-37, GW).

Praise the Lord. Today is March 25th and is day #84 in year 2019. The number of days remaining to end this year is 281. By God's grace, you shall serve the Lord more passionately this year, and you shall see the end of 2019 and beyond in Jesus name.

Believers are expected to be totally committed to God, not one leg in, one leg out or hot today cold tomorrow. We must all heed Apostle Paul's injunction to not let anything separate us from the love of God (Rom. 8: 35-39). In this regard, Prophetess Anna's case is noteworthy and instructive. She lived with her husband for only 7 years and became a widow for 84 years. Despite the loss of her husband, we are told she remained committed to the God of the Church and the Church of God where she was serving.

Thank God there are widows like Anna today in many of our Churches. However, we must pray constantly for all widows for God to comfort, encourage and strengthen them to continue serving Him according to His will for them. Note also that the Devil's battle cry is to use sin or disobedience or anything to separate believers from fellowshipping with God. The onus is on us to resist Devil's attempt of using ephemeral things to denying us of eternal blessings. Every effort of Satan concerning you shall fail in the name of Jesus.

Prayer: Father, let nothing separate me from You, IJN. Have a blessed day.

Tuesday March 26, 2019
Topic: YOU CAN STILL CONQUER MOUNTAINS

Scripture: "So look at me. The Lord has kept me alive as he promised. It's been 45 years since Israel wandered in the desert when the Lord made this promise to Moses. So now look at me today. I'm 85 years old. I'm still as fit to go to war now as I was when Moses sent me out. Now give me this mountain region which the Lord spoke of that day- -" (Joshua 14: 10-12, GW).

Praise the Lord. Today is March 26th and is day #85 in year 2019. The number of days remaining to end this year is 280. By God's grace, you shall wax stronger daily this year, and you shall see the end of 2019 and beyond in Jesus name.

Today let us look at what happened to Caleb at 85 years old! He was one of the 12 spies Moses sent to go and spy the promised land of Canaan prior to entry. Based on fear, doubt and unbelief, 10 of the spies gave negative report that Israel would not be able to take over the land. Only Caleb and Joshua, based on their trust and strong faith in God, reported that Israel would be able take over the land (Num. 13 & 14). God rewarded both Joshua and Caleb for their trust in Him and for positive confession.

When Israel under Joshua's leadership finally occupied Canaan, Caleb at age 85 came to Joshua to demand his own portion of the land as promised by God, some 45 years earlier. He was assigned Hebron which he conquered by overcoming its Anakin inhabitants (Joshua 14:6-14). Caleb said he was as strong at 85 as he was at 40. At 85 he was still looking for "mountain" to conquer!

No matter how old you are God can still give you "mountains" to conquer in the remaining 280 days of 2019 and beyond. You can still tell somebody about salvation through Jesus, spend more time in God's word, learn a new skill, work on improving your relationship, take up an assignment in God's house, read books, start writing books, etc.

Payer: Lord, keep me alive and let me be strong in You and in the power of Your might, IJN.

Wednesday March 27, 2019
Topic: HELPING GOD DO HIS WORK?

Scripture: "Abram was 86 years old when Hagar gave birth to Ishmael". (Genesis 16:16, GW).

Praise the Lord. Today is March 27th and is day #86 in year 2019. The number of days remaining to end this year is 279. By God's grace, you shall patiently await the performance of God's plans for your life this year, and you shall see the end of 2019 and beyond in Jesus name.

Sometimes circumstances force people to take actions that amount to helping God do His work without getting His approval for such actions. This happens when "flesh" is in control and believers must guide against this seriously. Sarah and Abraham fell into a kind of "faith ditch" when Sarah told Abraham to have Hagar, their maid as a "second wife". Sarah took this decision because, after 10 years of marriage there was still no child despite God's promise to make Abraham a great nation and make his seed as numberless as the stars of heaven (Gen 12: 1-4; 15:1-5). Without checking with God Abram consented to Sarah's suggestion and Ishmael was born by Hagar to Abraham at age 86.

It turned out that Ishmael (first child named prior to birth in Bible) was not the promised son to Abraham but Isaac who was later born to Abraham by Sarah. In the meantime, a lot of damages had been done some of which we are still suffering till today in terms of the Middle East conflicts and terrorism (read Gen. 16-17). Anytime man violates God's marriage policy of one man, one wife (Gen. 2:24) or engages in sexual love affairs outside marriage boundary, sins and other problems tend to ensue. These problems may include pride, jealousy, envy, favoritism, separation, divorce, abuse, murder, etc. To avoid these and many other problems married couples and those intending to get married should faithfully adhere to God's ordained plan of one man one wife for marriage.

Prayer: Father, let Your divine order, agenda and peace reign in all our families, IJN.

Thursday March 28, 2019
Topic: BETTER ENDING THAN THE BEGINNING

Scripture: "Though your beginning was small, Yet your latter end would increase abundantly." (Job 8:7, NKJV).

Praise the Lord. Today is March 28th and is day #87 in year 2019. The number of days remaining to end this year is 278. By God's grace, your influence shall increase more and more this year, and you shall see the end of 2019 and beyond in Jesus name.

At the time we first know about Job in the Bible, everything was going great for him spiritually, economically and otherwise. He was even described as the greatest of all the men of the east and God bragged about him to Satan (Job 1: 1-9). Suddenly, Satan attacked him and Job lost everything, including all his children. He was even so sick that his wife suggested to him to curse God and die, but job refused to sin or charge God foolishly (Job 2:9-10).

While commiserating with him one day, Bildad, one of Job's friends made the statement in Job 8:7 quoted above, not knowing he was been prophetic. When God turned the tide in favor of Job and restored him, he ended up having twice of everything he lost (Job 42: 10). The Bible says the end of a thing is better than the beginning thereof (Eccl. 7:8). It doesn't matter how you started this year and what has happened in the first 87 days of year 2019, so long as you remain faithfully connected to Jesus Christ each of the remaining 278 days of this year shall usher in greater glory and blessings for you. By God's grace, you will end year 2019 much better (spiritually, financially, etc.) than you started it, IJN.

Prayer: Father, restore unto me all I have lost and let my tomorrow be better in all areas, IJN.

Friday March 29th, 2019
Topic: MIRACULOUSLY MULTIPLIED MEALS

Scripture: "So they did eat, and were filled: and they took up of the broken meat that was left seven baskets." (Mark 8:8).

Praise the Lord. Today is March 29th and is day #88 in year 2019. The number of days remaining to end this year is 277. By God's grace, famine shall be far away from you this year and your cup of blessings shall overflow; you shall see the end of 2019 and beyond in Jesus name.

God does not want His people to suffer hunger or lack. His plan is to supply all our need according to His riches in glory by Christ Jesus (Phil. 4:19). Being a God of abundance who owns the heavens and the earth, God can take care of ALL the needs of those who will follow Him faithfully.

After a multitude had been with Jesus Christ 3 days in the wilderness receiving sound doctrines and getting healed in their bodies, He didn't want to send them away hungry, so that no one would faint on the way. Out of compassion He determined to feed the multitude, saying "-- because they have now been with me three days, --" (Mk. 8:2). He miraculously multiplied 7 loaves and a few fishes and got at least 4000 people sumptuously fed with a leftover of 7 baskets full of surplus food (Mk. 8: 5-9).

When you stay with Jesus Christ, He cares for you in all areas- spiritually, physically, etc. In the remaining 277 days of this year God's miracles of abundance will manifest in your life and you shall not lack any good thing in the mighty name of Jesus (Psalm 34:10, NLT).

Prayer: Father, let me remain with you perpetually to be fed spiritually and otherwise, IJN.

Saturday March 30th, 2019
Topic: SAFETY IS IN THE SAVIOR

Scripture: "For the Lord is our defence; and the Holy One of Israel is our king" (Psalm 89:18).

Praise the Lord. Today is March 30th and is day #89 in year 2019. The number of days remaining to end this year is 276. By God's grace, you shall not be a prey to the enemy this year, and you shall see the end of 2019 and beyond in Jesus name.

Man is constantly under the attack of Satan who operates restlessly in uncountable ways, visible and invisible. Satan (also called devil) is our adversary and he goes about seeking whom to devour (1 Pet 5:8). Therefore, Satan is a murderer, a destroyer, an oppressor, an accuser of the brethren, a thief that comes to steal, to kill and to destroy (Jn 10:10). In his attack Satan can use human beings, demons, serpents, animals, trees, water, etc. to do harm and havoc to his victims. Man is very limited on his own to fight against Satan.

The believer must completely depend on the LORD who is our defense and our King as indicated in today's opening scripture. The LORD can defend us because He has already defeated Satan and His power surpasses that of Satan. Only God is Omnipotent (all powerful), Omnipresent (present everywhere) and Omniscient (knows all things). God's defense mechanisms are multipronged and includes empowering us with some powerful weapons of warfare such as (a) Prayer (1Thes. 5:17, Jn 14:14), (b) Faith (1 Jn 5:4-5), (c) Holiness (Jn 14:30, Job. 11: 14-20, Job 17:9), (d) Using the name of JESUS (Jn. 14:13, Phil 2:10), (e) Serving God faithfully (Ps. 105:15).

To enjoy God's defense, the believer must remain connected, obedient and loyal to His maker. I decree that that in the remaining 276 days of year 2019, every weapon of the enemy designed to kill you or any member of your family shall fail and be destroyed by fire, IJN.

Prayer: Father, I know safety is of the LORD, therefore hide me and my family in Your secret place, IJN.

Sunday March 31, 2019
Topic: LAUGHTER INDEED AT LAST

Scripture: "Then Abraham fell upon his face, and laughed, and said in his heart, Shall a child be born unto him that is an hundred years old? and shall Sarah, that is ninety years old, bear?" (Genesis 17:17, NLT).

Praise the Lord. Today is March 31st and is day #90 in year 2019. The number of days remaining to end this year is 275. By God's grace, impossibility shall become possible for you this year, and you shall see the end of 2019 and beyond in Jesus name.

Permit me to say that Abraham received several "birthday gifts" from God to mark his 99th birthday anniversary. These birthday blessings are many and are well documented in Gen. 17: 1-26. Just to mention a few: (a) God appeared to Abraham and told him to walk before Him and be perfect (Gen. 17:1), (b) God would covenant with Abraham and multiply him exceedingly (Gen 17: 2 & 6-14), (c) Name change: Abram to Abraham (Gen 17:5) and Sarai to Sarah (Gen. 17: 15), (d) gift of a son born of Sarah a year later (Gen 17: 16-19).

God made good all his promises to Abraham and Sarah. In particular, Isaac was born to Abraham by Sarah exactly one year after the promises above were made and when Abraham was 100 and was Sarah 90 (Gen. 21:5). The name Isaac was pre-birth name chosen by God and it means "laughter". Both Sarah and Abraham laughed at the idea of having a child in their old age. Contrary to some popular opinions, Abraham's laughter was not in disbelief for the Bible says "No unbelief made him (Abraham) waver concerning the promise of God, but he grew strong in his faith as he gave glory to God" (Rom.4: 20).

Remember if you are born again you are a partaker of the Abrahamic covenant. Therefore, you are called to walk perfectly before God, be blessed and be a blessing, be fruitful, be great, have dominion, be above and not beneath, make it to heaven, etc. These are part of your bona fide promised entitlements. Claim them by faith like Abraham without wavering in Jesus name.

Prayer: Father, strengthen my faith and let all your promises about my life be fulfilled, IJN.

Monday April 1, 2019
TOPIC: LOVING THE LORD

Scripture: "The Lord says, "I will rescue those who love me. I will protect those who trust in my name?" (Psalm 91:14, NLT).

Praise the Lord and welcome to the second quarter, of year 2019. Today is April 1st and is day #91 in year 2019. The number of days remaining to end this year is 274. By God's grace, you will grow in love for the Lord this year, and you will see the end of this year and beyond, safe and sound in the mighty name of Jesus.

The most important thing to God in terms of His relationship with man and how men are expected to relate to one another is LOVE. This should not be too surprising given the nature of God. At least twice the Bible says "God is love" (1 John 4: 8, 16). It was because of love that God sacrificially gave up His only Son to redeem man back to Himself after the fall of man (John 3:16). During His ministry on earth, Jesus also emphasized the importance of love through His miracles (driven by compassion and love) as well as through His teachings. In answering the question of an expert Pharisee lawyer, "Master, which is the great commandment in the law?", Jesus proved that loving God and loving the neighbor are the greatest first and second commandments in the law (Matt 22: 34-37).

According to our opening scripture above those who will love God and trust in His name will enjoy divine insurance against evil occurrences. If you love God you will obey Him and do His will (John 14:21-23). Those who love God also position themselves to receive reciprocal love from God the Father and that of Jesus Christ His son. May your love for God and people count upward in the remaining part of year 2019 in Jesus name.

Prayer: Father, let my love for You and Your Church grow the more and please rescue and protect me and my family from all evils, IJN.

Tuesday April 2, 2019
Topic: FLOURSHING AMIDST THE FLOCK

Scripture: "Those that be planted in the house of the Lord shall flourish in the courts of our God. They shall still bring forth fruit in old age; they shall be fat and flourishing" (Psalm 92:13-14).

Praise the Lord. Today is April 2nd and is day #92 in year 2019. The number of days remaining to end this year is 273. By God's grace, your service to God and His house shall open doors of prosperity to you this year, and you will see the end of this year and beyond, safe and sound in the mighty name of Jesus

Anyone who is truly and faithfully connected with and committed to God of the Church and the Church of God can never be poor, all things considered. Such persons will constantly be in the presence of God and experience the joy and pleasures available in His presence (Psalm 16:11). Such persons will be rooted and unmovable, always abounding in the work of God, and God Himself will be their Rewarder (1 Cor. 15:58, Heb. 11:6). They will be partakers of the unsearchable riches of Christ (Eph. 3:8) and God will supply all their need according to His riches in glory by Christ Jesus (Phil. 4:19). Furthermore, the Bible says seekers of God "- -shall not lack any good thing" (Ps. 34:10, NKJV).

Aside from enjoying Godly prosperity in this world, those who will faithfully devote themselves to serving God and His gospel will inherit everlasting life and seat with Christ on His throne in heaven (Matt 19:27-29; Lk. 18: 28-30). Brethren, it pays to serve God and support His Church! Get on board and remain on board.

Prayer: Father, give me the grace to serve you and Your Church passionately till the end, IJN.

Wednesday April 3, 2019
Topic: DIVINE VISITATION

Scripture: "And as he journeyed, he came near Damascus: and suddenly there shined round about him a light from heaven:" (Acts 9:3).

Praise the Lord. Today is April 3rd and is day #93 in year 2019. The number of days remaining to end this year is 272. By God's grace, you will have glorious life changing encounters with the Lord this year, and beyond, safe and sound in the mighty name of Jesus.

Divine visitation is a life changing experience that usually adds tremendous value to the life of the one visited. Who to visit, when to visit, method of visitation and purpose visitation are usually God's prerogatives. No one visited by God ever remains the same. God visited Abraham and Sarah, Zachariah and Elizabeth, etc. and bareness came to an end in their lives. When Peter and also Paul and Silas had divine visitation encounter, the prison gates opened and they walked out gallantly free from the prison cell. Saul (who became Paul) was on his usual murder mission to Damascus when God visited Him in a bright light and changed his destiny from a persecutor (of believers in Christ) to a preacher of the gospel (Acts 9: 3-19). May you receive divine visitation such that any vice associated with your foundation shall be altered to glorious virtue in the mighty name of Jesus.

Although God has the final decision on visitation, believers can have the grace to provoke it through: (a) intensive praise and worship (Acts 25: 1-16), (b) prayer (Mt. 7:7, Jn 14:14), (c) generous giving (Acts 10: 1-8), etc. Divine visitation can bring about many blessings for the believer including termination of demonic activities, provision of needs, divine direction, open door, etc. May 2019 be your year of divine visitations

Prayer: Father, please visit me constantly to bless me and terminate my problems, IJN.

Thursday April 4, 2019
Topic: HOLDING ON TO HOPE

Scripture: "For to him that is joined to all the living there is hope: for a living dog is better than a dead lion" (Ecclesiastes 9:4).

Praise the Lord. Today is April 4th and is day #94 in year 2019. The number of days remaining to end this year is 271. By God's grace, your expectation shall not be cut short this season, and you will see the end of this year and beyond safe and sound in the mighty name of Jesus.

Hope is the anticipation of something good to come in the future. Hope is to have confidence in one's expectation. The redeemed or the one born again who is still breathing is joined to Christ and other like-minded believers and therefore has hope. Such a person should know that his/her tomorrow will be better because the Bible says Christ in you, the hope of glory (Col. 1:27). It is pertinent to keep holding on to hope.

The hope of the redeemed must transcend the present life for, "if in this life only we have hope in Christ, we are of all men most miserable" (1 Cor. 15:19). Do you know Jesus as your Lord and Savior? Do you have hope of reigning with Him in His kingdom? As a believer, you must keep hope alive and be optimistically expectant. You must resist the discouragement that tends to ensue when expectation seems to delay in materializing (Pro 13:12). It is then time to remember that delay may not necessarily be denial. Prayerfully back up your resistance with believing in hope like Abraham did (Rom 4:18). The good plans of God will unfold for you as you align your hope with the word of God. May the tide turn in your favor, IJN.

Prayer: Father, let my path be as the shining light, that shines more and more unto the perfect day, IJN.

Friday April 5, 2019
Topic: WORDS OF WISDOM

Scripture: "Then she said to the king: "It was a true report which I heard in my own land about your words and your wisdom" (2 Chron. 9:5).

Praise the Lord. Today is April 5th and is day #95 in year 2019. The number of days remaining to end this year is 270. By God's grace, your wisdom, word and work shall be wonders to many this season, and you will see the end of this year and beyond safe and sound in the mighty name of Jesus.

The words of God and the wisdom of God are among the key elements needed to live a successful Christian life. The Bible says "Let the word of Christ dwell in you richly in all wisdom ... " (Col. 3:16). God blessed king Solomon with so much words and wisdom. It is recorded that Solomon spoke 3000 proverbs and sang 1005 songs (1 kings 4:32). Solomon was also the richest king ever lived (2 Chron 9:22). Today we are still reading about his wisdom and affluence (1 kings 3: 10-14).

The queen of Sheba, one of the richest women in the Bible, heard of Solomon's fame and travelled a long way to visit Solomon and to verify what she heard. As indicated in today's opening scripture the queen confirmed that, what she heard about king Solomon was true. She further testified that Solomon exceeded the fame she heard of him (2 Chron 9:6).

The key to Solomon's wisdom and greatness was worship and giving unto God. One day Solomon went to God's altar and offered 1000 burnt-offerings. That same night God appeared to him and told him to ask anything he wanted. Solomon only asked for wisdom and knowledge. God granted his request and also gave him riches, wealth and honor in addition (1 Chron. 6-12). Do you want to be blessed with words of wisdom and riches like Solomon? Provoke God for these blessings with holy living, intensive praise and worship, generous giving and service to God.

Prayer: Lord Jesus, I want more of You, for You are the WORD, POWER and WISDOM of God, IJN.

Saturday April 6, 2019
Topic: SACRIFICIAL THANKSGIVING

Scripture: "At that time those who had come from captivity, the returned exiles, offered burnt offerings to the God of Israel, twelve bulls for all Israel, ninety-six rams, seventy-seven lambs, and as a sin offering twelve male goats. All this was a burnt offering to the Lord" (Ezra 8:35, NLT).

Praise the Lord. Today is April 6th and is day #96 in year 2019. The number of days remaining to end this year is 269. By God's grace, your offerings and gifts to the Lord shall make room for you this season, and you will see the end of this year and beyond safe and sound in the mighty name of Jesus.

After 70 years in captivity in Babylon, exiled Israelites began to return to their homeland as promised by God and prophesied by Jeremiah (Jer. 29: 10-14). Prophet Ezra led some of the exiles on their return journey to Jerusalem. At the beginning of their journey Ezra took good record of those in his company, had a camp meeting with them, selected leaders to help manage the people and declared a fast to pray for safe journey. God answered their prayers for, Ezra declared "- - and the hand of our God was upon us, and he delivered us from the hand of the enemy, and of such as lay in wait by the way. And we came to Jerusalem, and abode there three days" (Ezra 8: 31-32). All your trips and projects this year 2019 shall begin well and end well, IJN.

When the exiled Israelites returned to their homeland, the first thing they did was to give thanks unto God. Among other things they offered burnt offerings to the LORD including 96 rams as indicated in today's opening scripture. Some lessons to learn from the foregoing: (a) It's time to quit Babylon (Satan's captivity) and return to Jerusalem (Jesus Christ), (b) Life is a conglomerate of 'journeys" (moving from place to the other, growing up, going to school, marriage, working, etc. Begin and end each 'journey' with prayer, (c) form to time give sacrificial offerings to God as a sign of gratitude (Lev. 22:29). Have a blessed day, IJN.

Prayer: Father, by your mercies let me present my bodies a living sacrifice to You, IJN.

Sunday April 7, 2019
Topic: GIVING CHEERFULLY TO GOD

Scripture: "Every man according as he purposeth in his heart, so let him give; not grudgingly, or of necessity: for God loveth a cheerful giver." (2 Cor. 9:7).

Praise the Lord. Today is April 7th and is day #97 in year 2019. The number of days remaining to end this year is 268. By God's grace, giving to the Lord shall be a joy that will beget joy into your life, and you will see the end of this year and beyond safe and sound in the mighty name of Jesus.

As we count down the days left in this year, we must not lose sight of our blessings that are adding up as answers accrue to one of the prayer points in the model prayer Jesus taught His followers: "Give us this day our daily bread" (Mt. 6:11). God is a giver and He expects us to emulate Him in that regards. By His word and His action, God has demonstrated that giving attracts tremendous benefits. For example, God gave us His only Son, Jesus Christ as our Redeemer and today, He has countless number of children who are joint heirs with Jesus Christ.

God's word says, "Give and it shall be given unto you; good measure - -" (Lk. 6:38). Furthermore, the Bible tells us that it is more blessed to give than to receive (Acts 20:35). All things considered, every human being has something positive (tangible or intangible) that is givable. The list of givable items can be endless and may range from simple and less expensive things like a smile, a "thank you", to more complex higher-valued items like sharing God's word, tithes, offerings, cars, precious jewels, houses, etc.

There is no doubt that our world will be a better place if we heed God's injunction of giving cheerfully. Regrettably, many people today are pre-occupied with grabbing rather than giving. Any grabbing that will make anyone lose heaven is not worth it for, "For what shall it profit a man, if he shall gain the whole world, and lose his own soul?" (Mark 8:36). Let's be generous towards God and His gospel; we can never out give Him! Have a blessed day.

Action/Prayer: Prayerfully sing the Hymn, "Take My Life and Let it Be"

Wednesday April 10, 2019
Topic: GOOD CARE OF GOD

Scripture: "Then Isaac sowed in that land, and received in the same year an hundredfold: and the Lord blessed him" (Gen. 26: 12-13)

Praise the Lord. Today is April 10th and is day #100 in year 2019. The number of days remaining to end this year is 265. By God's grace, you will continue to sow and receive bountiful harvest, and you shall see the end of this year and beyond, safe and sound in the mighty name of Jesus.

In good times and in bad times, God usually takes good care of those who are His and do His will. The story of Elijah who was divinely fed by a raven bird illustrates this point (1 Kgs 17: 1-6). Another very instructive example is the case of Isaac who went to sojourn in a foreign land called Gerar. There was serious famine in the land and Isaac was about to depart for Egypt but God told him not to. Isaac's farming business yielded 100 % returns within one year despite the chronic famine. After the first year, Isaac's business flourished so much that his status changed and he "...waxed great, and went forward, and grew until he became very great" (Gen 26:13). In fact, God blessed Isaac and his business so much that the native Philistines envied him (Gen. 26:14).

From Isaac's experience described above, we can learn some lessons as to how to attract God's good care: (a) Whatever God says to you, do it, (b) Trust and thank God unwaveringly in any circumstance you find yourself, remembering that the current problem/circumstance you face may become your platform for promotion, (c) Don't eat all your seeds, sow some, (d) Live holy without compromising your faith in God, etc.

Prayer: Father, Thank You for the first 100 days of 2019, please grant me the anointing for 100-fold returns on my effort

Thursday April 11, 2019
Topic: SAVED TO SAVE

Scripture: "Brethren, my heart's desire and prayer to God for Israel is that they may be saved " (Rom. 10:1).

Praise the Lord. Today is April 11th and is day #101 in year 2019. The number of days remaining to end this year is 264. By God's grace, you will continue to yearn for the salvation of more souls, and you shall see the end of this year and beyond, safe and sound in the mighty name of Jesus.

In what is popularly known as the Great Commission, Jesus Christ essentially charged His followers to preach the good news of salvation to non-believers so that they too can be saved and become followers of Christ as well. In other words, as a follower / disciple of Jesus Christ you are saved to save others. The primary purpose God sent His Son, Jesus Christ into the world was to seek and to save that which is lost (Luke 19:10). Similarly, the primary assignment Jesus Christ commissioned His followers to do is to seek and to save the lost souls (Matt. 28: 19-20).

Regrettably, many believers today are not doing much in terms of evangelizing to get unbelievers saved as we are commissioned to do. We have become complacent, nonchalant and unconcerned while many of our family members, friends, classmates, neighbors, colleagues, etc. are heading to hell. Many of us are robbing the grace of God that saved us on the ground instead of passionately extending that grace to bring others to the saving knowledge of Jesus Christ. Oh Lord, have mercy on us.

The early Christians took the great commission very seriously and were aggressively spreading the gospel. No wonder saved souls were added to the Church daily (Acts 2:47). Believers of today will do a much better job if we would adopt Apostle Paul's mindset as in the opening scripture above. Knowing the devastating consequences of neglecting the great commission, Apostle Paul saw it a necessity to win souls and declared "woe is me if I do not preach the gospel" (1 Cor 9:16). May God have mercy on us and create in us a yearning for souls passionately, IJN.

Prayer: Father, thank You for saving me, please the give me wisdom, passion and everything g I need to win souls for You, IJN.

Friday April 12, 2019
Topic: SET FOR CHANGE OF STATUS

Scripture: "Thou shalt arise and have mercy upon Zion: for the time to favour her, yea, the set time, is come." (Psalm 102:13).

Praise the Lord. Today is April 12th and is day #102 in year 2019. The number of days remaining to end this year is 263. By God's grace, this is your set time for unstoppable divine favor, and you shall see the end this year and beyond, safe and sound in the mighty name of Jesus.

If you have given your life to Jesus Christ as your Lord and Savior, you are a member of Zion which is the Church of God. The scripture above is yours to claim at all times. Jesus Christ our Savior let us remember that it is by His grace, mercy and favor that He has set us free from the bondage of sin (Eph 2:8).

Aside from salvation, the mercy and favor of God can transform the life of recipients of these virtues in many other dramatic ways. Two examples will suffice to illustrate this point. The blind Bartimaeus who cried out adamantly to Jesus to have mercy on him, got his breakthrough when Jesus stopped, commended him for his faith and miraculously opened his eyes (Mk 10: 46-52). Joseph the son of Jacob was a great beneficiary of both the mercy and favor of God. As a result, any time evil was planned for him, God turned such plans to good outcomes for Joseph. For instance, the plot by his brothers to kill him and the false accusation of sexual assault by Potiphar's wife against Joseph both became the platform for Joseph to be promoted from the prison to become the prime minister of Egypt (Gen. 39:21-23 & 45: 1-8). Every evil plan against you shall become Godly exaltation, IJN

God who gave Bartimaeus and Joseph mercy and favor is not a respecter of persons. Your own set time for positive change of status has come. God's blessings (salvation, mercy, favor, peace, prosperity, etc.) are stocked up for you. Call upon God and He will answer you and show you great and mighty things yet unknown to you (Jer. 33:3).

Prayer: Father, let my set time for Your grace, mercy and favor come perpetually, IJN.

Saturday April 13, 2019
Topic: BLESSING GOD FOR HIS BENEFITS

Scripture: "Bless the Lord, O my soul: and all that is within me, bless his holy name. Bless the Lord, O my soul, and forget not all his benefits" (Psalm 103:1-2).

Praise the Lord. Today is April 13th and is day #103 in year 2019. The number of days remaining to end this year is 262. By God's grace, your voice of praising God throughout this year shall not be silenced by the enemy, and you will see the end of this year and beyond, safe and sound in the mighty name of Jesus.

David's focus in composing Psalm 103 was on counting up the wonderful and glorious deeds of God to him personally as well as to various other groups, and to accord praises and thanksgiving to God for His generous benevolence. Two times in verses 1 and 2 David commanded his own soul to bless the LORD. Similarly, he ordered all that is within him to bless the LORD's holy name. Continuing the charge, David implored his soul and all that is within him not to forget all God's benefits of which he provided a long list. How we all need to borrow a leaf from David in terms of acknowledging and appreciating God for all the benefits he loads us with daily!

Instead of complaining on things we don't have, we should do like David and praise God assiduously for: forgiving our sins, healing our diseases, redeeming us from eternal death, showing us mercy, crowning us with love and compassion, etc. Sometimes, you can get more mileage from praise than from prayer. I heard about the testimony of a brother who died during a worship service. The brethren gathered, prayed, loosed and bound for a long time over the brother and nothing happened. One of the brethren suggested they should all begin to just praise God. As soon as the intensive praise began, the dead brother came back to live and joined the praise team. As you increase your praise to God in this year 2019, your impossibility shall become possible, IJN.

Prayer: Father, let my soul, my spirit and my body praise you at all times, IJN.

Sunday April 14, 2019
Topic: PASCAL LAMB OF THE PASSOVER

Scripture: "In the fourteenth day of the first month at even is the LORD's Passover" (Lev. 23:5).

Praise the Lord. Today is April 14th and is day #104 in year 2019. The number of days remaining to end this year is 261. By God's grace, you will see the end of this year and beyond, safe and sound in the mighty name of Jesus.

A day like today, the 14th of the month is an important day in the life of all bona fide followers of Jesus Christ as it reminds us of the events surrounding the crucifixion of our LORD Jesus Christ. Coincidentally, the LORD's Passover was also on the 14th day of the month, as indicated in today's opening scripture above. Jesus Christ was crucified around the period of the annual feast of the Passover (Matt 26:2, Mk. 14:1).

Several similarities are notable between the Passover and the Crucifixion: (a) They both involved sacrificial lamb. The lamb without blemish (called the Paschal Lamb) used in the Passover feast is a pointer to the sinless Son of God that sacrificed His life to take away the sins of the world. Apostle Paul refers to Jesus Christ as "our Passover lamb" (1 Cor. 5:7). (b) They both signify freedom from bondage. After they finished eating the Passover lamb and the unleavened bread, the Israelites were free to get out of slavery and bondage unhindered. Similarly, Jesus' death and resurrection paved the way to every sinner who will accept Him by faith as their Savior to escape the bondage of sin (c) As death passed over all the people in Israeli houses with door posts marked with the blood of the Passover lamb, so also any one redeemed by the blood of Jesus has a covenant with God for divine protection and eternal life (Gal. 6:17; John 3:16). Accept Jesus Christ as your Lord and Savior today and begin your journey for eternal life and freedom from death.

Prayer: Lord Jesus, thank You for Your life, death and resurrection by which I know I shall live and not die, IJN.

Monday April 15, 2019
Topic: PROPAGATING GOSPEL OF PEACE

Scripture: "And into whatsoever house ye enter, first say, Peace be to this house" (Lk 10:5)

Praise the Lord. Today is April 15th and is day #105 in year 2019. The number of days remaining to end this year is 260. By God's grace, you shall live peaceably throughout this year, and you will see the end of this year and beyond, safe and sound in the mighty name of Jesus.

Let us look at the word peace from two definitional points of view. First, "peace" (or "shalom" in Hebrew) is often used to connote an appearance of calm and tranquility of individuals, groups of people and nations. Secondly, from the spiritual perspective, 'peace' can be taken to mean harmony brought about by an individual's restoration with God. When 'spiritual peace' is genuinely in a person or persons, 'shalom peace' is most likely to manifest in the person(s). The prevalence of violence and chaos in today's world is due largely to deficiency of 'spiritual peace'.

Jesus Christ is the principal propagator of peace. He is aptly called the 'Lord of peace' (2 Thess. 3:16) and the 'Prince of Peace' (Isa. 9:6) because He is the son of the 'God of peace' (Rm 15:33,16:20). Furthermore, Jesus came into this world not only to preach peace (Acts 10:36) but also to give peace (Jn 14:27; 20:21).

Like Himself, Jesus Christ expects His followers to be propagators of the gospel of peace. During His ministry here on earth He gave an example of this charge by sending out 70 of his disciples two by two ahead of Him to every city he planned to visit. As indicated in today's opening scripture part of the mandate for the seventy disciples was to declare peace to every house they entered. Today, followers of Jesus Christ have similar mandate often called 'the great commission' which is to go into the world and preach the gospel (Mk 16: 15-18). Have you accepted Jesus Christ as your Lord and Savior? To what extent are you sharing your faith with others, especially non-believers? Don't miss the blessing of obeying the great commission. The Bible says, "- -How beautiful are the feet of them that preach the gospel of peace, and bring glad tidings of good things!" (Rm. 10:15).

Prayer: Father, make me a peace maker and a passionate propagator of peace, IJN

Tuesday April 16, 2019
Topic: GOD IS GREAT

Scripture: " Forasmuch as there is none like unto thee, O Lord; thou art great, and thy name is great in might". (Jeremiah 10:6, KJV)

Praise the Lord. Today is April 16th and is day #106 in year 2019. The number of days remaining to end this year is 259. By God's grace, your enemy shall know beyond doubt that you are serving a great and mighty God, and you will see the end of this year and beyond, safe and sound in the mighty name of Jesus.

One unsearchable and inestimable attribute of God is His greatness. The Psalmist attests to this, saying, "Great is the Lord, and greatly to be praised; and his greatness is unsearchable" (Psalm 145:3). Furthermore, Job declares, "Behold, God is great, and we know him not, neither can the number of his years be searched out" (Job 36:26). God's greatness spans numerous areas. He is great in power (Neh. 1:3), in excellence (Ex.15:7), in love (Eph.2:4, 1Jn 3:1), in mercy (1 Chron. 21:13, 1 Pet 1:3), in compassion (Neh. 9:3). etc.

When the Jews were about to be carried into captivity, Prophet Jeremiah warned them against the superstition and idolatry of the country to which they were going, given that the inhabitants of the place (Chaldea) were greatly addicted to astrology (Jer. 10: 1-2). The prophet reminded the Israelites about how God's word forbade them from following the vain ways of the astrologers and their powerless gods. As indicated in today's opening scripture Jeremiah pointed out that the heathen gods are far inferior to the true God of Israel who is great and whose name is great in might. This true God is greater than all gods (Exo 18:11) and He is to be feared above all gods (2 Chron 2:5, Ps. 96:4).

A believer in Jesus Christ is a child of the Almighty God who is great in all areas and can use His greatness to meet the needs of any one that belongs to Him. It is an affront to God to put trust in astrology when God has promised to be our guide for ever (Ps. 48: 14).

Prayer: Father, please demonstrate Your greatness in all areas of my life, IJN

Wednesday April 17, 2019
Topic: THE CHANGELESS CHANGER

Scripture: "Then they cried unto the LORD in their trouble, and he delivered them out of their distresses." (Psalm 107:6).

Praise the Lord. Today is April 17th and is day #107 in year 2019. The number of days remaining to end this year is 258. By God's grace, you will not cry in vain this year, your solutions will come readily, and you shall see the end of this year and beyond, safe and sound in the mighty name of Jesus.

God is a changeless changer. While everything else in the universe is subject to change, God says: "-- I am the LORD, I change not--" (Mal. 3:6). Out of His abundance of mercy and goodness, the unchanging God has given the believer the power to change situations and circumstances simply by crying to Him. Today's opening scripture above alludes to how the redeemed Israelites cried to God in the wilderness when they were distressed in troubles and He delivered them. Psalm 107 catalogues at least 3 other times that God saved (or brought out) His people from troubles when they cried to Him. When they were homeless and hungry, He housed them and fed them to satisfaction, when they were sick, he sent His word to heal them, and when they faced violent stormy waves and were about to sink, He rescued them (verse 13, 19 and 28).

The Bible says God is mighty to save (Isaiah 63: 3) and that "Death and life are in the power of the tongue" (Pro 18:21). Cry to God regarding any situation or circumstance you are facing for which you desire a change. Engage intensive praise to God, the changeless Changer, He will come through for you and there shall be testimony, IJN.

Prayer: Father, change my circumstances (name them) to conform to your will, word and way, IJN.

Thursday April 18, 2019
Topic: BREAK NOT THE HEDGE

Scripture: "He that diggeth a pit shall fall into it; and whoso breaketh an hedge, a serpent shall bite him." (Ecclesiastes 10:8)

Praise the Lord. Today is April 18th and is day #108 in year 2019. The number of days remaining to end this year is 257. By God's grace, the divine hedge and shield protecting you shall not be broken, and you will see the end of this year and beyond, safe and sound in the mighty name of Jesus.

The wisdom and word of God enjoin us to do good to all men especially unto them who belong to the household of faith (Gal. 6:10). Regrettably, many people do the opposite and end up bringing mischief upon themselves. This was the case with Haman who prepared gallows for Mordecai and ended up hung on it himself (Esther 7:8-10). Also, two sets of 50 soldiers and their captains sent to arrest Elijah were roasted by fire from heaven (2 Kings 1: 9-11). God will always defend His own. I decree that every arrow of the enemy sent to destroy you shall backfire IJN.

Believers must heed the warning (as in today's opening scripture) against breaking an hedge so as to avoid been bitten by serpent. Sins and disobedience to God and His word are examples of what can easily break the hedge of God over your life. Are you paying your tithes faithfully and fully? are you tearing down the Church of God with your mouth instead of helping to build it? are you still guilty of any of the offences listed in 2 Tim 3: 2-5 and Rev. 21: 8? If you answer is "yes" to any of these, you are breaking the hedge and you must cry to God for deliverance today. You will not be a hedge breaker, IJN.

Prayer: Father, as mountains surround Jerusalem, surround me with Your hedge; don't let me do anything that will break Your hedge in my life, IJN.

Friday April 19, 2019
Topic: PRAYERFUL HANDLING OF PROBLEMS

Scripture: "For I know that my redeemer liveth, and that he shall stand at the latter day upon the earth: And though after my skin worms destroy this body, yet in my flesh shall I see God" (Job 19:25-26).

Praise the Lord. Today is April 19th and is day #109 in year 2019. The number of days remaining to end this year is 256. By God's grace, you will see the invisible and hear the inaudible this season to enhance your success, and you shall see the end of 2019 and beyond, safe and sound in the mighty name of Jesus.

Having Godly and positive attitude is germane to handling the issues of life. Additionally, the interplay between personal convictions and one's faith can determine how one reacts to the issues of life. In turn, how one reacts to these life's occurrences can make or break one's destiny. Consider the lives of two people, Cain and Job. When Cain's offering was rejected by God, he got angry, took matter in to his hands and killed his brother Abel instead of crying to God for mercy and possibly restituting. The consequence was that he lost his destiny and missed all the blessings of first born (Gen 4: 1-24). Unlike Cain, Job had a Godly and positive disposition about his woes and calamities. Faced with the loss of all his children and properties, a decaying skin and false accusations and ridicule from his friends Job was hopeful and optimistic, declaring the words in the opening scripture above, "...For I know that my redeemer liveth- - ". He looked beyond his problems and saw God, the Potentate. Job's convictions, strong faith in God, and the truth he knew about his redeemer kept him going and paved the way for his double blessings' restoration (Job 42:10).

What life problems are you facing? – health issues? financial shortage? children disobedience? spiritual uncertainties? Job stress? fruitlessness? academic problems? marital conflicts? etc. By faith, develop a positive attitude and look beyond the problem prayerfully to see God who can proffer solution and a way of escape (1 Cor. 10:13, Isa. 43: 1-3, Lk. 1:37). I pray that every problem you face shall become a platform for your promotion, IJN.

Prayer: Father, help me not to focus on crisis at the expense of Christ, IJN.

Saturday April 20, 2019
Topic: ADVERSITY TURNED TO ADVANTAGE

Scripture: "But as for you, ye thought evil against me; but God meant it unto good, to bring to pass, as it is this day, to save much people alive." (Genesis 50:20)

Praise the Lord. Today is April 20th and is day #110 in year 2019. The number of days remaining to end this year is 255. By God's grace, every evil plot meant to harm you shall help propel you to greater glory this year, and you shall see the end of 2019 and beyond, safe and sound in the mighty name of Jesus.

Joseph, the eleventh son of Jacob who said the profound statement in the opening scripture above lived for 110 years (Gen 50:26). You too will live long, IJN. Joseph was hated by his brothers because he was his father's favorite. The animosity from his brothers got to a climax when Joseph shared with them his dream of dominion over them. The brothers plotted against him and sold him into slavery in Egypt. However, God was with Joseph and almost everywhere he went in Egypt (e.g. Potiphar's house, prison, Pharaoh's palace) he was favored and put in leadership position.

Pharaoh promoted Joseph from prison to palace, second in command to Pharaoh because Joseph was the only one who could interpret Pharaoh's dreams (Gen. 41: 25-44). Joseph became the manager of grain granaries in Egypt to which his brothers and father (like other people all over the world) came to buy food. When they came, Joseph recognized his brothers but they couldn't recognize him. Joseph had an emotional reunion with his family. He took good care of his brothers and father, introduced them to Pharaoh and got them settled in the best part of Egypt (Gen. 47:11).

Some lessons to learn from Joseph: (a) Be careful and prayerful in how and to whom you share your dreams (b) Parents should teach Godly principles to all their children and love them equally; each child is God's heritage (c) prayerfully live purely (d) don't render evil for evil (1 Thes. 5:15).

Prayer: Father, in my life please turn every adversity to advantage and every evil to good, IJN

Sunday April 21, 2019
Topic: YOU ARE HIGHLY VALUABLE!

Scripture: "The works of the LORD are great, sought out of all them that have pleasure therein. His work is honourable and glorious: and his righteousness endureth forever." (Psalm 111: 2-3).

Praise the Lord. Today is April 21st and is day #111 in year 2019. The number of days remaining to end this year is 254. By God's grace, you will do great and honorable work this year, and you shall see the end of this year and beyond, safe and sound in the mighty name of Jesus.

God is a perfect worker. He created the entire universe in six days without making any mistake. Psalm 111, believed to be penned by king David, uses some noteworthy words to describe God's work. Thus, in counting up on God's work, David says it is: great and sought after (v.2), honourable and glorious (v. 3), wonderful and memorable (v.4), powerful (v6), truthful and just (v.7). The believer must see himself/herself in the light of these descriptive words for he/she is part of the handwork of God. As the Bible declares, " - - we are his workmanship, created in Christ Jesus unto good works, which God hath before ordained that we should walk in them" (Eph. 2:10). In other words, the believer's worth, work and walk must conform to the handwork of his/her maker.

You are highly valuable! Stop underestimating yourself. The perfect God who made you in His own image declared that you are "very good" (Gen 1:31). In addition, you are made great and expected to be great, work great, and live great. Similarly, you are made wonderfully (Ps. 139:13) and your worth, work and walk must reflect this attribute. This world will be a better place if we conduct ourselves in consonance with how God created us.

Prayer: Father, let my worth, work and walk reflect the attributes with which you made me, IJN.

Monday April 22, 2019
Topic: POWER PASS POWER

Scripture: "Now these were the people of the province who came up out of the captivity of those exiles whom Nebuchadnezzar the king of Babylon had carried captive to Babylonia. They returned to Jerusalem and Judah, each to his own town, The sons of Jorah, 112" (Ezra 2:1, 18, ESV).

Praise the Lord. Today is April 22nd and is day #112 in year 2019. The number of days remaining to end this year is 253. By God's grace, any limitation over you shall be lifted this year, and you see the end of this year and beyond, safe and sound in the mighty name of Jesus.

God is Omnipotent meaning He is the Almighty God whose power is unlimited and surpasses all other powers. The Bible says "- - power belongeth unto God" (Ps. 62:11) and that He has made the heaven and the earth by His great power (Jer. 32:17). With His power, nothing is too difficult for God to do (Gen 18:14). One use of God's power is to defend those that belong to Him including setting them free from captivity as He has promised (Isa. 49:25).

After 430 years in bondage, captivity and oppression in the land of Egypt God used His power to liberate the Israelites only in one night (Exo 12). As indicated in today's opening scripture some 112 exiles and their leader Jorah were taken away from Nebuchadnezzar who had kept them as captives in Babylon. At the appointed time God demonstrated to Nebuchadnezzar that power pass power by returning these exiles to Jerusalem (Ezra 2). You and your family shall not be taken captive, IJN.

Captivity (physical or spiritual) is any type of limitation or confinement that prevents people from maximizing their potential. There are two major categories of captivity - spiritual captivity and physical captivity. These two can give birth to numerous other types such as sins, poverty, sickness, addiction, unfruitfulness, joblessness, stagnation, failure, anger, etc. Of course, Satan is the chief architect of all forms of captivity. The good news is that God has made divine plan to deliver His own people from all types of captivity (John 8:32, Eph. 4:8). Keys to avoiding captivity or securing deliverance from it include (a) having a vibrant relationship with Jesus Christ, (b) pray fervently to avoid being a prey (c) live holy.

Prayer: Father, by Your divine power immunize me against all forms of captivity, IJN.

Tuesday April 23, 2019
Topic: GIVING THE BEST TO GOD

Scripture: "Then David the king addressed the congregation: "My son Solomon was singled out and chosen by God to do this. But he's young and untested and the work is huge - -Furthermore, because my heart is in this, in addition to and beyond what I have gathered, I'm turning over my personal fortune of gold and silver for making this place of worship for my God: 3,000 talents (about 113 tons) of gold—all from Ophir, the best—and 7,000 talents (214 tons) of silver for covering the walls of the buildings, and for the gold and silver work by craftsmen and artisans. "And now, how about you? Who among you is ready and willing to join in the giving?" (1 Chronicles 29: 1-5, MSG)

Praise the Lord. Today is April 23rd and is day #113 in year 2019. The number of days remaining to end this year is 252. By God's grace, your role in the Lord's Church shall not be taken from you, and you will see the end of this year and beyond, safe and sound in the mighty name of Jesus.

King David had great respect and honor for God as evident in several practical steps he took during his era. For example, he courageously fought and killed Goliath and defeated the Philistines when they defied and reproached the armies of Israel in an attempt to put the people of God to shame (1 Sam 17). David also desired to build God a Temple but God chose Solomon (David's son) to do the job because David had shed much blood and fought too many wars (Chron. 17: 4-12; 28:3).

Although David was not permitted to build God's Temple, he made adequate preparation to provide the necessary materials for building the Temple as indicated in today's opening scripture. In his own words David said, "- - I've done my best to get everything together for building this house for my God, all the materials necessary …". Notable among the best things David got ready were "3,000 talents (about 113 tons) of gold—all from Ophir, the best". God deserves the best from us because He gave us His best, Jesus Christ (John 3:16). Let us emulate David by honoring God with our best gifts beginning with our life and including our talents, treasure and time. The more you give to God, the more you get from God (Lk. 6:38, Gal. 6: 6-7).

Action/Prayer: Sing the Song "Take My Life and Let it Be" (by Frances R. Havergal, 1874). Then pray: Father, thanks for giving me Your best; please help me to give You my best, IJN.

Wednesday April 24, 2019
Topic: GIVING THE BEST TO GOD

Scripture: "Riches profit not in the day of wrath: but righteousness delivereth from death" (Proverbs 11:4)

Praise the Lord. Today is April 24th and is day #114 in year 2019. The number of days remaining to end this year is 251. By God's grace, you shall be delivered from death this year, and you will see the end of this year and beyond, safe and sound in the mighty name of Jesus.

It is very saddening to see many people mortgaging away their soul and losing the opportunity to spend eternity with God because of their greed and insatiable appetite for riches or wealth, often obtained by illicit means. Don't get me wrong; God is not against getting rich or being wealthy. As a matter of fact, God is interested in the prosperity and pleasures of his people (Ps. 35:27, Job 36:11, 3 John v.2). What God is against is acquiring riches or wealth by sinful means such as stealing and cheating. The Bible says it does not profit any one to gain the whole world and lose his/her soul (Mk 8:36). Yet, many of us forget that a "day of wrath" will arrive someday. This refers to the judgment day of God when each of us will stand alone before God to render an account for all our deeds.

On the day of wrath, ill-gotten wealth (such as embezzlement, bribery, payments for hired killing, cheating, etc.) will be worthless and incapable of buying reconciliation with God. God will pour his wrath on the guilty and send them to eternal damnation. The righteous on the other hand will be delivered from death into eternal life as the opening scripture above indicates. Receive the grace to live righteously, IJN.

Prayer: Father, don't let the riches of this world rob me of making it into heaven, IJN.

Thursday April 25, 2019
Topic: GOD OF INCREASE

Scripture: (a) "The LORD shall increase you more and more, you and your children."(Psalm 115: 14). (b) "Thou shalt increase my greatness, and comfort me on every side" (Psalm 71:21).

Praise the Lord. Today is April 25th and is day #115 in year 2019. The number of days remaining to end this year is 250. By God's grace, the supernatural increases you will experience this season will surprise your enemies, and you will see the end of this year and beyond, safe and sound in the mighty name of Jesus.

The word increase connotes addition, making greater (in number, size, strength, quality, value, etc.) than initial or previous level. Instead of decrease or stagnation God's plan is for increase to occur in anything of good value. This divine plan for increase is evident in God's own creative work. He gave all living things (He created) the ability to reproduce themselves based on His command to, "be fruitful and multiply- -"(Gen 1: 22, 28). In fact, the concept of increase was so important to God that He established a covenant about it with man beginning with Abraham.

As Abraham's progeny, believers are heirs to the covenant and promise of increase. Jacob increased exceedingly (Ge. 30:43), -"- children of Israel were fruitful, and increased abundantly, and multiplied-"(Ex. 1:7). Job declares, "Though thy beginning was small, yet thy latter end should greatly increase" (Job 8:7). Jesus Christ declared, "- - I am come that they might have life, and that they might have it more abundantly"(Jn 10:10). Several of the miracles in the Bible brought about large increases from nothing or little materials (e.g.1 Kgs 17: 7-15, Matt 14: 13-18).

Are you interested in receiving valuable increases in your life (marriage, children, wisdom, knowledge, understanding, honor, prosperity, peace etc.)? Call on the God of increase to make it happen. You can provoke your increase by (i) becoming an obedient covenant child of God (Isa 43: 1-6, Ex. 28: 1-13), (ii) giving of thanks and praise to God (Jer. 30:19; Psalm 67: 3-7), (iii) serving God faithfully (Ex.23: 25-31; Heb 11:6) (iv) praying for increase (Matt. 7:7), (v) giving generously (Lk. 6: 38; Pro 11:24), (vi) living righteously (Pro 28:28), etc.

Prayer: Use the opening scriptures (a) and (b) above to pray for yourself and your family.

Friday April 26, 2019
Topic: PRAISING AND PUBLICIZING GOD.

Scripture: "What can I offer the LORD for all he has done for me? I will lift up the cup of salvation and praise the LORD's name for saving me" (Psalm 116: 12-13, NLT)

Praise the Lord. Today is April 26th and is day #116 in year 2019. The number of days remaining to end this year is 249. By God's grace, you will never lack reasons to give thanks to the Lord, and you will see the end of this year and beyond, safe and sound in the mighty name of Jesus.

The answer to the question asked by David in the opening scripture above is simply that there is not enough, anyone can offer that can be commensurate with all God has done for him/her. The question should motivate us to humble ourselves, count our blessings and do something (no matter how small or how big) to let God know we do appreciate His deeds to us even though we cannot pay for all of them. That is part of the driving force behind this Countdown and Count Up platform. It is an attempt to emphasize that God has given us so much and we should give him something to show our gratitude.

If you are a Christian, how much can you pay for: the grace of God that saved you (Eph 2:8)?, His daily loads of benefits to you (Ps. 68:19)?; many of the afflictions He delivers you from (Ps. 34: 19)?; the sun He prevents from smiting you by day (Ps. 121:6)?; His good plans for you (Jer. 29:11)?, His eyes that run to and fro on you (2 Chron. 16:9)?; His presence that never leaves nor forsake you (Heb 13:5)?; etc. While God's benefits to us are innumerable and we cannot pay for them, we can, like David, demonstrate our gratitude and appreciation to Him in various ways, including offering thanksgiving, praising and proclaiming Him to others about His saving grace. We must constantly remember that everything we have / have received came from God and giving Him back a portion of what he has given us should not be too difficult. Based on the law of harvest if you appreciate God, God will appreciate you. As your praise goes up your perquisites (blessings) will come down. Hallelujah!

Prayer: Father, let me Praise and Publicize You at all times, IJN.

Saturday April 27, 2019
Topic: POWER OF PRAISE

Scripture: "O praise the LORD, all ye nations: praise him, all ye people. For his merciful kindness is great toward us: and the truth of the LORD endureth forever. Praise ye the LORD" (Psalm 117: 1-2).

Praise the Lord. Today is April 27th and is day #117 in year 2019. The number of days remaining to end this year is 248. By God's grace, you will help raise the tempo of praise to God this year in the country you reside in, and you will see the end of this year and beyond, safe and sound in the mighty name of Jesus.

Praise can be defined as offering grateful homage in words or song especially to God as an act of worship. When engaged appropriately, praise can be a powerful tool by which God can give us victory over our enemies and bring about desirable outcomes for His own. Our opening scripture above (Ps 117) is the shortest chapter in the Bible and also the middle chapter on either side of which there are 594 chapters. Incidentally, the Psalm 117 contains 33 words, the same number of years at which Jesus (the "Center" of believer's life) was crucified. It is also noteworthy that Psalm 117 calls on all people and all nations to praise the LORD for two major reasons - His merciful kindness that is great towards us and His truth which endures forever. By inference and extension, it is correct to say that the more we praise God, the greater His merciful kindness will flow towards us. And by similar reasoning we know that the more we praise God, the greater He can set us free since His word says "- - you will know the truth, and the truth will set you free" (Jn. 8:32).

We can see the manifestation of power of praise in several ways including (a) Merciful kindness of God given to Jehoshaphat and Judah (JJ) that enabled them defeat heavily-armed armies of 3 nations that attacked them. Without any weaponry, other than praise JJ defeated and killed all their attackers and spent 3 days collecting their wealth (2 Chron. 20). (b) Freedom from prison as we see in Acts 16: 25 - 34 when Paul and Silas and others were miraculously freed from prison when they engaged in midnight praise.

Action: Prayerfully, integrate more praises to God and more commendation (instead of condemnation) to people in your relationships and watch the win-win Power of Praise, IJN.

Sunday April 28, 2019
Topic: GOD IS A STATUS CHANGER

Scripture: "The stone which the builders rejected Has become the chief cornerstone" (Psalm 118:22, NKJV).

Praise the Lord. Today is April 28th and is day #118 in year 2019. The number of days remaining to end this year is 247. By God's grace, the tide will turn in your favor this year and you will be sought after; you will also see the end of this year and beyond, safe and sound in the mighty name of Jesus.

Rejection has been part of human problem since sin entered into the world. Cain rejected his own twin brother and even killed him (Gen 4: 8). Sarah rejected Hagar and orchestrated ostracizing her from the family of Abraham. Even Jesus Christ was rejected and killed by the same people He came to redeem. The opening scripture for today was a prophetic pointer to the rejection that Jesus Christ would face in the new Testament. During His earthly ministry, Jesus Christ told a parable to confirm the prophesy about His rejection (Luke 20:9-19). As Peter explained to the Jewish leaders Jesus is the rejected stone whom God, made to be the Chief cornerstone of salvation (Acts 4: 8-12).

As it turned out, the same Jesus rejected was not only accepted, but "- God also has highly exalted Him and given Him the name which is above every name that at the name of Jesus every knee should bow, - - and that every tongue should confess that Jesus Christ is Lord, to the glory of God the Father" (Phil 2: 9-11). Jesus Christ is a life and status changer. Confess Him today as your Lord and Savior. He will change your status. Joseph was rejected by his brothers but he became the prime minister of Egypt. Esther was a maid in a foreign country but she became the first lady of that land. It is your turn. I see favorable status changes manifesting very soon for many people reading this piece. The set time is NOW for: sinners to become saved, failure to become success, the jobless to gain profitable employment, the barren to become mother of children, the sick to become healed, etc. single to become happily married, the poor to become prospering, etc. Claim your own by calling "- - those things which be not as though they were" (Rm. 4:17). It will be unto you according to your faith, IJN. Have a blessed Sunday.

Prayer: Father, change my status such that I will achieve all Your good plans for me, IJN

Monday April 29, 2019
Topic: WORDS OF THE WORD

Scripture: "Forever, O LORD, thy word is settled in heaven" (Psalm 119:89).

Praise the Lord. Today is April 29th and is day #119 in year 2019. The number of days remaining to end this year is 246. By God's grace, the era has come that everything about will be settled in your favor; and you will see the end of this year and beyond, safe and sound in the mighty name of Jesus.

The entire Bible is the word of God and should be taken very seriously for many reasons including the fact that it is: (a) Inspired by God (breathed upon), (b) Inerrant (without error, perfect), (c) Infallible (incorruptible), (d) Invincible (incapable of being defeated, sovereign), (e) Immutable (unchangeable, changeless).

Psalm 119 with 176 verses is the longest chapter in the Bible and in the book of Psalms. Aside from its length, Psalm 119 is very rich in meaning. The theme that reverberates throughout the Psalm is the word of the Lord. This is what informed the choice of the topic above – words of the WORD since Jesus Christ is the Word (Jn 1:1). Various synonyms for logos ("God's word") used in Psalm 119 include: (1) law, ordinance, commandments, precepts, testimonies, statutes, judgments.

When written originally in Hebrew, the Psalm 119 was split into 22 sections, each section, containing 8 verses. There are important lessons to learn in terms of how the word of God in each of the 22 sections can significantly improve one's life. For brevity, only 5 of the sections with the associated verses and lessons are presented here as follows, (i) Follow God's word and ways and you will be blessed (v. 1-8), (ii) keeping God's word in your heart will keep sin away from you (v. 9-16), (iii) God's word can be your strength (v. 25-32) (iv) God's word can keep you pure and prospering (v. 33-40), (v) God's word provides comfort in times of need, produces joy in difficult times and hope when you are feeling down (v. 49 - 56). (vi) The word of God is settled; you can depend on it in time of trouble (v. 89-96), (vii). The word of God can give you wisdom and understanding (v. 97 - 104)

Prayer: Father, let me grow in Your word and Your wisdom that I may prosper and have good success, IJN.

Tuesday April 30, 2019
Topic: DANGER OF FORSAKING GOD

Scripture: "For Pekah the son of Remaliah killed 120,000 from Judah in one day, all of them men of valor, because they had forsaken the LORD, the God of their fathers." (2 Chron 28:6)

Praise the Lord. Today is April 30th and is day #120 in year 2019. The number of days remaining to end this year is 245. By God's grace, you will never forsake the Lord, and you see the end of this year and beyond, safe and sound in the mighty name of Jesus.

On His own, God does not want to lose any one who has entered a relationship with Him. In fact, His word declares, "I will never leave thee, nor forsake thee" (Heb. 13:5b). God will jealously guard those who belong to Him to the extent that He said,"-- I have graven thee upon the palms of my hands; thy walls are continually before me" (Isaiah 49:16). God's security system is divine and surpasses what any human arrangement can ever provide or understand.

God's Sovereignty allows Him to use any means He wants to ensure the safety of His children. For instance, if you give your life to Him, He can keep you under His shadow and you will become a tantalizing mirage which the enemy cannot touch (Ps. 91:1). Otherwise, He might choose to cover you with His feather like the mother hen broods over her chicks to protect them against the predator. God might just simply, hang you under His wings and fly you out of reach of the enemy (Ps. 91:4). Remember also that the Almighty God has angels at His disposal that He can command to be your body guards to protect you wherever you go (Ps. 91:11-12). There are innumerable other ways God can use to protect His own.

While God doesn't want to be separated from those belonging to Him, many people have separated themselves from God by committing sins. Sin is a separator (Isaiah 59: 1-2). It is dangerous to forsake God. The sins of the world that Jesus was carrying on the cross of Calvary caused a temporary separation of the father from the son (Mk 15:34). In Today's opening scripture above, Judah forsook God by worshipping images and idols (2 Chron 24:18) and God sent Pekah to kill 120,000 of their valiant men in one day.

Action / Prayer Avoid sins like a plague. Father, let nothing separate me from You, IJN.

Wednesday May 1, 2019
Topic: HELP FROM HEAVEN

Scripture: "I will lift up mine eyes unto the hills, from whence cometh my help. My help cometh from the Lord, which made heaven and earth" (Psalm 121: 1-2).

Praise the Lord. Today is May 1st and is day #121 in year 2019. The number of days remaining to end this year is 244. By God's grace, no help will elude you this season, and you will see the end of this year and beyond, safe and sound in the mighty name of Jesus.

Welcome to the month of May, the fifth month of the year. The number 5 connotes GRACE (God's Riches at Christ's Expense). Salvation through faith in Jesus Christ is made possible only by GRACE (Eph. 2:8). It is help from the LORD that makes grace available to man for salvation. This type of help can be called Spiritual help. Another type of help is physical help such as provisions, protection from body guards etc. In general, physical help is preceded by spiritual help. Help is inevitable in human existence and survival. From cradle to grave help is a sine qua non. Every human being is a receiver and giver of help in one form or the other in the cycle of life.

God, in His omniscient nature, foreknew human's need for help and made provision for it when he declared". It is not good that the man should be alone; I will make him an help meet for him" (Gen. 2:18). Consequently, the first help ever known to man came from God when Eve was created out of Adam to be his wife (Gen 2: 21-23). God became the ultimate helper of the human race. It is therefore not surprising that the Psalmist in the opening scripture above said his help cometh from the LORD (who resides in Heaven).

God's help is superior to that of man because it is divine, dependable and dynamic in the sense that it is a "present help in time of trouble" (Ps. 46:2). You shall not get in trouble IJN. Nevertheless, whatever help you need, whether spiritual (such as grace, salvation, favor, mercy, etc.) or physical help (such as procreation, protection, promotion, provisions, prosperity, etc.), look up, don't look down. Look unto the LORD, that's the only way you will count upwards on God's blessings. Happy month, IJN.

Prayer: Father, let every help I need to fulfill destiny be available to me unhindered, IJN.

Thursday May 02, 2019
Topic: PROSPERITY-PROVOKING PRAYER

Scripture: " Pray for the peace of Jerusalem: they shall prosper that love thee. Peace be within thy walls, and prosperity within thy palaces". (Psalm 122: 6-7).

Praise the Lord. Today is May 2nd and is day #122 in year 2019. The number of days remaining to end this year is 243. By God's grace, peace shall envelope you throughout this year, and you will see the end of year 2019 and beyond, safe and sound in the mighty name of Jesus.

God wants his children to prosper as indicated in His word: "Beloved, I wish above all things that thou mayest prosper and be in health, even as thy soul prospereth" (3 John v.2). One way the believer can access the prosperity ordained by God is by praying for the peace of Jerusalem, the capital of Israel, God's own chosen country. The primary reason God said He chose Israel is because of it's holiness, the love God has for Israel and because of the oath He made with Abraham (Deut. 7: 6-8). Additionally, God wanted Israel to be a model nation to other nations and that through them "all the families of the earth would be blessed (Gen. 12:3).

In a broad sense, Jerusalem referred to in the opening scripture above includes the nation of Israel and the Church of Jesus Christ, the Prince of Peace. As you pray for Jerusalem, live holy and do things that will advance the Kingdom of God, you will prosper IJN. As year 2019 counts down, may you count up in righteous prosperity, IJN.

Prayer: Father, give Jerusalem and the rest of the world the peace that comes through Jesus Christ, the Prince of Peace, IJN.

Friday May 03, 2019
Topic: LOOKING FOR MERCY?

Scripture: "Behold, as the eyes of servants look unto the hand of their masters, and as the eyes of a maiden unto the hand of her mistress; so, our eyes wait upon the Lord our God, until that he have mercy upon us." (Psalms 123:2).

Praise the Lord. Today is May 3rd and is day #123 in year 2019. The number of days remaining to end this year is 242. By God's grace, your eyes shall be focused on the Lord perpetually, and you will see the end of this year and beyond, safe and sound in the mighty name of Jesus.

Mercy and grace are 2 of God's most generous and most beneficial gifts to man because without them man will be dead spiritually and physically. Let's look at each briefly. Mercy has been defined by someone as, not receiving the punishment which one rightly deserves. For example, the sinful man deserved death as punishment (Rom 3:23). However, any man willing to repent of his sins is not consumed because of God's mercy (Lam. 3:22). One of the two thieves crucified with Jesus on the cross received mercy when he admitted his own guilt and said unto Jesus, "Lord, remember me when thou comets into thy kingdom.". Jesus said unto him, "Verily I say unto thee, Today shalt thou be with me in paradise" (Luke 23: 42-43). The unrepentant thief was condemned. (Luke 23: 39-43)

Grace has been defined as when God gives man what he does not really deserve. An example is man's salvation by grace, not by work (Eph 2:8). Man, in his sinful nature does not deserve salvation but Jesus Christ made man's salvation possible at the expense of His life. As servants look unto their masters and maids look unto their mistresses, children of God must look unto Jesus, the Author and Finisher of our faith (Heb. 12:1-2). Are your eyes focused on Jesus Christ?

Prayer: Father let the set time for more of Your favor, grace, mercy and peace in my life be now, IJN.

Saturday May 04, 2019
Topic: ESCAPING FROM THE ENEMIES

Scripture: "Blessed be the LORD, who hath not given us as a prey to their teeth. Our soul is escaped as a bird out of the snare of the fowlers: the snare is broken, and we are escaped" (Psalms 124:6-7).

Praise the Lord. Today is May 4th and is day #124 in year 2019. The number of days remaining to end this year is 241. By God's grace, your enemies will be frustrated to give up coming after you, and you will see the end of this year and beyond, safe and sound in the mighty name of Jesus.

Every day the enemy wages attacks against the believer (1 Peter 5:8). In fact, the Bible makes it clear that there is sufficient evil in each day (Matt 6:34b). The good news is that escape from the enemy is sure if the LORD is on the side of the one under attack. This is the point David makes in Psalm 124, where he reminds us that the LORD should be blessed because, by being on the side of the Israelites, He made it possible for them to escape the various attacks of their enemies. The LORD who did this for Israel is the same yesterday and today and forever (Heb 13:8). He will do it for anyone to whom He is an ally.

The Bible says "Many are the afflictions of the righteous: but the LORD delivereth him out of them all" (Psalm 34:19). King Saul made several attempts to kill David, but each time David escaped unhurt because the LORD was on his side. To enjoy the same divine deliverance and protection as David and the Israelites you must be on the Lord's side so that He can be on your side. Your "to do list" in this regard is to: (1) give your life to Jesus Christ (2), let your ways please God, (live obediently and holy), (3) bless / praise the LORD always (4), serve the Lord, (5) give generously to God. Like the Israelites, you too shall testify escaping the snare of the fowler, IJN.

Prayer: Father, in the remaining days of this year and forever, shield me against all enemy attacks, IJN.

Sunday May 05, 2019
Topic: SPIRITUAL AND PHYSICAL SECURITY

Scripture: "They that trust in the LORD shall be as mount Zion, which cannot be removed, but abideth forever" (Psalms 125:1).

Praise the Lord. Today is May 5th and is day #125 in year 2019. The number of days remaining to end this year is 240. By God's grace, your faith in the Lord shall be solid and strong like a rock, and you will see the end of this year and beyond, safe and sound in the mighty name of Jesus.

How to be safe and secure is a major problem faced all over the world. There are two types of safety and security – Spiritual and Physical. They are both intertwined and not mutually exclusive. However, it is the physical security that tends to receive almost all attention. Personal safety, family safety, financial safety, assets safety, border protection, national safety etc. are some of the dimensions of safety and security that dominate people's attention on a daily basis. Many people, organizations and government entities spend a ton of money and other resources on physical safety and security with little or no attention to the spiritual aspect of the problem. Yet the Bible says: "- - we wrestle not against flesh and blood, but against principalities, against powers, against the rulers of the darkness of this world, against spiritual wickedness in high places" (Eph. 6:12).

Most of the physical security issues we battle with have spiritual foundations which must be spiritually tackled before solution can be procured. The best security system any people, organization or government can have is that of the LORD for the Bible says "- -Safety is of the LORD" (Pro 21:31). As indicated in today's opening scripture above, putting trust in the LORD is the panacea for stable security. Mt Zion has a broad meaning and includes the City of the living God (Heb. 12:22) and the Church of Jesus Christ which the gates of hell cannot prevail against (Mt. 16:19). To be safe and secure, you must, (a) give your life to Jesus Christ and remain in Him, (b) study God's word to learn more about spiritual warfare (c) live holy, (d) pray for divine protection, (e) pay your tithes and don't rob God. In Jesus Christ and in His Father is the best security – spiritual and physical (John 10: 28-29). Have a blessed day.

Prayer: Father, I hide myself in You, let no weapon fashioned against me prosper, IJN.

Monday May 06, 2019
Topic: THE MAGNIFICIENT MAN

Scripture: "And God said, Let us make man in our image, after our likeness: and let them have dominion over the fish of the sea, and over the fowl of the air, and over the cattle, and over all the earth, and over every creeping thing that creepeth upon the earth. So, God created man in his own image, in the image of God created he him; male and female created he them" (Genesis 1:26).

Praise the Lord. Today is May 6th and is day #126 in year 2019. The number of days remaining to end this year is 239. By God's grace, your staff of authority shall wax stronger and stronger this season, and you will see the end of this year and beyond, safe and sound in the mighty name of Jesus.

Welcome to the 6th day of this month. Man, created on the 6th day, is the last of God's creation and is uniquely different from other creatures for many reasons including the following: (1) Man was made in God's own image. (2) Man was made to be magnificent (that is extra extraordinary) by the council of the Trinity – God the Father, the Son and the Holy Spirit. (3) Man is the only creature in which God "-- breathed into his nostrils the breath of life; and man became a living soul" (Gen 2:7). (4) Man is also unique and magnificent because God gave him dominion over all the earth and to replenish the earth. (5) Man was given the power to name all animals and birds whatever name he chose for each creature was final. Therefore, in His creation God has placed man on a high pedestal.

Though man abused his position, sinned against God and temporarily lost his relationship with God, Jesus Christ restored man to God by His sacrificial death and resurrection, hallelujah! Stop minimizing yourself when you are created to be great. You are not an ordinary person. You are fearfully and wonderfully made (Psalm 139:14). You are a king and a priest unto God (Rev. 1:6). You are carrying the DNA of the triune God in you; you are special! Let the mind of Christ be in you. Maximize your manhood by thinking great, act great, love great and work great as your Father. You shall be great indeed, IJN.

Prayer: Father let Your magnificence in me manifest to the utmost, IJN

Tuesday May 07, 2019
Topic: CHRISTLY CHILDREN.

Scripture: "Lo, children are an heritage of the LORD: and the fruit of the womb is his reward" (Psalm 127:3)

Praise the Lord. Today is May 7th and is day #127 in year 2019. The number of days remaining to end this year is 238. By God's grace, you shall be a delight to the Lord as His child, and you will see the end of this year and beyond, safe and sound in the mighty name of Jesus.

Children are important for numerous reasons including the following: (1) They belong to God – His heritage (best gifts) and reward, (2) Children belong to God's kingdom (Lk. 18: 15-17). (3) They are gifts to us from God (James 1:17). (4) They are God's miracles in terms of how they come into being. (5) They are part of God's blessings and manifestation of marriage covenant between a male and a female (Gen 1:28, 2: 24). (6) Right from conception to when they are little, God already has great plans for children including ordaining their careers and recruiting them as potential Kingdom dwellers (Jer. 1:4-5; Mark 10: 13-16). (7) Children are agents of continuity of the human race, etc. Therefore, we must count upwards on our blessings regarding our children and ensure Godly agenda is realized about them.

Our children have a key role to play in our future. Therefore, the following are some of the actions needed to make our children Christly: (a) Pray regularly for your children.

(b) Lead them to Jesus Christ for salvation. (c) Train your children in the ways of the Lord (Gen 18:19, Pro 22:6, Eph 6:4). (d) Teach them the words of God (Deut. 6: 6-9). (e) Teach your children self-esteem, work ethics and discipline (f) Be a good role model to your children.

Prayer: Father, terminate bareness in the life of any one reading this and let all our Children be Christ-like IJN

Wednesday May 08, 2019
Topic: RECEIVING GODLY REWARDS

Scripture: "Blessed is every one that feareth the Lord; that walketh in his ways. For thou shalt eat the labour of thine hands: happy shalt thou be, and it shall be well with thee" (Psalm 128:1-2).

Praise the Lord. Today is May 8th and is day #128 in year 2019. The number of days remaining to end this year is 237. By God's grace, you will not labor for the enemy to reap your harvest this season, and you will see the end of this year and beyond, safe and sound in the mighty name of Jesus.

The Bible makes it clear that God is a rewarder of those who diligently seek Him (Heb. 11:6). Rewards of God are His blessings that "--maketh rich and addeth no sorrow" (Pro 10:22). The opening scripture for today provides, succinctly, that the criteria for receiving rewards from God are to fear Him and walk in his ways, that is, to respect God and obey His laws. One beautiful nature of God is that He gives you more than He asks of you (Lk 6:38). He asked Abraham to give up his son so that he can father all the nations of the world, He says pay only a tenth of your income and receive ceaseless flow of blessings from heaven, He says confess and repent of your sins to receive salvation that will entitle you to be a joint heir with Jesus to sit with Him on His throne in heaven.

Psalm 128: 1-3 says everyone that will do just 2 things (respect and obey God's laws), will be blessed with so many rewards. I have categorized and condensed these rewards as follows: (1) possessing your possession, (2) productive (biologically and otherwise), (3) prosper, (4) pleasurable, (5) Problem-free (it shall be well with you). As year 2019 counts down your rewards shall count upwards, IJN

Prayer: Father give me the grace to respect You and obey all Your laws and let your blessings overflow in my life, IJN.

Thursday May 09, 2019
Topic: DEADLY DENIAL

Scripture: "But he that denieth me before men shall be denied before the angels of God." (Luke 12:9).

Praise the Lord. Today is May 9th and is day #129 in year 2019. The number of days remaining to end this year is 236. By God's grace, you never deny Jesus Christ, and you will see the end of this year and beyond, safe and sound in the mighty name of Jesus. One of the things Jesus Christ made clear to His followers during His earthly ministry, was the nature of reward/penalty that will accrue to those that confess or deny him before men. He said, "- - Whosoever shall confess me before men, him shall the Son of man also confess before the angels of God: But he that denieth me before men shall be denied before the angels of God" (Luke 12:8-9). Taking the matter of confession and denial of him to a higher level, Jesus declared, "- - Whosoever therefore shall confess me before men, him will I confess also before my Father which is in heaven. But whosoever shall deny me before men, him will I also deny before my Father which is in heaven" (Matt. 10: 32-33). From all indications Jesus took the issue of confession or denial of Him very seriously.

To confess Jesus means to acknowledge Him and make Him known to others as the Son of God sent to save the world (John 3:17). On the other hand, to deny Jesus means to reject and/or fail to tell others about Him. Jesus Christ said those that confess Him before men will be rewarded positively in the sense that He will speak well of them before angels of God or directly before His Father in heaven. In contrast, those that reject / fail to confess Him before men will be penalized (get negative rewards) in the sense that He will deny them before the angels of God or directly before His Father in heaven. Confessing Jesus Christ or denying Him can determine where one will spend eternity, hell or heaven. The Bible says, "- -whatsoever a man soweth, that shall he also reap" (Gal. 6:7). If you sow seeds of confessing Jesus Christ before men you will reap His confession of you before God and His angels and you will spend eternity with Jesus in heaven. On the other hand, sowing seeds of denial of Jesus Christ will provoke His denial and rejection of you before God and His angels which can result in eternal death. This will not be your portion in Jesus mighty name. **Prayer: Father, give me the grace to confess You to all people always in Jesus name. Amen**

Friday May 10, 2019
Topic: FORGIVING FATHER.

Scripture: "If thou, LORD, shouldest mark iniquities, O Lord, who shall stand? But there is forgiveness with thee, that thou mayest be feared." (Psalm 130:3-4).

Praise the Lord. Today is May 10th and is day #130 in year 2019. The number of days remaining to end this year is 235. By God's grace, Satan shall not succeed in luring you to sin this year, and you will see the end of this year and beyond, safe and sound in the mighty name of Jesus.

One grace given to all those Christ has redeemed is the forgiveness of their past, present and future sins. God Himself declares, "- -I will be merciful to their unrighteousness, and their sins and their iniquities will I remember no more" (Heb.8:12). The forgiveness of God the Father is amazing! Someone gave illustration of how superhydrophobic coating repels almost any liquid. No matter what material they coat (paint, ketchup, mustard, honey, etc.), the liquids just roll right off without even a faint of stain. The sacrifice of Jesus Christ on the cross and His blood operates even better than the superhydrophobic coating in terms of rolling off the past, present and future sins of the forgiven and redeemed believer. Unlike the priests of the Old Testaments Jesus Christ offered only one sacrifice for sins forever (Heb. 10: 11, 12, 14).

God's forgiveness of sins is a demonstration of His faithfulness and dispensation of His mercy which endureth for ever (Psalm 136:1, 145:8-9). It behooves the redeemed to live a life of complete obedience and loyalty to God and not abuse the fact that God is a forgiving Father. Furthermore, the redeemed believer must learn from God (and His word) and emulate Him about forgiveness. As the opening scripture for today indicates, there is forgiveness with God. Similarly, God has equipped every believer with the gift of forgiveness (Jn 20:23, 2 Pet 1:3). There is forgiveness with you as a child of the God.

Are you still marking iniquities and harboring unforgiveness? Use the forgiveness with you wisely so that your own sins can be forgiven and your prayer answered (Mt. 6:14, LK. 6:37)

Prayer: Father, thank You for the blood of Jesus that cleans all sins. Give me the grace to forgive readily and let Your grace continue to shield me from the power of sin, IJN

Saturday May 11, 2019
Topic: HAUGHTY OR HUMBLE HEART?

Scripture: "Lord, my heart is not haughty, nor mine eyes lofty: neither do I exercise myself in great matters, or in things too high for me." (Psalm 131: 1).

Praise the Lord. Today is May 11th and is day #131 in year 2019. The number of days remaining to end this year is 234. By God's grace, your humility will prepare the way for your upliftment this season, and you will see the end of this year and beyond, safe and sound in the mighty name of Jesus.

The point of David in Psalm 131 was to tell the people over whom he has been anointed to reign as king that he was not haughty in heart but humble to that which God has called him to do. As the Bible says, "The heart is deceitful above all things, and desperately wicked: who can know it?" (Jer. 17:9 KJV). Of course, the heart referred to in this scripture is the unregenerate heart, one not yet washed with the precious blood of Jesus, and one that is still ruled by the spirit of pride and pomposity.

One important lesson to learn from David's expressions in Ps 131 is the need for humility instead of haughty heart in service to God and humanity. Jesus also taught us humility when he became obedient unto death, even death on the cross (Phil 2:8). According to Psalm 34:18 "The LORD is nigh unto them that are of a broken heart; and saveth such as be of a contrite spirit". Have you humbled yourself to receive the salvation offered by Jesus Christ? Do it today. While "Pride goeth before destruction, and an haughty spirit before a fall." (Pro.16:18), numerous blessings accrue to those with humble spirit: They are saved and lifted up (Job 22:29, James 4:10); God hears their prayer (2 Chron 7:14, Ps 9:22, 10:22); they will not be destroyed (2 Chron 12:7, 12); they are not forgotten (Ps. 10:12); they shall be honored (Pro 29:23); they shall be exalted (Lk 14:11 & 18:14); they get grace from God (1 Pet 5:5, James 4:6), etc.

Prayer: Father, by Your grace destroy any haughty spirit from me and fill my heart with humility IJN.

Sunday May 12, 2019
Topic: WHEN GOD IS YOUR ALLY

Scripture: "His enemies will I clothe with shame: but upon himself shall his crown flourish (Psalms 132:18).

Praise the Lord. Today is May 12th and is day #132 in year 2019. The number of days remaining to end this year is 233. By God's grace, all your enemies shall realize their folly and come to you on bended knees this year, and you see the end of this year and beyond, safe and sound in the mighty name of Jesus.

If God is on your side you have a great and incomparable ally. Your enemies become His enemies and God can clothe your enemies with shame while He causes you to flourish as He did for David as indicated in today's opening scripture. Another king who benefitted from God's ally is king Jehoshaphat of Judah who was attacked by armies of three nations (2 Chron 20). Bewildered and feeling helpless from the attack, Jehoshaphat wisely cried to God for help. God answered his prayer and told him to use the 'weapon' of just to praise God and not fight during the battle. The result was that God made Jehoshaphat's enemies kill each other until they were all dead. In other words, Jehoshaphat's enemies were "clothed" with shame. Jehoshaphat and his people flourished because when they "- - came to take away the spoil of them, they found among them in abundance both riches with the dead bodies, and precious jewels, which they stripped off for themselves, more than they could carry away: and they were three days in gathering of the spoil, it was so much" (V. 25). The wealth of your wicked enemies shall be laid up for you, IJN.

David won God's heart by his passion to build a habitation for God and his unparalleled worship of God. God remembered David and promised to bless him in many ways. Solomon, David's son documents some of these ways in Psalm 132 which is one of the 15 Psalms (120-134) known as "Song of Degrees" or "Songs of Ascents.

Until you are reconciled with God through His Son Jesus Christ, you are the enemy of God. (Rm 5:10). Receive Jesus Christ as your Lord and Savior today and avoid garments of shame.

Prayer: Father clothe all my enemies with shame while You cause me and my descendants to flourish like the palm trees, IJN.

Monday May 13, 2019
Topic: Topic: GOD's GPS

Scripture: "And thine ears shall hear a word behind thee, saying, This is the way, walk ye in it, when ye turn to the right hand, and when ye turn to the left." (Isaiah 30:21, KJV)

Praise the Lord. Today is May 13th and is day #133 in year 2019. The number of days remaining to end this year is 232. By God's grace, you will be divinely guided in all that you will do this year, and you will see the end of this year and beyond, safe and sound in the mighty name of Jesus.

The modern Global Positioning system (GPS) otherwise called Navigator has become an indispensable gadget for many of us in efforts to find our ways. However, the GPS occasionally leads people to the wrong place. One time, I keyed the address of a conference I was attending into my GPS. It was taking me through series of turnings on what looked like a back route. Based on the estimated arrival time (EAT) displaced on the GPS I was rejoicing because I thought I was not going to be late for the conference. To my greatest shock, after a few more quick turnings, the GPS directed me to a dead-end road by a stream indicating I have arrived at my destination. Disappointingly, I retraced my way back to a major road. I turned off my GPS for a few minutes, repowered it and keyed in again the address of my conference. Eventually, I got to my desired destination, though a few minutes late.

God's GPS is divine and can never mislead. With God's GPS Abram left his country as instructed by God not knowing where he was going but God took him to Canan to possess the land (Gen 13:1-18). With God's GPS, Elijah made it to brook of Cherith and then to Zarepath where God met all his needs even in time of severe dryness and famine (1 kings 17:1-14). It was divine GPS that helped the Shepherds locate the manger in which Jesus was born in Bethlehem (Lk 2:8-18).

According to the opening scripture above God's GPS is available to tell you the directions to go in all the journeys of life - spiritual, geographical, marital, career wise, educational, etc.

With God's GPS, you will arrive safely, surely and successfully at your destinations in 2019 and beyond, IJN.

Prayer: Father, as you guide me with Your GPS, give me the grace to follow your perfect ways, IJN.

Tuesday May 14, 2019
Topic: LOVING LIKE THE LORD

Scripture: "Love is patient and kind; love does not envy or boast; it is not arrogant" (1 Corinthians 13:4, ESV).

Praise the Lord. Today is May 14th and is day #134 in year 2019. The number of days remaining to end this year is 231. By God's grace, you will be a pace setter with respect to love, patience and kindness and you will see the end of this year and beyond, safe and sound in the mighty name of Jesus.

Love can be defined as a feeling of warm and affectionate personal attachment to others and their well-being. Love can manifest in various ways. The ancient Greeks used 7 words to describe the different states love can be experienced: Storge, Philia, Eros, Agape, Ludus, Pragma and Philautia. A more condensed classification puts love types in 4 major categories: Agape, Storge, Philia and Eros.

Agape is the best kind of love and it defines the nature of God, how He relates with human beings and the best way He expects His followers to relate to Him and to each other. In terms of His nature, the Bible says God is love (1 John 4:8, 16). God's relationship with man is centered on love (John 3:16). Like Himself, God has endowed man with the capacity to love Him and to love one another. The importance of love in this context is best understood by the answer Jesus gave to a lawyer who asked him "- -what is the greatest command in the law?" (Mt. 22:36). Essentially, Jesus told the lawyer that all the law and the prophets hang on two great commandments": (1) to love God and (2) to love the neighbor (Mt. 22: 37-40). Today's opening scripture describes some of the characteristics of agape love exemplified by Jesus Christ. Other attributes of agape type of love can be found in the same chapter, often called the love chapter of the Bible. Jesus expected his followers (born again believers) to practice agape love when He said "A new commandment I give unto you, That ye love one another; as I have loved you, that ye also love one another" (John 13:34).

Prayer: Father, give me the grace to practice agape love like You and Your Son Jesus Christ

Wednesday May 15, 2019
Topic: GOD WANTS YOU GREAT

Scripture: "For I know that the Lord is great, and that our Lord is above all gods." (Psalms 135:5 KJV).

Praise the Lord. Today is May 15th and is day #135 in year 2019. The number of days remaining to end this year is 230. By God's grace, you shall not be small this year, and you will see the end of this year and beyond, safe and sound in the mighty name of Jesus.

What you know and believe in can significantly influence what you become. The Bible says "- - the people that do know their God shall be strong, and do exploits." (Dan.11:32b, KJV)

God is good and He is great meaning He has unlimited power, and is aptly described as the Omnipotent God who reigns (Rev. 19:6). No matter which aspect one views God, His greatness is unquestionable. He is great in His works of creation, work of redemption, in perfection, holiness, providence, faithfulness, grace, etc.

The Bible is replete with testimonies about God's greatness. David declares, "Great is the LORD, and greatly to be praised--" (Psalm 48:1) and that "the Lord is a great God, and a great King above all gods" (Psalm 95:3). Job pointed out that because of God's greatness we are unable to know Him completely neither can we search out the number of his age (Job 36:26). Moses describes God as "- - God of gods, and Lord of lords, a great God, a mighty, and a terrible, which regardeth not persons, nor taketh reward" (Deut. 10:17). Solomon said it is the great God that formed all things (Pro.26:10).

Knowledge of the greatness of God should serve as a catalyst for a believing follower of Jesus Christ to strife for greatness. God created you to be great and you are carrying the seed of greatness in you because the great God made you in His own image (Gen 1:26). Moreover, the covenant of greatness God made with Abraham extends to all Christians through Jesus Christ (Gal, 3:14). Water that seed with righteous living, hard work, service to God and humanity and your greatness shall manifest, IJN.

Prayer: Father, empower me to surmount all limitations to my greatness, IJN

Thursday May 16, 2019
Topic: MAGNIFYING GOD'S MERCY.

Scripture: "O give thanks unto the Lord; for he is good: for his mercy endureth forever." (Ps. 136:1, KJV)

Praise the Lord. Today is May 16th and is day #136 in year 2019. The number of days remaining to end this year is 229. By God's grace, you will increase in giving thanks to God and receiving His mercy this season, and you will see the end of this year and beyond, safe and sound in the mighty name of Jesus.

God's mercy is uniquely magnified in Psalm 136 in the sense that each of the 26 verses of this Psalm ends with the same phrase: "for his mercy endureth forever". God's mercy is one of the blessings we can correctly say counts upward as the year counts down for the Bible says the earth is full of God's mercy (Ps. 119:64) and that God keeps mercy for thousands (Exo 34:7). Furthermore, God's mercy and compassion are new every morning (Lam 3:32-23). I decree that God will shower you with mercy perpetually in the mighty name of Jesus.

Magnifying the mercy of God by acknowledging the continuity and enduring nature of it is a great way of thanking and praising God. As a matter of fact, the song/phrase "for his mercy endureth forever" has a miracle-provoking attribute. For example, when it was sung during Solomon's time, the temple was filled with a cloud (2 Chron. 5: 13). On another occasion, Jehoshaphat and his army sang this same phrase and God miraculously gave them victory over the armies of 3 nations that invaded them (2 Chron. 20:21,22).

In this season and forever, as you engage in thanking and praising God for His enduring mercy, all your oppressors shall be suppressed and you shall enjoy total victory over your enemies IJN

Prayer: Father, let your tender mercy flow into my life ceaselessly, IJN

Friday May 17, 2019
Topic: THE DAY OF THE LORD

Scripture: "Howl ye; for the day of the Lord is at hand; it shall come as a destruction from the Almighty. Therefore, shall all hands be faint, and every man's heart shall melt:" (Isaiah 13:6-7 KJV)

Praise the Lord. Today is May 17th and is day #137 in year 2019. The number of days remaining to end this year is 228. By God's grace, your name shall remain in the good book of the Lord, and you will see the end of this year and beyond, safe and sound in the mighty name of Jesus.

Events that have definite known termination date (e.g. Year 2019) are easier to countdown on than those without specific known date or time to man. An example of the latter is "the day of the Lord".

The day of the Lord refers to the time when God will come on the scene in a powerful way to execute His wrath on the earth because of the iniquities of man and unbelief (Jer. 30:1-17; Joel 1-2). The Bible catalogues some of the events that will take place at the end of history (Isaiah 7:18-25). Several of the passages dealing with the day of the Lord in the Old Testament (including today's opening scripture and Isaiah 13:6 and Ezekiel 30:3) portray a sense of imminence and nearness of its occurrence. In the New Testament the day of the Lord is called variously as a day of "wrath," (Rev. 6:17), a day of "visitation" (1 Pet 2:12), and the "great day of God Almighty" (Rev.16:14).

Not only will "the day of the Lord" come quickly, like a thief in the night (Zep. 1:14-15; 2 Thess.) it shall come as a destruction (of the unsaved) from the Almighty. Followers of Christ must therefore be watchful and ready for the coming of Christ at any moment.

No one, except God knows the exact date and time for the day of the Lord. However, we know that every day we see, brings that day nearer than the previous day. Only those who have received Jesus Christ as their Lord and Savior will escape the destruction of the day of the Lord. Give your life to Jesus Christ today to avoid the destruction that is associated with the day of the Lord. Your hand shall not faint neither shall your heart melt, IJN.

Prayer: Father, deliver me and my household from the destruction of the end time, IJN

Saturday May 18, 2019
Topic: PURSUE PERFECTION

Scripture: "The Lord will perfect that which concerneth me: thy mercy, O Lord, endureth forever: forsake not the works of thine own hands." (Psalms 138:8 KJV)

Praise the Lord. Today is May 18th and is day #138 in year 2019. The number of days remaining to end this year is 227. By God's grace, excellent spirit will be your portion in all that you do this year, and you will see the end of this year and beyond, safe and sound in the mighty name of Jesus.

Everything about God is perfect, including His word / law (Ps. 18:30), His way (2 Sam 22:31), His work (Deut. 32:4). Since you and I are part of His work we carry the genes of perfection in us. God told Abram: "--I am the Almighty God; walk before me, and be thou perfect" (Gen 17:1). Jesus Christ told his followers (including you) "Be ye therefore perfect, even as your Father which is in heaven is perfect" (Mt 5:48).

On this 138th day of year 2019, God is saying to you to walk before Him and be perfect in the remaining 227 days of the year and of course for the rest of your life. If God says it, it is possible; you just have to believe it, claim it and live it. That is what the Psalmist (David) is doing in today's opening scripture above. He confidently declares that the Lord will perfect everything concerning Him. The same God can do the same for you.

Are there things that need perfection in your life right now? Your relationship with God, your health, work, finances, marriage, academics, etc.? Look beyond these problems and keep your gaze and trust on the perfect God who is able to make the crooked way straight (Isaiah 40:4).

Action: Prayerfully pursue perfection by handing over your concerns to the God of grace and mercy, His good plans shall soon manifest for you as He brings perfection to you, IJN.

Prayer: Father, by Your power please provide solutions to all my problems and perfect me in every area. Name them.

Sunday May 19, 2019
Topic: WONDERS OF GOD'S WORKMANSHIP

Scripture: "I will praise thee; for I am fearfully and wonderfully made: marvelous are thy works; and that my soul knoweth right well." (Psalms 139:14 KJV).

Praise the Lord. Today is May 19th and is day #139 in year 2019. The number of days remaining to end this year is 226. By God's grace, you will remain misery to your enemies, and you will see the end of this year and beyond, safe and sound in the mighty name of Jesus.

Look at yourself in the mirror. What you see (yourself) is a demonstration of the wonderful work of God who made you in his own image. Right now, myriads of events are taking place in your body including the beating of your heart. If you're in average physical condition, it is likely your heart beats between 60 and 70 times per minute, averagely 93,000 times per day, 651,000 times per week and about 34 million times per year. At God's control, your heart fuels itself, paces itself, repairs itself, and alters itself in response to lifestyle changes, with no conscious effort on your part.

There are many striking revelations about your wonderful body in Ps 139. These include:

God is omniscient and knows everything about your body (v 1-6). God is omnipresent and you cannot hide from him (v. 7-12). God is omnipotent and not only did He make you fearfully and wonderfully, He has a book in which all your body parts are written even before they were fashioned (v 13-16). One implication of this is that you can mention any part of your body to him to heal, strengthen or replace. God loves you and has precious thoughts about you that outnumber the count of sand (v 16-17).

God's foremost thought about you is that He wants you saved, for Jesus declares "--seek ye first the kingdom of God, and his righteousness; and all these things shall be added unto you." (Matt. 6:34).

Action / Prayer: Take time to praise God and pray that your wonderfully and fearfully made body will bring glory to God continuously, IJN

Monday May 20, 2019
Topic: WOES TO THE WICKED

Scripture: "Keep me, O Lord, from the hands of the wicked; preserve me from the violent man; who have purposed to overthrow my goings." (Psalms 140:4 KJV).

Praise the Lord. Today is May 20th and is day #140 in year 2019. The number of days remaining to end this year is 225. By God's grace, you will not be a prey to any violent man, and you will see the end of this year and beyond, safe and sound in the mighty name of Jesus.

Persecution is inevitable in the Christian race. The Bible declares that all who will live godly in Christ Jesus will suffer persecution (2 Tim 3:12). Fervent and effective prayer is a powerful weapon by which anyone who is determined to serve the Lord faithfully can overcome persecution. Even Jesus Christ was persecuted, but because of His commitment to prayer He victoriously finished the work of redemption He was sent to do. You will finish yours too, IJN.

David was destined to be a king of Israel but Saul and other enemies mounted up various persecutions to derail Him. Psalm 140 is part of the prayer assault used by David to defeat his enemy and it provides some useful insights and lessons for engaging in spiritual war fare. In His prayer in this Psalm, David described his enemy variously as the evil man, the wicked, the violent man, the proud, etc. In the name of Jesus that is above all other names, all your enemies, no matter what they are called shall be shamefully defeated.

Action / Prayer: Pray the following prayer points based on Psalm 140 as used by David:

Deliver me O Lord from the evil man, preserve me from the violent man (v 1).

Keep me, O LORD, from the hands of the wicked; preserve me from the violent man; who have purposed to overthrow my goings (v2)

O God, my strength, cover my head in the day of battle (v7)

Grant not, O LORD, the desires of the wicked and further not his wicked device IJN (v 8)

Father, let the mischief of my enemies' own lips cover them, IJN (v 9)

Father, let no evil speaker against me be established IJN (v11)

O Lord of hosts, let evil hunt the violent man against me until he is overthrown IJN (v 11)

Father, thank You for giving me total victory over my enemy. Shout 7 Hallelujahs

Tuesday May 21, 2019
Topic: FOLLY OF DENYING THE FATHER

Scripture: "The fool hath said in his heart, There is no God. They are corrupt, they have done abominable works, there is none that doeth good" (Psalms 14:1, KJV).

Praise the Lord. Today is May 21st and is day #141 in year 2019. The number of days remaining to end this year is 224. By God's grace, you will never deny that Jesus is Lord, and you will see the end of this year and beyond, safe and sound in the mighty name of Jesus.

Atheism is the doctrine or belief that there is no God. It is estimated that about 7% of the world population are atheists, with China and Russia being major contributors to this 7%. In the U.S. proportion of people subscribing to atheism has grown over the years. A recent poll by Pew Research show that between 2007 and 2012 the percentage of Christians in U.S population declined from 78% to 73% while that of atheists increased from 1.6% to 3.1%.

Disbelief in the existence of God stems from foolishness according to God's word, for the Bible declares twice that, "- -The fool hath said in his heart, There is no God" (Psalm 14:1, 53:1). Those who deny the existence of God are victims of deceit and wickedness of their own hearts since the Bible says, "The heart is deceitful above all things, and desperately wicked: who can know it?" (Jer. 17:9). It is clear from this scripture that, evil, corrupt and ungodly thoughts are bound to proceed from the hearts of those who deny that there is God. No wonder today's opening scripture indicates that such people are corrupt and do abominable works.

What will happen to those who deny that there is God? There is hope for them for salvation provided they repent of their unbelief and accept Jesus Christ as their Lord and Savior (John 3:16, Psalm 55:16, Rm. 10:13). It is therefore imperative that we believers in God should continue to pray and embark on aggressive evangelism to reach out to unbelievers with the Gospel of Jesus Christ. However, if unbelievers die without knowing and accepting Jesus Christ, the Bible says they will face judgement and be denied by Jesus Christ before His father (Heb. 9:27, Matt. 10:33). Hell fire will not be your portion, IJN.

Action / Prayer: Quit been a fool. Confess Jesus as the Son of God (Mk 1:1) and ask Him to have mercy on you and forgive you your sins. Invite Him to come into your life and be your Savior.

Wednesday May 22, 2019
Topic: RELIABLE REFUGE

Scripture: "I cried unto thee, O Lord: I said, Thou art my refuge and my portion in the land of the living." (Psalms 142:5, KJV)".

Praise the Lord. Today is May 22nd and is day #142 in year 2019. The number of days remaining to end this year is 223. By God's grace, you will reside in the land of the living, not of the dead throughout this year, and you will see the end of this year and beyond, safe and sound in the mighty name of Jesus.

God is the most reliable refuge as we face the troubles of life. His word declares "When thou passest through the waters, I will be with thee; and through the rivers, they shall not overflow thee: when thou walkest through the fire, thou shalt not be burned; neither shall the flame kindle upon thee." (Isaiah 43:2 KJV). Notice this verse starts with "when" not "if", indicating the inevitability of troubles or problems in life. King David, who had his own share of life's troubles knew the value of crying to God in prayer. Psalm 142 is another prayer believed David composed when he ran for his life to hide either in the cave of Adullam, (1 Sam. 22:1) or in the cave at Engedi, where he cut off Saul's skirt (1 Sam. 24:3).

So far this year 2019 do you feel you are being pursued by enemies? Are you distressed, discouraged, disappointed, disillusioned as a result of problems arising from sickness? joblessness? barrenness? failure? debt? etc.? Cry to Jesus. He is the present help in time of trouble and the most reliable refuge. He will provide solution and a way of escape IJN.

Prayer: O Lord be my rock, and my fortress, and my deliverer; my God, my strength, in You I will trust; my buckler, and the horn of my salvation, and my high tower. (Psalms 18:2)

Thursday May 23, 2019
Topic: WALKING IN GOD'S WILL

Scripture: "Teach me to do thy will; for thou art my God: thy spirit is good; lead me into the land of uprightness". (Psalms 143:10, KJV).

Praise the Lord. Today is May 23rd and is day #143 in year 2019. The number of days remaining to end this year is 222. By God's grace, all that you will do this year shall be according to the will of the Lord, and you will see the end of this year and beyond, safe and sound in the mighty name of Jesus.

Knowing and doing the will of God is important as this can make or break a person spiritually, economically and otherwise. In fact, Jesus Christ declared that only those that do the will of His Father would enter the kingdom of heaven (Mt. 7:39). Jesus Christ also taught His disciples to pray that God's will be done on earth as it is in heaven (Mt. 6:10).

There are several connotations to the phrase, "the will of God". According to 1 Thess. 5: 18 the will of God is that we give thanks in everything. Some people have opined that God's will can be dichotomized into 'Perfect will' and 'Permissive will'. Leslie Weatherhead says that God's will falls into three distinct categories; intentional, circumstantial, and ultimate. John Piper has categorized God's will into two perspectives. One perspective regards the will of God as the sovereign plan (Will of God or decree) that comes to pass irrespective of human reaction. For example, it was the will of God that Jesus Christ would die to redeem sinners. The second perspective of the will of God refers to the laws or commandments of God to guide how human beings are to relate to God (vertical relationship) and to relate to other human beings (horizontal relationship).

God wants us to do His will, irrespective of the type. It is in our own interest to seek out God's will and act in total obedience. The word of God, counselling, prayer, divine revelation, etc. are some of the ways by which we can know God's will. The wills of God common to all who will put faith in and follow Jesus Christ include salvation, sanctification, service (e.g. witnessing), praying without ceasing, etc.

Prayer: Father, make your will known to me and give me the grace to act accordingly in obedience.

Friday May 24, 2019
Topic: MOVING THE MOUNTAINS

Scripture: "Bow thy heavens, O LORD, and come down: touch the mountains, and they shall smoke" (Psalms 144:5, KJV).

Praise the Lord. Today is May 24th and is day #144 in year 2019. The number of days remaining to end this year is 221. By God's grace, you will have divine encounter Jehovah Sharma, this season, and you will see the end of this year and beyond, safe and sound in the mighty name of Jesus.

In spiritual parlance, mountains can symbolize good and evil. Examples of good symbolism include (a) Mount Sinai where Moses received the gift of the Law, the Ten Commandments (Ex. 20), (b) The appointment of the Twelve by Jesus on a mountain (Mk 3:13-19), (c) Jesus' healing of the lame, blind, dumb, maimed and many others on a mountain (Mt.15:29). In the remaining days of this year you will be on the mountain of God's goodness, IJN.

Examples of evil connotation of mountains include when it symbolizes sabotage, distraction, obstacles, evil embargoes, problems, hindrances, prohibitions, stumbling blocks, etc. We see a clear evidence of this in the temptation of Jesus by the Devil in which Jesus was taken into a high mountain, shown all the kingdoms of the earth with a promise to be given the glory and power of them if he would worship Satan (Lk. 4: 5-8). Other examples are the obstacles that stood in the way of Israel's returning from Babylonian exile and those that later prevented progress in the temple rebuilding work that were compared to mountains. (Isa 40:1-4; Zech. 4:7).

As believers, God has given us the privilege to call on Him any time and that He will answer us and show us great and mighty things (Jer.33:3). As we journey through each day of 2019, let us do like the Psalmist in the opening scripture above. Invite the LORD to open the heavens and come down into your life. He is a consuming fire and He will set ablaze every mountain of problem militating against you, IJN.

Prayer: Father, come down with Your fire to consume poverty, sickness, failure, delay, stagnation and other mountain of problems in my life, IJN.

Saturday May 25, 2019
Topic: TRULY BALANCED DIET

Scripture: "The eyes of all wait upon thee; and thou givest them their meat in due season" (Psalms 145:15, KJV).

Praise the Lord. Today is May 25th and is day #145 in year 2019. The number of days remaining to end this year is 220. By God's grace, you will not lose your blessings this year because of impatience, and you will see the end of this year and beyond, safe and sound in the mighty name of Jesus.

For proper growth, development and functionality, our body needs a balanced diet. There are 2 types of diets – physical and spiritual. Physical diet is attainable through proper combination of fresh fruits, fresh vegetables, whole grains, legumes, nuts and lean proteins with appropriate exercise. In the same token our spiritual diet is important because the word of God declares that "--Man shall not live by bread alone, but by every word that proceedeth out of the mouth of God." (Mt. 4:4). Spiritual food is the word of God which also includes the flesh and blood of Jesus Christ (John 6:54).

Today's opening scripture talks about how God provides the food needs of all those who will look up to Him. We must be grateful to God for giving us our daily bread. At the same time, we must pray for the 780 million (or 1 in 8) people in developing countries that still suffer from chronic hunger.

One of the names of God is Jehovah Jireh meaning "The LORD Will Provide" (Gen. 22:14). When it comes to provisions God's records are unmatchable and unbeatable. For example, the 40 years the Israelites spent in the wilderness God ensured they lacked nothing (Deut. 2:7). As year 2019 counts down your supplies will count up and Jehovah Jireh will ensure that you lack nothing, IJN.

The food God provides for us is meant to encompass both the physical and spiritual diets, the 2 must reinforcing each other. Regrettably, most people focus only on the physical diet and neglect the spiritual aspect. The extent to which you effectively and prayerfully integrate both diet types is the extent to which you can fulfill destiny. ***Prayer: Father feed me with both physical and spiritual balanced diets to enable me fulfill destiny IJN***

Sunday May 26, 2019
Topic: CHURCH REGULAR ATTENDANCE CUSTOM

Scripture: "And he came to Nazareth, where he had been brought up, and as his custom was, he went into the synagogue on the Sabbath day, and stood up for to read." (Lk. 4:16).

Praise the Lord. Today is May 26th and is day #146 in year 2019. The number of days remaining to end this year is 219. Today is also to the 21st Sunday of year 2019. It is that Lord's day and it shall be glorious for you IJN. If the Lord tarries, we shall see and live beyond the remaining 31 Sundays in this year, safe and sound in the mighty name of Jesus.

Jesus took Church attendance very seriously because He knew the value of Church. As indicated in today's opening scripture, it was customary of Jesus to attend Church. What one does regularly plays a major role in defining that person. Being the Lord of the Sabbath (Mk 2:28), it is not surprising that Jesus attended Church regularly.

Jesus did not only attend Church, He was active in the Church, doing things like reading the scripture, teaching and preaching (Lk 4: 21-28), healing the sick (Lk 6:6-11), cleaning and ensuring orderliness in the Church (Mk 11: 15-17).

Today, many people are deserting the Church or go there only sporadically. Some people substitute watching telecast services on TV for regular Church attendance. This is not Christ-like and it's wrong. Remember the injunction in Heb.10:25 that says, we should not neglect assembling together for worship. Furthermore, Jesus Christ said His house should be a house of prayer (Mt. 21:13) and the Bible commands us to pray without ceasing (1 Thes 5:17). Praying and praising God together with the brethren is one of the reasons to go to Church regularly.

Aside from demonstrating that you have the mindset of Jesus Christ and that you are obedient to God's injunction to fellowship and pray, you should go to Church regularly to nurture your spiritual life with the word of God, increase your joy (Ps 16:11), avail yourself with the possibility of receiving miracles (Lk 6:6-11; Mk 1: 21-27) and be blessed and be a blessing.

Prayer: Father let nothing separate me from your Church and the blessings of enquiring in your holy Temple.

Monday May 27, 2019
Topic: PARTAKING IN GOD'S PLEASURE

Scripture: "The Lord taketh pleasure in them that fear him, in those that hope in his mercy" (Psalms 147: 11, KJV).

Praise the Lord. Today is May 27th and is day #147 in year 2019. The number of days remaining to end this year is 218. By God's grace, everything you do henceforth will be pleasing to God, and you will see the end of this year and beyond, safe and sound in the mighty name of Jesus.

Pleasure refers to delight or feeling of being pleased. Pleasure can also mean enjoyment or satisfaction derived from what is to one's liking. Some people think God is against pleasure and that Christians should not have fun. This is not true. God loves pleasure and wants His people to partake in it, so long it is devoid of sins (see Galatians 5:19-21; Colossians 3:5-10)

We know God loves pleasure because the Bibles says He created all things for His pleasure: "Thou art worthy, O Lord, to receive glory and honour and power: for thou hast created all things, and for thy pleasure they are and were created" (Rev. 4:11). Furthermore, anywhere God is, pleasures are there for the Bible declares, "- - in His presence is fulness of joy; at thy right hand there are pleasures for evermore" (Ps. 16:11). Throughout this year 2019 and forever the pleasures of God will envelop you IJN.

What then does it take to be a partaker in God's pleasure? The list can be long but let's focus on the following three points: (1) Fear of God (see today's opening scripture). Fear refers to respect for God that will draw one to Him in love and service. (2) Hope in His mercy. His mercy and grace by which we receive His salvation and become His (Col. 1:27, Ps. 149: 4). (3) Faith and obedience. That is to believe that you were created for God's pleasure and must accept His invitation to come to Him by faith (Rev. 4:11, Matt 11:28). The Bible says the just shall live by faith (Heb 10:38). Determine by faith to live a life of pleasure and joy in the Lord.

Prayer: *Father, let me proper to the level that will give you pleasure,* **IJN**

Tuesday May 28, 2019
Topic: LIVING FOR THE LORD?

Scripture: "For whether we live, we live unto the Lord; and whether we die, we die unto the Lord: whether we live therefore, or die, we are the Lord's" (Romans 14:8).

Praise the Lord. Today is May 28th and is day #148 in year 2019. The number of days remaining to end this year is 217. By God's grace, the devil has lost all claims on you, you belong to Jesus Christ, and you will see the end of this year and beyond, safe and sound in the mighty name of Jesus.

The way many people live their lives show that they are ignorant or are carefree about the fact that a day of accountability to God will ensue one day. Confirming this fact, the Bible declares, ". .it is appointed unto men once to die, but after this the judgment" (Heb.9:27). Furthermore, the Bible says that God, "- - hath appointed a day, in the which he will judge the world in righteousness by that man whom he hath ordained; whereof he hath given assurance unto all men, in that he hath raised him from the dead" (Acts 17:31).

The judgement will entail each person giving an account of himself/herself to God (Rm. 14:12). Jesus Christ will be the ultimate judge who will evaluate each person's faith, work and lifestyle (John 3:16, 18; 2 Tim 4:1)

Simply put, God's judgement will be favorable for believers in Jesus Christ as they will not perish but go to heaven. On the other hand, God's judgement will be unfavorable for unbelievers as they will be sent to hell (Mt. 13: 41-42; Mt. 25:4, Jn 14:2, Rev 20:11-15).

What is your choice, hell or heaven? Where you will go depends on the decision you make while you are still alive in terms of who you live for - the Lord Jesus or for Satan. Jesus Christ said, "He that is not with me is against me –" (Lk. 11:23). He further said, "-- whosoever shall deny me before men, him will I also deny before my Father which is in heaven" (Mt. 10:33). Accept Jesus Christ as Lord and Savior and live for the Lord. If you do so you will go to heaven and reign with Jesus Christ, IJN. ***Prayer: Father, by Your grace and power let me live, move and have my being in Jesus Christ forever. Amen.***

Wednesday May 29, 2019
Topic: SINGING A NEW SONG

Scripture: "Praise ye the LORD. Sing unto the LORD a new song, and his praise in the congregation of saints." (Psalm 149:1).

Praise the Lord. Today is May 29th and is day #149 in year 2019. The number of days remaining to end this year is 216. By God's grace, your passion for praising God shall never diminish, and you will see the end of this year and beyond, safe and sound in the mighty name of Jesus.

God is very interested in newness especially if it is tailored towards preserving the perfect world He created. This fact is evident throughout the Bible. God Himself declares "A new heart also will I give you, and a new spirit will I put within you: and I will take away the stony heart out of your flesh, and I will give you an heart of flesh" (Ezek. 36:26). It is this gift of a new heart and a new spirit that makes it possible for one to have a new nature in Jesus Christ and be in right relationship with God: "Therefore, if any man be in Christ, he is a new creature: old things are passed away; behold, all things are become new" (2 Cor. 5:17).

God is blessing us daily, doing many new things as He has promised: "Behold, I will do a new thing; now it shall spring forth; shall ye not know it? I will even make a way in the wilderness, and rivers in the desert" (Isaiah 43: 19). The singing of new songs is just one way we can express our appreciation of God's daily blessings unto us. Psalm 98:1 declares "O sing unto the LORD a new song; for he hath done marvelous things". New songs are refreshing and renewing.

Hannah sang to God when her prayer for a son was answered and her bareness was terminated (1 Sam 2: 1-10). Mary the mother of Jesus sang a song called the Magnificat when she was favored to be the mother of Jesus Christ (Lk.1:45-55). For the remaining days of this year, God will do many new things in your life and you will sing new songs, IJN.

Prayer: Father, thank you for done for me already. Please continue to do marvelous things for me that will provoke laughter and new songs of praise from me to You, IJN.

Thursday May 30, 2019
Topic: REST FROM AIMLESS ROAMING

Scripture: "So the floodwaters gradually receded from the earth. After 150 days, 4 exactly five months from the time the flood began, the boat came to rest on the mountains of Ararat." (Genesis 8:3-4, NLT).

Praise the Lord. Today is May 30th and is day #150 in year 2019. The number of days remaining to end this year is 215. By God's grace, every disarray in your life shall disappear permanently, and you will see the end of this year and beyond, safe and sound in the mighty name of Jesus.

When human wickedness and evil activities reached intolerable level for God, He decided to send floodwaters to destroy every living thing, except Noah, his family and few selected creatures that were with them in the ark (Gen. chap 6 and 7). Noah and those with him were spared from destruction because Noah found grace in the eyes of the Lord (Gen 6:8). In this year, you and your family shall be saved from all forms of destruction, IJN

Although Noah and his family escaped the flood destruction, they faced the challenge of not been able to dock as the floodwater prevailed upon the earth carrying their boat (ark) about restlessly for 150 days. As indicated in the opening scripture above, after the 150 days were over the boat (ark) came to rest on the mountain of Ararat. The boat came to a rest because God remembered Noah (Gen. 8:1). From today, anything constituting flood of problems lingering in your life shall dry up and be terminated, in the mighty name of Jesus. Your season to rest from persistent sickness, bareness, joblessness, miscarriages, recurring marital disputes, evil dreams and other problems in the market place of life has come, in Jesus mighty name.

Action: If you have not, accept Jesus Christ as your Lord and Savior today by confessing your sins, repenting of them and asking Him to forgive you and give you the grace to serve Him for the rest of your life. He will accept you and keep you in His ark of safety.

Prayer: Father, remember me and don't let my life's boat sink or roam about aimlessly, IJN

Friday May 31, 2019
Topic: DIVINE INCREASE

Scripture: "Though thy beginning was small, yet thy latter end should greatly increase." (Job 8:7, KJV).

Praise the Lord. Today is May 31st and is day #151 in year 2019. The number of days remaining to end this year is 214. By God's grace, you will enjoy divine increases in all areas you desire (spiritually, financially, etc., and you will see the end of this year and beyond, safe and sound in the mighty name of Jesus.

When it comes to positive things. God wants his people to enjoy an increase rather than a decrease. This fact is evident in God's work of creation regarding living creatures. For example, after creating fishes and the birds on the fifth day, God blessed them saying:"- Be fruitful, and multiply, and fill the waters in the seas, and let fowl multiply in the earth" (Gen 1:22). In like manner, after God created man, male and female on the sixth day, He added His blessing, saying "--Be fruitful, and multiply, and replenish the earth, and subdue it: and have dominion over the fish of the sea, and over the fowl of the air, and over every living thing that moveth upon the earth" (Gen 1: 28).

From the foregoing, it is clear that God's blessing is the primary ingredient that brings about divine increase. No wonder the Bible declares "The blessing of the Lord, it maketh rich, and he addeth no sorrow with it" (Pro. 10:32). God blessed Abraham and took him from no child to become father of nations (Gen. 12: 1-4, Gen 15. 22).

Aside from God's blessings (#1), other factors that can provoke divine increase include: (#2) giving (Lk. 6:38, 1 Chron. 1: 6-12), (3) prayer (Mt. 7:7-8, Jn 16:24) and (4) praise (Psalm 67: 3-7), etc. As the opening scripture above indicates God expects progressive increase in believers' lives. He told Abraham, "That in blessing I will bless thee, and in multiplying I will multiply thy seed as the stars of the heaven- -" (Gen 22:17). God enabled Hannah to move progressively from no child to one son (Samuel) and ending up with a total of 6 children (1 Sam 2:21). By divine mathematical multiplication God promised that "A little one shall become a thousand- - "(Isa. 60:22)

Action / Prayer: Intensify your praise to God. Give a sacrificial gift to provoke your divine increase. Father, bless me indeed and let me enjoy divine increases in all areas (be specific)

Saturday June 01, 2019
Topic: DIVINE VISITATION

Scripture: "And in the sixth month the angel Gabriel was sent from God unto - - - a virgin espoused to a man whose name was Joseph--and the virgin's name was Mary - - - And the angel - - - said, Hail, thou that art highly favoured, the Lord is with thee: blessed art thou among Women- - And, behold, thou shalt conceive in thy womb, and bring forth a son, and shalt call his name Jesus " (Luke 1:26- 31).

Praise the Lord. Today is June 1st and is day #152 in year 2019. The number of days remaining to end this year is 213. By God's grace, you will receive several visitations from the Lord this season for upgrading your life, and you will see the end of this year and beyond, safe and sound in the mighty name of Jesus.

Glory be to God who has brought us to the sixth month of this year. The 6th month is very important in the history of the believer as it is the month that the announcement was made that Jesus Christ, the Savior of the world would be conceived by a virgin called Mary.

Divine visitation is a life changing experience; no one receives it and remain the same. Positive divine visitation is what every believer in Jesus Christ should pray, thirst and hunger for.

According to today's opening scripture, the Angel who visited Mary decreed and prophesied over her as instructed by God. The Angel's profound statements are suggestive of some personal prayer points that can enhance our lives for God's glory. These statements and the associated suggested prayer points are as follow:

(1)" though art highly favored". Prayer: Father let me experience higher level of favor, IJN

(2) "the Lord is with thee". Prayer: Father, let Your presence be with me always, IJN

(3) "blessed art thou among women". Prayer: Father, if you are looking for one person to bless, let me be the one, IJN

(4) "thou shalt conceive and bring forth a son and shalt call his name Jesus"

Prayer: Father, let me bring forth what will make me a blessing to my generation, IJN. Prayer: Father, visit me with good news throughout this month and forever, IJN.

Sunday June 02, 2019
Topic: SCARCITY TURNED TO SURPLUS

Scripture: "So Simon Peter went aboard and hauled the net ashore, full of large fish, 153 of them. And although there were so many, the net was not torn" (John 21:11, ESV)

Praise the Lord. Today is June 2nd and is day #153 in year 2019. The number of days remaining to end this year is 212. By God's grace, the era of fruitless labor are over in your life, and you will see the end of this year and beyond, safe and sound in the mighty name of Jesus.

God is a status changer. Given that the earth is the LORD's and the fullness thereof (Ps. 24: 1), He can easily move somebody from having zero to having surplus. Peter and 6 other disciples had this experience during one of Jesus' post resurrection appearances (John 21: 1-12). These disciples had fished all night and caught nothing (zero) at the Sea of Siberia. Jesus then appeared to them and said "Cast the net on the right side of the boat, and you will find some.". The disciples obeyed and their net caught so much as indicated in today's opening scripture. They ended up with surplus catch.

Do you have any area(s) your efforts have not yielded the desired result? Don't give up. Connect with Christ and pray to Him to show you the "right side" to direct your efforts (Ps. 32: 8). Do like the Psalmist says: "Commit your way to the Lord, Trust also in Him, And He shall bring it to pass (Ps. 37:5). Obey God, persevere and be patient like Hannah who kept on going to Shiloh until she got Samuel and five other children (1 Sam 2:21). Very soon you will testify for your scarcity shall turn to surplus

Prayer: Father give me the grace to do whatever it takes for You to supply all my need according to Your riches in glory by Christ Jesus.

Monday June 03, 2019
Topic: MY PURSUERS MUST PERISH

Scripture: "Pharaoh's chariots and his host he cast into the sea, and his chosen officers were sunk in the Red Sea" (Exo 15:4, ESV).

Praise the Lord. Today is June 3rd and is day #154 in year 2019. The number of days remaining to end this year is 211. By God's grace, those enemies pursuing you shall drown to disappear from your radar, and you will see the end of this year and beyond, safe and sound in the mighty name of Jesus.

There is no doubt that believers are targets of the enemy because the enemy is not happy that we have left his camp. Just as Pharaoh and the Egyptian army pursued the Israelites after their exodus from Egypt, the same way Satan and his demons pursue the believers of Jesus Christ on a constant basis. Satan pursues believers to kill, to steal and to destroy (John 10:10a). The word of God also warns us against Satan's strategy that we should "Be sober, be vigilant; because your adversary the devil, as a roaring lion, walketh about, seeking whom he may devour"(1 Peter 5:8). You will not be his victim IJN.

Faced by the Red Sea (with no bridge to take them to the other side) and Pharaoh's army pursuers behind them, Moses cried to God for help. God told him to stretch his rod over the sea to part the Red Sea. When he did the Red Sea parted and the Israelites crossed over on dry ground. When Pharaoh and his army attempted to cross over like the Israelites, God told Moses to stretch the rod over the sea again to close back the parted Sea. When he did all Pharaoh and his army were drowned in the Red Sea as indicated in today's opening scripture. God fought for the Israelites and gave them victory.

The same God that fought for the Israelites will do the same for you if you are His follower, because He is a defender of His people (Isa. 52:22; 43: 1-4; Ps 7:10; 62:6). As believers God has given us "spiritual staff" and other weapons to use as He leads us in the fight against the enemy. These weapons include (1) The Name of Jesus, (2) Holy living, (3) Prayer, (4) The Word of God, (5) Praise, (6) Obedience, (7) Giving. As you use these weapons, all your pursuers are in trouble, IJN.

Prayer: Let all my unrelenting pursuers and destiny snatchers perish in the Red Sea, IJN

Tuesday June 04, 2019
Topic: AVOIDING ABOMINATIONS

Scripture: "And it came to pass --- in the sixth month, in the fifth day of the month, as I sat in mine house, ---- the hand of the Lord God fell there upon me.------ and took me by a lock of mine head; and the spirit lifted me up between the earth and the heaven, and brought me in the visions of God to Jerusalem, --where was the seat of the image of jealousy, which provoketh to jealousy. And, behold, the glory of the God of Israel was there, according to the vision that I saw in the plain. --- He said furthermore unto me, Son of man, seest thou what they do? even the great abominations that the house of Israel committeth here, that I should go far off from my sanctuary? but turn thee yet again, and thou shalt see greater abominations" (Ezekiel 8: 1-6, KJV).

Praise the Lord. Today is June 4th and is day #155 in year 2019. The number of days remaining to end this year is 210. By God's grace, you will not partake in any abomination this year, and you will see the end of this year and beyond, safe and sound in the mighty name of Jesus.

The only place where the exact phrase "the hand of the Lord GOD" is mentioned in the Bible (KJV) is in Ezekiel 8:1. When the hand of the Lord GOD was upon Prophet Ezekiel, the spirit lifted him up and he saw visions of God about Jerusalem, and the temple. I pray the hand of the Almighty God will be upon you to lift you up and show you divine revelations, IJN.

Among the things God showed Prophet Ezekiel was the glory of God of Israel and the idolatry of the people. Also, Ezekiel saw image of jealousy in the entry at the gate of the altar northward and greater abominations (Ezek. 8:5-6). Regrettably, jealousy and many other abominable vices are rampant in Churches of today. O Lord have mercy!

See the list in Proverbs 6: 16-19, KJV, these sins are especially enraging to God because of how they can destroy lives and society. Since God hates them, we must pray against them and hate them in ourselves and in others.

Prayer: Father, deliver me from the lust of the flesh, the lust of the eyes, and the pride of life and all things abominable to You, IJN.

Wednesday June 05, 2019
Topic: BANISHING BARRENNESS

Scripture: "And, behold, thy cousin Elisabeth, she hath also conceived a son in her old age: and this is the sixth month with her, who was called barren." (Luke 1:36).

Praise the Lord. Today is June 5th and is day #156 in year 2019. The number of days remaining to end this year is 209. By God's grace, your name will not be associated with barrenness, reproach or failure, and you will see the end of this year and beyond, safe and sound in the mighty name of Jesus.

God is a status changer and with Him nothing is impossible (Lk. 1:37). The way He changed the statuses of women like Sarai, Rachael, Hannah, Manaoh's wife and Elisabeth from barrenness to bearing of children should provide hope and encouragement to all couples who have been unable to have children. Barrenness is against the will of God who said, "- -There shall nothing cast their young, nor be barren, in thy land" (Ex. 23:26a).

Among the initially barren women mentioned above, Elisabeth's case stands out. Her barrenness was so serious she became an object of mockery, reproach and shame.

An important lesson from Zacharias and Elisabeth is that they did not allow their problem to stand between them and their devotion and dedication to the service of God. Though stricken in age, Zacharias neither relented nor retired from faithfully executing the priest's office before God in the order of his course. While serving in the Temple one day, an angel of God (Gabriel) appeared to Zacharias and said "-Fear not, Zacharias: for thy prayer is heard; and thy wife Elisabeth shall bear thee a son, and thou shalt call his name John" (Luke 1:13). Zacharias received the news with doubt and was cursed (by Gabriel) to be dumbed until the fulfillment of the prophecy (Luke 1:20). As the angel said, Elisabeth conceived and brought forth a baby boy who was named John (Luke 1: 57- 64). God terminated Elizabeth's barrenness, and the one called "barren" became the mother of the greatest prophet among those born of women in his time (Matthew 11:11). **Prayer: *Father, please terminate all forms of barrenness (biological, soul winning, financial, talents, etc.) in my family, IJN.***

Thursday June 06, 2019
Topic HARMONIOUS RELATIONSHIP

Scripture: "Wherefore receive ye one another, as Christ also received us to the glory of God" (Romans 15:7).

Praise the Lord. Today is June 6th and is day #157 in year 2019. The number of days remaining to end this year is 208. By God's grace, you will honor people and be honored by people this season, and you will see the end of this year and beyond, safe and sound in the mighty name of Jesus.

Harmonious relationship is important to God and beneficial to man at all levels. God created man in His own image for fellowship with him and to give Him praise. God himself declares in His word, "for them that honour me I will honour--"(1 Sam 2:30). Additionally, God created Eve for Adam as a help mate. They were to relate to each other as husband and wife and to become one (Gen. 2:24). It is all about relationship. As man increased in number, God gave the 10 commandments, the first 5 to guide loving and peaceful relationship between man and God (vertical relationship) and the second 5 to foster loving and peaceful relationship between man and his neighbors (horizontal relationship).

As the opening scripture for today indicates mutual acceptance of one another is what God expects among believers. Every believer is saved by the same grace and love of Jesus Christ. The same way Jesus received us to Himself and to His Father is how we are to receive one another. That is, believers are to see themselves as members of one body as the Bible declares: "So we, being many, are one body in Christ, and every one members one of another" (Rom. 12:5). We should be able to dwell together in unity which the Bible says is good and pleasant (Psalm 133:1).

Regrettably, there is still so much hatred, division, backbiting, unforgiveness, jealousy, envy, and other vices going on among believers. Among other things we must (1) love one another as Christ commands (Jn 13:34,35), (2) live peaceably with others (Rm 12:18), (3) bear each other's burdens (Gal. 6:12), (4) pray for and forgive one another readily (James 5:6).

Prayer: Father, give me the grace to receive, respect and love others, **IJN**

Friday June 07, 2019
Topic OPENING WIDE TO GOD

Scripture: "I am the Lord thy God, which brought thee out of the land of Egypt: open thy mouth wide, and I will fill it" (Psalm 81:10).

Praise the Lord. Today is June 7th and is day #158 in year 2019. The number of days remaining to end this year is 207. By God's grace, your mouth shall be full of words of grace released to you by the Lord, and you will see the end of this year and beyond, safe and sound in the mighty name of Jesus.

God is mightily big and does big things which no one else can do. In the opening scripture above God introduced Himself to the Israelites as the one who brought them out of the land of Egypt. The Israelites concurred with this when they proclaimed that "- -With a powerful hand the LORD brought us out of Egypt, from the house of slavery" (Exodus 13:14). Like His Father, Jesus Christ is a powerful liberator. He was anointed to do good works including bringing you out of sins, sickness, stagnation, poverty, barrenness, loneliness, or anything that amounts to the Egyptian bondage (Acts. 10:38; Lk. 4:18)

Aside from deliverance from bondage, God has power to bless (Gen. 12: 1-3; Eph. 1:3) Sometimes, God may give you the privilege to determine the size of your blessing. As in today's opening scripture above, God said to the Israelites "open thy mouth wide, and I will fill it". God is saying the same to you by principle. What you open your mouth for and how wide you open it will determine what you get and how much you get. For example, if you open your mouth wide in praising Him He can bless you in various ways including: letting the earth yield its increase to you (Ps. 67: 3-7), opening the prison gate to set you free as He did for Paul and Silas (Acts 16: 25-40), fighting your battle and defeating your enemy as He did for Jehoshaphat and Judah (2 Chron 20: 1-25).

As year 2019 counts down, don't limit yourself and don't limit God. Prayerfully "open your mouth wide" and watch God fill it. That is, do more for God, for yourself and for others. Pray more, evangelize more, serve more, give more, study more, plan more, eat healthier, exercise more, rest more, love more, help more, save more, invest more, spend more time with your family, etc. God will bring you out to bless you, IJN. *Prayer: Father, let me open wide to You to receive Your blessings without sorrows, IJN.*

Saturday June 08, 2019
Topic: PERSONALITY PANORAMA –KING ASA (I)

Scripture: "In the twentieth year of Jeroboam king of Israel, Asa began to reign over Judah," (1 Kings 15:9).

Praise the Lord. Today is June 8th and is day #159 in year 2019. The number of days remaining to end this year is 206. By God's grace, your life will witness a new dimension of upliftment this season, and you will see the end of this year and beyond, safe and sound in the mighty name of Jesus.

There are about 3237 different names of people mentioned in the Bible. However, only about 1794 of these people (55 %) have a unique name meaning that only nearly half the people mentioned in the Bible share the same name with at least one other individual. For example, the Bible has 31 Zechariahs, 13 Josephs and 5 different Johns. There are many lessons we can learn from the lives and experiences of many Bible personalities.

Asa was the grandson of Rehoboam, the son of Solomon. He reigned in Jerusalem for 41 years. Asa started well with God but did not finish well. The Bible declares that "-Asa did that which was right in the eyes of the Lord, as did David his father" (1 Kings 15:11). On ascension to the throne, Asa got rid of all the idols his ancestors had made and promoted, honoring the Lord and His temple (1 kings 15: 12-15).

Later in his reign, Asa abruptly abandoned his commitment to God, entered into an unholy treaty with Benhadad king of Syria to help him fight against Basha, the king of Israel. He trusted the arm of flesh rather than that of God. When Hanani, the Seer, challenged Asa about his disbelief in God, Asa was infuriated and had Hanani thrown in the prison (2 Chron 16: 7- 10). Asa's disregard for God and maltreatment of the anointed man of God cost him dearly. He was afflicted with a severe disease in his feet that took his life (2 Chron 16: 12). Thus, Asa died, neglecting the God he started with. That will not be your portion, IJN.

Prayer: Father, whatever I do in the market place of life, let me start and end with You successfully, IJN.

Sunday June 09, 2019
Topic: PERSONALITY PANORAMA – KING ASA (II)

Scripture: "So the Lord smote the Ethiopians before Asa, and before Judah; and the Ethiopians fled. And Asa and the people that were with him pursued them unto Gerar: and the Ethiopians were overthrown, that they could not recover themselves; for they were destroyed before the Lord, and before his host; and they carried away very much spoil" (1 Chron 14: 12-13).

Praise the Lord. Today is June 9th and is day #160 in year 2019. The number of days remaining to end this year is 205. By God's grace, you will see the end of this year and beyond, safe and sound in the mighty name of Jesus.

Yesterday's countdown ministration was on Asa, the king of Judah for 41 years. We learnt that he did what was right in the eyes of God especially at the beginning of his reign. Among other things, he cleansed the land of foreign gods and idol worship and commanded Judah to seek the LORD God of their fathers. We also learnt that king Asa did not finish well in that he abandoned God towards the end of his reign and that he died shamefully.

The focus of today's ministration is on how Asa, when he was still trusting God, sought and received divine assistance from God to defeat his enemies. There is a tendency for the enemy to strike when things are going well. This was the case with Asa and Judah who decided to build fortified cities with walls, towers, gates, and bars after the Lord has given them rest on every side (2 Chron 14: 6-7).

With an army of only 580,000 warriors, Asa of Judah were attacked by an Ethiopian named Zerah whose army numbered 1,000,000 men and 300 chariots. Asa cried out to the Lord his God for help (2 Chron 14:11, NLT). God answered Asa's prayer and gave him and Judah amazing victory over the Ethiopian enemies as indicated in today's opening scripture above (2 Chron 14: 12-13).

Are you, your family or any one you know facing any type of attack? Remember James 5:16, your fervent prayer avails much. Who (or what) is that intimidating "Zerah" attacking (or plans to attack) your health, children, career, business, marriage, etc.? Cry fervently to God for help as Asa did. You shall overcome, IJN. ***Prayer: Father, please help and empower me to defeat and destroy all my enemies, IJN.***

Monday June 10, 2019
Topic: PETITION FOR PROTECTION

Scripture: "Preserve me, O God: for in thee do I put my trust" (Psalm 16:1).

Praise the Lord. Today is June 10th and is day #161 in year 2019. The number of days remaining to end this year is 204. By God's grace, no weapon fashioned against you this season shall prosper, and you will see the end of this year and beyond, safe and sound in the mighty name of Jesus.

The best security any one can have is that of God. This is why the Bible says "The horse is prepared against the day of battle: but safety is of the Lord" (Pro. 21:31). God has already made many promises to keep safe any one that belongs to Him and trust Him. For example, the Lord that created Jacob said to him "- - Fear not: for I have redeemed thee, I have called thee by thy name; thou art mine. When thou passest through the waters, I will be with thee; and through the rivers, they shall not overflow thee: when thou walkest through the fire, thou shalt not be burned; neither shall the flame kindle upon thee" (Isa. 43: 1-2). When Jesus sent out 70 of his disciples, He gave them power to tread on serpents and scorpions and promised that "- -nothing shall by any means hurt you" (Luke 10: 19b).

The Psalmist also declares that "They that trust in the Lord shall be as mount Zion, which cannot be removed, but abideth forever" (Ps. 125:1).

If you have given your life to Jesus Christ as your Lord and Savior, you are entitled to the same covenant of protection like Abraham, Isaac and Jacob. This does not necessarily mean that one problem or the other will never confront you. When such problems come to you God says He will be with you to take you through it safely. As a matter of fact, with the right attitude of response, problems are often platform for promotion for a child of God.

To enjoy maximum protection from God, the believer must at least do the following: (1) maintain constant and unwavering trust in the Lord, (2) live holy, (3) pray and fast regularly (4) serve the Lord (5) obey God completely. As you observe these faithfully God will preserve you from all dangers in the remaining 204 days in year 2019.

Prayer: Father, put the mark of Jesus Christ on me and let nothing harm me for the rest of my life, IJN

Tuesday June 11, 2019
Topic: SHUN SELF-RIGHTEOUSNESS

Scripture: "All the ways of a man are clean in his own eyes; but the Lord weigheth the spirits" (Proverbs 16:2).

Praise the Lord. Today is June 11th and is day #162 in year 2019. The number of days remaining to end this year is 203. By God's grace, the Lord's yardstick of you will see the end of this year and beyond, safe and sound in the mighty name of Jesus.

One common error people tend to commit is that of self-righteousness (SR). The dictionary defines SR as "confident of one's own righteousness, especially when smugly moralistic and intolerant of the opinions and behavior of others.". One reason why one can be prone to the error of SR is that there is a tendency to evaluate oneself using own yardstick or own standard exclusive of that of others and particularly that of God's.

Today's opening scripture points out a marked difference between human evaluation and divine evaluation of the ways of man. Essentially, human's evaluation of their ways is usually based on physical criteria in terms of what their limited eyes can see while God's approach to evaluation is based on spiritual dimension which encompasses His omniscience. Since the spirit controls the physical, God's perspective is far superior to that of man. No wonder the Bible declares that, "all our righteousnesses are as filthy rags" (Isa. 64:6), and, "there is none righteous, no, not one" (Rom 3:10).

A rich ruler came to Jesus to ask what he must do to inherit eternal life. Jesus told him to obey the commandments. In his own eyes, the rich ruler told Jesus that he had kept all the commandments (LK. 18: 18-30). However, based on divine standard, Jesus told the man, "Yet lackest thou one thing: sell all that thou hast, and distribute unto the poor, and thou shalt have treasure in heaven: and come, follow me" (v. 21). When the ruler heard what Jesus said he was very sorrowful for he was very rich. The ruler's self-righteousness closed his eyes from seeing the need to help the poor and to love his neighbor.

The believer's life is largely plagued by innate tendency for self-righteousness. Therefore, to shun self-righteousness we must prayerfully trust and depend on God for guidance in all things, for our righteousness is in Him (2 Cor. 5:21). **Prayer: Father deliver me and don't let me be guilty of self-righteousness, IJN.**

Tuesday June 12, 2019
Topic: WHEN GOD HANDLES YOUR WORK

Scripture: "Commit thy works unto the Lord, and thy thoughts shall be established" (Psalm 16:3).

Praise the Lord. Today is June 12th and is day #163 in year 2019. The number of days remaining to end this year is 202. By God's grace, you shall be established and successful in all that you do this year, and you will see the end of this year and beyond, safe and sound in the mighty name of Jesus.

When God handles your work, all will be well. Anything committed in to God's hand can never suffer or fail. The Bible says, "Except the Lord build the house, they labour in vain that build it" (Ps. 127:1). You will not labor in vain IJN. God is a perfect worker whose works are wondrous (Ps.105:2). He has total control over all the works in the world because He put each one of them in place. He finished the work of creation only in 6 days. Jesus Christ also successfully completed the work of redemption and declared "it is finished" (Jn. 19:30). God knows the ins and out of every work and it behooves you to let Him be in charge of your works.

To hand your works over to God entails depending on God completely for wisdom, strength, help and all it takes to get the works done in the fashion that will glorify God. It calls for prayerfully casting all concerns about the works upon God and His providence for supply, support and sustenance. Ask for His grace to be diligent and proficient in doing each work as unto the Lord. Start each day's work with prayer for guidance and divine assistance for excellent performance. At the end of the day give thanks to God for helping you accomplish what has been achieved for the day. Don't let your work stand in the way of serving the God who provided you the work. Pay your tithes and give generously to God.

What are the benefits of handing over your works to God? They are many and may include getting your thoughts (or desires, aspirations, etc.) established. For instance, God can grant you rapid promotion, He can facilitate your works, He can divinely connect you with your destiny helpers. In summary, honor God on, and with your works and He will do for you what will exceed your thoughts and imagination, JN. ***Prayer: Father, take total control of my works and be glorified by what I do, IJN.***

Thursday June 13, 2019
Topic: MANAGING YOUR "MANNA"

Scripture: "Then said the Lord unto Moses, Behold, I will rain bread from heaven for you; and the people shall go out and gather a certain rate every day, that I may prove them, whether they will walk in my law, or no." (Exodus 16:4 KJV).

Praise the Lord. Today is June 13th and is day #164 in year 2019. The number of days remaining to end this year is 201. By God's grace, you and your family shall never suffer hunger, and you will see the end of this year and beyond, safe and sound in the mighty name of Jesus.

Manna is God's supernatural edible substance provided for the Israelites during their forty-year period of travels in the desert following the Exodus from Egypt and prior to the conquest of Canaan. Manna was made available to Israel following their complaint and murmuring for lack of food in the wilderness.

In Biblical account, the name manna is said to derive from the question "man-hu" seemingly meaning "What is it?". Therefore, in the context of the opening scripture above what is it that you want God to rain down for you in this year 2019? Name them and God says He will answer you, IJN.

Note that it is important to follow divine direction in the use of Godly provisions in order to maximize the benefits. When Israel collected manna according to divine direction, there was no problem. However, when they collected manna with greed, manna started producing maggots (Ex.16:19-24).

In the remaining days of year 2019, God will give you your manna but you must guide against greed and other maggot-producing sins.

Prayer: Father, give me the grace to follow divine directions in the use of all that you provide for me, IJN

Friday June 14, 2019
Topic: CARING FOR THE CHURCH

Scripture: "So the churches were strengthened in their faith and grew larger every day." (Acts 16:5, KJV).

Praise the Lord. Today is June 14th and is day #165 in year 2019. The number of days remaining to end this year is 200. By God's grace, your faith shall be stronger and larger this year than ever before, and you will see the end of this year and beyond, safe and sound in the mighty name of Jesus.

Part of the responsibilities of a Christian is to care and support the Church of God, particularly to ensure its stability and its growth. The Church has always been very important to Jesus Christ. With unwavering determination Jesus Christ declared "I will build my church; and the gates of hell shall not prevail against it" (Mt. 16:18). He purchased the Church with His blood by dying for it (Acts 20: 28, Eph. 5:26).

Like Jesus Christ, believers must be totally committed to the Church. Aside from Jesus the Bible is replete with examples of many people who demonstrated strong commitment and support for the Church. Foremost among this group is Paul who, ironically used to be a staunch enemy and persecutor of the Church. It was because of support from Paul and his protégé, Timothy that Churches in Derbe and Lystra were strengthened in faith and grew larger every day as indicated in the opening scripture above. During his second missionary journey, Paul recruited young Timothy, circumcised him and went with him from town to town instructing believers to follow decrees and decisions approved by apostles and Church elders in Jerusalem (Acts 16:1-4).

You can support the Church of Christ in various ways including (1) Praying for the Church, (2) evangelizing to recruit members for the Church, (3) planting new Churches (4) giving generously to help fund the Church activities such as building, mission, etc. (5) praying for and encouraging the Pastor, ministers, etc. For other ideas of how to support the Church and advance the work of God contact Phebe, Tryphena, Tryphosa and more than 20 other names listed by apostle Paul in Romans chapter 16. As year 2019 counts down let your support for the Church count up so that your blessings can count upwards, IJN

Prayer: *Father, make me an assiduous supporter of Your Church, IJN.*

Saturday June 15, 2019
Topic: CHOOSING GOD'S CHOICE

Scripture: "And it came to pass, when they were come, that he looked on Eliab, and said, Surely the LORD's anointed is before him" (1 Samuel 16:6, KJV).

Praise the Lord. Today is June 15th and is day #166 in year 2019. The number of days remaining to end this year is 199. By God's grace, you will not make errors in all your choices this year and you will see the end of this year and beyond, safe and sound in the mighty name of Jesus.

Life is full of choices. The intricacies of choices and their effects on our lives can be enormous and overwhelming. For example, our entry and exit into this world, our growing up, our career, destiny, etc. are influenced by myriads of choices, some made by us others made for us or on our behalf. Therefore, it is expedient that we engage prayer and care to ensure that our choices and those made about us are correctly made. After God rejected king Saul, He instructed prophet Samuel to go to the house of Jesse to anoint one of His sons as a replacement for Saul, according to 1 Sam 16:3.

Without any evidence of praying or seeking God's confirmation Samuel looked at the outward appearance of the first son (Eliab) and said surely, he was the one. God quickly intervened and rejected Samuel's choice that was based solely on outward (v. 7). As it turned out, David, the youngest of Jesse's sons was the correct choice meant by God. David was not even present at the coronation venue but had to be sent for at the field where he was busy tending his father's sheep. When David arrived, God said to Samuel "...Arise, anoint him: for this is he" (v 12). I decree that you will be the next "this is he/she" for salvation, favor, blessings, promotion, freedom from sickness, debt, shame, reproach, IJN.

Consider the following actions in making correct choices (1) prayerfully seek God's Direction (Ps. 32:8, Pro 3:5-6), (2) Dig out all the relevant information about the issue (2 Tim 2:15), (3) Determine and evaluate possible alternatives (Eccl. 11:6), (4) Discuss with reliable confidant(s) (Pro 11:14; 24:6), (5) Don't rush (2 Tim. 2:24,1 Thess. 5:14). As year 2019 count down, may correct and optimal choices about you count up, IJN. **Prayer: *Let every choice and decision concerning my life be made correctly according to Your will IJN***

Sunday June 16, 2019
Topic: FAULTLESS FATHER

Scripture: "Furthermore we have had fathers of our flesh which corrected us, and we gave them reverence: shall we not much rather be in subjection unto the Father of spirits, and live" (Hebrews 12:9).

Praise the Lord. Today is June 16th and is day #167 in year 2019. The number of days remaining to end this year is 198. By God's grace, you will give the Lord your total allegiance forever, and you will see the end of this year and beyond, safe and sound in the mighty name of Jesus.

Welcome to June 16, 2019, the Father's Day for this year. Countdown begins today for the next one in (June 21, 2020), which is about 371 days from today. By God's grace we shall see that day and beyond, IJN.

Kudos to all fathers and fathers to be. Father's Day provide the opportunity to appreciate, honor and celebrate fathers for their important roles in the family. It should also be an opportunity to remind fathers the awesome responsibility God expects them to shoulder as His representative in terms of spiritual leadership in the family and elsewhere. Hear what God said about Abraham, the Father of Faith: "For I know him, that he will command his children and his household after him, and they shall keep the way of the Lord, to do justice and judgment; that the Lord may bring upon Abraham that which he hath spoken of him" (Gen.18: 19, KJV). I pray that as fathers we will not disappoint God in training our children the words and ways of God and leading our entire family to love Him with all our heart, soul, mind and strength as well as love our neighbors as ourselves.

It must be noted that God is the ultimate Father of every human being. Unlike earthly father, God is faultless, always faithful and will never fail. God is the perfect model all earthly fathers must follow. The Bible says without Him we can do nothing (John 15:5). Through His Son Jesus Christ, God is the one who can clean sins away and teach/show how to father in the fashion that will qualify us to have the eternal life that He gives. It will be a tragedy to be a father here on earth and spend eternity in hell fire. That will not be your portion, IJN. **HAPPY FATHER'S DAY**. *Prayer: My Heavenly Father, hallowed by thy name. Please help me to be a father as You expect me be, IJN.*

Monday June 17, 2019
Topic: BE UNMOVEABLE

Scripture: "I have set the Lord always before me: because he is at my right hand, I shall not be moved". (Psalms 16:8 KJV).

Praise the Lord. Today is June 17th and is day #168 in year 2019. The number of days remaining to end this year is 197. By God's grace, the Lord will be set perpetually before you forever, and you will see the end of this year and beyond, safe and sound in the mighty name of Jesus.

Everything in life (objects or issues/situations) can assume only one of two possible positions at a given time: stable (unmoved) or unstable (moved or displayed). As used here, stability connotes normal undisturbed circumstance or situation while instability refers to abnormal circumstance accompanied with some discomfort, inconvenience or unsatisfactory deviation from the status quo.

The good plan of God for His people is to always have stable and smooth circumstance in which to operate under His watch. For example, God made adequate provision to ensure smooth and safe journey for the Israelites during their exodus from Egypt to the Promised Land. The Bible declares, "And the Lord went before them by day in a pillar of a cloud, to lead them the way; and by night in a pillar of fire, to give them light; to go by day and night:" (Ex. 13:21, KJV).

King David must have been aware of God's plans and promises for guidance and protection for His people when he boldly made the statement in today's opening scripture. As you journey through year 2019, resolve to do like David in this scripture. When you set the Lord always before you, He will be with you, guide you and teach you the way to go (Psalm 32:8, Isaiah 43: 1-3, Heb. 12:2). When you trust in Jesus you will be like mount Zion which cannot be moved (Ps. 125:1-2). You must resist the following possible agents of instability: Greed, Love of money more than God, Avoiding Fellowship, Fear, Pride, Doubt, Disobedient, Anger, Prayerlessness, Neglecting God's word etc.

Prayer: (a) Father, destroy anything that will destabilize or derail my walk with You, IJN.

(b) Father, give me the grace to be steadfast, unmovable, always abounding in the work of the Lord.

Tuesday June 18, 2019
Topic: PEACE FROM PRINCE OF PEACE

Scripture: "When a man's ways please the Lord, he maketh even his enemies to be at peace with him" (Proverb 16:7 KJV)

Praise the Lord. Today is June 18th and is day #169 in year 2019. The number of days remaining to end this year is 196. By God's grace, all your ways shall be pleasing to Jesus Christ, and you will see the end of this year and beyond, safe and sound in the mighty name of Jesus.

Peace is a scarce commodity today almost at all levels, worldwide, national, organizations, family, etc. The main reason for this is because the author and custodian of peace, JESUS CHRIST, is missing in the lives of many people. Jesus Christ is the PRINCE OF PEACE (Isaiah 9:6). Evidences abound for this. Before he departed this world, He told His followers, "Peace I leave with you, my peace I give unto you: not as the world giveth, give I unto you. ..." (Jn 14:27). When a great storm arose against the ship, He and His disciples were travelling in one day, He rebuked the wind and said unto the sea, "Peace be still" and the wind ceased and there was great calm (Mk. 4: 35-40). After His resurrection he appeared miraculously to His disciples on several occasions declaring, "Peace be unto You" (Luke 24:36, Jn 20:19, 21, 26).

The opening scripture for today's ministration (Pro. 16:7) provides the answer to how we can have peace in the world. It is by ensuring that every person's ways please the LORD. To please God you must know Him, His dos and don'ts and be obedient to Him. The implication of this for peace of the world is that the more people we can get to please the LORD, the more peace there will be.

As Christians, we have our work cut out for us. We must be more aggressive and more effective in evangelizing the whole world if we want peace. Let's use all means possible to prayerfully introduce Jesus Christ, the prince of peace to everybody we come across. The seed of peace you sow today will yield harvest of peace that you or somebody else will reap later for, "- - whatsoever a man soweth, that shall he also reap" (Gal. 6:7b). As year 2019 counts down let your soul winning activities for Christ count up. You will increase peace of the world and increase your chance of receiving the crown of rejoicing and Soul Winner's crown (Phil 4:1; 2 Thess. 2:19). *Prayer: Father, help us to be more serious and more successful in getting the world know Your Son Jesus Christ as the Prince of Peace, IJN.*

Wednesday June 19, 2019
Topic: DIVINE DELIVERANCE

Scripture: "Let my supplication come before thee: deliver me according to thy word" (Psalm 119:170, KJV)

Praise the Lord. Today is June 19th and is day #170 in year 2019. The number of days remaining to end this year is 195. By God's grace, total deliverance shall be your deliverance this year, and you will see the end of this year and beyond, safe and sound in the mighty name of Jesus.

Praying for deliverance constantly is critical to the survival of followers of Jesus Christ given the constant attack we face from the devil (1 Pet. 5: 7-8). No wonder one of the prayer points Jesus Christ taught His followers to pray goes like this "And lead us not into temptation but deliver us from evil" (Matthew 6:13). God has already promised to deliver the righteous for He knew afflictions of all kinds will arise: "Many are the afflictions of the righteous: but the Lord delivereth him out of them all" (Psalm 34:19). Afflictions can take various forms including sins, sickness, slavery, death, imprisonment, temptations, joblessness, miscarriage, evil dreams, stagnation, marital problems, fear, witchcraft, etc.

The good news is that God has the power to deliver you from any form of affliction or bondage if only you will cry to him. When Peter was imprisoned, and the Church prayed for him, God sent an Angel to deliver him (Acts 12: 5-17). Daniel, an unstoppable prayer champion, was thrown into the den of lions and God delivered him by shutting the mouths of the lions so they could not consume him (Dan 6). Esther and her Jewish refugees were scheduled to be killed on Dec. 13, but when they prayed and fasted for 3 days the decree was revoked (Esther chaps. 8 & 9).

As year 2019 counts down remember God's promises for you are yea and Amen. God says no weapon fashioned against you shall prosper (Isaiah 54:17). Pray daily to God to deliver you and your family from evil; be specific in your supplication to Him and He will deliver you, IJN. ***Prayer: Father, deliver me from evil and the afflictions of .... (name them), IJN***

Thursday June 20, 2019
Topic: DIVINE VISITATION

Scripture: "And when Abram was ninety years old and nine, the Lord appeared to Abram, and said unto him, I am the Almighty God; walk before me, and be thou perfect" (Genesis 17:1, KJV)

Praise the Lord. Today is June 20th and is day #171 in year 2019. The number of days remaining to end this year is 194. By God's grace, you will receive divine visitations this year, and you will see the end of this year and beyond, safe and sound in the mighty name of Jesus.

Divine visitation refers to the appearance of God or His designee (e.g. Angel, Holy Spirit, etc.) to an earthly person or persons for a specific purpose. In general, divine visitation can either be positive (involving blessings) or negative (involving punishment). Positive divine visitation is a great honor which every true child of God should yawn and pray for.

As in the opening scripture for today God visited Abram when he was 99 years old. God introduced Himself to Abram as the Almighty God (El shaddai meaning "strengthener and satisfier of His people" or All-Sufficient God). God then told Abram to do 2 main things: (1)" walk before me", (2) "be thou perfect (i.e. blameless)". The same charge still applies to Christians today. We are to walk before God by faith in terms of depending on Him for everything we want and to walk in complete obedience to all His commandments and ordinances. Furthermore, we are to be upright and sincere and be perfect as He is perfect (Mt. 5: 48).

The benefits of positive divine visitation are many and include (1) termination of bareness and reproach (e.g. Sarah, Hannah, Elizabeth), (2) turning away captivity (Zeph. 2:7), (3) supernatural provisions (1 kgs. 19:5), (4) turning failure to success (Luke 5:1-11), (5) raising the dead (Lk 7: 15-16), (6) to give peace (Jn 20: 19) (7) protection (Ex. 23:20)

Prayer: *Father, as year 2019 counts down visit me and put laughter in my mouth, IJN.*

Friday June 21, 2019
Topic: SAVED TO SERVE

Scripture: "From the gatekeepers: Akkub, Talmon, and 172 of their associates, who guarded the gates." (Nehemiah 11:19 KJV)

Praise the Lord. Today is June 21st and is day #172 in year 2019. The number of days remaining to end this year is 193. By God's grace, angels will guard all the gates of the Lord's temple in your life and you shall not be defiled or destroyed; you will see the end of this year and beyond, safe and sound in the mighty name of Jesus.

Rendering service(s) to God is a mandate that many Christians neglect deliberately or due to ignorance of what to do or the value of such service(s). The work of God is so much that no member of the Church should be without serving in one capacity or the other. From general to specific duties there is plenty of work to go around. For example, the 'great commission' / command of Jesus to His disciples "-Go ye into all the world and preach the gospel to every creature" (Mk. 16:15) has room for every saved person to be fully engaged in service. If you are not serving in one way or the other in the house of God, then how are you obeying the injunction "Serve the Lord with gladness"? (Ps. 100:2a)

From today's opening scripture, we see that two leaders (Akkub and Talmon) and 172 associates found their own work niche as gatekeepers guarding the gates of the wall of Jerusalem after it was rebuilt by Nehemiah and his team. Gatekeepers are responsible for safety and security. Spiritually speaking, every believer is of necessity a gatekeeper because "your body is the temple of the Holy Ghost which is in you, which ye have of God" (1 Cor. 6: 19). The onus to guard this 'Temple" against pollution is on the believer. This is the starting point of the service you are saved to do.

Aside from your service to your body and your role in the great commission there are numerous other things you can do in the body of Christ to do like He said, "Occupy till I come" (Lk. 19:13). Talk with your Pastor or spiritual leader, let him/her know your skills and talent and how much time you can volunteer. You very much needed than you think. The benefits for serving the LORD are varied, numerous and of eternal values. God is a rewarder of those who diligently seek Him (Heb 11:6). Furthermore, He has promised in Exo. 23:25 that when you serve Him, He will bless us.

Prayer: Father empower me to do greater works for You IJN.

Saturday June 22, 2019
Topic: HIS HAND OF HELP

Scripture: "Let thine hand help me; for I have chosen thy precepts" (Psalm 119: 173)

Praise the Lord. Today is June 22nd and is day #173 in year 2019. The number of days remaining to end this year is 192. By God's grace, the helping hand of the Lord will wrought you victories, and you will see the end of this year and beyond, safe and sound in the mighty name of Jesus.

The hand of God is a helping hand. Everybody in life needs help at one time or the other and/or for one thing or the other. Help is usually needed for various reasons including making impossible things possible or getting things done faster, easier, cheaper, more efficiently, etc. Help is one of the ways our lives can be facilitated by bringing comfort, joy and peace. We are created to receive help and to give help as necessary (Gen. 2:18).

The best help anyone can have is that of God. Unlike human help God's help can never fail because He is "--very present help in trouble" (Psalm 46: 1b). In fact, the Bible declares, "There is no one like the God of Israel. He rides across the heavens to help you, across the skies in majestic splendor". (Deut. 33:26, NLT).

While God is generous and merciful, He will be more prone to provide help to those who belong to Him and walk in His ways than to those who are not His. For example, God, describing Israel as His servant and Jacob His chosen one, said to him, "Fear thou not; for I am with thee: be not dismayed; for I am thy God: I will strengthen thee; yea, I will help thee; yea, I will uphold thee with the right hand of my righteousness" (Isa 41: 8, 10). When attacked by the armies of three nations, Jehoshaphat and Judah sought help from God and were able to defeat and destroy their attackers (2 Chron 20: 1-34).

If you give your life to Jesus Christ, remain His and follow His precepts, you will never lack divine help. May your help from God count up even as year 2019 countdown.

Prayer; Father, let Your helping hand be upon me and my family perpetually, IJN.

Sunday June 23, 2019
Topic: Topic: GETTING RID OF "GOLIATHS

Scripture: "And there went out a champion out of the camp of the Philistines, named Goliath, of Gath, whose height was six cubits and a span" (1 Sam 17:4)

Praise the Lord. Today is June 23rd and is day #174 in year 2019. The number of days remaining to end this year is 191. By God's grace, you will demolish every Goliath threatening your life, and you will see the end of this year and beyond, safe and sound in the mighty name of Jesus.

The story of how the anointed youthful David felled and decapitated the giant Philistine champion (as recorded in 1 Samuel chapter 17) is a reminder that total dependence on God is the only way to win the battles of life against the enemy.

For 40 days Goliath defied and terrorized against the army of Israel and challenged them to present a man to fight against him. When the young David learnt about the challenge of Goliath and the reproach against Israel he said to Saul "- -Let no man's heart fail because of him; thy servant will go and fight with this Philistine" (1 Sam 17:32). David shared with Saul his previous experience of killing a lion and a bear that took a lamb from his flock and emphasized his confidence that God can grant him victory over Goliath again. Then Saul was convinced to let David go to combat Goliath (1 Sam 17:34-37).

While Goliath was heavily protected with heavy military wares and equipped with weapons, David only had his staff, five smooth stones and his sling in his hand. Seeing the small stature and youthfulness of David, Goliath disdained and cursed him saying he would give his flesh to the fowls and the beasts. David said to Goliath, "- - Thou comest to me with a sword, and with a spear, and with a shield: but I come to thee in the name of the Lord of hosts, - - " (v.45). As Goliath arose to approach David, David hastened towards him and, "--put his hand in his bag, and took thence a stone, and slang it, and smote the Philistine in his forehead - -and he fell upon his face to the earth" (V. 49).

Believers must be aware of possibility of physical and spiritual "giants" or "Goliaths" that can threaten their faith and existence in this world. Total dependence on God by faith, prayer, fasting, boldness, etc. are some of the ways to slay these giant "Goliaths". ***Prayer: Father, empower me to slay all "Goliaths" challenging my faith and life, IJN.***

Monday June 24, 2019
Topic: LIVING LONG

Scripture: "These are the days of the years of Abraham's life, 175 years" (Gen. 25:7, ESV)

Praise the Lord. Today is June 24thand is day #175 in year 2019. The number of days remaining to end this year is 190. By God's grace, you will be wise and obey the injunction to number your days; and will you will see the end of this year and beyond, safe and sound in the mighty name of Jesus.

The plan of God for His people is that they will live long provided certain conditions are followed. These conditions include the following: (1) fearing the LORD God and keeping all His statutes and His commandments (Pro 10:27; Deut. 6:2), (2) Loving the LORD and receiving His salvation (Jn. 3:16; Psalm 21: 1-4; 91:14-16), (3) obeying and honoring earthly parents (Eph. 6:1-3), (4) living righteously and healthily (Pro 11:19, 1 Cor. 6:19), (5) serving the Lord (Exo. 23: 25-26), (6) possessing Godly wisdom and understanding (Pro 3:16; 9:11), etc.

God blessed Abraham's lineage with long life. He lived for 175 years, his son Isaac lived 180 years (Gen 35:28), and Jacob his grandson lived 147 years (Gen 47:28). Not only did Abraham lived long, he had good life with no record of sickness. Concerning him the Bible declares "Abraham died in a good old age, an old man and full of years- -"(Gen. 25:8).

Do you want to live long like Abraham? The Bible says it is possible: "That the blessing of Abraham might come on the Gentiles through Jesus Christ; that we might receive the promise of the Spirit through faith" (Gal. 3:14). In other words, all you have to do is give your life to Jesus Christ and you will partake in the blessing of long life here on earth and in eternity (John 11:25-26). Of course, the aforementioned condition, presupposes healthy lifestyle in nutrition, hygiene and exercise, appropriate rest, etc.

Prayer: Father, please satisfy me with long life full of blessings and let me reign with You in eternity, IJN.

Tuesday June 25, 2019
Topic: FRUITFULNESS

Scripture: "And I will make thee exceeding fruitful, and I will make nations of thee, and kings shall come out of thee." (Gen. 17:6)

Praise the Lord. Today is June 25th and is day #176 in year 2019. The number of days remaining to end this year is 189. By God's grace, you shall be bountifully fruitful this year, and you will see the end of this year and beyond, safe and sound in the mighty name of Jesus.

Fruitfulness is defined as producing good results, beneficial and profitable. The key word in this definition is "producing". We can think of different types of fruitfulness such as (a) biological fruitfulness (as in having children), (b) spiritual fruitfulness (as in winning souls for Christ), (c) other types of fruitfulness that can bring about increased number of inanimate or non-organic materials (e.g. an idea or wisdom that leads to developing products that brings wealth).

In God's creation, fruitfulness was wired into living creatures. In particular, after creating male and female humans in His own image God blessed them and said "--Be fruitful, and multiply, and replenish the earth, and subdue it: and have dominion over the fish of the sea, and over the fowl of the air, and over every living thing that moveth upon the earth" (Gen 1:28). The seed of fruitfulness God put in you shall bring forth Godly harvest, IJN.

The opening scripture above was part of the blessings bestowed on Abraham when God appeared to him (perhaps on his birthday) at the age of 99 years (Gen 17:1). According to God's word every believer in Jesus Christ is a beneficiary or partakers of God's covenant of blessings with Abraham: "That the blessing of Abraham might come on the Gentiles through Jesus Christ; that we might receive the promise of the Spirit through faith" (Galatians 3: 14). Therefore, I decree that you shall be fruitful in all areas, IJN. Today marks the end of bareness in your life, IJN.

Prayer: Father, let me be fruitful in all areas that will bring glory to You, enhance my life and make me a blessing to my generation, IJN.

Wednesday June 26, 2019
Topic: BLESSINGS OF TRUSTING GOD

Scripture: "Blessed is the man that trusteth in the LORD, and whose hope the LORD is" (Jeremiah 17:7)

Praise the Lord. Today is June 26th and is day #177 in year 2019. The number of days remaining to end this year is 188. By God's grace, the LORD you are trusting shall bless you beyond description this season, and you shall see the end of this year and beyond, safe and sound in the mighty name of Jesus.

There is a big difference between putting trust in man versus putting trust in God. God Himself pointed out this difference, "--Cursed are those who put their trust in mere humans, who rely on human strength and turn their hearts away from the LORD. They are like stunted shrubs in the desert, with no hope for the future. They will live in the barren wilderness, in an uninhabited salty land. "But blessed are those who trust in the LORD and have made the LORD their hope and confidence. They are like trees planted along a riverbank, with roots that reach deep into the water. Such trees are not bothered by the heat or worried by long months of drought. Their leaves stay green, and they never stop producing fruit" (Jer. 17: 5-8, NLT).

Therefore, in general, it can be summarized that putting trust in God attracts blessings while putting trust in man attracts curses. A survey of the scripture reveals numerous blessings of trusting God including: (a) Salvation (Ps. 18:30, Isaiah 12:2), (b) Everlasting strength, (c) Divine shield, refuge and fortress (2 Sam22:31, Ps. 91:2), (d) Victory (2 Chron 13:18), (e) deliverance from persecution (Ps. 7:1), (f) divine direction (Pro 3: 5-6), (g) Divine confidence (Ps. 37:5; 56:3), etc.

You might ask How can I trust in God? The simple answer is to give your life to Jesus Christ and abide in Him for He declares, "- -I am the way, the truth, and the life: no man cometh unto the Father, but by me"(John 14:6).

Prayer: Father, as year 2019 counts down let my trust in You wax stronger and let my blessings multiply and count upwards, IJN.

Thursday June 27, 2019
Topic: THE BANE OF BRIBERY

Scripture: "A bribe is like a bright, precious stone that dazzles the eyes and affects the mind of him who gives it; [as if by magic] he prospers, whichever way he turns" (Proverbs 17:8, AMPC).

Praise the Lord. Today is June 27th and is day #178 in year 2019. The number of days remaining to end this year is 187. By God's grace, will you not give nor receive bribes capable of bastardizing your testimony, and you will see the end of this year and beyond, safe and sound in the mighty name of Jesus.

The Bible's position on bribery is clear and cut dry, it is an evil that can destroy destinies if it is not nipped in the bud. Bribery can be defined as anything (e.g. money or favor) given or promised to influence or twist the judgment or conduct of the recipient in favor of the giver or his/her client. Unfortunately, bribery has become a serious cankerworm eating ferociously into the fabric of many nations.

God's law given to Moses for the Israelites abhors bribery because of its tendency to pervert judgment: Bribery played a major role in the death of Jesus Christ. Judas accepted a bribe of 30 pieces of silver ("blood money") to betray Jesus Christ. Consequently, the innocent Jesus was arrested and crucified (Matthew 27:3-9). Another example of the bane of bribery is when Simon the sorcerer, after seeing the Holy Ghost given to those the apostles laid hands on, offered the Apostles money saying, "--Give me also this power, that on whomsoever I lay hands, he may receive the Holy Ghost" (Acts 8:19). Peter refused Simon's request and condemned him for attempting to 'bribe' to receive God's free gift. Simon realized his mistake and requested Peter to pray for him (Acts 8: 20-24).

Bribery creates a platform for multiple sins including perversion of justice, lying, greed corruption, mischief, wickedness, affliction, deprivation, etc. Are you a giver or receiver of bribes? You are toiling with sin and inviting God's consuming fire, for the Bible says, "- - fire shall consume the tabernacles of bribery" (Job 15:34, KJV). Every believer must avoid bribery at all costs and preach against it. Repent and restitute as needed. **Prayer: *Father, in any way I have given, received or encouraged bribery, have mercy on me and forgive. Please wipe out bribery from my environment***

Friday June 28, 2019
Topic: ATTACKED BY AMALEKITES?

Scripture: "And Moses said unto Joshua, choose us out men, and go out, fight with Amalek: tomorrow I will stand on the top of the hill with the rod of God in mine hand" (Ex. 17:9, KJV)

Praise the Lord. Today is June 28th and is day #179 in year 2019. The number of days remaining to end this year is 186. By God's grace, you will defeat every Amalekite warring against you this season, and you will see the end of this year and beyond, safe and sound in the mighty name of Jesus.

During their journey to the promised land, the Israelites faced many obstacles that would have stopped them from getting to their destination. However, through the help of God they eventually made it to the land that "flow with milk and honey". At Rhiphidim, the Israelites suffered two major setbacks. First, they lacked water which prompted them to murmur against Moses to the extent of wanting to stone him. Moses took the matter to God and God miraculously solved the problem by instructing Moses to strike the rock with his rod to bring out water (Exo 17: 1-7).

Soon after the water problem was solved, the nation of Amalek came and attacked Israel without any provocation. Moses told Joshua to choose some men and go out to fight the aggressors while he, Aaron and Hur would go to the top of the hill with the rod of God in Moses' hand. Joshua obeyed and led the chosen men to fight the Amalekites as directed. It turned out that whenever Moses raised up the rod in his hand Joshua and his people defeated the Amalekites and whenever his hands were down the Amalekites prevailed (Exo. 17: 8-11).

Obviously, Israel defeated Amalek through the help of God. It is instructive that Israel's victory was possible due to the interplay of prayer, dependence on God, obedience to spiritual leaders, division of labor and unity. Notably, Joshua obeyed Moses without argument, Aaron and Hur provided Moses with the needed assistance and the men chosen by Joshua to fight did so devotedly as directed. The result was that the Amalekite attackers were defeated (Exo 17: 8-16). All your attackers shall be defeated, IJN.

Prayer: Father, attack and destroy all my destiny attackers, IJN.

Saturday June 29, 2019
Topic: PARTYING OR NO PARTYING?

Scripture: "In the third year of his reign he (Ahasuerus) gave a feast for all his officials and servants. The army of Persia and Media and the nobles and governors of the provinces were before him, while he showed the riches of his royal glory and the splendor and pomp of his greatness for many days, 180 days" (Esther 1:3-4, ESV).

Praise the Lord. Today is June 29th and is day #180 in year 2019. The number of days remaining to end this year is 185. By God's grace, you shall be connected with men and women of caliber this year, and you will see the end of this year and beyond, safe and sound in the mighty name of Jesus.

Two of the questions that often loom in the mind of some believers are (1) should I attend parties? (2) If I do should I drink alcohol or not? I know some people believe that these are controversial issues. However, I like to predicate my answer on two scriptures: (a) "Whether therefore ye eat, or drink, or whatsoever ye do, do all to the glory of God" (1 Cor. 10:31, KJV), (b) "Abstain from all appearance of evil" (1 Thess.5:22, KJV).

Whether or not a Christian should attend a party depends on factors such as the purpose, location, attendees and outcomes of the party. For example, it is not advisable for a bona fide Christian to go to an idol worship center to participate in sacrificing to idols and eating and drinking with idol worshippers. In general, any party / thing that will grieve the Holy Spirit in you, take you further away from God and mars your testimony (e.g. drunkenness, drug use, sexual immorality, gossiping, etc.) should be avoided. On the other hand, parties that provide peaceful and fun atmosphere to relax, fellowship with other Christians, share the gospel with potential converts should be cautiously and prayerfully considered to prevent been lured into and falling into temptation.

There are several Christ centered celebrations (or parties) in the Bible that are worthy of emulation. Jesus attended the wedding at Cana where he did his first recorded miracle of converting water to wine. There was no indication of any one getting drunk or any act of violence at that party. Christians should avoid parties that can provide platforms for breeding of sins (such as those engaged in by Job's sons and daughters (Job 1:5). **Prayer: Father, please don't let me attend parties that will spoil my testimonies, IJN.**

Sunday June 30, 2019
Topic: POWER PASS POWER

Scripture: "And it came to pass after many days, that the word of the Lord came to Elijah in the third year, saying, Go, shew thyself unto Ahab; and I will send rain upon the earth " (1 Sam 18:1, KJV).

Praise the Lord. Today is June 30th and is day #181 in year 2019. The number of days remaining to end this year is 184. By God's grace, you will be a vessel through which the Lord will provide solutions to worldwide problems, and you will see the end of this year and beyond, safe and sound in the mighty name of Jesus.

Elijah was a powerful and highly anointed prophet of God. The Bible says he was a man subject to like passions as we are, and he prayed earnestly that it might not rain: and it did not rain for 3 1/2 years (James 5:17). I pray that this kind of power of old will manifest in us in this end time, IJN.

Ahab, the 8th king of the northern kingdom of Israel, ruled for 22 years. The Bible declares that Ahab "did what was evil in the LORD's sight, even more than any of the kings before him" (1 Kings 16:30). Ahab violated the biblical prohibition of marriage to pagans by marrying Jezebel, an immoral and fanatical pagan (Dt.7: 1-5). Our children will not marry unbelievers, IJN.

Under the influence of Jezebel, Ahab gave up the worship of God and encouraged the worship of an idol called Baal. In response to Ahab's and Israel's mounting sins, God sent Elijah to Ahab to predict 3 1/2 years of drought and famine as punishment (1 Kgs 17:1; 18: 16-18). The prophecy came true and brought severe sufferings of famine and drought to people and animals during the stipulated period. At the end of the 3 1/2 years, Elijah challenged Ahab for a contest between God and Baal on Mount Carmel (Kgs 18: 16-40).

Elijah taunted and ridiculed the 450 prophets of Baal for the failure of their false and dead god to call down fire to consume the alter they had prepared. Elijah then repaired the altar and prayed to his God: "Immediately, God answered, and fire fell from heaven and consumed everything on the altar to the amazement of all those present (vv. 38-39). At Elijah's command all the pagan prophets were seized and executed, and the drought ended immediately (1 Kgs 18: 41-46). **Prayer: *O Lord of hosts, consume by fire all the enemies attempting to consume me, IJN.***

Monday July 01, 2019
Topic: FEAST OF THE TRUMPET

Scripture: "Tell the people of Israel: 'On the first day of the seventh month you must have a special day of rest, a holy meeting, when you blow the trumpet for a special time of remembering" (Leviticus 23:24, NCV).

Praise the Lord. Today is July 1st and is day #182 in year 2019. The number of days remaining to end this year is 183. By God's grace, you will have rest and perfect peace this year, and you will see the end of this year and beyond, safe and sound in the mighty name of Jesus. Welcome to the first day of second half, and to the third quarter of year 2019. You shall rejoice in this 2nd half, IJN.

The feast of the trumpet (FOT) is one of the 7 feasts in the Bible that are called "the feasts of the Lord" (Lev. Chap. 23). As noted in today's opening scripture, the FOT began on the first day of the 7th month and called for blowing trumpets in remembrance of the goodness of God to the Israelites. During the FOT celebration, no work was to be performed, but burnt offerings and a sin offering were to be brought before the Lord.

Among many lessons we can learn from the Feast of the Trumpets (and the other Feasts of the LORD) are the following: (1) Feasts and trumpets in general signify celebrations and call for assembling (Lev. 23, Num 10: 1-10). (2) Blowing of trumpets signified victory as evidenced by Israelites' defeat of the Midianites under the leadership of Gideon (Judges 7:16-25). (3) Blowing of trumpets removes obstacles as it happened to the wall of Jericho that crumbled before Israelites when they matched round it blowing trumpets (Joshua 6:1-20).

The greatest feast yet to be known to man is called The Marriage Supper of the Lamb and it will take place in heaven (Rev 19: 8-10). Preceding this feast Jesus Christ will return to take His own in what is called the rapture and it will be accompanied by a loud sound of a trumpet. Anybody who misses these 2 events will burn in hell fire forever. To be a partaker of these 2 events and to avoid hell fire, you must give your life to Jesus Christ as your Lord and Savior. If you haven't, do so today and begin eternal celebrations, IJN. **Prayer: Father, let my Trumpet of Thanksgiving and celebrations always be loud and clear, IJN**

Tuesday July 02, 2019
Topic: POWER OF PRAISE

Scripture: "I will call upon the LORD, who is worthy to be praised: so, shall I be saved from mine enemies" (Psalm 18:3, KJV).

Praise the Lord. Today is July 2ndand is day #183 in year 2019. The number of days remaining to end this year is 182. By God's grace, your intensive praise of the Lord shall cause all your enemies to be destroyed, and you will see the end of this year and beyond, safe and sound in the mighty name of Jesus.

Both praise and prayer are vital to Christian living. Praise is the offering of grateful homage to God in words, song, dance or other forms of admiration, exaltation, or appreciation. Prayer on the other hand focuses more on devout petition to God to meet some need. Ideally, both prayer and praise should not be mutually exclusive. The model prayer Jesus taught His followers begins with praise: "Our Father which art in Heaven, Hallowed be thy name" and ends with praise: "For thine is the kingdom, and the power, and the glory, forever. Amen." (Matt 6: 9-13, KJV).

Praise carries unique power that the believer can tap into to have an advantage over the enemy. Judging by the frequency of occurrences in the KJV of the Bible, "praise" (214 times) is more emphasized in the Bible than prayer (128 times). Alluding to the importance and power of praise, the Bible says God inhabits the praises of Israel (Psalm 22:3) and that every believer is chosen to show forth the praises of God (1 Peter 2:9).

One area we can easily see the manifestation of the power of praise is with respect to protection and deliverance. This is alluded to in today's opening scripture. Likewise, we see the power of praise demonstrated when Paul and Silas were miraculously set free from prison when they sang praises to God at midnight (Acts 16:25-40). As you intensify your praise to God in the remaining half of 2019, all your enemies shall be defeated, God will bless you and the earth will yield its increase unto you, (Ps. 67:6), IJN.

Prayer: Father, give me the grace to praise You at all times and let the power of praise pursue and paralyze all my, IJN

Wednesday July 03, 2019
Topic: WHO OWNS YOUR SOUL?

Scripture: "Behold, all souls are mine; as the soul of the father, so also the soul of the son is mine: the soul that sinneth, it shall die" (Ezekiel 18: 4, KJV).

Praise the Lord. Today is July 3rdand is day #184 in year 2019. The number of days remaining to end this year is 181. By God's grace, all members of your family shall remain the Lord's and the enemy cannot touch any of you, and you will see the end of this year and beyond, safe and sound in the mighty name of Jesus.

God is the one speaking in the opening scripture above. The Bible says, "The earth is the LORD's, and the fulness thereof; the world, and they that dwell therein" (Ps. 24:1). Therefore, all souls definitely belong to Him. I am so glad I belong to Jesus. What about you?

There is no partiality with God. The same love He has for the father's soul is also what He has for the souls of other members of the family. However, salvation is a personal matter. Each member of the family must repent of his/her sins, ask for forgiveness and receive Jesus Christ as his/her personal Savior because the Bible says, "For all have sinned, and come short of the glory of God" (Rom. 3:23). As the last portion of today's opening scripture says, "the soul that sinneth, it shall die". That is, unrepented and unregenerated souls shall be separately permanently from God.

The good plan of God is that all members of the family be saved and go to heaven (Acts 17:30). Therefore, let evangelism begin with your family. Parents should teach their children the ways of the Lord as Abraham did (Gen. 18:19). We must use all available strategies (family altar, prayer, social media, tracts distribution, hosting group Bible study, visitations, etc.) to ensure that the souls of all our family members (as well as other souls) belong to God and not to Satan.

Prayer: Father, help me to do my part in winning souls for You, IJN

Thursday July 04, 2019
Topic: SILENCING SENNACHERIB

Scripture: "And that night the angel of the LORD went out and struck down 185,000 in the camp of the Assyrians. And when people arose early in the morning, behold, these were all dead bodies." (2 Kings 19:35, ESV).

Praise the Lord. Today is July 4th and is day #185 in year 2019. The number of days remaining to end this year is 180. By God's grace, an angel of the Lord will strike down all those enemies who don't want you to survive this year, and you will see the end of this year and beyond, safe and sound in the mighty name of Jesus.

Freedom was a scarce commodity for king Hezekiah and the people of Judah until God miraculously delivered them from the oppression and terrorism of 2 consecutive kings of Assyria - kings Sennacherib and Shalmaneser. Unlike these 2 wicked kings Hezekiah was a Godly king with a lot of good things said about him in the Bible: May the testimony about your relationship with God surpass that of Hezekiah's, IJN.

Shalmaneser besieged Samaria and carried Israel into exile in Assyria because "they (Israel) did not obey the voice of the LORD their God, but broke His covenant- -" (2 Kings 18:12). Disobeying God and breaking His covenant (such as failure to pay you tithes) can make you vulnerable to attacks of the enemy. That will not be your portion, IJN.

After Shalmanesser came Sennecherib to invade Judah in the 14th year of Hezekiah's reign. Sennacherib took all Judah's fortified cities. He required Hezekiah to pay tribute to him thereby creating economic hardship that forced Hezekiah to stripe treasures away from God's house. Furthermore, he made mockery of Hezekiah for trusting a God that he claimed would not be able to deliver him from the impending attack. Hezekiah took Sennecharib's letter of ridicule and reproach to God in praise and prayer, requesting God to please save them from Sennacherib's hand (2 kings 19:14-19). God answered Hezekiah's prayer and sent an angel who, in one night, struck down and killed 185,000 Assyrians in the camp. Shamefully, Sennacherib king of Assyria went home and lived at Nineveh where he was struck down with the sword by 2 of His sons (2 Kings 19:34-35). I decree that every "Shalmaneser" and "Sennecherib" terrorizing, oppressing and exploiting you shall die,

Prayer: Father, silence and put to shame all who are mocking You in my life, IJN.

Friday July 05, 2019
Topic: MARCHING INTO LEADERSHIP

Scripture: "The total number of men assigned to Judah, troop by troop, is 186,400. They will lead the march." (Numbers 2:9, MSG).

Praise the Lord. Today is July 5th and is day #186 in year 2019. The number of days remaining to end this year is 179. By God's grace, anointing to be head and not tail shall be yours this season in good things, and you will see the end of this year and beyond, safe and sound in the mighty name of Jesus.

After the Israelites had left Egypt, God spoke to Moses and said, "Number the congregation of the People of Israel by clans and families, writing down the names of every male" (Numbers 1: 1-2, MSG). With the help of Aaron Moses carried out the instruction and the sum total were 603,550 (Num 1:46). Of this total, the largest number of enlisted people from one tribe (74,600) came from the tribe of Judah. Again, God spoke to Moses and Aaron with specific instructions how to regroup the troops such that troops from 3 tribes would camp next to each other and stay on one side of the Tent of Meeting facing it. By this arrangement Judah's camp had the largest number of 186,400 men as indicated in the opening scripture above.

Judah was the 4th of Jacob's 12 sons and his name means "praise" (Gen 35:1 & 29:35). The position and role of Judah in the journey to the promised land is instructive. He became the founder of one of Israel's 12 tribes. His tribe had the largest number of able-bodied men of war and he was chosen to lead the march, though he was not the oldest among the 12 sons of Jacob. At the time of Jacob's blessing Judah was granted the birthright privileges of the first born (Gen. 49: 8-9). You will not lose your birthright, IJN. Judah was a foreshadower of Jesus Christ according to the book of Hebrews: "- -it is evident that our Lord was descended from Judah, - - ". (Heb. 7:14, ESV). Furthermore, Jesus is described as a member of the tribe of Judah by lineage (Matt 1:16; Luke 3:31–34).

As a redeemed child of God, you have leadership traits in you after the order of Judah and Jesus. You are created to have dominion and to be head and not tail (Gen.1 :28; Deut. 28.13). So, shall it be, IJN. Pray to God to see how He can use you to lead in one way or the other in your family, Church, choir, community, work place, Bible study groups.

Prayer: Father, lift away any lid on my leadership traits IJN

Saturday July 06, 2019
Topic: BARNISHING BARRENNESS

Scripture: "And Abraham ran unto the herd, and fetch a calf tender and good, and gave it unto a young man; and he hasted to dress it." (Genesis 18:7, KJV).

Praise the Lord. Today is July 6th and is day #187 in year 2019. The number of days remaining to end this year is 178. By God's grace, your generosity will prepare you for greatness and seemingly impossible miracles, and you will see the end of this year and beyond, safe and sound in the mighty name of Jesus.

Aside from his faith, patience, obedience, giving, courage, worshipping spirit, etc., the lives of Abraham and Sarah point to the fact that hospitality can attract blessings. The scripture says, "Be not forgetful to entertain strangers: for thereby some have entertained angels unawares" (Heb. 13:2). Today's opening scripture relates to Abraham's hospitable reaction to three men he saw while relaxing under the shade of a tree in plains of Mamre (Gen 18: 1-15). Without knowing that the three men were the LORD and 2 angels, Abram took the following steps: (1) he ran to meet them, (2) he bowed himself toward the ground to honor them, (3) he persuaded them to stop over to rest and be refreshed, (4) he hastened to tell his wife about them and requested 3 good meals with choicest meat be made ready quickly for them, (5) he stood by them (i.e. waited on them) under the tree while they ate.

What happened after the meal is instructive. As indicated in the Bible that, "A man's gift maketh room for him, and bringeth him before great men (Pro.18:16), Abraham's gift of hospitality brought him before 3 divine guests. After eating the delicious meal Abraham provided for the guests, they asked for Sarah his wife and one of them (the LORD) said, "- -I will certainly return unto thee according to the time of life; and, lo, Sarah thy wife shall have a son" (Gen. 18:10). Additionally, the LORD gave Abraham privileged divine revelation about the imminent destruction that was coming to Sodom and Gomorrah (Gen 18: 17-32).

As a believer, hospitality can markedly change your destiny in a positive way and make room for you with God. About a year after the promise of a son to Sarah, Isaac was born (Gen 21:1-2). This put an end to bareness, reproach, shame and poverty in the lives of Abraham and Sarah and they have continued to be a blessing to the world (Gal 3:14).

Prayer: Father, please give me a heart of hospitality, IJN.

Sunday July 07, 2019
Topic: GOD'S HOUSE OF HEALING

Scripture: "And the blind and the lame came to him in the temple; and he healed them" (Matthew 21:14).

Praise the Lord. Today is Sunday, July 7th and is day #188 in year 2019. The number of days remaining to end this year is 177. Today is also the 26th Sunday in 2019. By God's grace, you shall not miss any miracle that takes place in the house of God this year, and you you will see the end of this year and beyond, safe and sound in the mighty name of Jesus.

The Church (called variously as Temple, Sanctuary, House of God, Worship Center, etc.) is a place where people gather together to worship God. It originated from Greek word "ecclesia" meaning an assembly (or body) of believers in Christ. Therefore, Church has a broader meaning than physical building. For example, Church has "organic" and spiritual characteristics as it involves the dynamics of divine and human nature. The Church belongs to Jesus who said, "- -I will build my Church; and the gates of hell shall not prevail against it" (Matt 16:18). The Church is one of the greatest institutions Jesus left behind here on earth through which people are to be saved, baptized and discipled and fellowship together. (Acts 2:46 -47).

The house of God is a fertile ground for miracles to take place. There are 7 recorded miracles that Jesus performed on the Sabbath (our equivalence of Sunday). The number 7 connotes perfection. Every one of your miracles shall be perfected, IJN. Out of the 7 Sabbath healing miracles of Jesus, 3 were done directly in the Church and the 4th one done right after Church. The 4 miracles are: (a) healing a man with unclean spirit (Mk. 1:21-28), (b) healing of a man with withered hand (Mk. 3: 1-6), (c) healing a woman crippled 18 years by evil spirit (Luke 13: 10-17). (d) healing of Simon's mother in law and many others after Church.

Today or any time you go to worship God expect miracles to take place in your life. Jesus Christ (that healed the lame and the blind according to the opening scripture above) is still doing miracles because He is "- -the same yesterday, and today, and forever" (Heb. 13:8). Your will testify of your miracles soon, IJN. ***Prayer: Father, don't let the enemy debar me from getting to the place of worshipping you and the place of getting my perfect miracles, IJN.***

Monday July 08, 2019
Topic: SPEAKING ABOUT SALVATION

Scripture: "And the Lord said to Paul one night in a vision, "Do not be afraid, but go on speaking and do not be silent- -" Acts 18:9, ESV).

Praise the Lord. Today is July 8th and is day #189 in year 2019. The number of days remaining to end this year is 176. By God's grace, you will not quit speaking about salvation to many people, and you will see the end of this year and beyond, safe and sound in the mighty name of Jesus.

Right from the time Paul, formerly known as Saul, was converted he got his marching order from God in terms of his mission: "But the Lord said unto him, Go thy way: for he (Paul) is a chosen vessel unto me, to bear my name before the Gentiles, and kings, and the children of Israel" (Acts 9:15). From that time Paul used every opportunity he had to speak the word of God. He was so committed to the great commission that he cursed himself if he did not preach the gospel: "For though I preach the gospel, I have nothing to glory of: for necessity is laid upon me; yea, woe is unto me, if I preach not the gospel!" (1 Cor. 9:16). When Silas and Timothy came from Macedonia to visit Paul, they found him "- occupied with the word, testifying to the Jews that the Christ was Jesus" (Acts 18: 5).

After sometime Paul began to face resistance and opposition from the Jews who were arguing against themselves and reviling Paul. He then shook out his garments and said to them, "Your blood be on your own heads! I am innocent. From now on I will go to the Gentiles" (Acts 18: 6). As Paul continued his preaching among the Gentiles many people believed and were baptized. As instructed in today's opening scripture Paul was not silent.

Here are some lessons we can learn from Paul's experience in Corinth (1) fear not to speak about salvation always (2) be occupied with the word, that is, " preach the word; be ready in season and out of season (1Tim 4:2), (3) be prepared for possible opposition or rejection (4) when rejected in one place, peacefully explore other areas doing as Christ suggests in Matt 10:14, (5) devotion to God's work and winning souls can provoke divine visitation. When last did you speak about salvation? Let your effort count up in this regard.

Prayer: Father, move me to proclaim the good news daily that You save (Ps. 96:2), IJN.

Tuesday July 09, 2019
Topic: BLESSING OF BETHLEHEM

Scripture: "The Savior—yes, the Messiah, the Lord—has been born today in Bethlehem, the city of David!" (Luke 2:11, NLT)

Praise the Lord. Today is July 9th and is day #190 in year 2019. The number of days remaining to end this year is 175. By God's grace, you will be alive to celebrate Christmas this year, and you will see the end of this year and beyond, safe and sound in the mighty name of Jesus.

Scripturally, spiritually and otherwise, Bethlehem is an important city with many blessings of particular interest to Christians. Foremost among these blessings is the messianic significance of Bethlehem being the birthplace of Jesus Christ as it was prophesied long before his birth: "But thou, Bethlehem Ephratah, ---- out of thee shall he come forth unto me that is to be ruler in Israel; - - "(Mic. 5:2; cf. Matt. 2:6; John 7:42). Given that the scripture cannot be broken, the prophecy was fulfilled and Jesus was born in Bethlehem (Matt. 2:1,5; Luke 2:4,15). Consequently, Bethlehem has achieved worldwide recognition primarily for being the birthplace of Jesus Christ, the Savior of the world.

Bethlehem was originally called Ephratah meaning "fruitful". No wonder Jesus Christ demand his followers to abide in Him so that they can bear fruit and bring forth much fruit (Jn 15: 1–6). Furthermore, when God created man, he commanded him to "be fruitful and multiply" (Gen. 1:28). All promises of God about you including fruitfulness, shall be fulfilled and every attempt of the enemy to tamper with your foundation shall fail, IJN.

The word Bethlehem means "house (place) of bread," and its significance lies in the fact that it is located in a fertile region characterized by an abundance of corn (for making bread). Is it any wonder then that Jesus Christ, born in Bethlehem said "I am the bread of life- -?" (John 6:35, 48). Sometimes I jokingly tell people that the reason I like bread a lot is because of the LORD who is the bread of life. More seriously, the bread element of the Holy Communion reminds us of the body of our LORD Jesus Christ broken for us and his ties to Bethlehem (1 Cor. 11:21). What a blessing!

Prayer: Father, thank You for the gift of Jesus Christ born in Bethlehem as planned. Please let me remain connected with the Him and be fruitful all the time, IJN.

Wednesday July 10, 2019
Topic: ESCAPE FROM THE ENEMIES

Scripture: "And Saul spake to Jonathan his son, and to all his servants, that they should kill David." (1 Samuel 19:1, KJV).

Praise the Lord. Today is July 10th and is day #191 in year 2019. The number of days remaining to end this year is 174. By God's grace, any one attempting to kill you this year will fail, and you will see the end of this year and beyond, safe and sound in the mighty name of Jesus.

Our greatest enemy as believers is Satan whose job is to kill, to steal and to destroy (John 10:10). Satan and his demons are constantly making efforts to achieve their evil ultimate goal of killing their potential victims. That is why the scripture warns us to be vigilant about Satan's evil agenda: "Be sober, be vigilant; because your adversary the devil, as a roaring lion, walketh about, seeking whom he may devour" (1 Pet 5:8).

As indicated in the opening scripture for today Saul commissioned his son (Jonathan) and his servants to kill David. Even Saul himself attempted to kill David: "And Saul sought to smite David even to the wall with the javelin: but he slipped away out of Saul's presence, and he smote the javelin into the wall: and David fled, and escaped that night" (1 Sam. 19:10). Between his own personal attempts and those of the agents he engaged, Saul made at least 12 attempts to kill David (1 Sam Chaps. 18-22). With the help of God, David was able to escape all Saul's attempts to kill him. In appreciation of God's divine deliverance for him from all his enemies, David spoke the song documented in 2nd Sam 22 which is essentially the same as Psalm 18. I pray that you too will escape all your enemies' attempts to harm you and you will celebrate, IJN.

The surest escape route from all our enemies is Jesus Christ, the way, the truth and the life. (Jn. 14:6). Give your life to Jesus and hide yourself in Him. He will be your shield and your refuge and help you escape from all your enemies, IJN.

Prayer: Father thank You for being my Lord, my rock, and my fortress, and my deliverer; The God of my rock; in You will I trust: You are my shield, ... so shall I be saved from mine enemies, IJN (2 Sam 22: 2-4).

Thursday July 11, 2019
Topic: HEAVENLY SONG OF HALLELUJAH

Scripture: "His judgments are true and just. He has punished the great prostitute who corrupted the earth with her immorality. He has avenged the murder of his servants." (Revelation 19:2, NLT).

Praise the Lord. Today is July 11th and is day #192 in year 2019. The number of days remaining to end this year is 173. By God's grace, you will not be corrupted with immorality or any other sin this season, and you will see the end of this year and beyond, safe and sound in the mighty name of Jesus.

The book of revelation contains detail on hope and warning messages Jesus Christ revealed to John the beloved when he was banished to the Isle of Patmos (Rev 1:9). As he received, John proclaimed the hope that the victorious Lord would surely return to vindicate the righteous and judge the wicked. As indicated in today's opening scripture God's judgment for the wicked are true and just, involving severe and destructive punishment for His enemies such as people with Jezebel and Babylonian spirit. The great prostitute is said to represent the early Roman empire with its seductiveness, many gods and the blood of Christian martyrs on its hands.

In John's vision, it was the combination of God's true and just judgment, the destruction of idolatry and the blood of martyred saints being avenged that provoked a loud sound of a great multitude "- - in heaven singing, Hallelujah! The salvation and glory and power are God's " (Rev. 19:1, MSG). Thus, John saw multitude in heaven singing "Hallelujah" (praise the Lord) and ascribing also to God Salvation, glory and power.

The Bible makes it clear that there will be singing in heaven since heaven is a place of joy (Isa. 49:13; Jer. 51:48). Only those who have received Jesus Christ as their Lord and Savior will enter the kingdom of heaven (John 3:16; 1:12; Acts 16:31; Rom 10:9). They will be among the multitude that will sing Hallelujah unto the Lord. Repent of your sins and accept Jesus Christ as your Lord and Savior if you want to be part of the Choir of heaven. You shall not miss heaven, IJN.

Prayer: Father grant me the grace to overcome so as to be able to sit with You in Your throne in heaven, IJN.

Friday July 12, 2019
Topic: RESPECT FOR PARENTS

Scripture: "Each of you must show great respect for your mother and father, and you must always observe my Sabbath days of rest. I am the Lord your God." (Leviticus 19:3, NLT).

Praise the Lord. Today is July 12th and is day #193 in year 2019. The number of days remaining to end this year is 172. By God's grace, you will see the end of this year and beyond, safe and sound in the mighty name of Jesus.

In this era, problems relating to children and young people (drugs, stealing, fighting, vandalism, cheating, assaults, trespassing, etc.) are mounting up on a daily basis. In the U.S, statistics indicates that in 24 hours cycle 15,006 teens will use drugs for the first time and 1,439 teens will attempt suicide. Today, in every 4 minutes a youth is arrested for an alcohol-related crime. Just as the saying goes that, "charity begins at home", the root causes of the problems described above (and many more) can be traced to the homes in which children disrespect and disobey their parents. The Bible says, "If the foundations be destroyed, what can the righteous do?" (Psalm 11:3). The righteous had better cried to God for divine intervention before destruction takes place.

In His wisdom and mercy, God has made provisions for man to avoid destruction of the foundation. Today's opening scripture is one of such provisions which require children to respect their parents. Incidentally, this provision is akin to what Apostle Paul called the first law with promise, succinctly put as, "Children, obey your parents in the Lord: for this is right.2 Honour thy father and mother...That it may be well with thee, and thou mayest live long on the earth" (Eph. 6: 1-3).

Children must be taught very early about the importance of this and other laws of God so that when they grow up, they will not depart from observing them (Pro. 22:6). They must be made aware of the example of Jesus Christ who was subject and obedient to his parents (Luke 2: 51-52). To prevent the enemy from truncating the destinies of our children, they must be properly guided and encouraged to know and serve God and to adhere to the "honor your parents" law.

Action/Prayer: Lead your children to Jesus Christ (as their Lord and Savior) as early as possible and pray regularly that they will be obedient children, IJN.

Saturday July 13, 2019
Topic: SEEKING THE SAVIOR

Scripture: "And he ran before, and climbed up into a sycamore tree to see him: for he was to pass that way." (Luke 19:4, KJV).

Praise the Lord. Today is July 13th and is day #194 in year 2019. The number of days remaining to end this year is 171. By God's grace, you will have a life transforming encounter with Jesus Christ this season, and you will see the end of this year and beyond, safe and sound in the mighty name of Jesus.

God has promised that anyone who will seek Him sincerely with all his heart will find Him (Jer. 29:13). The same thing can be said of Jesus Christ His Son. He was (and is still) a man in high demand. On one occasion Simon and many others with him were searching for Jesus and when they found Him, they said "All men seek for thee" (Mk. 1:37b). On this 194th day of 2019, may you seek Jesus and find Him.

One of the blessings of looking for Jesus is that you get more than you ask of Him when you find Him. For example, consider a rich man named Zacchaeus. The Bible says, "he sought to see Jesus who he was; and could not for the press, because he was little of stature" (Luke 19:3). Having heard so much about Jesus, Zacchaeus simply wanted to know who Jesus was (may be his completion, stature, how he did his miracles, etc.).

As indicated in today's opening scripture above, Zacchaeus ran and climbed up into a sycamore tree to catch a glimpse of Jesus who was passing by. Jesus spotted him on the tree and asked him to come down, and that He would visit Zacchaeus at his home that same day. In the presence of Jesus Christ, the rich man repented and promised to restitute for those he has defrauded, and also to give away 50% of his fortunes. Jesus Christ forgave Him and told him salvation has come to his house that day (Luke 19: 1-10). Thus, Zacchaeus got much more than he sought Jesus for. He saw Jesus Christ, got salvation, was privileged to receive Jesus as a guest in his house, and much more (vv. 9 &9).

As year 2019 counts down, "climb" your own "sycamore trees" to gain greater spiritual visibility of Jesus. Think of what you can do to honor and appreciate Him the more.

Prayer: Father, please give me the grace to do all I have to do to have more of You, IJN.

Sunday July 14, 2019
Topic: PECULIAR PEOPLE OF GOD

Scripture: "Now therefore, if ye will obey my voice indeed, and keep my covenant, then ye shall be a peculiar treasure unto me above all people: for all the earth is mine:" (Exodus 19:5)

Praise the Lord. Today is July 14th and is day #195 in year 2019. The number of days remaining to end this year is 170. By God's grace, you will be an obedient and keeper of the Lord's covenant this season, and you will see the end of this year and beyond, safe and sound in the mighty name of Jesus.

God is a promise keeper. He appeared to Moses in a burning Bush at mount Horeb and told him that he would be sent to bring the Israelites out of the land of Egypt. God then promised Moses a sign saying, "--Certainly I will be with thee; and this shall be a token unto thee, that I have sent thee: When thou hast brought forth the people out of Egypt, ye shall serve God upon this mountain" (Exo. 3:12).

God fulfilled His promise to Moses in that three months after they left Egypt they arrived at the wilderness of Sinai where Israel camped, and Moses went up to God on the mountain. God told Moses specific instructions to pass on to the Israelites (Exo. 19: 1-25). Today's opening scripture above is the most important message God gave Moses on mount Sinai for the Israelites prior to the delivery of the 10 commandments in Exodus 20. God made it clear that if the Israelites would be obedient and keep His covenant, they would be the most treasured and most preferred people to Him. God chose the Israelites to this exalted position not because of anything they had done to deserve it; it was simply because of His love and mercy for them.

The same love and mercy of God is available through Jesus Christ under the new covenant and new dispensation of grace to anyone who will repent of his/her sins and accept Jesus Christ as his/Savior. In other words, if you are born again you are a chosen generation and a peculiar person to God (1 Pet. 2:9), you are precious in the eye of God and honored (Isaiah 43: 4), God sets His love on you (Deut. 7:7-8). You are of great value to God.

Prayer: Father, let me remain peculiar and precious unto You, IJN.

Monday July 15, 2019
Topic: DETESTING DIVORCE

Scripture: "Wherefore they are no more twain, but one flesh. What therefore God hath joined together, let not man put asunder." (Matthew 19:6, KJV).

Praise the Lord. Today is July 15th and is day #196 in year 2019. The number of days remaining to end this year is 169. By God's grace, you will always be an agent of unity and peace, and you will see the end of this year and beyond, safe and sound in the mighty name of Jesus.

Divorce rate in America is said to loom around 40% to 50 % with variations in rate influenced by a myriad of socio economic and other factors (age, income, race, type of work, religious affiliation, etc.). A recent study reported 8 most frequently cited reasons for divorce to include: (1) Lack of commitment, (2) too much argument, (3) infidelity, (4) marrying too young, (5) unrealistic expectation, (6) lack of equality, (7) lack of preparation, and (8) abuse.

No matter the rate of or reason for divorce, the critical fact is that it is against the will and plan of God who says he hates divorce (Mal. 2:16). In today's opening scripture Jesus Christ stated categorically that no man should put asunder (separate) what God has joined together. The context of Jesus' statement (Mt. 19: 1-13) is in answering a question posed to him by vicious Pharisees who came to tests him: "Is it lawful for a man to put away his wife for every cause?" (Mt. 19:6b). Jesus answered them with scriptural facts proving that God's plan for marriage is monogamy and permanence until death do the them part (Gen 1: 27; 2:24; Mt. 19:6b). Jesus then told the Pharisees that fornication was the only ground to permit divorce (see Mt.19: 1-12).

Husband and wife should always remember that the Bible says, "For thy Maker is thine husband; - - " (Isaiah 54:5). Can you imagine what will happen to you if God leaves you or you leave God? Talk about hell fire! That will not be your portion. Don't put yourself, either let anyone put you asunder from your God-given spouse. Detest and avoid divorce at all costs. Stay in and enjoy your marriage, IJN.

Prayer: Father, arrest and annihilate any power trying to put my marriage asunder, IJN.

Tuesday July 16, 2019
Topic: WONDERS OF GOD'S WORD

Scripture: "The law of the Lord is perfect, converting the soul: the testimony of the Lord is sure, making wise the simple." (Psalm 19:7, KJV).

Praise the Lord. Today is July 16th and is day #197 in year 2019. The number of days remaining to end this year is 168. By God's grace, you will increase in the word of God and in wisdom this season, and you will see the end of this year and beyond, safe and sound in the mighty name of Jesus.

God's word is full of wonders far beyond complete human comprehension. First, note that the word of God in the opening scripture above and the rest of the chapter is described variously as the "law of the LORD", "testimony of the LORD", "statutes of the LORD", "commandment of the LORD" and "judgments of the LORD" (Ps. 19:7-9). Throughout the Bible there are other descriptions of God's word alluding to its wonders. For example, God's word is described as "life and Spirit" (John 6:63), "sword of the Spirit" (Eph. 6:17).

In terms of the wonders of God's word, let us look at two characteristics and two corresponding capabilities of God's word mentioned in the opening scripture above:

(1) God's word is perfect and capable of converting the soul. God's word is pure and complete and contains the whole mind and will of God and can save man and make him perfect and thoroughly furnished to all good works (2 Tim 3:16). Salvation is a wonder such that a sinner can hear God's word, get convicted of his/her sins, repent and accept Jesus by faith and become redeemed. (2) God's word described as testimony of the LORD, is sure and can make the simple wise. The Gospel is the testimony of Jesus Christ to which He himself testify and others testify of Him (2 Tim 1:8). The Gospel and the whole Bible is true and anyone who is humble and simple enough to believe in it will be wise. Wisdom comes from God and His word (James 1:5).

Other notable wonders of God's word are: it can heal and deliver from destruction (Ps. 107:20), it can prevent us from sinning (Ps. 119:11), it can light our path (Ps. 119:105), it can be our shield (Pro 30:5), It can prosper us and give us success (Jos. 1: 8), etc. Get deeper into the word of God and see wonderful thigs happen in your life.

Prayer: Father, let your word do wonderful miracles in my life, IJN

Wednesday July 17, 2019
Topic: ELIJAH DIVINELY ENERGIZED

Scripture: "And he arose, and did eat and drink, and went in the strength of that meat forty days and forty nights unto Horeb the mount of God." (1 Kings 19:8, KJV).

Praise the Lord. Today is July 17th and is day #198 in year 2019. The number of days remaining to end this year is 167. By God's grace, you shall be fed by the Lord and your household shall not suffer hunger this season, and you will see the end of this year and beyond, safe and sound in the mighty name of Jesus.

One of the promises of God to those that belong to Him is they "- - shall eat in plenty, and be satisfied, and praise the name of the LORD your God, that hath dealt wondrously with you: and my people shall never be ashamed" (Joel. 2:26). I am sure Prophet Elijah can organize a special praise service onto God for fulfilling this promise in His life. At least on 3 occasions God miraculously fed Elijah - by a raven bird at brook Cherith (1 Kings 17: 1-7), by a widow woman of Zarephath. (1 Kgs 17: 8-16), and by an Angel as indicated in the opening scripture above (1 Kings 19: 4-8).

The incident that led to the feeding of Elijah by an angel is interesting and instructive. He (Elijah) had just stood on Mount Carmel and prayerfully called down fire from heaven to consume a repaired altar, thereby woefully defeating idol Baal and its 450 prophets all who Elijah slaughtered. Also, Elijah who was on "foot wagon" outran and got to Jezreel before Ahab who was on a Chariot. When Ahab reported these achievements of Elijah to Jezebel his wife, she sent a message to Elijah that he would be killed within 24 hours. Immediately, Elijah resulted into running for his life to escape the threat of death by Jezebel. Lacking food, tired of running and depressed, Elijah requested God to take his life (v. 4). Elijah who had by prayer called down fire from heaven temporarily forgot all God had done and acted in fear rather than faith. However, God had mercy on him and sent an angel to bring him food while he slept under a juniper tree. Elijah eat, was satisfied and got enough strength to last him 40 days and 40 nights on his journey to Mount Horeb, the mount of God.

Prayer: Father, please jettison every Jezebel pursuing me; feed me spiritually and otherwise until I want no more, IJN.

Thursday July 18, 2019
Topic: DAVID RESTORED TO THE THRONE

Scripture: "And throughout all the tribes of Israel there was much discussion and argument going on. The people were saying, "The king rescued us from our enemies and saved us from the Philistines, but Absalom chased him out of the country" (2 Sam. 19:9, KJV).

Praise the Lord. Today is July 18th and is day #199 in year 2019. The number of days 2remaining to end this year is 166. By God's grace, and as the Lord lives, you shall not be deposed or demoted, you shall be promoted this season, and you will see the end of this year and beyond, safe and sound in the mighty name of Jesus.

The Bible says "- - a person's enemies will be those of his own household" (Mt. 10:36). This scripture cannot be truer than the case of David who was dethroned as king of Israel by his own rebellious son Absalom in a fierce internal conspiracy that made David to flee from Jerusalem (2 Sam Chaps. 14 -19). After Absalom got to the throne in Jerusalem, Ahithophel, one of David's wisest counselors who has decamped to join Absalom asked permission to attack David with 12,000 troops. However, Hushai, David's secret agent in Absalom's palace advised Absalom to mobilize the entire nation against David and flattered Absalom, by asking him to lead the attack by himself. Absalom accepted Hushai's idea over that of Ahithophel. Out of desperation, Ahithophel, who felt his advice was rejected committed suicide (2 Sam. 17:23). Hushai gave David's troop tips about Absalom's war plans.

When battle ensued, David's army had upper hand and Absalom's army took to flight and Absalom was eventually killed (2 Sam. 18:1-18). David lamented over his son's death: David's love for his son Absalom despite his rebellion, typifies Christ's love for sinners. Jesus commands us to love tour enemies (Mt. 5:44).

As David persistently cried, mourning the death of his son Absalom, one of his military leaders, Joab, challenged him for not showing appreciation to his troops who risked their lives to save David and his family members from death (2 Sam 19:1-7). By consensus, David returned to Jerusalem and was restored as king (2 Sam 19:8-15). Have you lost any position or something of value? As we count down year 2019, I decree that your season of restoration has come, IJN. **Prayer: Father, don't let the rebellious spirit of Absalom creep into my household, business, ministry, etc.**

Friday July 19, 2019
Topic: SURPASSING RICHES OF SOLOMON

Scripture: "King Solomon made 200 large shields of hammered gold, each weighing more than fifteen pounds" (1 Kings 10:16, NLT).

Praise the Lord. Today is July 19th and is day #200 in year 2019. The number of days remaining to end this year is 165. By God's grace, you shall be blessed with riches that will glorify God this season, and you will see the end of this year and beyond, safe and sound in the mighty name of Jesus.

Solomon's riches and wisdom surpassed that of all the kings of the earth (1 Kings 10:23). The inventory of his assets includes 200 large shields of hammered gold as indicated in the today's opening scripture above.

What was the secret behind Solomon's wisdom and riches? The simple answer is love for God and giving as the following scripture testifies: "And Solomon loved the Lord, walking in the statutes of David his father: - -And the king went to Gibeon to sacrifice there; --- a thousand burnt offerings did Solomon offer upon that altar. 5 In Gibeon the Lord appeared to Solomon in a dream by night: and God said, Ask what I shall give thee." (1 king 3: 3-5). Solomon only asked for a wise and an understanding heart to be able to rule as a king. God gave Solomon all he asked for. Even what he didn't ask for was added to him such as riches and honor and that he would exceed everyone before and after him (1 Kgs 3: 12-13).

There is nothing wrong in getting rich so long it is achieved in a Godly way and glorifies God. The Bible says that God gives power to get wealth (Deut. 8:18)

Many of us are not yet rich because we are not sowing the kind of seed that can bring riches. The quality and quantity of your seed will determine the level of your riches (2Cor 9: 6). Love God and sow generously at His "altar" like Solomon did and watch God responding to you generously.

Prayer: Father, you gave me Your best, please give me the grace to give You my best, IJN

Saturday July 20, 2019
Topic: WHEN GOD FIGHTS FOR YOU

Scripture: "When thou goest out to battle against thine enemies, and seest horses, and chariots, and a people more than thou, be not afraid of them: for the Lord thy God is with thee, which brought thee up out of the land of Egypt." (Deut. 20:1, KJV).

Praise the Lord. Today is July 20th and is day #201 in year 2019. The number of days remaining to end this year is 164. By God's grace, all your life's battles shall be handled by the Lord, and you will see the end of this year and beyond, safe and sound in the mighty name of Jesus.

Life is a battlefield in which we are faced with many overwhelming oppositions just like the Israelites in the wilderness. Note that in this world the believer's life is not devoid of enemy's attacks. We are told to "Be sober, be vigilant; because your adversary the devil, as a roaring lion, walketh about, seeking whom he may devour" (1 Pet. 5:8). Jesus Christ told His followers that "---in me ye might have peace. In the world ye shall have tribulation: but be of good cheer; I have overcome the world (John 16:3b).

In today's opening scripture God bolstered Israelites' confidence by reminding them that He was always with them and had already saved them from potential danger. The same God can help you fight the battles of life irrespective of its nature, anytime anywhere. When God fights for you your victory is guaranteed. He is a man of war (Ex. 15:3) and He has never lost any battle. He helped David defeat Goliath, He rescued Daniel from the dens of lions, He healed Job and restored his loses.

What challenges or "battles" are you facing? - at home, on the job, in the ministry, at school, in sickness, in finances, in your family? etc. Your problems may seem overwhelming but be not afraid of them for the Lord God is with you (especially if you are His child). Just let God be your battle axe as He was for Jeremiah who declares "Thou art my battle axe and weapons of war: for with thee will I break in pieces the nations, and with thee will I destroy kingdoms (Jer. 51:20). God has all that is necessary to give you total victory. Do what apostle Paul did with his problems - he trusted the Lord and endured. The Lord delivered him. Forever, you shall be delivered from all afflictions, IJN **Prayer: Father, in the battles of life please be my battle axe and weapons of war, IJN.**

Sunday July 21, 2019
Topic: OBEYING GOD EVEN WHEN IT SEEMS ILLOGICAL

Scripture: "At the same time spake the Lord by Isaiah the son of Amoz, saying, Go and loose the sackcloth from off thy loins, and put off thy shoe from thy foot. And he did so, walking naked and barefoot". (Isaiah 20:2, KJV).

Praise the Lord. Today is July 21stand is day #202 in year 2019. The number of days remaining to end this year is 163. By God's grace, all the Lord's injunctions shall be easy for you to obey, and you will see the end of this year and beyond, safe and sound in the mighty name of Jesus.

Complete obedience of the believer is important to God. No wonder He ties blessings to obedience and curses to disobedience (Deut. 11: 27-28 & Deut. 28). It is never foolish to obey God, though God may choose the foolish things of this world to confound the wise (1 Cor 1:27). If God says it, we must obey no matter how foolish or illogical it may seem to us. In this regard, Prophet Isaiah's obedience to God as indicated in today's opening scripture is instructive. God told Isaiah to take off his clothes and shoes and walk about naked and barefooted for 3 years. As humiliating, debasing and illogical this instruction seemed, Isaiah obeyed God without question.

There may be times God may ask us to do things we don't understand. We must obey God in complete faith knowing that He is omniscient and will never ask us to do something that is wrong in His sight. Abraham was asked to sacrifice Isaac and he obeyed in his heart ready to carry the instruction out until God stopped him and provided a ram to substitute for the sacrifice. By His sacrificial death, Jesus Christ obeyed God his father completely.

God may not ask you to walk naked and barefooted. But, to what extent are you obeying what He has already said about receiving eternal life (John 3:16)? preaching and proclaiming salvation to unbelievers (Mk. 16:15)? paying your tithes and offering (Mal. 3:10-12)? living holy (1 Pet 1:16)? Remember, you must give an account to God for everything you do (Eccl. 11:9b, NLT).

Prayer: Father, whatever, You say to me, let me hear and obey You completely, IJN

Monday July 22, 2019
Topic: 'GETTING RID OF OTHER 'gods'

Scripture: "Thou shalt have no other gods before me " (Exodus 20:3, KJV).

Praise the Lord. Today is July 22nd and is day #203 in year 2019. The number of days remaining to end this year is 162. By God's grace, you shall not be deceived to follow any false god, and you will see the end of this year and beyond, safe and sound in the mighty name of Jesus.

What we have in the opening scripture for today is the first of the 10 commandments (commonly called the Decalogue) given by God to man through Moses on Mount Sinai. Before God spoke these 10 commandments out, He introduced Himself: "I am the Lord thy God" (Exo 20:2). By this, God established His ownership of the people and His authority over them. The first 4 of these commandments concern our duty to God and are commonly called 'THE FIRST TABLES' (Exo. 34:1). Our primary duty to God is to worship Him, that is to give to Him the glory due to His holy name. The first commandment (Exo 20:3) concerns the object of our worship, Jehovah, and him only should be worshipped.

The sin against this first commandment which we are most in danger of is giving the glory and honor due to God only to other creature(s). What constitute 'other god' is anything esteemed or loved, feared or served, delighted in or depended on more than God.

Prohibition of 'other gods' is the foundation of the whole law and it requires we take the Lord for our God, acknowledge that He is God, accept Him for ours, adore Him with admiration and humble reverence, and set our affection entirely upon Him.

In this era of materialism and insatiable desires, the believer must prayerfully resist the temptation of violating the first and other laws of God. Get rid of 'other gods' such as pride, greed, alcoholism, sexual sins, drug addiction, jealousy, etc. If you love and treasure your family, job, pursuit of money, fashion, food, or anything more than God, you will be in violation of the first law. The consequence of violating this law is to miss heaven. This will not be your portion, IJN.

Prayer: Father, I have no other God but You; I need no other god, IJN.

Tuesday July 23, 2019
Topic: CONQUERING CONSPIRACY THROUGH CHRIST

Scripture: "And Judah gathered themselves together, to ask help of the Lord: even out of all the cities of Judah they came to seek the Lord". (II Chronicles. 20:4, KJV).

Praise the Lord. Today is July 23rd and is day #204 in year 2019. The number of days remaining to end this year is 161. By God's grace, every all enemies conspiring to fight you shall be confounded to turn their weapons upon themselves, and you will see the end of this year and beyond, safe and sound in the mighty name of Jesus.

The word of god says "Behold, they shall surely gather together, but not by me: whosoever shall gather together against thee shall fall for thy sake" (Isaiah 54:15). God manifested the efficacy of this scripture for the people of Judah when suddenly people of 3 nations (Moabites, Ammonites and Edomites) gathered together to invade Judah (2 Chron. 20: 1-32). As indicated in today's opening scripture above, Judah also smartly gathered together to seek help from the Lord as directed by its king, Jehoshaphat.

As Judah, with their little ones, wives, and children were fasting and praying in a general assembly before the Lord, the Spirit of God fell on a man called Jahaziel who declared to the congregation "Thus saith the LORD unto you, Be not afraid nor dismayed by reason of this great multitude; for the battle is not yours, but God's - - - Ye shall not need to fight in this battle: set yourselves, stand ye still, and see the salvation of the LORD with you,---- tomorrow go out against them: for the LORD will be with you" (2 Chron 20: 15-17).

On the day of the battle, as Judah sang praises, The LORD set ambushments against the enemies who were all smitten as Judah's enemies set their own weapons upon themselves. Judah found all their enemies dead, leaving behind great spoil of riches that took them 3 days to carry away (vv. 24-25).

As you connect and remain connected to Jesus Christ, He will fight for you and you will conquer. *Prayer: Father, fight for me and consume all conspirators against me with Your fire, IJN.*

Wednesday July 24, 2019
Topic: PERSONALITY PANORAMA: TERAH

Scripture: "Terah lived for 205 years and died while still in Haran". (Gen 11:32, NLT).

Praise the Lord. Today is July 24th and is day #205 in year 2019. The number of days remaining to end this year is 160. By God's grace, you will not die this year, you will live your full age, and you will see the end of this year and beyond, safe and sound in the mighty name of Jesus.

Believer's knowledge of his/her foundation and background is important. This information can prove useful in knowing how to pray and what to do about one's destiny. Terah, mentioned in today's opening scripture can be described as the 'grandfather of Faith' since he is the father of Abraham who is often described as the 'father of faith' (Rom. 4:16). The pedigree of every follower of Jesus Christ is rooted in Terah, the father of Abraham.

Abraham 's delay in child bearing (at 100 years old) was probably generational as Terah his father had no children until he was 70 years old (Gen 11:26). Aside from Abraham, Terah had 2 other sons: Nahor and Haran. Haran was the father of Lot. Unfortunately, "- - Haran died in Ur of the Chaldeans, the land of his birth, while his father, Terah, was still living" (Gen. 11:28). Our children shall live long, and they will not die before us, IJN.

Terah moved away from Ur of the Chaldeans and was on his way to Canaan. However, he settled in Haran for a stopover. On his journey, Terah took with him his son Abram, his daughter-in-law Sarai, and his grandson Lot. (Gen. 11:31). As indicated in today's opening scripture, Terah died at age 205 in Haran. After his father's death, Abram moved to Canaan as instructed by God (Gen 12:1, 5). One of the first things Abraham did on arrival at the promised land of Canaan was that he built an altar unto the LORD who appeared unto him (Gen 12: 5-7). Whenever God relocates you, worship Him to show appreciation.

God's will for our lives may come in stages with possible transition periods just as Abram's stay in Haran was a transition period for him. Believers can use transition periods to wait patiently and prayerfully on God in preparation for better service to Him when the time for the calling matures. Your transition periods shall not be wasted, IJN. ***Prayer: Father, visit and perfect my foundation and let live my full age, IJN***

Thursday July 25, 2019
Topic: MOSES MISSED THE MARK

Scripture: "And Moses and Aaron went from the presence of the assembly unto the door of the tabernacle of the congregation, and they fell upon their faces: and the glory of the Lord appeared unto them". (Numbers 20:6).

Praise the Lord. Today is July 25th and is day #206 in year 2019. The number of days remaining to end this year is 159. By God's grace, anger or any other vice shall not rob you of fulfilling your destiny, and you will see the end of this year and beyond, safe and sound in the mighty name of Jesus.

During the journey to the promised land, the Israelites came to the wilderness of Zin and stayed at Kadesh. There, they suffered two major setbacks - Miriam died and there was no water for the community. The people gathered together in opposition to Moses and Aaron. They murmured against Moses saying "- - why have ye brought up the congregation of the Lord into this wilderness, that we and our cattle should die there? -- it is no place of seed, or of figs, or of vines, or of pomegranates; neither is there any water to drink" (Num. 20:4-5).

Moses and Aaron took the matter to God in worship and prayer. God told Moses to take the rod, gather the assembly together with Aaron and speak to the rock to bring forth (Num. 20: 8). In carrying out this instruction, Moses made the following mistakes (1) he called the people complaining "rebels" (2) he said, "must we fetch you water out of this rock?", (3) he smote the rock twice instead of speaking to it as he was instructed to do (vv.9 – 13). Although water came out abundantly from the rock for people to drink, God was upset with Moses and Aaron for their unbelief that led to striking the rock instead of speaking to it (vv. 9-12). God then said to them "-- therefore ye shall not bring this congregation into the land which I have given them" (v.12). Thus, Moses missed the opportunity to enter the promised land. He missed the mark! There are several lessons to learn from Moses' failure to get to the promised land: (1) God's instructions must be obeyed carefully and completely, (2) we must deliberately heed the injunction, "Be ye angry, and sin not." (Eph. 4:6); etc The rock that produced water in this case is symbolic of Jesus Christ who is the Living Water (John 4:10, 1 Cor. 10:4). **Prayer: *Father, deliver me from anger and anything that can deny me of making heaven, IJN***

Friday July 26, 2019
Topic: REWARDS FOR RIGHTEOUSNESS

Scripture: "The righteous lead blameless lives; blessed are their children after them". (Proverbs 20:7, NIV).

Praise the Lord. Today is July 26th and is day #207 in year 2019. The number of days remaining to end this year is 158. By God's grace, you shall be blameless before the Lord, and you will see the end of this year and beyond, safe and sound in the mighty name of Jesus.

The word righteous is an adjective meaning being just or morally right and justified. A Righteous life is the one lived in obedience according to the words and ways of God. Some of the synonyms for righteousness are fairness, goodness, justness, uprightness, virtue, honor, etc. God is a righteous God and He expects us to be righteous. God appreciates those who believe in Him and endeavor to live a righteous life. The Bible says, "And he (Abram) believed in the LORD; and he counted it to him for righteousness" (Gen 15:6).

Rewards for righteousness are numerous according to the word of God. For example, Noah's righteousness was the main reason he and his household escaped the destruction of the flood: "Then the LORD said to Noah, "Go into the ark, you and all your household, for I have seen that you are righteous before me in this generation (Gen 7:1; 11:7). There are other rewards for righteousness such as life instead of death (Pro. 11: 19); peace and flourishing (Psalm 72:7; 85:10); exaltation (Pro. 14:34) etc.

As indicated in today's opening scripture one of the major rewards for the righteous is the blessing of his/her children after them. We see example of this in the life of Abraham. Blessings increased progressively in the generations that follow him. The rewards for righteousness are not only spiritual but are in other dimensions – physical, economic, social etc. The best reward for righteousness is to make it to the kingdom of God. Our righteousness is made possible through our faith in Jesus Christ. Have you received Him as your Lord and Savior? Do so today and become a new person heading for heaven (1 Cor. 5:17; John 3:16, 6:37,)

Prayer: Father, give me the grace to live righteously and please bless all my children, IJN

Saturday July 27, 2019
Topic: LIE OF ABRAHAM'S AND ABIMELECH'S LUST

Scripture: "Therefore Abimelech rose early in the morning, and called all his servants, and told all these things in their ears: and the men were sore afraid". (Genesis 20:8).

Praise the Lord. Today is July 27th and is day #208 in year 2019. The number of days remaining to end this year is 157. By God's grace, you will see the end of this year and beyond, safe and sound in the mighty name of Jesus.

Abraham and Abimelech (the king of Gerar) were men with flaws who enjoyed God's mercy like most of us. The relationship between the 2 of them started on a bad note but ended on a good note (Gen. 20). The summary is that Abraham went to Gerar with his wife Sarai to sojourn. There, Abraham, for the fear he might be killed because of his beautiful wife, lied about Sarai saying: "- She is my sister" (v.2). On hearing this, Abimelech who has lusted after Sarai quickly sent to get her into the palace. The same night, before he could sexually molest Sarai, God appeared in a dream to Abimelech saying "Behold, thou art but a dead man, for the woman which thou hast taken; for she is a man's wife" (v.3). Abimelech was told to restore Sarai to her husband and get Abraham to pray for him (vv. 6- 10).

Here are some lessons from this story: (1) Heaven-bound believers must avoid lies for they have consequences. (2). Heaven-bound believers must avoid greed and lust and adultery. Abimelech already had his wife, why bother Sarah, no matter her beauty. (3) It is dangerous to tamper with servants of God for God says "- -Touch not mine anointed and do my prophets no harm" (Psalm 105:15). God will always fight for His own. Immediately he took Abraham's wife, God slammed Abimelech's household with bareness. Thank God this curse was later revoked when Abraham prayed for Abimelech (v. 17). You may be tampering with your destiny when you maltreat anointed men and women of God. That will not be your portion, IJN.

Prayer: Father deliver us from lying and lusting capable of destroying Your servants, IJN

Sunday July 28, 2019
Topic: NO UNEMPLOYMENT IN GOD'S ECONOMY

Scriptures: "And when they came that were hired about the eleventh hour, they received every man a penny". (Matthew 20:9).

Praise the Lord. Today is July 28th and is day #209 in year 2019. The number of days remaining to end this year is 156. By God's grace, you will neither labor in vain this season, nor denied what is due to you, and you will see the end of this year and beyond, safe and sound in the mighty name of Jesus.

High unemployment rate is a major economic problem in many countries of the world today. It can contribute significantly to socio economic problems like poverty, hunger, high crimes rates, armed robbery, high mortality rate, etc. Recent unemployment rate data of nations show big disparities among nations, ranging from as low as 0.4% in Romania to as high as 95% in Zimbabwe.

Today's opening scripture is in regard to a parable of Jesus to clarify the membership rule of the kingdom of God. In the parable, a householder went out early to hire laborers into his vineyard at an agreed wage rate of a penny per day. He went out again at the 3rd, 6th and 9th hours and hired idle laborers for the same condition as the first set. At the 11th hour he went out and hired idle laborers who told him they were idle because no man had hired them. At the end of the workday he paid them same rate of one penny beginning with the last hired to the first hired.

Here are some lessons to learn from this parable: (1) God is the householder /landowner and believers are the laborers / workers, the vineyard represents the kingdom of God, (2) In God's vineyard / service, there is work for every one willing to work, (3) God is generous and gracious in rewarding those that work for Him, He does no wrong, (4) Salvation and entrance to God's kingdom is strictly by grace alone and not by position, how much work or how long one has worked, (5) the prerogative to save any one anytime is God's as He wishes, (6) don't be jealous of what God has given to other people who you consider are less qualified than you. (7) Don't consider yourself (or anyone) too late to be blessed. God is cars for all. **Prayer: *Father, let me be profitably engaged and receive my blessings at the appointed time, IJN.***

Monday July 29, 2019
Topic: WISDOM FROM THE WORD

Scriptures: "For wisdom will enter your heart, and knowledge will fill you with joy". (Proverbs 2:10).

Praise the Lord. Today is July 29th and is day #210 in year 2019. The number of days remaining to end this year is 155. By God's grace, you will be endowed with wisdom that will produce joy in all you do this season, and you will see the end of this year and beyond, safe and sound in the mighty name of Jesus.

The value of wisdom, knowledge and understanding in handling the issues of life cannot be over emphasized. Simply put, wisdom is to have keen insight into the true nature of things or to have skill, tact, or expertise in something. Knowledge involves the accumulation of correct information or facts about a certain object or thing. Understanding refers to good judgment, or the skill to govern our life in a careful, successful manner.

One common thing among wisdom, knowledge and understanding is that they all come from the LORD: "For the LORD giveth wisdom: out of his mouth cometh knowledge and understanding"(Pro 2:6). Jesus Christ is described as the Word in John 1:1 and in Him all things consist (Col. 1:17b). In today's opening scripture above, Solomon indicates that his son (and all believers in the LORD) can become carriers of wisdom and understanding. This is through receiving the LORD's words and hiding His commandments within us (Pro 2:1). In other words when any one receives Jesus Christ as his/her Savior, the person receives the power of God and wisdom of God (1 Cor. 1:24).

When God gives you wisdom, knowledge and understanding there is nothing you embark upon that will not be successful. Jesus Christ successfully completed His earthly ministry largely because the spirit of the LORD rested upon him, the spirit of wisdom and understanding, and the spirit of knowledge (Isaiah 11:2). As year 2019 counts down prayerfully let your desire for Godly wisdom, knowledge and understanding from the LORD count up.

Prayer: Father, let me remain connected with Jesus Christ and let me increase in wisdom, knowledge and understanding, IJN.

Tuesday July 30, 2019
Topic: VANITY OF VANITIES; ALL IS VANITY

Scriptures: "Then I looked on all the works that my hands had wrought, and on the labour that I had laboured to do: and, behold, all was vanity and vexation of spirit, and there was no profit under the sun". (Ecclesiastes 2:11).

Praise the Lord. Today is July 30th and is day #211 in year 2019. The number of days remaining to end this year is 154. By God's grace, you will not put major efforts on minor things, Godly agenda shall be your priority, and you will see the end of this year and beyond, safe and sound in the mighty name of Jesus.

Solomon is man of great wisdom who achieved so much during his life time (1 Kgs 4:30 Ecc.4-10). In spite of all his achievements, Solomon declares the shocking but true statement in the opening scripture of today. In fact, the phrase "vanity of vanities; all is vanity" is repeated 2 times by Solomon, at the beginning and end of his Ecclesiastical write up (1:2 & 12:8). In other words, emptiness prevails in anything liable to change and corruption. All human efforts to amass riches, wealth, fame, laureates, houses, etc. are vanities as they have no eternal value. At some time, man will be unavoidably separated from those things: "For we brought nothing into this world, and it is certain we can carry nothing out" (1 Tim. 6:7).

The lesson Solomon wants us to learn is to bear in mind that all human accomplishments will one day disappear and become meaningless. We must therefore live wisely to honor and satisfy God in all we say, think and do (1 Cor. 10:31; Col. 3:23). Only the things we do for God with our time, talents, and treasures (or money) will have eternal values. Examples include winning souls, helping to build God's Church, helping the poor, etc. Do as Jesus Christ advise: " Lay not up for yourselves treasures upon earth, where moth and rust doth corrupt, and where thieves break through and steal: But lay up for yourselves treasures in heaven, where neither moth nor rust doth corrupt, and where thieves do not break through nor steal" (Matthew 6:19-20). May your blessings count upwards, IJN.

Prayer: Father, don't let my efforts result in vanities, let me layup treasures in heaven, IJN.

Wednesday July 31, 2019
Topic: GATEKEEPERS OF HOUSE OF GOD

Scriptures: "In all, there were 212 gatekeepers in those days, and they were listed according to the genealogies in their villages. David and Samuel the seer had appointed their ancestors because they were reliable men" (1 Chronicles 9:22, NLT).

Praise the Lord. Today is July 31st and is day #212 in year 2019. The number of days remaining to end this year is 153. By God's grace, you will see the end of this year and beyond, safe and sound in the mighty name of Jesus.

The Bible says " Let all things be done decently and in order" (1 Cor 14:40). If there is anywhere order is needed it is in the house of God. Based on today's opening scripture, let us talk about the 212 gatekeepers of the house of God in Judah who ensured orderliness in worship services. The main criterion for their selection was that they were "reliable men".

These gatekeepers had returned from captivity in Babylon to which they had been exiled because of their transgression against the Lord. Upon return from exile these Levites were chosen to guard the gates of God's house, the house of worship. Gates are very important and so is the responsibility of serving as the keepers of them. Gates serve many purposes including entry points - for both good and bad things. Examples of good things happening at gates: (a) The Lord loveth the gates of Zion more than all the dwellings of Jacob (Psalm 87:2); (b) The Lord, strong and mighty can come in through the gates (Ps.24:7-10); (c) Job saw his help at the gate (Job. 31:21); (d) there are gates of nobles (Isa. 13:2). Examples of bad occurrences / roles of gates include (i) enemies can cause distress at gates (Deut. 28:55); (ii) there are gates of death (Ps. 9:13); (iii) there are gates of hell (Matt 16: 18). The keepers of gates must stay prayed up for divine protection and provision.

Note also that your body, as a believer, "is the temple of the Holy Ghost which is in you, which ye have of God..." (1 Cor. 6:19, KJV). Do you know that your body consists of many "gates" including the eyes, ears, nose, anus, pours in the skins, etc. What are you doing to keep the gates of your body from been polluted and invaded by the "enemies"? You can pray, serve God, live healthy, use God's word, etc. ***Prayer: Father, the Lord strong and mighty, let all the gates of my life and those of Your Church open to You to come in, IJN.***

Thursday August 01, 2019
Topic: NEW BEGINNING

Scriptures: "Behold, I will do a new thing; now it shall spring forth; shall ye not know it? I will even make a way in the wilderness, and rivers in the desert." (Isaiah 43:19).

Praise the Lord. Today is August 1st and is day #213 in year 2019. The number of days remaining to end this year is 152. By God's grace, you will receive new blessings from the Lord this month, and you will see the end of this year and beyond, safe and sound in the mighty name of Jesus.

Welcome to the new month of August, the 8th month of the year. The number 8 connotes a new beginning. When Abraham was 99 years old God gave him a new beginning by establishing an everlasting covenant with him. The covenant was marked with a token that called for the circumcision of every male child on the 8th day (Gen 17: 11-12). The 8th day's circumcision was a pointer to the true circumcision of the heart made without hands by Jesus Christ (Col. 2:11). It is symbolic of putting away old nature to have a new beginning of life in Jesus Christ (1 Cor. 5:17). God's covenant with Abraham ushered him into a new era of many blessings including fruitfulness, exceeding multiplication, becoming the father of many nations, etc. (Gen 17: 1-17).

Noah had a new beginning to commence a new order of things in a regenerated world after he became the 8th (and last) person saved from the flood that destroyed the rest of the world (2 Pet. 2:5). Every "flood of hindrance" that has limited your achievement hitherto, shall dry up this month in Jesus name. Beginning this month your feet shall be set on new grounds of productive ventures and fruitfulness in Jesus name. God gave Joseph a new beginning and he left the prison dungeon one day to become the prime minister of Egypt on the same day (Gen. 39: 20; 41: 41-44). The beggar man at the beautiful gate who was lame from his mother's womb was given a new beginning by the power of God through the hands of Peter. He rose, walked and started jumping up praising God (Acts 3: 1-11). Lazarus and the son of the woman of Nain were given a new beginning when Jesus brought them back from death to life (Lk 7: 11-17; Jn 11: 34-44). Beginning this month, your life shall witness new wonderful transformations that will glorify God, IJN.

Prayer: Father, please give me a new beginning of living holy and prospering in all areas of my life, IJN

Friday August 02, 2019
Topic: GIVING TOWARDS HOUSE OF GOD

Scriptures: "Then David the king addressed the congregation: "My son Solomon was singled out and chosen by God to do this. ---. I've done my best to get everything together for building this house for my God, all the materials necessary: gold, silver, bronze, - - - 3,000 talents (about 113 tons) of gold - -all from Ophir, the best - - and 7,000 talents (214 tons) of silver for covering the walls of the buildings, - - " (1 Chron. 29: 1-5, MSG).

Praise the Lord. Today is August 2nd and is day #214 in year 2019. The number of days remaining to end this year is 151. By God's grace, you and your children will be vessels of honor the Lord will use to promote his kingdom agenda in this era, and you will see the end of this year and beyond, safe and sound in the mighty name of Jesus.

God described David as "a man after mine own heart"... (Acts 13:22). The main reason for this exalted description ascribed to David was because God said, of David, he "shall fulfil all my will". Essentially, obedience and other reasons such as his love for God and for God's house are key factors that made David win the heart of God. Many of David's expressions show that he loved God's house very deeply. For example, he said he was glad when invited to go to God's house, (Ps. 122:1).

In appreciation of what God had done for him, David loved God and placed a high premium on loving His house. He wanted to build a house for God, but God disapproved of it saying, "thou hast shed blood abundantly, and hast made great wars: - " (1 Chronicles 22:7). God would only allow his son, Solomon, to be the builder of the Temple. Although David was not allowed to build God's house directly, he made ample building materials ready for his son as can be seen in today's opening scripture above. Among his best personal resources David contributed towards building God's house were 7,000 tablets or 214 tons of silver. This is instructive and should be challenging to us on this 214th day of year 2019. What are you doing in building God's house and His Church?

Prayer: Father, You gave me your best, please help me to give You my best in building Your house, Your Church and Your kingdom here on earth, IJN.

Saturday August 03, 2019
Topic: CLEANSING THE CHURCH

Scriptures: "And when he had made a scourge of small cords, he drove them all out of the temple, and the sheep, and the oxen; and poured out the changers' money, and overthrew the tables" (John 2:15).

Praise the Lord. Today is August 3rd and is day #215 in year 2019. The number of days remaining to end this year is 150. By God's grace, your body, being the temple of Holy Ghost shall not be polluted, and you will see the end of this year and beyond, safe and sound in the mighty name of Jesus.

Shortly after performing His first miracle of converting water into wine, Jesus went to Jerusalem in preparation for the Passover. There He entered a Temple and found "those that sold oxen and sheep and doves, and the changers of money sitting" (John 2:14). Jesus was angry and He cleansed the Temple taking the action described in the opening scripture above. Chasing them out He said to those that were trading in the Temple, "make not my Father's house an house of merchandise" (John 2:16b). In Matthew's account of the same event it is recorded that Jesus chided the merchandisers saying, "It is written, My house shall be called the house of prayer; but ye have made it a den of thieves" (Matthew 21:13).

Here are some lessons to learn from the incident above: (1) Jesus seized every opportunity to attend Church and so we, His follower, must do the same. Quit giving excuses for missing Church. When you deliberately miss Church, you may be missing miracles, joy and other blessings. (2) It is in order to be angry at wrong doings so long the anger is not allowed to escalate to sin (Eph. 4: 26). Jesus was angry at the merchants who were exploiting those who have come to worship in God's house. He could not withstand the rowdy, disrespectful and dishonoring actions of these merchants to His father's house. (3) The Church is a place to come to worship, praise and pray to God, not a marketplace. Anything done in the Church must be done decently and in order (1 Cor. 14:40). (4). Given that our body is the Temple of the Holy Ghost, we must "drive out" any "merchandising activity" that can pollute our body and grieve the Holy Spirit.

Prayer: Father, consume by fire every spirit of disorderliness and evil merchandising of buying and selling in Your Church, IJN.

Sunday August 04, 2019
Topic: READY FOR THE NEW JERUSALEM?

Scriptures: "The angel who talked to me held in his hand a gold measuring stick to measure the city, - - - When he measured it, he found it was a square, as wide as it was long. In fact, its length and width and height were each 1,400 miles. --Then he measured the walls and found them to be 216 feet thick- - " (Revelations 20:15-17, NLT).

Praise the Lord. Today is August 4th and is day #216 in year 2019. The number of days remaining to end this year is 149. By God's grace, you will make it to heaven, the New Jerusalem whenever Jesus comes to take his own, and if He tarries, you will see the end of this year and beyond, safe and sound in the mighty name of Jesus.

The city whose walls measured 216 feet in thickness referenced in today's opening scripture above is the "Holy City" also called "The New Jerusalem". A summary of the place, the proportions and the people of this city is the focus of this ministration.

The Place: After the great judgment, God will create a new earth (Rm. 8:18-21; 2 Peter 3:7-13). This is consistent with the vision John said he saw (Rev. 21: 1-2). While its exact location is unknown, the Bible says it will come down from heaven and it will be eternal (Rev. 21: 2, 10; Isa 65:17; 66:22). The place will be new and brilliantly shining with the glory of God.

The Proportions: In addition to the description in today's opening scripture, the city was pure gold, as clear as glass. There are 12 gates all made of pearls. No temple in the city, for the Lord God Almighty and the Lamb are its temple (Rev. 21: 18-22). The new Jerusalem is a perfect cube, same shape as the Most Holy Place in Solomon's temple (1 kings 6:20).

The People: The citizens of the new Jerusalem are God and his followers - those whose names are written in the book of life. Those who will have no place there include, "unbelievers, the corrupt, murderers, liars.

I admonish you to give your life to Jesus Christ today so that you can qualify to reign with God in the New Jerusalem and avoid hell fire. Just ask Jesus Christ to forgive you your sins and come into your life to be your Lord and Savior. See you in the New Jerusalem. *Prayer: Father, help me to live for You so I can reign with You in the New Jerusalem, IJN.*

Monday August 05, 2019
Topic: DEATH FROM DISOBEDIENCE

Scriptures: "But of the tree of the knowledge of good and evil, thou shalt not eat of it: for in the day that thou eatest thereof thou shalt surely die" (Genesis, 2:17).

Praise the Lord. Today is August 5th and is day #217 in year 2019. The number of days remaining to end this year is 148. By God's grace, you will not partake in anything forbidden by the Lord, and you will see the end of this year and beyond, safe and sound in the mighty name of Jesus.

When God created him in the Garden of Eden, man had the potential to live forever without dying physically and spiritually. From the scripture above, man knew that the condition for immortality was to obey God and not eat from the tree of the knowledge of good and evil. God made it clear that disobedience would attract death.

Regrettably the serpent came and deceived Eve to eat the forbidden fruit, saying "Ye shall not surely die" (Gen 3:4b). Eve and Adam succumbed to the offer of the serpent and became victims of "the lust of the flesh, and the lust of the eyes, and the pride of life" (1 John 2: 15-17). They then faced the terrifying prospect of death, as forewarned by the Almighty God as in today's opening scripture. Thus, Adam and Eve, by their disobedience introduced sin to mankind and its consequent penalty of death (Rom. 5:12; Heb. 9:27).

Fortunately, man didn't have to remain permanently dead and separated from God due to the redemptive work of Jesus Christ: "For if by one man's offence death reigned by one; much more they which receive abundance of grace and of the gift of righteousness shall reign in life by one, Jesus Christ" (Romans 5:17). Redemption means Jesus Christ, through His sacrificial death, paid the penalty for sin (which is death) and purchased believers in Him back from sin and death for reconciliation with God, their maker.

Anyone who wants to have eternal life instead of permanent death must not live a life of disobedience. Be obedient to God and choose life instead of death: "- -I have set before you life and death, blessing and cursing: therefore, choose life, - - -" (Deut. 30:19). You can choose life by accepting Jesus Christ as your Lord and Savior.

Prayer: Father, please give me the grace to live and not die by obeying You completely, IJN

Tuesday August 06, 2019
Topic: PERSONALITY PANORAMA: EZRA

Scriptures: "From the family of Joab: Obadiah son of Jehiel and 218 other men." (Ezra 8:9).

Praise the Lord. Today is August 6th and is day #218 in year 2019. The number of days remaining to end this year is 147. By God's grace, you will be relevant and outstanding among the people the Lord will use and bless in this season, and you will see the end of this year and beyond, safe and sound in the mighty name of Jesus.

Ezra was a priest, a scribe and a great leader. His name mean help. He led the second group of exiles (about 2000) from Babylon to Jerusalem. Notable among this group were 218 exiles from the family of Joab headed by Obadiah as indicated in the opening scripture above. Ezra was committed to study, follow, and teach God's word as pointed out in Ezra 7:10: "- Ezra had determined to study and obey the Law of the Lord and to teach those decrees and regulations to the people of Israel". In addition, Ezra is credited with the authorship of most of 1 and 2 Chronicles, Ezra, Nehemiah, and Psalm 119 and that he led the council of 120 men who formed the Old Testament canon.

After the city of Jerusalem was rebuilt, Ezra instituted a religious reformation in which the ancient Torah (the Law) made the norm of the Jewish life. He also demanded that Jews who had married foreigners to divorce them to maintain the Jewish purity the Torah required. Ezra set an example of piety and dedication through prayer and fasting.

Some of the lessons we can learn from Ezra's life include (a) need to have strong commitment to serving God and people (b) serving God in multiple capacities is possible. Are you maximizing your potential in multitasking? (c) we must be committed to studying and teaching God's word (Joshua 1:8-9), (d) always be a helper (e) pray and fast regularly (f) strive to be a reformer in your community in terms of doing what is right and consistent with God's word. e.g. don't engage in or encourage adultery, bribery, drugs, stealing, etc.

Prayer: Father, let me know more about You and Your word that I might be more effective in fulfilling my destiny and being a blessing, IJN.

Wednesday August 07, 2019
Topic: EARTH ABOUT TO END?

Scriptures: "And when you hear of wars and insurrections, don't panic. Yes, these things must take place first, but the end won't follow immediately." (Luke 21:9, NLT)

Praise the Lord. Today is August 7th and is day #219 in year 2019. The number of days remaining to end this year is 146. By God's grace, the signs of the end time will not cause any panic attack to, and you will see the end of this year and beyond, safe and sound in the mighty name of Jesus.

When will the world come to an end is a common question that reverberates through the minds of many people? There have been over 200 predictions of the end of the world none of which has come true. For example, Harold Camping predicted the world would come to an end in 1994 and it did not happen. Again, he gave another one with exact date of May 21, 2011 at 6 pm. To his disappointment and that of his followers the prediction was a wash. The truth of the matter is that no one, except God, knows the exact time this world will cease to exist. Jesus Christ declares, "Heaven and earth shall pass away, but my words shall not pass away. But of that day and hour knoweth no man, no, not the angels of heaven, but my Father only". (Matt. 24: 35-36).

Although we are not privileged to know the exact day the earth will end, we do have pointers from God's word in terms of signs of the nearness of the end of time. Today's opening scripture and the few verses that follow provide us with a catalog of events that will precede the coming of the Lord. These include: wars and commotions, nation rising against nation, and kingdom against kingdom: great earthquakes in divers places, famines, etc. (Luke 21:9 -12). All these are already happening in our time!

What then should be the believer's reaction be to the issues about the end of the earth? The believer should do what the Bible says in 1 Peter 4:7: "- - the end of all things is at hand: be ye therefore sober and watch unto prayer." The believer must not be swayed by human predictions, instead he/she must faithfully wait, live holy and hold fast to God and His word, and be prepared for the return of Jesus Christ which can happen at any time.

Prayer: Father, let me be ready to go with You any time You return, IJN.

Thursday August 08, 2019
Topic: GOD'S ARK IS PRESENCE OF GOD

Scriptures: "Then David summoned all Israel to Jerusalem to bring the Ark of the Lord to the place he had prepared for it. This is the number of the descendants of Aaron (the priests) and the Levites who were called together: From the clan of Merari, 220, with Asaiah as their leader" (1 Chronicles 15; 3, 4, 6, NLT).

Praise the Lord. Today is August 8th and is day #220 in year 2019. The number of days remaining to end this year is 145. By God's grace, the presence of the Lord will be perpetual in your habitation, and you will see the end of this year and beyond, safe and sound in the mighty name of Jesus.

The Israelites carried the AOC with them everywhere they went during the journey to the promised land. On one occasion it was captured by the Philistines (1 Sam 4). While the AOG was in their possession, the Philistines suffered unexplainable calamities that forced them to return it to the Israelites after 7 months (1 Sam 5 & 6). Any one that has hijacked your blessings shall suffer, IJN.

After the Ark of God got back to Israel, Eleazar the son of Abinadab kept it for about 70 years before David, the King of Israel made arrangement to move it to Jerusalem. The first attempt resulted in calamity in that Uzzah who mishandled the cart carrying the AOG was struck dead by God (2 Sam 6: 6-7). David, fearful of what happened to Uzzah, commanded the Ark to go to Obededom's house instead of his own (2 Sam. 6:10–11). During the 3 months the AOG stayed in Obededom's house, " - -the Lord blessed Obededom and his entire household" (2 Sam 6:11). David arranged to transfer the AOG to the City of David when he leant about how God blessed Obededom's household. This transfer was done with great care and celebrations. Among the 862 Levites involved as carriers of the AOG were 220 clan members of Merarias (1 Chron 15:6). David's wife (Michal) despised him for dancing before the AOG and she became barren all her life (II Sam. 6:14, 16, 20, 23).

Some lessons to learn from this story include (1) Believers should know they are carriers of God's presence. (2) Therefore, believers must be holy (3). It is dangerous to despise anyone praising God. *Prayer: Father, from now till eternity, let your presence be with me, IJN.*

Friday August 09, 2019
Topic: SPEAKING TO JESUS FOR SALVATION

Scriptures: "And it shall come to pass, that whosoever shall call on the name of the Lord shall be saved" (Acts 2:21).

Praise the Lord. Today is August 9th and is day #221 in year 2019. The number of days remaining to end this year is 144. By God's grace, you and your family shall be saved, and you will see the end of this year and beyond, safe and sound in the mighty name of Jesus.

The profound statement in today's opening scripture is about the condition for salvation which Apostle Peter made on the Pentecost day. The Holy Spirit first manifested itself to the disciples on the Pentecost day (Acts 2:1-4). The coming of the Holy Spirit on the disciples is in fulfilment of two Biblical promises: (a) one in the Old Testament – Joel 2:28, which says "I will pour out my Spirit on all people". (b) another in the New Testament, where Jesus says he will send another Counselor, the Spirit of truth (John 16: 5-15). Whatever the word of God has said about you shall be fulfilled IJN.

Several spectacular miracles happened on the Pentecost day two of which are (a) baptism of the disciples with the Holy Spirit evidenced by their speaking in different languages such as those from different nations present could hear in their own language (v.13), and (b) the salvation of about 3000 souls after Peter preached to them about Jesus Christ (Acts 2:38-41). When Peter's audience were amazed and some mocked the disciples saying they were drunk, Peter quickly dismissed their claim and pointed out that what the audience saw was the effect of the outpouring of the Holy Spirit prophesied by Joel and promised by Jesus Christ. The Holy Spirit is an enabler being a great source of power (Acts 1:8). The Holy Spirit has an essential and indispensable role in salvation. The Holy Spirit works in unity with God, the Father and the Son to bring about to salvation in the one that believes.

Like the 3000 souls at Peter's first sermon, you too can receive salvation today speaking to Jesus Christ for your salvation. When you call on the name of Jesus Christ and tell Him (1) You are a sinner (Rm 3:23), (2) you repent of your sins and ask Jesus to (by His mercy) forgive you your sins and be your Lord (Acts 2:38, Romans 10: 9, Jn. 1:12), (3) tell Him to give you the Holy Spirit to help you live and serve Him forever (v. 38, Lk. 11:13). *Prayer: Father, please cause many sinners to speak and plead for their salvation through Jesus to Jesus Christ Your Son, IJN.*

Saturday August 10, 2019
Topic: ANY FOOD EATING IN HEAVEN?

Scriptures: "In the midst of the street of it, and on either side of the river, was there the tree of life, which bare twelve manner of fruits, and yielded her fruit every month: and the leaves of the tree were for the healing of the nations." (Revelation 22:2).

Praise the Lord. Today is August 10th and is day #222 in year 2019. The number of days remaining to end this year is 143. By God's grace, you enjoy heaven on earth as the Lord wills, and you will see the end of this year and beyond, safe and sound in the mighty name of Jesus.

Some interesting questions I have heard people ask include, "will there be eating of food in heaven? If Yes, what type? Will I find my favorite there? etc. While answers to these questions are not easy, scripture can provide us with some clues. Interestingly, the first and last books of the Bible (Genesis and Revelation) each has something to say about the "tree of life"(Gen 1:29, Rev. 2:7).

There are scriptural references that seem to suggest there will be food eating in heaven (Mark 14:25, Rev 19:9). There are also scriptures that suggest the contrary, an example being "- - the kingdom of God is not meat and drink; but righteousness, and peace, and joy in the Holy Ghost" (Rom. 14:17). The Bible is silent as to whether the tree of life in Revelation as mentioned in today's opening scripture is for human consumption or not. If they are not for human consumption what will happen to so much output of 12 different varieties of fruits produced by the tree every month? Some people are of the opinion the tree of life refers to the Gospel, the 12 fruits are the 12 apostles, and the leaves are Gospel doctrines by which the nations are healed of the disease of sin.

The summary is that since, for now we only "know in part" (1 Cor13:9), we don't really know if, or what, we will eat in heaven. What is most important now is to focus on making it to heaven where we shall be overwhelmed with joy of seeing Jesus and being like Him forever (1 John 3:2-3). He is the Bread of life and if we need food there, He will ensure all our need will be met. Hallelujah!

Prayer: Father, please grant me my utmost desire to make it to Your heavenly kingdom and to reign with You forever, IJN.

Sunday August 11, 2019
Topic: JUDAS' BETRAYAL OF JESUS

Scriptures: "Then entered Satan into Judas surnamed Iscariot, being of the number of the twelve" (Luke 22:3).

Praise the Lord. Today is August 11th and is day #223 in year 2019. The number of days remaining to end this year is 142. By God's grace, you shall not succumb to the temptation Satan, and you will see the end of 2019 and beyond, safe and sound in the mighty name of Jesus.

Satan's constant and primary assignment is to kill to steal and to destroy (John 10:10). Most often Satan engages the help of his servants called demonic agents to get His evil work done. One of such agents is Judas, one of the 12 disciples of Jesus. As the opening scripture above indicates Satan came and entered Judas Iscariot's heart convincing him to betray Jesus. Immediately, Judas went to the Sanhedrin (the Israeli leading priests and teachers of religious law) to discuss the best way to betray Jesus to them. (Lk. 22:4-6).

What motivated Judas to commit this heinous act against Jesus? Here are some suggestions: (1) The betrayal was to bring about believer's redemption and to fulfill a prophecy made hundreds of years before: " Even my close friend in whom I trusted, who ate my bread, has lifted his heel against me" (Psalm 41:9, ESV). (2) Judas was pushed to do this evil because of greed. Being the treasurer of Jesus' ministry (John 12:6), Judas most likely had his eyes on inheriting the money in the coffer after Jesus' death. (3) Being in Jesus' "inner circle," Judas had a closer relationship to Jesus than most people such that he could easily give Him away with a kiss. etc. Judas betrayed Jesus by kissing him to signal to his arresters that He was the one He "sold" to them. Then said Jesus to him, "Judas, would you betray the Son of Man with a kiss?" (Lk. 22:48). Then they seized Jesus and led him away.

Lessons to learn from Judas' story include: (1) We must constantly resist and pray against Satan's ceaseless attempts to 'enter' into us. (Mt. 6: 13), (2) we must guard against small, gradual failings (e.g. small steals, lies, etc.) that can gain strength and power in our lives and could open the door to more deadly influences (3) we should be aware that human beings are capable of pretense and deceit (4) Judas' evil action reminds us of Shakespeare's wise saying that "the evil that men do lives after them- -"***Prayer: Father, don't let me be an object or subject of betrayal, IJN***

Monday August 12, 2019
Topic: SPYING THE LAND SUCCESSFULLY

Scriptures: "And they said unto Joshua, Truly the Lord hath delivered into our hands all the land; for even all the inhabitants of the country do faint because of us" (Josh. 2:24).

Praise the Lord. Today is August 12th and is day #224 in year 2019. The number of days remaining to end this year is 141. By God's grace, you will see the end of this year and beyond, safe and sound in the mighty name of Jesus.

As an ex spy himself (Num. chapter 13), Joshua knew the value of spying a land earmarked for possession. Now that he has become the one to take the Israelites to the promised land, he sent 2 spies to examine the state of the inhabitants of the land especially of Jericho prior to their entering the place. The 2 spies returned to Joshua with positive report as indicated in today's opening scripture. Every report that will come to you this year (medical, academic, legal, business, marital etc. shall be according to your desire and shall give you joy, IJN.

God favored the 2 spies with respect to their mission. On reaching Jericho they were received and entertained by a harlot called Rahab. When the king of Jericho was informed of the presence of these 2 spies in the town, he sent message to Rahab commanding her to deliver them up (Josh. 2:2). Rahab hid the spies in the house-top and told the messengers that the men were departed and gone towards the mountain (vs. 2-4). In the meantime, she told the spies that the fear of the Israelites had fallen on all the inhabitants of the country on hearing of their victories over the Amorites. Also, that she knew none could resist the God of Israel, and therefore she desired them to give her an oath that, when they took Jericho, they would preserve her life and that of her family (Josh. 2:8-13).

The spies swore to her in agreement with the deal and she let them down by a cord from their hiding place at the house-top, giving them directions how to proceed, in order to avoid the pursuers (Josh2:14-16). Rahab was told to tie a scarlet line to the window, through which she had let them down, which should be the sign to the Israelites to spare that house and its inhabitants whenever the city would be captured (Josh 2:17-19). Let us learn from Rahab that every human being is a potential destiny helper. **Prayer: *Father, send me helpers who will facilitate my success in everything I embark upon henceforth IJN.***

Tuesday August 13, 2019
Topic: WHO TO BLAME: ELI OR HIS SONS?

Scriptures: "If someone sins against another person, God can mediate for the guilty party. But if someone sins against the Lord, who can intercede?" But Eli's sons wouldn't listen to their father, for the Lord was already planning to put them to death" (1 Samuel 2:25).

Praise the Lord. Today is August 13th and is day #225 in year 2019. The number of days remaining to end this year is 140. By God's grace, you will not deliberately sin against the Lord, and you will see the end of this year and beyond, safe and sound in the mighty name of Jesus.

The sons of Eli - Hophni and Phinehas, were described as sons of Belial meaning worthless and wicked children of the devil. Unlike the young Samuel who ministered unto the LORD before Eli the priest (1 Sam 2:11), Hophni and Phinehas were perverse and "they knew not the Lord" (1 Sam. 2:12) See also 1 Sam 2: 13-17 and 22-25.

Despite persistent reports of the sons' malpractices, Eli merely complained without doing anything serious to discourage or stop their abominable practices. The Bible says sin, when it is finished, bringeth forth death (James 1:15b). When God could no longer tolerate the sins of Eli sons, He sent a man of God to Eli to deliver a woeful message in which God revoked the priestly role of Eli's family and imposed a curse on his household and lineage (1 Sam 2: 32-34). As it turned out Hophni and Phinehas were slain on the same day in a battle between Israel and Philistines (1 Sam 4: 11). On the same day, Eli also died at age 98 (1 Sam 4: 14-18) and so did Phinehas' wife who died after a delivering a baby she named Ichabod (1 Sam 4: 20-22).

In this tragic story it is fair to say that both Eli and his sons have failed in one way or the other. Although Eli warned his sons against their sinful practices, he did not back up his warning with adequate supervision, firmness, penalty for disobedience and prayer. As regards the sons, they are to blame for greed and disobedience to God and Eli.

Raising up children is obviously a big challenge in this technologically advanced era, but it can still be done with the help of God. To raise your children successfully seek God's help in carefully integrating love, discipline, listening, observing, communication, rewards, clear instructions, moderate punishment, word of God, prayer and assigning responsibility. **Prayer: *Father, let our children be brought up in the nurture and admonition of the Lord.***

Wednesday August 14, 2019
Topic: ARE YOUR CHILDREN GOD'S HERITAGE?

Scriptures: "Train up a child in the way he should go: and when he is old, he will not depart from it." (Proverbs 22:6).

Praise the Lord. Today is August 14th and is day #226 in year 2019. The number of days remaining to end this year is 139. By God's grace, neither you nor your children shall be wayward, and you will see the end of this year and beyond, safe and sound in the mighty name of Jesus.

The Bible declares, "Lo, children are an heritage of the Lord: - -" (Psalm 127:3). That is, children really belong to God, though they are gifts from Him to us as earthly parents. Therefore, as today's opening scripture above suggests, God expects our children to be trained up in His way. Notice we are to train them "up" not down. To train children "up" means to add value to their lives such that they grow up to know, love and obey God, honoring their parents and useful in their society.

God's testimony about Abraham is instructive regarding His expectation and how we are to train up our children in Gen 18:19.

From this we can see that training up our children begins with us living a Christ-like life as an example for our children to follow. At the same time, instruct and command them to do what is right and play by the rule consistent with the word of God. Share the message of salvation with them as early as they can understand what it means. This must be reinforced consistently with other pertinent instructions to strengthen their faith in the LORD.

Godly discipline is also important in training up children according to Eph. 6:4, ESV. Parents must exercise virtues such as tender love, patience, endurance, firmness, in handling issues concerning children training. Chances are that children will make a lot of requests many of which may not be good for them at all or at the time they want such. Don't hesitate to deny such requests but provide adequate explanation for denial. Where possible, suggest and provide possible alternatives that will be more appropriate and beneficial to the children. Jesus and Joseph are perfect examples of children God expects us to train up. I decree that none of us will raise up Belial children.

Prayer: *Father, please let our children be trained up to love and serve You and to fulfil their destinies, IJN.*

Thursday August 15, 2019
Topic: RETURNING TO GOD FOR RESTORATION

Scriptures: "And ye shall know that I am in the midst of Israel, and that I am the Lord your God, and none else: and my people shall never be ashamed" (Joel 2:27).

Praise the Lord. Today is August 15th and is day #227 in year 2019. The number of days remaining to end this year is 138. By God's grace, no sin or any other thing will bring shame to you this season, and you will see the end of this year and beyond, safe and sound in the mighty name of Jesus.

Joel was a prophet in Judah sent to warn the Jews of God's impending judgment because of their sins and to urge them to repent and turn back to God. Having become prosperous, the people of Judah took God for granted and turned to self-righteousness, idolatry and sin. Joel warned them that this type of lifestyle would inevitably attract God's judgment on them. Joel pointed out that the punishment would include a terrible plague of locusts that would cover the land and devour the crops. Furthermore, the devastation wrought by locusts, cankerworm, caterpillars and palmerworms described as "my great army which I sent among you" (Joel 2:25) would be a foretaste of the coming judgment of God called "the day of the Lord" (Joel 2:1).

Included in Joel's message of judgment and need for repentance is an affirmation of God's kindness and grace and His readiness to forgive and restore that which had been lost to the plaque of locust (Joel 2: 12-25). In addition to restoration God made some wonderful promises that would follow their return and repentance in Joel 2: 26-27.

Have you sinned against the LORD and /or lost anything this year or in the past? God, who is not a respecter of persons, will do for you what he did for the people of Judah if you will repent and return to Him today. I see restoration galore in the horizon, IJN. Here is just a sample of scenarios from which you can prayerfully claim your own restoration by faith: a broken relationship with God due to sexual sin, a recent divorce, recently withdrawn from Choir, persistent head ache, a struggling business about to collapse, expired job contract, denied admission, denied business contract. **Prayer: *Father, restore unto me my lost glories and don't let me ever be put to shame, IJN.***

Friday August 16, 2019
Topic: GOD IS OMNISCIENT

Scriptures: "But there is a God in heaven that revealeth secrets, and maketh known to the king Nebuchadnezzar what shall be in the latter days. Thy dream, and the visions of thy head upon thy bed, are these" (Daniel 2:28).

Praise the Lord. Today is August 16th and is day #228 in year 2019. The number of days remaining to end this year is 137. By God's grace, you will receive divine revelation from the Lord in your activities this season, and you will see the end of this year and beyond, safe and sound in the mighty name of Jesus.

God is omniscient meaning God has complete or unlimited knowledge. The past, the present and the future are known to God. God can declare the end from the beginning because He is the Alpha and Omega (Isaiah 46:10; Rev. 1:8). All secrets are known to God as indicated in today's opening scripture and supported by Deuteronomy 29:29.

One king who was humbled by the power of God to reveal dreams is Nebuchadnezzar, king of Babylon. This king had a dream that troubled him such that he could not sleep. Worse still, he neither remembered the dream nor its interpretations. He commanded to call the magicians, and the astrologers, and the sorcerers, and the Chaldeans, to show the king his dreams and its interpretation but none could solve the mystery. Nebuchadnezzar sent out a decree that all the aforementioned people and other wise men of Babylon would be slain if no one could tell the king his dream and its interpretation (Dan 2: 2-13).

When Daniel learnt of the king's decree he arranged to meet with the king and requested for more time to be able to show the king all about the dream. When his request was granted, Daniel called his companions prayer partners Hananiah, Mishael, and Azariah for a night vigil. (Dan. 14-18). The outcome was that God revealed the secret of the dream unto Daniel in a night vision and he praised the Lord intensively (Dan. 2:19-23). Daniel requested a meeting with the king during which he gave the king detail of the dream and its interpretation. The king was very happy, gave thanks to God and promoted Daniel and his companions (see Dan. 2: 31-49). You too shall be promoted soon, IJN.

Actions /Prayer: (a) Pray for divine revelation that will make you a problem solver. (b) Read Isaiah 45:3 and pray for access to resources that will enhance your life and make you a blessing to God's work.

Saturday August 17, 2019
Topic: PERSECUTOR TURNED PREACHER

Scriptures: "And they that were with me saw indeed the light, and were afraid; but they heard not the voice of him that spake to me." (Acts 22:9).

Praise the Lord. Today is August 17th and is day #229 in year 2019. The number of days remaining to end this year is 136. By God's grace, you hear the inaudible and see the invisible this season, and you will end this year gloriously in the mighty name of Jesus.

The conversion of Saul from a persecutor of Christians to a preacher of the Gospel is a vivid demonstration of the power of God. The opening scripture above is in reference to his testimony about his own conversion, the detail of which is recorded in Acts. 9:1-17; 22:6–11; 26:12–18). Paul (whose pre-conversion name was Saul) was an aggressive persecutor of Christians in Jerusalem Acts 7: 54-60. Shortly after Stephen's death Saul mounted great persecution against the Church, arresting Christians and putting them into prison. He sought and received permission from the high priest to proceed to Damascus for the purpose of imprisoning more followers of Christ.

On his way to Damascus a bright light from heaven shone around Paul and his travelling companions. They all fell to the ground (Acts 26: 13-14). Only Paul heard the voice of Jesus, "Saul, Saul, why persecutest thou me?" (Acts 9:4b). Jesus told him he would become a minister to the Gentiles and was told to go to Damascus for further instruction. Temporarily blind, Paul was led into Damascus where a disciple called Ananias met him and prayed for him and he regained his sight after 3 days of fasting. Thereafter, he was baptized and "- -straightway he preached Christ in the synagogues, that he is the Son of God" (Acts 9:20). Among Paul's achievements are that he became the greatest apostle and he wrote (under the influence of the Holy Spirit) about 14 of the 27 books of the New Testament. Furthermore, he preached for Christ throughout the Roman empire on 3 missionary journeys. In addition, after his conversion no amount of persecution was able to stop him from serving God faithfully. ***Action/Prayer: If God can change a persecutor of Christians to a preacher of Christ, your own case shall not be impossible, IJN. Cry to God to transform your life for better, as you desire: From sinner to saint, barren to mother of many, poor to rich, sick to healthy, etc.***

Sunday August 18, 2019
Topic: PERSONALITY PANORAMA: SIMEON

Scriptures: "For mine eyes have seen thy salvation," (Luke 2:30).

Praise the Lord. Today is August 18th and is day #230 in year 2019. The number of days remaining to end this year is 135. By God's grace, Jesus Christ shall be honored in your life, and you will see the end of this year and beyond, safe and sound in the mighty name of Jesus.

There is so much we can learn from Bible personalities, especially those that are Godly and had strong connection with Jesus Christ. There are 5 people called Simeon in the Bible and we shall focus on one of them today: the one who met and received Jesus in the Temple in Jerusalem when He was brought for presentation to the Lord (Luke 2: 22-36). The other Simeons in the Bible can be found in Gen 35:23; Lk. 3:30; Acts 13:1 and Acts 15:14.

The Simeon who received Jesus Christ as a child in the Temple has so many wonderful virtues worthy of our emulation (Lk. 2: 25-35). These virtues include (1) he was just and devout (that is he was pious, holy, feared God and devout to God), (2) he was waiting for the consolation of Israel, (3) the Holy Ghost was upon him, (4) he had the gift of revelation and knew the promise that the Holy Ghost teaches all things (5) he came by the Spirit into the Temple with the right attitude to worship in Spirit and in truth, (6) he loved Jesus, took him up in his arms, and blessed God (7) he prayed to God to be permitted to depart this world in peace, having lived his full age according to the promise in Exodus 23:26. (8) he also blessed the parents of Jesus and prophesied into the life of Jesus (he knew the value of edifying words (Eph. 4:29).

How important is salvation to you? Simeon took it so seriously that he refused to die until his eyes have seen it as it was prophesied to him. If you have not accepted Jesus Christ as your Lord and Savior, do it today before it is too late. May you not die without seeing your Salvation, IJN. Every one of us must do as apostle Paul admonishes us, "- - work out your own salvation with fear and trembling". (Phil. 2:12).

In the remaining 135 days of this year God wants you to still "see" many blessings that you can possess. Without vision you can't have possession. Therefore, begin to see what you desire to possess: healing, peace, joy, job, saved souls, fruit of the womb, victory, ..., etc. ***Prayer: Father, thank You for my salvation; please anoint me afresh with the oly Ghost and with power, let me see and possess, favor, honor, peace, IJN.***

Monday August 19, 2019
Topic: THE SHEEP AND THE SHEPHERD

Scriptures: "The Lord is my shepherd; I shall not want." (Psa. 23:1, KJV)

Praise the Lord. Today is August 19th and is day #231 in year 2019. The number of days remaining to end this year is 134. By God's grace, all your needs shall be met this season, and you will see the end of this year and beyond, safe and sound in the mighty name of Jesus.

David is said to be the writer of Psalm 23, verse 1 of which is the focus of today's ministration. A shepherd is a person who herds, tends and guards sheep. A shepherd can also refer to a person who protects, guides, or watches over a person or group of people. David fits very well to each of these 2 definitions. In both cases he had tremendous experiences. He even fought and killed a lion and a bear to protect the sheep under his care (1 Sam. 17:34-36). When the time for career change was ripe for David God chose him over all his brothers to be anointed as king of Israel. He ruled as a king for 40 years during which he learnt many lessons in terms of looking after people and himself been looked after by God when he was running for his life from his enemies.

In terms of Shepherd-hood, David had threefold experience: (a) he was a shepherd of sheep, (b) he was a shepherd of people, and (c) he was under the shepherd-hood of God. Based on these balanced experiences David penned Psalm 23 under the inspiration of God. He saw himself as the sheep and the Lord his Shepherd. As verse one of this Psalm says when the Lord is your shepherd you will lack nothing. The remaining verses of this Psalm focus on possible needs of the sheep and how the shepherd meets all of them. It is a covenant relationship in which the sheep stays peaceful, protected and provided for so long she remains in the sheepfold of the Shepherd.

Jesus Christ is the good Shepherd (John 10:11, 14). Anyone who gives his/ her life to Him automatically becomes a sheep in His pasture (Psalm 100:3). Such people, as long as they remain connected with the good Shepherd, will enjoy divine peace, provisions and protection because God's goodness and mercy will follow them all the days of their life. Are you in the sheepfold of Jesus? If not get in today, IJN

Prayer: Father, I am Your sheep, let Your goodness and mercy follow me forever, IJN

Tuesday August 20, 2019
Topic: THE SHEEP AND THE SHEPHERD II

Scriptures: "He maketh me to lie down in green pastures: he leadeth me beside the still waters." (Psalm. 23:2, KJV)

Praise the Lord. Today is August 20th and is day #232 in year 2019. The number of days remaining to end this year is 133. By God's grace, you will enjoy a serene life this season, and you will see the end of this year and beyond, safe and sound in the mighty name of Jesus.

The opening scripture for today is alluding to how the sheep is so well catered for by the shepherd such that the sheep is satisfied that she is resting, lying down in green pasture by the still waters. Hunger is not a problem for the sheep as she is protected and guided to the place where she always has easy access to fresh pasture and water to satisfy her needs.

The work of the shepherd in ensuring the sheep is well fed and catered for appropriately depicts the work of Jesus Christ (the Good Shepherd) to His redeemed followers (the flock). In a prophecy Ezekiel received God characterizes this work declaring, "I will feed them in a good pasture, and upon the high mountains of Israel shall their fold be: there shall they lie in a good fold, and in a fat pasture shall they feed upon the mountains of Israel" (Ezek. 34:14).

In his exposition, John Gill surmises that the green pasture in today's opening scripture may symbolize the covenant of grace, its blessings and promises, where there is delicious feeding; likewise, the fulness of grace in Christ, from whence grace for grace is received. Furthermore, Gill also suggests that the still water may designate the everlasting love of God which is like a river, the streams whereof make glad the hearts of his people.

Do you have an established relationship with Jesus Christ as your Lord and Savior? Jesus Christ declares "I am the good shepherd, and know my sheep, and am known of mine" (John 10:14). Why not be one of His sheep today so that you can begin to enjoy satisfactory livelihood in His green pasture!

Prayer; Father, feed me physically and spiritually until I want no more. Let Your praise be in my mouth continually, IJN

Wednesday August 21, 2019
Topic: THE SHEEP AND THE SHEPHERD III

Scriptures: "He restoreth my soul: he leadeth me in the paths of righteousness for his name's sake." (Psalm. 23:3, KJV)

Praise the Lord. Today is August 21st and is day #233 in year 2019. The number of days remaining to end this year is 132. By God's grace, you shall be fully restored (spiritually, physically and otherwise to the level ordained for you by the Lord, IJN

The ministrations in the past two days have focused on Psalm 23 which is an allegory in which David uses the relationship between a sheep and a shepherd to describe the relationship between himself (or Christ followers) and the Lord. In verse 1 we have established that just as the sheep lacks nothing because all her needs are met by the shepherd, so also followers of Christ are well catered for by the Lord (Jesus Christ) who is all sufficient. God's loving, protective care is perfect, his sheep (believers) need nothing else. Yesterday, we looked at verse 2 and pointed out the adequacy of the provisions of the shepherd for the sheep which enables the sheep to lie down peacefully at the green pasture. So also, the Good Shepherd leads His beloved ones to place of sustenance and rest.

Today's ministration focuses on verse 3 of the Psalm 23. Occasionally, a sheep may be temporarily separated from the shepherd / rest of the flock for one reason or the other. In such cases the loving shepherd will do what is necessary (diagnose and treat for sickness, feeds, refreshes, search for, etc. to restore (bring back) the erring sheep to the fold as illustrated by the parable of the lost sheep told by Jesus (Luke 15: 1-7). In like manner, followers of Jesus Christ need soul restoration whenever backsliding occurs due to spiritual carelessness, secret sins, falling into temptation, etc. The good shepherd, Jesus Christ, desires intimate involvement with his followers wanting to lead them in the right way, in truth and holiness.

God's restoration is all encompassing, spiritually, financially, etc. All the believer has to do is to heed God's loving call for the him/her to repent and return to Him. As the father of the prodigal son did, God is willing to receive and restore any sinner or backslider who will repent and return to Him (Joel 2: 12-27). I decree full restoration for you this year, IJN. **Prayer: Father, restore unto me in full the joy of thy salvation and any other blessings I have lost, IJN.**

Thursday August 22, 2019
Topic: THE SHEEP AND THE SHEPHERD IV

Scriptures: "Yea, though I walk through the valley of the shadow of death, I will fear no evil: for thou art with me; thy rod and thy staff they comfort me." (Psalm. 23:4, KJV)

Praise the Lord. Today is August 22nd and is day #234 in year 2019. The number of days remaining to end this year is 131. By God's grace, fear and death shall not come near you this season because of the Lord's presence with you, and you will see the end of this year and beyond, safe and sound in the mighty name of Jesus.

Today we continue our study of Psalm 23 in terms of David's allegory of likening the relationship between himself and the Lord to that of the sheep and the shepherd. Our application so far has shown that the Lord, the good Shepherd, (a) loves and cares for His flock (followers) and doesn't want them to lack anything, (b) keeps them in peace and adequately provided for, and (c) always ready to restore back to the fold / Himself any erring or backsliding follower that repents and returns to Him.

Another lesson we can learn from the sheep-shepherd relationship is divine protection. This can be seen in the opening scripture for today. While going through the valleys and hills and hazardous terrain, the sheep is constantly facing the risk of death from enemies such as dogs, wolves, bear, lions, snakes, cold, heat, etc. However, the shepherd is there to guide, guard and defend the sheep from potential predators. The shepherd uses his rod and staff to stop the sheep from going to dangerous zone. Like the sheep, followers of the Lord are also constantly facing the risk of death from the devil who goes about as a roaring lion seeking whom to devour (1 Pet 5:8). The ceaseless job of the devil is to steal, to kill and to destroy (Jn 10:10b). However, faithful believers are secured and protected in the presence and power of the good Shepherd.

The valley of the shadow of death the followers of Christ walk through include many afflictions they face, sickness, principalities, powers and spiritual wickedness in high places. The good news is that the believers do not have to fear; the mighty hand of the believer's Lord can save, (Ps. 138:7). As 2019 counts down your divine protection will count upward, IJN.

Prayer: Father, deliver me from all evils and let my faith in You swallow all fears, IJN

Friday August 23, 2019
Topic: THE SHEEP AND THE SHEPHERD V

Scriptures: "Thou preparest a table before me in the presence of mine enemies: thou anointest my head with oil; my cup runneth over" (Psalm. 23:5 KJV)

Praise the Lord. Today is August 23rd and is day #235 in year 2019. The number of days remaining to end this year is 130. By God's grace, you shall be satisfied to the overflow this season, and you will see the end of this year and beyond, safe and sound in the mighty name of Jesus.

In the first 4 verses of Psalm 23, David has already pointed out to us that he suffers no lack because His God provides for him, his God protects him, and His God restores him. In today's opening scripture David continues his testimony and appreciation of what God has done for him. David describes how a bountiful and sumptuous banquet is provided by a most liberal and benevolent God who has power to protect him though he is surrounded by enemies. Furthermore, David said God anoints his head with oil and his cup runs over.

David's main point is that God can give life in abundance and can decorate those who honor him with honor though they be surrounded by enemies. On God's table of abundance for the believer there is "all you can eat" including the daily loads of benefits from God (Psalm 68:19). I decree this will be your portion, IJN.

Prayer: Father, let me be a reference point in terms of your abundant blessings and let my testimony be 'I never know You will honor me this way', IJN

Saturday August 24, 2019
Topic: THE SHEEP AND THE SHEPHERD VI

Scriptures: "Surely goodness and mercy shall follow me all the days of my life: and I will dwell in the house of the LORD forever" (Psalm. 23:6 KJV).

Praise the Lord. Today is August 24th and is day #236 in year 2019. The number of days remaining to end this year is 129. By God's grace, your testimony this season shall be 'I never know You can honor me this way, thank You JESUS', and you will see the end of this year and beyond, safe and sound in the mighty name of Jesus.

Let us recap major application lessons we have Learnt so far from Psalm 23, verse by verse: v1: The all sufficient Lord is the Shepherd, therefore His followers (the sheep) suffer no lack. v2: The Lord provides, satisfies and gives peace to his followers. v3: The Lord receives and restores completely all erring followers that returns to Him in repentance. v4: The Lord protects his followers from death and evil by His power and ever presence with them. v5: The Lord prepares a table of 'all you can eat' for His followers and decorates them with overflowing anointing of gladness.

Having recounted the blessings which God had bestowed upon him in verses 1-5, David now in verse 6, as in opening scripture for today, expresses his confidence of the flow of these blessings continuously from the Lord to him perpetually. This is the lot of the believer as well.

David said goodness and mercy will follow him all the days of his life and that he will dwell in the house of the Lord forever (v6). David's confidence in declaring this resolution is based on his knowledge of the Lord's track record of goodness (Ps. 73:1) and of God been plenteous in mercy (Ps. 86:5). Furthermore, David knew that the Bible declares, "Blessed are they that dwell in thy house: they will be still praising thee" (Ps. 84:4). Therefore, the more you want your blessings to count up this year, the more you should 'dwell' in the house of the Lord. In other words, let the zeal of God's house consume you, and you shall be blessed tremendously, IJN.

Prayer: Father, let Your goodness and mercy follow me all the days of my life and let me dwell in Your house forever, IJN.

Sunday August 25, 2019
Topic: BLESSING, NOT CURSE FROM BALAAM

Scriptures: "And he took up his parable, and said, Balak the king of Moab hath brought me from Aram, out of the mountains of the east, saying, Come, curse me Jacob, and come, defy Israel" (Numbers. 23:7).

Praise the Lord. Today is August 25th and is day #237 in year 2019. The number of days remaining to end this year is 128. By God's grace, you shall be blessed and be a blessing and every curse concerning you is broken; you will see the end of this year and beyond, safe and sound in the mighty name of Jesus.

Balaam was a prophet hired by Balak the king of Moab to curse Jacob and defy Israel as indicated in today's opening scripture. Balak felt intimidated and was afraid of the large number of the Israelites who have just defeated the Amalekites. Balak felt if the Israelites were cursed it would be easier for the Moabites to defeat them. Balaam enquired from God if he should consent to Balak's request. God said unto Balaam, "Thou shalt not go with them; thou shalt not curse the people: for they are blessed" (Num 22:12).

Although Balak increased the value of the reward for cursing and made several other attempts to get Balaam to curse Israel, Balaam refused to be an accomplice without getting clearance from God. On one occasion Balaam sent Balak's servants back to Him in Num 22:18. Due to Balak's insistence on getting Israel cursed, coupled with Balaam's apparent interest in the rewards offered by Balak, God gave Balaam his permissive will to go to meet Balak. However, that mission was aborted as God angrily sent an angel to withstand Balaam's ash (Num 23: 22-35).

Despite several sacrificial and burnt offerings by Balak and Balaam (to win God's approval) God was adamantly against cursing Jacob and Israel. Instead Balaam was commanded to bless Jacob and Israel. God sent several messages through Balaam to Balak, that Jacob and Israel could not suffer any hurt or harm (Num. 23:23).

Do you know there are still many 'Balaks' today hiring 'Balaams' to curse and hurt other people? You can sanitize and immunize yourself against such curses by giving your life to Jesus and asking Him to cover you with His blood. You are blessed and cannot cursed, IJN.

Prayer: Father, break and render null and void all curses existing or potential over me and my family, IJN.

Monday August 26, 2019
Topic: HAVING GODLY MINDSET

Scriptures: "How shall I curse, whom God hath not cursed? or how shall I defy, whom the LORD hath not defied?" (Num. 23:8)

Praise the Lord. Today is August 26th and is day #238 in year 2019. The number of days remaining to end this year is 127. By God's grace, no one will be able to tamper you're your destiny this season, and you will see the end of this year and beyond, safe and sound in the mighty name of Jesus.

In yesterday's ministration we saw how God told Balaam to reject the invitation of Balak to curse Jacob and Israel. Instead of cursing them Balaam was commanded to bless them and that is what he did.

What Balak wanted Balaam to do is akin to the function of a hired killer. Though the reward offered was tempting to Balaam, thank God he listened to God's counsel and did not succumb to the temptation.

Not only should a Christian not be an accomplice, the believer must have the mindset of Jesus Christ (Phil 2:5). This is the point expressed in today's opening scripture. God put in the mind of Balaam to declare to Balak that it is futile of him (or any one) to curse Jacob or defy Israel when God has not done so. The believer must guard his/her mouth and bridle his/her tongue to avoid anti God communication (James 1:26). If God has not called a person 'a fool', 'a failure', 'hopeless', etc., don't call such person those names.

Prayer: Father, let me have the mindset of Jesus Christ and don't let me be the object or subject of whatever You have not ordained, IJN

Tuesday August 27, 2019
Topic: DISSENSION AMONG DETRACTORS

Scriptures: "And there arose a great cry: and the scribes that were of the Pharisees' part arose, and strove, saying, we find no evil in this man: but if a spirit or an angel hath spoken to him, let us not fight against God" (Acts: 23:9).

Praise the Lord. Today is August 27th and is day #239 in year 2019. The number of days remaining to end this year is 126. By God's grace, every conspiracy to attack you shall fail woefully, and you will see the end of this year and beyond, safe and sound in the mighty name of Jesus.

Shortly after his conversion Paul began to face persecutions. In Jerusalem, he was accused and brought to defend himself before the Sanhedrin (a council of high priests made up of Pharisees and Sadducees sects). The 2 sects have fundamental differences in their beliefs. For example, the Sadducees say that there is no resurrection, neither angel, nor spirit: but the Pharisees confess both. (Acts 23:8).

In his defense strategy Paul took advantage of the differences between the 2 sects by revealing that he was of the Pharisee sect. No sooner had he done this that a dissension and a division arose between the 2 sects. God used this division to save Paul from been killed by his detractors: "As the conflict grew more violent, the commander was afraid they would tear Paul apart. So, he ordered his soldiers to go and rescue him by force and take him back to the fortress." (Acts 23:10, NLT).

I decree that anyone or group of persons planning to detract or derail you or destroy your destiny shall be struck by dissension and confusion IJN.

Prayer: Father, teach me strategies that will bring dissension and confusion into the camp of my enemies and scatter all my dream killers, IJN

Wednesday August 28, 2019
Topic: RAISING CHRIST-LIKE CHILDREN

Scriptures: "And the child grew, and waxed strong in spirit, filled with wisdom: and the grace of God was upon him" (Lk 2:40)

Praise the Lord. Today is August 28th and is day #240 in year 2019. The number of days remaining to end this year is 125. By God's grace, you will increase in strength, wisdom and grace of God this season, and you will see the end of this year and beyond, safe and sound in the mighty name of Jesus.

Jesus Christ was a perfect child. He grew up to become very relevant and accomplished great things because he had very strong foundation. The upbringing of Jesus provides us with some insights how we can raise successful children like Him

Today's opening scripture talks about 3 main attributes noticeable in baby Jesus (1) he grew and waxed strong in the spirit, (2) filled with wisdom, and (3) and the grace of God was upon him. These key attributes are essential elements that must accompany the upbringing of any child that will be Christ-like.

The Holy Spirit (HS) does many things in the life of a person including supply of power (Acts 1:8) and comforting and teaching of all things (Jn. 14:26). Jesus Christ had abundance of the HS because he was conceived by it (Lk 1:28-35) and was anointed with it (Acts 10:38). The generosity of God makes the HS available to anyone who will ask Him by faith (Lk 11:13).

Parents or guardians should start praying for their children from conception to receive the HS. The same goes for wisdom, grace and other desirable spiritual gifts that will help the child become like Jesus. Samuel started hearing from God very early in his life. The same can happen for your children, IJN.

In addition to the 3 attributes discussed above we must train our children in the words, ways and works of the Lord right from when they are young so that when they are old, they will not depart from God (Pro 22:6). Invest in the spiritual and other aspects of your children and they shall be great and Christ like, IJN.

Prayer: Father, please bless my children and let them be like Jesus Christ, Amen.

Thursday August 29, 2019
Topic: ATTRACTING BLESSINGS LIKE ABRAHAM

Scriptures: "Now Abraham was old, well advanced in years. And the Lord had blessed Abraham in all things." (Gen. 24:1)

Praise the Lord. Today is August 29th and is day #241 in year 2019. The number of days remaining to end this year is 124. By God's grace, the anointing for long life and for being blessed on Abraham will rob on you this season, and you will see the end of this year and beyond, safe and sound in the mighty name of Jesus.

When it comes to Godly blessings Abraham can be described as a reference point. In today's opening scripture we are told God had blessed Abraham in all things. Additionally, When God told Abraham to sacrifice his only son and he was ready to do it, God swore by himself telling Abraham, "in blessing, I will bless thee." (Gen. 22:17). Abraham was so blessed that a type of blessing was specifically called "the blessing of Abraham " (Gen. 28:4). The first time the word 'blessing' occurred in the Bible was in reference to Abraham whom God told, "--I will bless thee, and make thy name great; and thou shalt be a blessing (Gen. 12:2). In other words, Abraham would be a source of blessing to others.

The Bible declares that, "Through Christ Jesus, God has blessed the Gentiles with the same blessing he promised to Abraham, so that we who are believers might receive the promised Holy Spirit through faith."(Gal 3:14, NLT). Thus, anyone who, by faith, has received Jesus Christ as his/her Savior can attract the same blessings that Abraham received.

The most important blessing we should secure first is the blessing of salvation through faith in Jesus Christ (Matt 6:33). Then other blessings can be attracted as we incorporate into our faith other virtues (as did Abraham) such as work, worship, prayer, righteous living, obedience, giving, hope, patience, God's word. As believers we are destined to be blessed and we shall be blessed, IJN.

Prayer: Father, Like Abraham let me live long and be blessed in all things, including those in Deuteronomy 28:1-14, IJN.

Friday August 30, 2019
Topic: SERVING GOD STEADFASTLY

Scriptures: "And they continued stedfastly in the apostles' doctrine and fellowship, and in breaking of bread, and in prayers" (Acts 2:42).

Praise the Lord. Today is August 30th and is day #242 in year 2019. The number of days remaining to end this year is 123. By God's grace, you will be devoted and steadfast in serving the Lord this season, and you will see the end of this year and beyond, safe and sound in the mighty name of Jesus.

The Christian race is a marathon one that has no stop until Jesus comes to take the believer. Once you have a relationship with Jesus, loyalty and continuity are required for deriving maximum benefits from the relationship. Several scriptures support this fact. The Bible says only "-- he that endureth to the end shall be saved" (Matt. 10:2). Furthermore, God said his soul will have no pleasure in any one that accepts Him by faith and then draw back (Heb. 10:38). What a serious warning to backsliders!

In today's opening scripture, we see that the early Christians had no room for backsliding. Instead, they served master Jesus steadfastly. They embraced His doctrines of peace, pardon, righteousness, and salvation without looking back. In fact, they took ownership of Christ's doctrine to the extent it was called the 'apostles' doctrine'. How passionate are we about the Gospel of Jesus? If we own it, get committed to it and preach salvation as if our life depends on it, there will be many more souls saved in the world today.

The early believers did not only preach the gospel with passion, they also put into practice what they preached. Furthermore, they integrated fellowshipping together, having holy communion and/or food together and praying together into their preaching. The result was that a conducive atmosphere was created for more miracles, signs and wonders and winning of more souls to take place.

In this end time, we can still enjoy revival like the early believers if we are determined to serve God with gladness and obey Paul's injunction: "Therefore, my beloved brethren, be ye stedfast, unmoveable, always abounding in the work of the Lord, forasmuch as ye know that your labour is not in vain in the Lord" (1 Cor. 15:58). Strife for steadfastness! *Prayer: Father, please give me the grace to serve You with gladness and with steadfastness, IJN.*

Saturday August 31, 2019
Topic: CRITERIA FOR BEING IN GOD'S PRESENCE

Scriptures: "Who shall ascend into the hill of the LORD? or who shall stand in his holy place?" (Psalm 24:3)

Praise the Lord. Today is August 31st and is day #243 in year 2019. The number of days remaining to end this year is 122. By God's grace, you will see the end of this year and beyond, safe and sound in the mighty name of Jesus.

The opening scripture for today asks 2 questions whose answers are in verses 4 and 5 of the same chapter. Every question of your life shall receive answers that will favor you, IJN. Briefly, salvation, holy and righteous living will be primary requirements to ascending to heaven to be in God's presence in His abode. You will not miss heaven, IJN.

This last day of the month of August will be the last day of sickness, sorrow, poverty, problems, fruitlessness, failure, and anything evil in your life, IJN. From now and henceforth, God will clean your hands, purify your heart and sanctify your entire body and you will ascend to peace, prosperity and be in God's presence always, IJN. Happy month ending!

Prayer: Father, let me be worthy of ascending to Your holy place to dwell in Your presence forever, IJN.

Sunday September 1, 2019
Topic: KNOWLEDGE FACTOR IN HOUSE BUILDING

Scriptures: "And by knowledge shall the chambers be filled with all precious and pleasant riches" (Proverbs 24:4)

Praise the Lord. Today is September 1st and is day #244 in year 2019. The number of days remaining to end this year is 121. By God's grace, you will have the wisdom, knowledge, understanding and riches you need to build and furnish you house to glorify God, and you will see the end of this year and beyond, safe and sound in the mighty name of Jesus.

Welcome to the September, the 9th month of the year. There are 9 virtues constituting the "fruit of the spirit" viz: love, joy, peace, longsuffering, gentleness, goodness, faith, meekness, temperance (Gal. 5: 22-23). May each one of these 9 virtues count upward in your life this month and forever IJN.

One critical and common factor necessary to be in place for optimal operation of the aforementioned-virtues of the fruit of the spirit is wisdom. No wonder the Bible says, "Wisdom is the principal thing; therefore, get wisdom: and with all thy getting get understanding" (Pro 4:7). Indeed, wisdom is the principal thing because the Bible equates Jesus Christ to "wisdom of God" (1 Cor. 1:24). Thus, Jesus Christ is the most superior and most foundational wisdom any one needs. If you give your life to Jesus Christ as your savior, not only will He endow you with wisdom, He can add all other things to you (Matt. 6:33).

Today's opening scripture and the verse preceding it declares "By wisdom a house is built, and by understanding it is established; by knowledge the rooms are filled with all precious and pleasant riches" (Pro. 24: 3-4, ESV). There are physical and spiritual houses. Wisdom, knowledge and understanding are needed to build and furnish every type of house as implied in today's opening scripture. Jesus Christ is the ultimate source of wisdom. He is generous and liberal, and He has promised to give wisdom to anyone that will ask Him by faith without doubting (James 1:5-8).

Prayer: Father, endow me with the wisdom I need to build all the physical and spiritual houses of my life, IJN.

Monday September 2, 2019
Topic: REVIEWING AND RECOMMITTING TO GOD

Scriptures: "I sent Moses also and Aaron, and I plagued Egypt, according to that which I did among them: and afterward I brought you out" (Josh. 24:5).

Praise the Lord. Today is September 2nd and is day #245 in year 2019. The number of days remaining to end this year is 120. By God's grace, you will see the end of this year and beyond, safe and sound in the mighty name of Jesus.

Appreciation is one thing that believers must learn to do more of, both to God and to each other. Appreciation is a form of testimony and the Bible says we overcome by the blood of the Lamb (Jesus) and the word of our testimony (Rev. 12:11).

The opening scripture for today is part of Joshua's testimony about how God has helped the Israelites to get out of bondage in the land of Egypt. Shortly before he died Joshua summoned all the tribes of Israel to present themselves before the Lord at Shechem. Then, Joshua, in the name of the Lord, rehearsed to them the many great and good things the Lord had done for them, from the time of their ancestor Abraham to the time God freed them and settled them in Canaan. Furthermore, Joshua exhorted them to fear and serve the Lord, and reject idols.

The people agreed and said to Joshua "--The LORD our God will we serve, and his voice will we obey". So, Joshua made a covenant with the people that day, and set them a statute and an ordinance in Shechem (Josh, 24: 24-25).

Like Joshua did for the Israelites, we should review what the Lord has done for us and recommit to Him. In year 2019 alone, the Lord has loaded you with benefits for 245 days as of today. He has fought many battles for you seen and unseen. What bondage (sins, sickness, temptations, lack, enemy attack, etc.) has He brought you out of? Why don't you praise Him and recommit to serve Him better in the remaining 120 days of this year and forever. He will bless your bread and your water, IJN (Exo. 23:25)

Prayer: Father, give me a heart of gratitude and appreciation, and let me be an overcomer perpetually, IJN

Tuesday September 3, 2019
Topic: AVOID HARMING THE LORD'S ANOINTED

Scriptures: "And he said unto his men, The LORD forbid that I should do this thing unto my master, the LORD'S anointed, to stretch forth mine hand against him, seeing he is the anointed of the LORD" (1 Sam 24:6).

Praise the Lord. Today is September 3rd and is day #246 in year 2019. The number of days remaining to end this year is 119. By God's grace, you will not maltreat or dishonor the anointed people of God, and you will see the end of this year and beyond, safe and sound in the mighty name of Jesus.

It is important to avoid hurting or harming anointed servants of God even when it is obvious, they are wrong. David's refusal to accept the advice of his men to kill Saul (his pursuer) even when he had the opportunity is instructive as to how to treat erring anointed servants of God.

Saul started chasing David to kill him shortly after David was anointed as king to replace Saul. On one occasion Saul gathered 3000 strong men to pursue David to the wilderness of Engedi. David had the opportunity to kill Saul inside a cave in Engedi where Saul was deep asleep. David merely cut off the skirt of Saul's robe privily. As indicated in the opening scripture above David said he would not stretch forth his hand against Saul, seeing he is the anointed of the LORD (1 Sam. 24:1-22)

Be careful how you treat anointed servants of God. God specifically said, "Touch not mine anointed, and do my prophets no harm" (Ps.105:15). If you have issues with an anointed servant of God, use every available means to resolve things prayerfully and peacefully. Don't make decisions based on rumors. Humbly approach anointed servants of God to confirm what you have heard. Don't play God in the life of an anointed servant of God. Let God to whom they will be answerable be the judge.

Remember also that through your love, care and prayer an erring servant of God may be forgiven and restored by God. I believe divine credits will accrue to you from the restoration of such anointed servant of God. **Prayer: *Father, instead of hurting and harming those You have anointed, make me a destiny helper to them, IJN.***

Wednesday September 4, 2019
Topic: GIVE GOD YOUR LIFE'S GATES

Scriptures: "Lift up your heads, O ye gates; and be ye lift up, ye everlasting doors; and the King of glory shall come in" (Ps. 24:7).

Praise the Lord. Today is September 4th and is day #247 in year 2019. The number of days remaining to end this year is 118. By God's grace, the devil shall fail in any attempt to stop the Lord from showing up for you, and you will see the end of this year and beyond, safe and sound in the mighty name of Jesus.

Gates and doors are important particularly for providing, security and entry and exit to a place. The Ark of God represents the awesome presence of God and David's point in today's opening scripture is that the glorious God should have free, unhindered and majestic entry to the place prepared for Him. God is still interested in coming into the lives of those who will allow Him. He says, "Behold, I stand at the door, and knock: if any man hear my voice, and open the door, I will come in to him, and will sup with him, and he with me" (Rev 3:20). If you open the door of your life to God, He will come in and make you a new person full of abundant life.

Just as God wants to come into your life so does Satan. Apostle Paul said, "For a great door and effectual is opened unto me, and there are many adversaries". (1 Cor. 16:9). When the children of God gathered, Satan came to gather with them (Job 1: 6 & 2:1). Who comes in to your life depends largely on you. Sin and ungodly living will grant Satan easy entry into your life while acceptance of God's invitation to come in and living righteously will ward Satan off as God would have already been in control.

Note that the believer's life is inseparable from 'gates'. The body is full of gates (mouth, nose, ears, anus, countless hair pores, etc. Furthermore, in pursuit of daily activities, the believer inevitably enters and exits all kinds of gates. The more the believer connects with God the more these gates will lift up their heads for God to come in. The reverse is true because where God is absent Satan will gladly take dominion. Satan will fail concerning you, IJN.

Prayer: Father, let all the gates of my life be opened to You to come in and let my life's gates be shut against Satan, IJN.

Thursday September 5, 2019
Topic: PREVENTING PRIDEFUL PROJECTS

Scriptures: "Having gone through the entire land for nine months and twenty days, they returned to Jerusalem. Joab reported the number of people to the king. There were 800,000 capable warriors in Israel who could handle a sword, and 500,000 in Judah." (2 Sam 24: 8-9).

Praise the Lord. Today is September 5th and is day #248 in year 2019. The number of days remaining to end this year is 117. By God's grace, you will see the end of this year and beyond, safe and sound in the mighty name of Jesus.

As believers we cannot afford to allow pride to drive our activities. Among the 7 things that God hates that are an abomination to Him, pride is the first one (Pro. 6:16-19). Incidentally, it is the same pride that tends to rank number one in terms of Satan's temptations thrown at the believer. The believer must prayerfully be on guard to prevent engaging in projects motivated by pride.

Today's opening scripture has to do with one of the projects David embarked upon towards the end of his life - census of Israel and Judah. Unfortunately, it was Satan, not God that pushed David to doing this: "Satan rose up against Israel and caused David to take a census of the people of Israel" (1 Chron. 21: 1-2, NLT). David assigned Joab the commander of the army to conduct the census.

As soon as Joab brought the census result to David his heart smote him because David realized he had sinned greatly. In the meantime, God had sent prophet Gad to David to inform him the nature of his punishment. David was asked to make a choice out of 3 punishments for Israel: (1) "three years of famine throughout your land", (2) "three months of fleeing from your enemies", or (3) "three days of severe plague throughout your land" (2 Sam 24: 13). David was in a dilemma, but he chose option 3 saying he would rather fall into God's hand than into man (v. 14). So, the Lord sent a plague that killed 70,000 people in 3 days. As the angel was preparing to destroy Jerusalem, the Lord relented and said to the death angel, "Stop! That is enough (v 16). Gad directed David to build an altar to the Lord at the place where the plagued was stopped and David did so in appreciation of God's answer to his prayer for stopping the plague. I decree that no death angel will come near you and your family, IJN. ***Prayer: Father, deliver me from Satanic temptations and don't let me embark on anything that You have not ordained, IJN.***

Friday September 6, 2019
Topic: BUSY DOING GOD'S BUSINESS?

Scriptures: "And he said unto them, How is it that ye sought me? wist ye not that I must be about my Father's business?" (Luke 2: 49).

Praise the Lord. Today is September 6th and is day #249 in year 2019. The number of days remaining to end this year is 116. By God's grace, you accord the Lord's work the highest priority, and you will see the end of this year and beyond, safe and sound in the mighty name of Jesus.

Today's opening scripture contains the first recorded spoken words of Jesus Christ. When Jesus was 12 years old His earthly parents (Joseph and Mary) took Him along to Jerusalem for the Passover Feast. After the feast, "- -they returned, the child Jesus tarried behind in Jerusalem; and Joseph and his mother knew not of it" (Lk. 24:43). The parents of Jesus continued their journey for one day seeking Jesus, assuming He was in the company of other family members who were ahead in the journey. When they didn't find him, they returned to Jerusalem looking for him. After three days, "they found him in the temple, sitting in the midst of the doctors, both hearing them, and asking them questions" (v.46).

All the people who heard Jesus discussed and asked questions in the Temple were astonished at His understanding and answers. When His parents saw him, they were amazed, and Mary couldn't help but asked, "Son, why hast thou thus dealt with us? behold, thy father and I have sought thee sorrowing" (v.48). Jesus answered this question with the 2 questions contained in the opening scripture above. Jesus then travelled back to Nazareth with His parents "--and was obedient to them - -" (vv. 51-52).

The lessons to learn from this story include: (1) God is the ultimate and preeminent Father and His business must be accorded the highest priority (Mt. 6:33; Lk. 19:13). (2) We must not neglect our responsibility to our family because of divine assignment. In the story above we see that Jesus was obedient to His parents while doing His Father's business" (4). Doing God's business, the right way attracts divine rewards as it did for Jesus in this story: "And Jesus increased in wisdom and stature, and in favour with God and man" (v. 52). Receive your own rewards, IJN. **Prayer: *Father, give me the grace to do Your business satisfactorily to You, IJN.***

Saturday September 7, 2019
Topic: REBELLION AGAINST MOSES

Scriptures: "They (Korah, Dathan and Abiram) incited a rebellion against Moses along with 250 other leaders of the community, all prominent members of the assembly, Then fire blazed forth from the LORD and burned up the 250 men who were offering incense" (Numbers 16: 2 & 35).

Praise the Lord. Today is September 7th and is day #250 in year 2019. The number of days remaining to end this year is 115. By God's grace, you will never be involved in rebellion against your God-ordained leader, and you will see the end of this year and beyond, safe and sound in the mighty name of Jesus.

Moses was specially chosen by God to be the leader used to deliver the Israelites from the bondage of Pharaoh and Egypt (Exo. 3). Aside from Jesus, there is probably no other prophet on earth closer to God than Moses. God's testimony of Moses' closeness to Him supports this claim (Num 12: 6-8).

As indicated in the opening scripture for today, Korah, Dathan and Abiram conspired with 250 other community leaders to rebel against Moses and Aaron. They accused them in Num 16:3. Moses knew that greed, jealousy and hunger for power of the priesthood primarily motivated the rebellion. Moses then told Korah "The Lord is the one you and your followers are really revolting against! For who is Aaron that you are complaining about him?" (v. 11, NLT).

Moses arranged a "contest" similar to what Elijah did with the prophets of Baal on Mount Carmel (1 Kgs. 18: 20-40). The contest was a means for God to show who is holy (Num 16:16-36). As Moses predicted, an unusual thing happened: The earth opened its mouth and swallowed Korah and all his coconspirators and their families and belongings (v. 32). Only Korah's sons were spared (Num 26:11).

Some of the lessons to learn in this story include (1) Be content and thankful for what you have instead of trying to get more than you deserve, (2) Avoid envy and jealousy, they are counterproductive (3) Rebellion, conspiracy and complaining against God's servants may be a deadly mission, avoid it. ***Prayer: Father, Let the earth open to swallow all my problems and anything and anybody anywhere who has resolved relentlessly to tamper with my destiny and life, IJN.***

Sunday September 8, 2019
Topic: BE A PRAISE FANATIC

Scriptures: "O Lord, thou art my God; I will exalt thee, I will praise thy name; for thou hast done wonderful things; thy counsels of old are faithfulness and truth." (Isaiah 25:1).

Praise the Lord. Today is September 8th and is day #251 in year 2019. The number of days remaining to end this year is 114. By God's grace, you will increase your praise to God, and you will see the end of this year and beyond, safe and sound in the mighty name of Jesus.

As we countdown this year, believers must not lose sight of counting up praise to the Almighty God. Any believer who does not accord high priority to praising God is not living his/her full potential for the Bible says we are chosen to "shew forth His praise" (2 Pet. 2:9). Furthermore, the Bible gives one of the reasons God created human beings as being to give Him pleasure (Rev. 4:11, KJV). The best way you can give pleasure to God is by living holy and praising Him because God "-inhabitest the praises of Israel" (Ps. 22:3). You are part of His Israel. It is mentioned, at least 6 times the Bible (NIV), that "God is worthy of praise" (2 Sam 22:4, 1 Chron 16:25, Ps. 18: 3; 48:1; 96:4; 145:3).

In today's opening scripture, prophet Isaiah tells us (1) the Lord is his God, (2) he will exalt Him (3) he will praise His name. Isaiah gives 2 main reasons why he will praise the name of the Lord: (a) because God has done wonderful things (b) God's counsels of old are faithfulness and truth. God has done countless wonderful things for you (salvation, provision, protection, healing, guidance, victories, etc.). God has also been faithful and true to his counsels (His wills and promises) about your life. God who is never tired of doing wonders is even named Wonderful (Isaiah 9:6). The more you praise Him the more wonderful things He will do in your life (Ps. 67: 1, 3- 6). Praise God with your time, talent and treasures. Praise God like David (Ps. 34:1). Praise God with your breath (Ps. 150:6). Be a praise divine fanatic.

Prayer: Father help me to pray to You and praise You ceaselessly and to experience overflowing blessings, IJN.

Monday September 9, 2019
Topic: REWARDS FOR TRUSTING GOD

Scriptures: "O my God, I trust in thee: let me not be ashamed, let not mine enemies triumph over me" (Psalm 25:2).

Praise the Lord. Today is September 9th and is day #252 in year 2019. The number of days remaining to end this year is 113. By God's grace, the enemy shall not triumph over you neither will you will be ashamed this season, and you will see the end of this year and beyond, safe and sound in the mighty name of Jesus.

By saying, "O my God, I trust in thee" in today's opening scripture David is saying he will depend on the infinite goodness and mercy of God for everything. In whom or in what are you trusting? Regrettably, in today's world many people and nations put their trust in ephemeral things such as riches, arms, jewelry, technology, political leaders, etc. Because these things are transient and man-made, trusting them is bound to lead to failure (Ps. 118:9, 146:3; Jer. 17:5). Instead, the believer's trust (like David's) must be in God: "Some trust in chariots, and some in horses: but we will remember the name of the Lord our God (Ps. 20:7). See also Ps.62:8, Isaiah 50:10, 2 Cor. 1:9).

Beloved, as a follower of Jesus Christ you too have been given immunity against shame and defeat by the enemy. These are just 2 of the many benefits derivable from trusting the lord. Through prophet Joel, God declares twice that "my people shall never be ashamed" (Joel 2: 26 & 27). Shame may arise from many things such as bareness, poverty, sickness, failure, etc. If per adventure you have suffered shame from these or other things, I decree that shame is terminated now IJN. In place of shame you shall receive double honor, IJN (Isaiah 61:7).

Child of God you are born to have to dominion (Gen. 1:28). Instead of the enemy triumphing over you, the Bible says " - - they shall come out against thee one way and flee before thee seven ways (Deut. 28:7). Are there people laughing at you because you haven't gotten a job? gotten your immigration paper? passed that exam? not yet married? etc., I have good news for you, you are about to arise from that 'problem' and, those laughing at you will soon laugh with you, IJN (Micah 7:8). All you have to do is keep trusting God.

Prayer: Father, let me deepen my trust in You and let me be shielded against shame and being a laughing stock, IJN.

Tuesday September 10, 2019
Topic: GIVING GOD BEST GIFTS

Scriptures: "And this is the offering which ye shall take of them; gold, and silver, and brass," (Exodus 2:53).

Praise the Lord. Today is September 10th and is day #253 in year 2019. The number of days remaining to end this year is 112. By God's grace, you will give high quality and acceptable offering to the Lord this season, and you will see the end of this year and beyond, safe and sound in the mighty name of Jesus.

Have you thought about the type of offering you give to God, whether it represents your best gifts to Him? God gave us His best, and deserves the best from us. It is obvious that God is interested in the quality and the quantity of our offerings to Him for the Bible says your seed will determine your harvest (Gal 6:7). The Bible further declares: "-- He which soweth sparingly shall reap also sparingly; and he which soweth bountifully shall reap also bountifully" (2 Cor. 9:6). Note that your offerings can determine the offers you get from God.

When God wanted a Sanctuary built by the Israelites, He sent Moses to them saying, " Speak unto the children of Israel, that they bring me an offering: of every man that giveth it willingly with his heart ye shall take my offering. And this is the offering which ye shall take of them; gold, and silver, and brass," (Exo. 25: 1-3). The following points are noteworthy and instructive about the offering God asks for: (a) From phrases like "bring me an offering", "take my offering" we know the offering is for God, not man. How do you view your offering? (b) the offering is to be given willingly, not grudgingly (2 Cor. 9:7), (c) by every man, that is by everybody. Ideally no one should be left out (including our children). The Bible enjoins us not to appear before the Lord empty (Duet 16:16). (d) the offering should be the best (as indicated in the opening scripture above).

Prayer: Father, everything I own comes from You, give me the grace to give You the best offering, including myself, IJN

Wednesday September 11, 2019
Topic: WALKING IN GOD'S WAYS

Scriptures: "Shew me thy ways, O Lord; teach me thy paths" (Psalm 25:4).

Praise the Lord. Today is September 11th and is day #254 in year 2019. The number of days remaining to end this year is 111. By God's grace, you will never depart from the Lord's ways and paths, and you will see the end of this year and beyond, safe and sound in the mighty name of Jesus.

Today, brings back to memory the 2001 September 11 attacks on the U.S by the Islamic terrorist group (al-Qaeda) using 4 hijacked aircraft by 19 suicide terrorists. The attacks killed 2,997 people, injured over 6,000 others, and caused at least $10 billion in infrastructure and property damage. Our prayer goes to the families of the victims involved that the Father of mercies and God of all comfort will continue to uphold and comfort them. We must also express gratitude to God and all security personnel that have since ensured safety and protection in this great nation. I decree that all forms of terrorism in your life shall be terminated, IJN.

The opening scripture today is part of David's prayer believed to be made when he faced an unusual attack by some of his subjects headed by his own son, Absalom. May God deliver us from household enemies (Matt 10:36). It is pertinent for the believer to seek ways and paths from the Lord because He is the Way, the truth and life (Matt 14:6). Furthermore, the Bible says, "As for God, his way is perfect --" (2 Sam 22:31; Ps. 18:30). In addition, it is written "All the paths of the Lord are mercy and truth- - "(Ps. 25:10). We can never go wrong if we walk in the ways and paths of the Lord. In His way and path are grace, mercy, peace, honor, favor, forgiveness, protection, promotion, direction, fruitfulness abundance, etc.

Fortunately, God has promised to teach and instruct us the way we should go - His way (Ps. 32:8). One of the means of knowing the ways and paths of God is through His word: "Thy word is a lamp unto my feet, and a light unto my path" (Ps. 119:105). Other approaches include prayer and fasting, dreams, visions, prophecy, divine revelations, etc.

Prayer: Father, teach me Your ways and guide me in all my decisions that I may walk before you in perfection, IJN.

Thursday September 12, 2019
Topic: READY FOR CHRIST'S RETURN?

Scriptures: "While the bridegroom tarried, they all slumbered and slept." (Matthew 25:5).

Praise the Lord. Today is September 12th and is day #255 in year 2019. The number of days remaining to end this year is 110. By God's grace, you will not sleep off to miss your blessings when arrive, and you will see the end of this year and beyond, safe and sound in the mighty name of Jesus.

In ancient Jewish tradition, the bridegroom would go to the bride's home to claim his bride. There, several festivities will be done including the wedding ceremony. After the ceremonies the couple make their way back to the bridegroom home, usually after sunset. All guests who wish to accompany the couple in a procession would be required to bring their lamps.

In the parable of the ten virgins (Matthew 25: 1-13), (5 of them were foolish, other 5 were wise were waiting to participate in the procession / wedding banquet. The 5 foolish virgins took their lamps without extra oil. The 5 wise virgins took extra oil along with their lamps. As stated in today's opening scripture, "While the bridegroom tarried, they all slumbered and slept" (v.5). By the time the bridegroom arrived, the 5 foolish virgins were out of oil and could not trim their lamps. They tried to borrow oil from the wise virgins but were denied for fear of insufficient oil for the 2 groups. The foolish virgins were advised to go and buy their own. Upon returning from extra oil purchase, it was too late for the foolish virgins to join the procession and the banquet.

Lessons to learn from this parable include: (1) Like "Eveready battery" whenever Jesus returns to take his people to heaven (for the marriage supper of the Lamb) we must be ready, living in righteously. (2) Salvation through faith in Jesus Christ is a primary requirement for making it to heaven. Be born again, IJN. (3) Spiritual preparation cannot be bought or borrowed at the last minute; it is an individual and personal responsibility (4) Adequate preparation is required for success in anything we plan to do. As the adage goes failure to plan amounts to planning to fail. You will not fail. IJN.

Prayer: Father, let me be ready and be among those You will take with You anytime You return, IJN

Friday September 13, 2019
Topic: GETTING RID OF OTHER "gods"

Scriptures: "And go not after other gods to serve them, and to worship them, and provoke me not to anger with the works of your hands; and I will do you no hurt." (Jeremiah 25:6).

Praise the Lord. Today is September 13th and is day #256 in year 2019. The number of days remaining to end this year is 109. By God's grace, you will serve the only true God and will have nothing to do with other god, and you will see the end of this year and beyond, safe and sound in the mighty name of Jesus.

Not serving other gods is so important to God that He made it the foremost of all the Decalogue (the 10 commandments): "Thou shalt have no other gods before me" (Exo. 20:3). Over and over again in the scriptures this commandment (and the consequence of violating it) is brought to the attention of the Israelites and other followers of God: (Deut.8:19; Exo. 5: 6-7; Josh. 24: 16-17, Josh 23:7-16, Isa 44:6; 2 Sam 5: 2-7, Hos. 13:4)

Jeremiah told the people of Judah and Jerusalem that he and other prophets faithfully passed on God's message to them but they "have not listened" (Jer. 25:3, NLT). The opening scripture for today is inclusive in God's message through Jeremiah (and other Prophets) to people of Judah (see Jer. 25: 5-6). Anything you love and consider more important than God is "other god" and should be avoided and not allowed to supersede God in your life so as not to provoke Him into anger. Examples of 'other gods' are money, job, sex, alcohol, drugs, sports, music, cell phone, etc.

Although Judah did not listen to Jeremiah's warning, the Prophet did not give up delivering God's message to them. This should be instructive to us. While rejection of God's message is still rampant today, like Jeremiah, we must not give up regardless of people's response. God never stops loving us, even when we reject him. We must be thankful to God that He won't give up on us and like Jeremiah we can commit ourselves to never forsaking Him. No matter how people respond when we tell them about God, we should remain faithful to God's high calling and continue to witness for Him.

Prayer: Father, let anything striving to compete with You in my life die now and please give me the grace and the courage to proclaim You as the only true God, IJN.

Saturday September 14, 2019
Topic: PARTAKING IN COVENANT OF PEACE

Scriptures: "And when Phinehas, the son of Eleazar, the son of Aaron the priest, saw it, he rose up from among the congregation, and took a javelin in his hand;" (Numbers 25:7).

Praise the Lord. Today is September 14th and is day #257 in year 2019. The number of days remaining to end this year is 108. By God's grace, you will not condone sinful actions and you will make a difference in your generation, and you will see the end of this year and beyond, safe and sound in the mighty name of Jesus.

Peace is a state of tranquility or quietness of spirit that transcends circumstances. No human being can give peace anywhere close to the peace God gives. God's peace surpasses all understanding (Phil 4:7). God is described, at least 5 times (in KJV), as "God of peace " (Rm 15:33, 16:20, Phil 4:9, 1 Thess. 5:23, Heb. 13:20). When you have peace of God, you will stay calm, cool and collected (like Jesus) while others may be running helter-skelter when disequilibrium sets in (Mt. 8: 23-27).

Phinehas, the son of Eleazer and grandson of Aaron (Ex. 6:25) attracted a covenant of peace and priesthood from God simply by being zealous for sanctity in the service of God. While Israel was staying in Shittim, on their way to the Promised Land, they began to indulge in sexual immorality with Moabite women and worshiping of Baal of Peor (Num. 25: 1-3). This action drew anger from God who sent a plague that started killing the men. While everyone was weeping in penitence at the entrance of the Tabernacle, an Israelite man brought a Moabite woman, flaunting his behavior before Moses and the assembly and went in to have sex with her. Phinehas rose among the congregation, took a javelin, followed them into room and thrust both of them through. That stopped God's anger and the plague after 24,000 men had already died (Num. 25:6-9).

God appreciated Phinehas for his zeal and action and rewarded him, saying,"- -Behold, I give unto him my covenant of peace: And he shall have it, and his seed after him, even the covenant of an everlasting priesthood- -" (Nu 25:10-13). Can God avert His anger / punishment because of you? What can you do to make a positive difference in your family, place of work, nation, etc. Be a Phinehas and change the world for better, IJN. *Prayer: Father, give me the grace to be zealous for You and let me be a partaker of Your peace covenant, IJN.*

Sunday September 15, 2019
Topic: DYING GRACEFULLY

Scriptures: "Then Abraham gave up the ghost, and died in a good old age, an old man, and full of years; and was gathered to his people" (Genesis 25:8).

Praise the Lord. Today is September 15th and is day #258 in year 2019. The number of days remaining to end this year is 107. By God's grace, you will be a parker of Abraham's blessing (Gal. 3:14), and you will see the end of this year and beyond, safe and sound in the mighty name of Jesus.

Physical death is an inevitable end of man here on earth. However, death is a subject that many people fear and don't want to talk about. Right from birth, each person's death date begins to countdown. A born again, heaven-bound child of God should not fear death because for the believer, death is expected to be a smooth transition to eternal life. Someone has said the last day for a believer here on earth is his/her birthday in eternity. The Bible says the day of death is better than the day of birth (Eccl. 7:1); and that the death of saints is precious in the sight of God (Ps. 116:15). Death opens the gate for the believer to be present perpetually with Jesus Christ (John 14:1-3; 2 Cor. 5:8, 1 Thess. 4:17; Rom 8: 35-39).

As indicated in the opening scripture above Abraham died in good old age. It can be said of Abraham that he died gracefully because he fulfilled his destiny in the sense that all God's promises about him were fulfilled. A few example to illustrate this point are: (1) God said He would bless him and make him a great nation (Gen 12: 1-3) and it is recorded that Abraham was blessed in all things (Gen 24:1), (2) God said Abraham would live long and buried in old age (Gen 15:15) and Abraham lived for 175 years before God called him home (Gen 25:7),

If you have given your life to Jesus Christ as your personal Savior, you don't have to fear death. You cannot die until you have fulfilled your destiny as ordained by God. As a matter of fact, you become a partaker of Abraham's blessing and promise which include long life (Gal 3:14; Psalm 91:16; 118:17). You shall live long and not die untimely, IJN.

Prayer: Father satisfy me with long life and let me fulfill destiny, IJN.

Monday September 16, 2019
Topic: WAITING FOR THE LORD

Scriptures: "And it shall be said in that day, Lo, this is our God; we have waited for him, and he will save us: this is the Lord; we have waited for him, we will be glad and rejoice in his salvation." (Isaiah 25:9).

Praise the Lord. Today is September 16th and is day #259 in year 2019. The number of days remaining to end this year is 106. By God's grace, you will lose your rewards and blessings because of impatience, and see the end of this year and beyond, safe and sound in the mighty name of Jesus.

In this era of automation and "fast food", "fast lane", "fast marriage" fast everything, waiting is almost becoming an anathema. People are detesting waiting for doctors, traffic light, waiting for their turns, etc. Yet today's opening scripture points out that the best thing that can ever happen to anyone (salvation) requires some level of waiting. The long-awaited promised Messiah came into the world as promised bringing salvation with him. With joy and praise will those who have been waiting and looking for Him (as did Simeon and Anna in Lk 2: 25-38) entertain the glad tidings of the Redeemer. With a triumphant song will glorified saints enter into the joy of their Lord (Matt 25:23). And it is not in vain to wait for Him; for the mercy comes at last, with abundant reward for the delay.

The scriptures point out several benefits can accrue to those that wait for the Lord: (a) They will be blessed (Isa. 30:18). (b)They are not put to shame (Isa. 49:23), (c) They enjoy the Lord's goodness (Lam 3:25). (d) God hears and answers their prayers (Micah 7:7). (e) They will gain new strength (Isa 40:31) etc. Are you waiting for the second coming of Jesus Christ? Don't give up and don't be tired of waiting. His coming is for an appointed time and it will surely happen. Believers must wait for the LORD patiently, prayerfully and living purely.

Take the following prayer Points:
1. Father, please renew my strength and give me the grace to wait patiently for Your return

2. Father, as I wait for You don't let any of my blessings elude me because of impatience.

3. Father, whenever You come to take Your own, don't let be left behind, IJN

Tuesday September 17, 2019
Topic: WHO AND WHOSE ARE YOU?

Scriptures: "Ye shall make you no idols nor graven image, neither rear you up a standing image, neither shall ye set up any image of stone in your land, to bow down unto it: for I am the LORD your God" (Leviticus 26:1).

Praise the Lord. Today is September 17th and is day #260 in year 2019. The number of days remaining to end this year is 105. By God's grace, the Devil has lost ownership of you; you shall belong to God only, and you will see the end of this year and beyond, safe and sound in the mighty name of Jesus.

Many people live their lives forgetting who and whose they are. Yet these 2 personality traits play large roles in defining the course of one's life including one's destiny. The believer cannot afford to forget who and whose he/she is. Your identity matters a lot. It was so important to God that the Israelites would remember they are His, that the statement, "I am the LORD your God", reflected in today's opening scripture, is repeated at least 33 times in King James version of the Holy Bible. (e, g. Ex. 6:7; 16:12; Lev. 11:44; Ezek. 20:20; etc.). Furthermore, God let the Israelites know who they are and nature of their relationship with Him by declarin in Deut. 14:2. In addition, God gave the Israelites several laws and instructions to guide how they were to relate with Him and to each other with corresponding rewards for obedience and penalties for disobedience (Ex. 20; Lev. 25 & 26).

Like the Israelites you are a chosen and peculiar person to God if you have given your life to Jesus Christ as your Savior and Redeemer (2 Pet. 2:9). You are a new person delivered from the bondage of sins and have become joint heir of God with Jesus Christ (2 Cor. 5:17; Rom 8:17). You are fully entitled to the blessing of Abraham and the promise of the Spirit through your faith in God (Gal. 3:14). Akin to what God told the Israelites, He is the LORD your God and you cannot have any other god beside Him. If you walk in His statutes and keep His commandments and do them, as He told the Israelites, you too will enjoy same (and possibly more) promises he made to the Israelites in Lev. 26: 3-13 and Deut. 28, 1-14). May you receive the grace to obey God and walk in His ways, IJN, **Prayer: Father, help me to constantly be mindful of who I am and that I belong to You, IJN**

Wednesday September 18, 2019
Topic: HONORING GOD WITH FIRSTFRUIT

Scriptures: "And it shall be, when thou art come in unto the land which the Lord thy God giveth thee for an inheritance, and possessest it, and dwellest therein; That thou shalt take of the first of all the fruit of the earth, which thou shalt bring of thy land that the Lord thy God giveth thee, and shalt put it in a basket, and shalt go unto the place which the Lord thy God shall choose to place his name there. - - And the priest shall take the basket out of thine hand, and set it down before the altar of the Lord thy God" (Deuteronomy 26:1, 2,4).

Praise the Lord. Today is September 18th and is day #261 in year 2019. The number of days remaining to end this year is 104. By God's grace, you will be faithful in giving first fruit offering and also be a partaker in its blessings, and you will see the end of this year and beyond, safe and sound in the mighty name of Jesus.

One of the ways God wants His people to honor Him is by giving Him "first fruit" from any increase He enables them to have: "Honor the Lord with thy substance, and with the first fruits of all thine increase. So, shall thy barns be filled with plenty, and thy presses shall burst out with new wine" (Pro. 3: 9-10). The opening scripture above and the rest of Deuteronomy 26 provide detailed guidelines for presenting first fruits unto the Lord.

At the time the First fruit injunction was given, it was to people who were mostly engaged in agriculture practices. However, the principle remains the same today. God says bring to Him your first blessing of increase arising from any new thing you engage in doing. Examples may include first salary in a new year, new job, new promotion, first profit in a business, first harvest from a venture, etc. Giving first fruit attracts many benefits to the giver including (a) rewards for obedience (Duet 28: 1-14) (b) provokes God to make what is left holy (Rom. 11:16) (c) breeds abundant supply (Lk. 6:38; Mal. 3:10-12), etc.

Prayer: Father, give me the grace to always have the opportunity to honor You with first fruit offering, IJN.

Thursday September 19, 2019
Topic: CONTRIBUTING CHRISTIANS

Scriptures: "I am donating more than 112 tons of gold from Ophir and 262 tons of refined silver to be used for overlaying the walls of the buildings" (1 Chronicles 29:5).

Praise the Lord. Today is September 19th and is day #262 in year 2019. The number of days remaining to end this year is 103. By God's grace, you will be one of the people Jesus Christ will use to build His Church, and the gates of hell shall not prevail against you, and you will see the end of this year and beyond, safe and sound in the mighty name of Jesus.

David desired to be the one to build the house of God (the Temple) but he was denied because of his abundance of wars and shedding of blood (1 Chron. 22: 8). Knowing that Solomon his son would be the chosen one to build the Temple David donated a good portion of the needed materials from his personal fortune and encouraged his followers to follow his example which they did willingly (1 Chron. 29: 1-9). Among the materials David prepared for building God's Temple were 262 tons of refined silver as reflected in today's opening scripture above. Before he died, David ensured that adequate preparation (materials and manpower) was in place for Solomon to build the Temple. Solomon successfully completed the building of the house of God in 7 years (1 Kings 6: 1, 38).

In the old Testament it was through the voluntary contributions of people that both the Sanctuary and the Temple were built (Exo. 35: 5-36: 7 & 1 Chron 29: 1-9). The same spirit of giving was pervasive among the early Christians many of who sold their houses and land and brought the proceeds to lay at the apostles' feet to support God's business (Acts 2: 44-47 & 4: 32-35).

Are you a contributing Christian? God is counting on you in building His Church so that the gate of hell will not prevail against it (1 Cor 3:9; Mt 16: 18). Allow the zeal of God's house consume you (Ps. 69:9) and you will be amazed what contributions God can empower you to make towards His Church. Provoke your miracles by supporting Christ's Church; shame and sorrow will depart from you and you will find ready solution to any problem that arises for you, IJN.

Prayer: Father, please give me the grace to do more for Your Church, IJN.

Friday September 20, 2019
Topic: PROCURING PERFECT PEACE

Scriptures: "Thou wilt keep him in perfect peace, whose mind is stayed on thee: because he trusteth in thee" (Isaiah 26:3).

Praise the Lord. Today is September 20th and is day #263 in year 2019. The number of days remaining to end this year is 102. By God's grace, you will be a beneficiary of peace from the Prince of peace, and you will see the end of this year and beyond, safe and sound in the mighty name of Jesus.

From today's opening scripture we can learn several lessons about peace. In particular, let us prayerfully answer the following questions about peace. (1) What is peace? (2) Source of perfect peace?, (3) Criteria for obtaining perfect peace?

(1) What is Peace? Peace can be defined as freedom of the mind from annoyance, distraction, anxiety, an obsession, fear, etc.; it is a state of tranquility and serenity.

The Bible talks about great peace (Ps 119:165), perfect peace (Isa 26:3) and worldly peace (John 14:27). May great peace and perfect peace be your portion henceforth, IJN.

When the disciples of Jesus were in disarray because of strong wind that brought turbulence to their boat Jesus brought tranquility into the situation by saying 'peace be still' (Mk 4:35-41)

(2) Source of perfect peace. The word "Thou" in today's opening scripture refers to God who is the owner and source of perfect peace. Jesus Christ, the Son of God is the embodiment of peace, hence one of His names is "Prince of Peace" (Isa. 9:6). If you are looking for perfect peace, turn to Jesus Christ

(3) Criteria for obtaining perfect peace: (a) fixing our mind /thought on God steadfastly and (b) Trusting God perpetually.

Prayer: Father, as I fix my mind and trust on You steadfastly, please take turbulence out of my life and give me great and perfect peace IJN.

Saturday September 21, 2019
Topic: BLESSINGS OF OBEDIENCE

Scriptures: "Then I will give you rain in due season, and the land shall yield her increase, and the trees of the field shall yield their fruit" (Leviticus 26:4).

Praise the Lord. Today is September 21st and is day #264 in year 2019. The number of days remaining to end this year is 101. By God's grace, you will receive showers of blessings this season, and you will see the end of this year and beyond, safe and sound in the mighty name of Jesus.

God gave the Israelites a set of statutes and commandments known as Levitical laws. They were called Levitical Laws ('Mosaic' or 'the Old Covenant') because they were delivered by God to Moses (on Mt Sinai) who was of the tribe of Levi, one of the 12 sons of Jacob.

God started His introduction to the Law with the Ten Commandments, but the entire Law encompasses 613 commandments, as detailed in the rest of the books of Moses. Jesus summarized the Law as having two emphases: love for God and love for neighbors (Matthew 22:37–39).

The focus of Leviticus chapter 26, from which today's scripture comes, is on laws concerning forbidden idolatry, sanctification of the Sabbath and reverence for the sanctuary. The laws of God carry blessings for obedience and punishment for disobedience. Today's opening scripture contains 3 of the 26 blessings (or there about) that God said will accrue to the people who would walk in His statutes, keep His commandments, and do them. The 3 blessings are, (1) they will be given rain in due season, (2) their land will yield its increase, (3) trees of the field shall yield their fruit. I decree that all the blessings listed in Leviticus chapter 26 and many more shall be your portion. Also, in the name of Jesus you will not partake in the punishments for disobedience that are listed in the chapter (Lev. 26: 15-39)

Prayer: Father Thank You for justifying me not by the works of the law but by the faith of Jesus Christ (Gal. 2:16). By Your grace I shall fulfill the Law by loving You and my neighbors, IJN

Sunday September 22, 2019
Topic: AVOIDING UNGODLY ASSOCIATIONS

Scriptures: "I have hated the congregation of evil doers; and will not sit with the wicked." (Psalm 26:5).

Praise the Lord. Today is September 22nd and is day #265 in year 2019. The number of days remaining to end this year is 100. By God's grace, you will be separated from all evil, and you will see the end of this year and beyond, safe and sound in the mighty name of Jesus.

One of the challenges some Christians face is knowing what type of association to keep and which not to keep. The correct way to approach this issue is to pray for the leading of the Holy Spirit and search the word of God for direction. While advising the Christians in Corinth on this same subject Apostle Paul said "-- Be ye not unequally yoked together with unbelievers: for what fellowship hath righteousness with unrighteousness? and what communion hath light with darkness?" (2 Cor. 6:14). What this scripture is saying is that as a born-again Christian you must not be too involved with unbelievers to the extent of participating in their sinful activities. As a follower of Jesus, the Bible says you are in the world but not of the world (Jn. 17:14).

In today's opening scripture David, the writer of Psalm 26 said in order not to engage in evil and wicked activities he deliberately refused to join the groups of those doing such businesses. Similarly, as a believer, you must not be entrenched in the lives and activities of unbelievers. There is an adage that say one should not smell what you are not supposed to eat. For example, as a Christian, don't court a non-Christian, don't go to drinking parlors with unbelievers, etc. Even when you think you are not going to participate in their activities "don't smell what you are not supposed to eat" so as not to destroy your testimony or expose yourself to the risks of losing your faith.

Prayer: Father separate me from all sinful activities and all hell-bound associations, IJN

Monday September 23, 2019
Topic: PROSPERING IN 'GERAR'

Scriptures: "And Isaac dwelt in Gerar" (Genesis 26:6).

Praise the Lord. Today is September 23rd and is day #266 in year 2019. The number of days remaining to end this year is 99. By God's grace, you will prosper wherever you go this season, and you will see the end of this year and beyond, safe and sound in the mighty name of Jesus.

Isaac relocated from Beersheba to Gerar mainly because of famine. God appeared to him and warned him not to go to Egypt but to settle in Gerar and any other place he would be shown. When Abimelech king of Gerar discovered Isaac's insincerity for calling Rebekah his sister instead of his wife he reproached Isaac. The king then gave strict command to all his people not to molest either Isaac or his wife (Gen 26: 7-11). The God of mercy who is the King of kings will overlook your errors and bless you IJN.

Isaac had a pleasant experience in Gerar. God reaffirmed to him the covenant of blessing made with his father Abraham and to his seed (Gen 22: 15-18). The Bible declares:

"Then Isaac sowed in that land, and received in the same year an hundredfold: and the Lord blessed him. And the man waxed great, and went forward, and grew until he became very great -- and the Philistines envied him" (Gen 26:12-14). I have good news for you, you are in (or God will soon show you) your "Gerar" - your place of prosperity, IJN. For this to happen, you must (a) sow in your 'Gerar" and work hard like Isaac did, (b) serve God and pray for Him to bless your effort.

Prayer: Father, wherever you lead me to dwell, let my efforts produce glorious and envy- provoking blessings which no one can tamper with, IJN.

Tuesday September 24, 2019
Topic: GOOD WORK FOR GOD

Scriptures: "There came unto him a woman having an alabaster box of very precious ointment, and poured it on his head, as he sat at meat." (Matt 26:7).

Praise the Lord. Today is September 24th and is day #267 in year 2019. The number of days remaining to end this year is 98. By God's grace, you will value Jesus highly and do your best for His body, the Church, and you will see the end of this year and beyond, safe and sound in the mighty name of Jesus.

Have you done any good work for God lately? As far as God is concerned, good work includes good gifts also. The woman in referred to in today's opening scripture above brought a precious gift of oil and poured it on the head of Jesus. According to John 12: 1-3, this woman was Mary, the sister of Martha and Lazarus who lived in Bethany. All the disciples were indignant (asking "why this waste?") but John's gospel singles Judas Iscariot out as the sole complainer of wastage (John 12:4). He (being a thief who wanted access to the money as the treasurer) said the oil could have been sold and the money given to the poor.

Jesus Christ told the disciples to leave the woman alone and that "-- she hath wrought a good work upon me" (Mt. 26: 10). He said they would always have the poor with them but not Himself. In appreciation of Mary's work of anointing His body for burial, Jesus decreed that wherever the gospel is preached all over the world, the woman's good work will be told as a memorial of her (Mt. 26: 11-13).

What is that precious thing that you have to let go for Jesus? Give God a good gift and let Him and the world testify of your good work akin to Mary's. I believe Mary's good work/gift motivated Jesus to raise Lazarus (Mary's brother) back to life after he was dead 4 days and stinking (John 11: 1-45). Your good work will provoke great miracles for you IJN. Happy Sunday.

Prayer: Father give me the grace to give You good gifts and do good work for You IJN

Wednesday September 25, 2019
Topic: BROUGHT OUT OF BONDAGE

Scriptures: "And the Lord brought us forth out of Egypt with a mighty hand, and with an outstretched arm, and with great terribleness, and with signs, and with wonders:" (Deuteronomy 26:8).

Praise the Lord. Today is September 25th and is day #268 in year 2019. The number of days remaining to end this year is 97. By God's grace, you will see the end of this year and beyond, safe and sound in the mighty name of Jesus.

A bondage is defined as the state of being bound by or subjected to some external power or control. It connotes subjugation and lack of freedom for the one on being bound. The Israelites were in bondage in Egypt for about 430 years (Exo. 12:40). They were subjected to hard labor, treated harshly, humiliated, afflicted and oppressed. When they cried to the LORD God of their fathers, he heard their cry and the result is what is recorded in today's opening scripture - God brought them out of bondage with signs and wonders (Deut. 26: 6-8).

Anything that imposes undesirable limitations, affliction and hardship on anyone can be regarded as bondage. There are physical and spiritual bondages such as imprisonment, sickness, sins, debts, joblessness, bareness, sickness, failure, imprisonment, etc. Are you a victim of any type of bondage? Cry to Jesus Christ in earnest and He will bring you out of that bondage with outstretched arm and with signs and wonders IJN. He is not a respecter of persons, your own will not be difficult for Him, IJN

Prayer: Father, today, please bring me out of the bondage of poverty, sickness, etc. IJN

Thursday September 26, 2019
Topic: SEPARATING FROM SINNERS

Scriptures: "Gather not my soul with sinners, nor my life with bloody men" (Psalm 26:9).

Praise the Lord. Today is September 26th and is day #269 in year 2019. The number of days remaining to end this year is 96. By God's grace, you will see the end of this year and beyond, safe and sound in the mighty name of Jesus.

David had great love and affinity for God's house (Psalm 26:8; 27:4 & 122:1). Some of the reasons he gave for loving God's house include the fact that it is place where God's honor dwell, it is a place to behold the beauty of the LORD and to enquire in his temple as well as a hiding place in the time of trouble. Knowing that God cannot harbor sinners in His house David offered the prayer/desire in today's opening scripture: "Gather not my soul with sinners, nor my life with bloody men".

The company you keep may determine the camp in which you will spend eternity. Like David, the believer who wants to make heaven must eschew sins and evil. Such a person must also heed apostle Paul's warning not unequally yoked with unbelievers and hell-bound candidates that have made things like unrighteousness, work of darkness, infidelity, idol worship and other devilish lifestyles their cup of tea (2 Cor 6: 14-16). Avoid such like a plague and "- -come out from among them, and be ye separate, saith the Lord, and touch not the unclean thing; and I will receive you. And will be a Father unto you, and ye shall be my sons and daughters, saith the Lord Almighty" (2 Cor. 6: 17-18). May you hearken to this injunction from God, IJN.

Prayer: Father, separate me from unrepentant sinners, IJN.

Friday September 27, 2019
Topic: SETTING CAPTIVES FREE

Scriptures: "So the priests, the Levites, the singers, the gatekeepers, the Temple servants, and some of the common people settled in villages near Jerusalem. The rest of the people returned to their own towns throughout Israel" (Ezra 2:70, NLT).

Praise the Lord. Today is September 27th and is day #270 in year 2019. The number of days remaining to end this year is 95. By God's grace, you will see the end of this year and beyond, safe and sound in the mighty name of Jesus.

The bible declares "- - "Even the captives of the mighty shall be taken, and the prey of the tyrant be rescued, for I will contend with those who contend with you, and I will save your children" (Isaiah 49:25, NLT). One instance of the fulfillment of this scripture occurred when God enabled the return of a total of 42,360 exiles to Judah, from their captivity in Babylon to which King Nebuchadnezzar had deported them. The categories of the returning exiles are indicated in today's opening scripture while a detailed list of numbers by family and other resources brought back can be found in Ezra 2:2-67). Your season of full restoration has come, IJN.

When the exiles arrived at the Temple of the Lord in Jerusalem, special offering was taken and some of the leaders made generous voluntary donations toward the rebuilding of God's Temple. The total of their gifts came to 61,000 gold coins, 6,250 pounds of silver, and 100 robes for the priests (Ezra 2: 68-69). The giving attitude of these exiles is worthy of emulation as they gave their best, not leftover, towards God's work. God still expects us to give willingly and bountifully to His work 2 Cor. 8:12, 9:6).

Prayer: Father, restore all our losses; set us free from whatever constitutes captivities in our lives and terminate the activities of kidnappers in our countries, IJN.

Saturday September 28, 2019
Topic: FAITH NOT FEAR

Scriptures: "The Lord is my light and my salvation; whom shall I fear? the Lord is the strength of my life; of whom shall I be afraid? " (Psalm 27:1).

Praise the Lord. Today is September 28th and is day #271 in year 2019. The number of days remaining to end this year is 94. By God's grace, you will see the end of this year and beyond, safe and sound in the mighty name of Jesus.

Is fear good or bad? The answer depends on which kind of fear we are talking about. From Biblical perspective there are 2 kinds of fear - (a) beneficial (or good) fear and (b) detrimental (or bad) fear. Type (a) is the fear of God in a reverential way. The reverence may pertain to God's awesome power and glory or in terms of proper respect for His wrath and anger. Blessings of beneficial fear are many and include: attracting wisdom and understanding (Ps.111:10), goodness of God (Ps.31:19), it leads to life, rest, peace, and contentment (Pro.19:23), it is the fountain and life (Pro. 14:27), etc. Fear type (b) is what the Bible calls "the spirit of fear" which is not from God (2 Tim 1:7). It brings snares (Pro 29: 25). It torments or punishes the victim who focuses on fears and anxiety instead of maximizing faith in loving God perfectly (1 John 4:8).

Detrimental fear manifests itself in so many forms such as fear of rejection, sickness, losing job, failing exam, etc. In today's opening scripture, David said he would not fear or be afraid of any one because to him God is light (or word of God), salvation and strength. Anyone who will by faith accept /have accepted Jesus Christ as LORD and Savior can avoid or conquer fear by exercising that same faith to trust in Jesus Christ. Throughout the Bible the believer is warned not to fear (Gen 15:1, Exo 20:20, Ps. 55:19, Rev. 15:1). It is said that there are 365 'fear not" or it's equivalence in the Bible, one for each day of the year! Therefore, fear not, just have faith, IJN.

Prayer: Father please give me mountains-moving faith that will also drown all my fears, IJN

Sunday September 29, 2019
Topic: DIVINE SUBSTITUTION

Scriptures: "When the wicked, even mine enemies and my foes, came upon me to eat up my flesh, they stumbled and fell " (Psalm 27:2).

Praise the Lord. Today is September 29th and is day #272 in year 2019. The number of days remaining to end this year is 93. By God's grace, you will see the end of this year and beyond, safe and sound in the mighty name of Jesus.

David's enemies and foes were many and included: lions and bears (1 Sam 17:34), Philistines, including Goliath (I Sam 17: 1-57), Saul (1 Sam 18:25; 19:1), the Amalekites (1 Sam 30:1-19) the Moabites and the Syrians (Chron 18), Absalom (2 Sam 15-19), etc. As indicated in his testimony in today's opening scripture almost all David's enemies who sought to kill him stumbled and died in his place. Your unrelenting foes shall stumble, IJN

Beloved, like David we have enemies and foes who are seeking whom to devour (1 Pet 5:8). The good news however is that with God as our ally our victory over the enemies is guaranteed. We have wonderful promises of protection from the God that keeps covenants. Has He not said, "No weapon that is formed against thee shall prosper? (Isaiah 54:17). Did he not say "- - I will contend with him that contendeth with thee, - - - And I will feed them that oppress thee with their own flesh; and they shall be drunken with their own blood"? (Isaiah 49: 25-26). When Haman plotted to kill Mordecai Did God not divinely substitute Haman to be hung on the gallows that he had prepared for Mordecai? (Esther 10:7). Your enemy will die in your place, IJN. Shout Hallelujah!

Prayer: Father, fight for me such that those that are determined to kill me will die in my place

Monday September 30, 2019
Topic: SAVED TO SERVE

Scriptures: "There are 273 more firstborn sons of Israel than there are Levites. To redeem these extra firstborn sons, collect five pieces of silver[e] for each of them (each piece weighing the same as the sanctuary shekel, which equals twenty gerahs). Give the silver to Aaron and his sons as the redemption price for the extra firstborn sons."" (Numbers 3: 46-48, NIV).

Praise the Lord. Today is September 30h and is day #273 in year 2019. The number of days remaining to end this year is 92. By God's grace, you will see the end of this year and beyond, safe and sound in the mighty name of Jesus.

If you are a believer / follower of Christ you must be actively involved in doing God's work especially at where you worship; otherwise you will be missing some blessings (Exo 23:25; Luke 19:13-26). You are created and saved to serve (Eph. 2:10). If you are not doing that you are not fulfilling destiny.

In the old Testament time, not everybody was privileged to serve in the Church (Tabernacle). Initially, the Tabernacle work was restricted to Aaron and his 4 sons. After 2 of Aaron's sons died (because they offered strange fire) God authorized Moses to assign the Levites to Aaron to assist with the Tabernacle duties which must have increased greatly (Num. 3: 1-13). At God's instruction the Levites were numbered and they became the only privileged "workers" in God's house while Aaron and his sons were the only one authorized to be priests (Num. 3: 6-10)

Today, Jesus Christ is our High Priest and anyone who follows Him is also called a priest (1 Peter 2: 5, 9; Rev 1: 5-6). Serving in God's house and partaking in the blessings that appertain is no longer restricted as it was during Aaron's era. If you are saved you must consider it a necessity to work for God for "faith without works is dead also" (James 2:26).

Action /Prayer: Aside from your role in the Great Commission (Mk 16:15), let the zeal of God's house consume you to the level of becoming part of a "ministry" in God's house e.g. hospitality, cleaning, choir, ushering, finance, etc. If need be, ask your Pastor for help. May you serve the Lord with gladness, IJN.

Tuesday October 1, 2019
Topic: JUDAS' BETRAYAL OF JESUS

Scriptures: "I have sinned," he declared, "for I have betrayed an innocent man. "What do we care?" they retorted. "That's your problem." (Matthew 27:4).

Praise the Lord. Today is October 1st and is day #274 in year 2019. The number of days remaining to end this year is 91. By God's grace, you will not never betray Jesus, you will be faithful to the end, and you will see the end of this year and beyond, safe and sound in the mighty name of Jesus.

Welcome to the first day of October, the 10th month of this year. In terms of important Biblical events it was a day like this, ("the tenth month, on the first day of the month") that the tops of the mountains of Ararat were seen (Gen 8:5). What a sigh of relief, hope and joy Noah and his family of 8 must have had for seeing the top of the mountains! That was after at least 150 days of floating aimlessly and desperately about on the flood that destroyed everyone else in the whole world. Throughout this month of October and beyond, you will not be a victim of any destructive flood (physical and/or spiritual). Furthermore, you will "see" and attain life and not death, hope and not despair, joy and not sorrow, prosperity and not poverty and everything that will lead to the fulfillment of your destiny IJN.

The ark in which Noah and his family found safety, despite the flood, is symbolic of the salvation that Jesus Christ provides for any one that will believe in Him and accept Him as LORD and Savior. As the flood was not able to abort God's plan for safety of Noah and his family, Judas' betrayal was not able to stop God's plan for the salvation of man. Jesus Christ died (and resurrected) because He was the only one qualified to pay the penalty for the sins of man and pave the way for salvation (John 14:6, Heb. 9:22, Col. 1:22). With his own mouth Judas condemned himself as indicated in today's opening scripture. He wanted to change his mind but it was too late. He paid dearly for betraying Jesus. He couldn't spend the money he sold Jesus for and ended up hanging himself (Matt. 27:5).

Prayer: LORD Jesus, thank You for my salvation, don't let me ever betray You, IJN

Wednesday October 2, 2019
Topic: REBUKING LOVINGLY AND RIGHTEOUSLY

Scriptures: "Open rebuke is better than secret love" (Proverbs 27:5).
Praise the Lord. Today is October 2nd and is day #275 in year 2019. The number of days remaining to end this year is 90. By God's grace, you will not rebuke nor be rebuked unlovingly, and you will see the end of this year and beyond, safe and sound in the mighty name of Jesus.

Rebuke refers to sharp, stern disapproval, reproof or reprimand. Secret love is the kind that will fail to tell the one loved his/her faults for fear of grieving or losing the relationship. The way you rebuke can make or mar (partially or totally) the person being rebuked. A believer should rebuke with the goal of correcting in love the one being rebuked. Our model in this regard should be the word of God: "As many as I love, I rebuke and chasten. Therefore, be zealous and repent" (Rev. 3:19).

Rebuking should be done in such a way to avoid hatred and sins (Lev.19:17). Paul rebuked Peter openly in love without sins when Peter was found guilty of hypocrisy with respect to eating or not eating with Gentiles (Gal. 2: 11-16). Believers must not handle rebuking as unbelievers. For example, it is wrong, and against God for a believer wife/husband to be violent, screaming and/or beating her/his husband/wife in the public or anywhere for that matter (Psalm 11:5, Pro. 3: 31-33). Rebuking should be done not only in love but with a goal of correcting and building up instead of tearing down the target of rebuke.

Prayer: Father in all forms of rebuke, let love and righteousness prevail, IJN

Thursday October 3, 2019
Topic: SAILING SAFELY THROUGH STORM

Scriptures: "We were in all 276 persons in the ship" (Acts 27:37).
Praise the Lord. Today is October 3rd and is day #276 in year 2019. The number of days remaining to end this year is 89. By God's grace, you will not lose any member of your family, ministry or organization this year, and you will see the end of this year and beyond, safe and sound in the mighty name of Jesus.

During his conversion, one of the things the LORD said about Paul (formerly Saul) was "I will shew him how great things he must suffer for my name's sake" (Acts 9:16). It turned out that Paul did suffer greatly for Christ, including reproach, beatings, imprisonments, false accusations, hunger, etc. (2 Cor.11:21-33).

Some of Paul's sufferings occurred when he was sailing to Italy in Rome (for trial before Caesar) in the company of 276 persons as reflected in today's scripture. Paul predicted a disastrous voyage, but his warning was ignored by the centurion (Julius) and the ship owner (Acts 27: 9-11). After sailing past Crete, as Paul predicted, they met with a tempest, and were brought into extreme peril and distress. In addition, they faced total darkness for many days to the extent of almost losing all hope of safety (Acts 27:12-20). Paul told them they could have avoided the tempest if they had harkened to his warning and tarried in Crete.

Paul then encouraged his fellow travelers saying, "- - be of good cheer: for there shall be no loss of any man's life among you, but of the ship. For there stood by me this night the angel of God, - - Saying, Fear not, Paul; - -, God hath given thee all them that sail with thee" (Acts 27:22-24). According to the word of God all the 276 persons arrived safely at their destination (Acts 27:44). I decree that in the remaining 89 days of this year there shall be no loss of any life in your family and you shall all end the journeys of year 2019 and beyond safely, IJN.

Prayer: Father, terminate all turbulence in my life and let all my earthly and heaven-bound journeys end safely and smoothly at the expected destinations, IJN.

Friday October 4, 2019
Topic: SEEKING SAFETY IN ENEMY'S CAMP?

Scriptures: "And the time that David dwelt in the country of the Philistines was a full year and four months." (1 Samuel 27:7).

Praise the Lord. Today is October 4th and is day #277 in year 2019. The number of days remaining to end this year is 88. By God's grace, you shall be unreachable and untouchable to every enemy pursuing you, and you will see the end of this year and beyond, safe and sound in the mighty name of Jesus.

As part of his strategy to escape Saul's plan to kill him, David went with his two wives and 600 men followers (and their households) to seek refuge with king Achish of Gath in Philistine (1 Sam 27: 1-12). When Saul was told that David had fled to Gath, the Bible says "- - he sought no more again for him" (2 Sam 27:4). From today every enemy that has been pursuing you shall become frustrated and give up because you shall be unreachable and untouchable in Christ, IJN.

As today's scripture indicates David spent a year and 4 months in the Philistines. While in Gath David requested a place in the country side to settle and the king gave him the city of Ziklag. From there David raided some Philistines communities, killing everyone there and taking all their livestock and belongings. When Achish asked David where he raided, he lied and told him he raided Israeli territory since there was no one left alive in the raided place to bringing tidings to Achish and Gath.

There is no human being that is faultless. Apart from telling lies, David committed adultery with Beersheba and killed her husband Uriah (2 Sam. 11). These character flaws of David portray instances he yielded to his flesh rather than to his faith in God and to the spirit of God. However, David did not let his weakness and sins stop him from worshipping God and crying to Him for help. His penitence and repentance in Psalm 51 is a case in point of how David secured his restoration to the point that God described David as "a man after my own heart--"(Acts 13:22). Have you sought help, protection or refuge in ungodly places, or committed sins unbecoming of a Christ follower? Repent today like David and ask for restoration.

Prayer: Father order my steps and never let me go anywhere without seeking approval from You, IJN

Saturday October 5, 2019
Topic: WANDERING CAN BE WASTEFUL

Scriptures: "As a bird that wandereth from her nest, so is a man that wandereth from his place." (Proverbs 27:8).

Praise the Lord. Today is October 5th and is day #278 in year 2019. The number of days remaining to end this year is 87. By God's grace, you will not wander aimlessly this season, and you will see the end of this year and beyond, safe and sound in the mighty name of Jesus.

Simply put, to wander is to go about aimlessly. Wandering can be wasteful, frustrating, time consuming, energy sapping and deadly. When the Israelites came out of bondage in Egypt and were on their way to the promised land, God cursed them for not believing that He was able to give them the land He had promised to their fathers. As a result of the curse they wandered 40 years in the wilderness and all those over 20 years old were slain and forbidden from seeing the promised land (Num 14: 11-19).

In today's opening scripture a stern warning is given against haphazardly forsaking or leaving one's place, that is where God has put you. We are told such a person will wander as a bird wanders from her nest. A bird that wanders from her nest may face several risks including becoming a prey, disoriented, hunger, lost, etc. Your place is your space, physical and spiritual. Your place may be where you worship, your marriage, your job/position, etc.

Abdicating your 'place' without hearing from God can expose you to enemy's attack, thereby messing up your destiny. King Uzziah of Judah, who was not a priest, wandered from his place and went into the temple of the Lord to burn incense upon the altar of incense. He was smitten with leprosy which remained with him until his death (2 Chron 26: 1-21). Beware and be warned.

Prayer: Father let nothing (not even myself) make me wander away from my place of blessings and breakthrough, IJN.

Sunday October 6, 2019
Topic: PRAYING LIKE DAVID

Scriptures: "Hide not thy face far from me; put not thy servant away in anger: thou hast been my help; leave me not, neither forsake me, O God of my salvation" (Psalm 27:9).

Praise the Lord. Today is October 6th and is day #279 in year 2019. The number of days remaining to end this year is 86. By God's grace, you will not do anything that will make the Lord to forsake you, and you will see the end of this year and beyond, safe and sound in the mighty name of Jesus.

At least 4 prayer points (PP) are discernible in today's opening scripture as offered by David. There is at least one possible reason (PR) behind each prayer point. These prayer points and the possible reasons are as follows: A prayer suggestion is also given for each.

PP#1: Hide not thy face far from me. PR for PP #1: " - - thou didst hide thy face, and I was troubled" (Ps. 30:7b). Prayer: Father hide not Your face from me so that I will not be troubled

PP #2: Put not thy servant away in anger. PR for PP#2 David remembers how God's anger took Uzzah away (2 Sam 6:7) and his own personal experience with numbering Israel (2 Sam 24). Prayer: Father don't let me do anything to provoke Your anger. Have mercy on me, IJN

PP#3: Thou hast been my help; You will help me again. PR for PP#3: "God - - a very present help in trouble" (Ps. 46:1). Prayer: Father help me in all my endeavors, IJN.

PP#4: Leave me not neither forsake me: PR for PP#4: "When my father and my mother forsake me, then the Lord will take me up" (Ps. 27:10). Prayer: Father, let me always be in Your presence, IJN

Monday October 7, 2019
Topic: GUARNTEED VICTORY IS IN GOD

Scriptures: "King Asa had an army of 300,000 warriors from the tribe of Judah, armed with large shields and spears. He also had an army of 280,000 warriors from the tribe of Benjamin, armed with small shields and bows. Both armies were composed of well-trained fighting men." (2 Chronicles 14:8, NLT).

Praise the Lord. Today is October 7th and is day #280 in year 2019. The number of days remaining to end this year is 85. By God's grace, you will be adequately equipped (spiritually, physically, financially, etc to fight the battles of life, and you will see the end of this year and beyond, safe and sound in the mighty name of Jesus.

Life is a battle field. We fight to come into the world and we fight to get out of it. In between life and death there are various battles. When you let God fight your battles, your victory is guaranteed. This was the experience of Moses and Israel (Exo 15), David (1 Sam 17), Jehoshaphat (2 Chron 20), Elijah (1 Kings 18) etc. Your own battles shall not be difficult for God to win, IJN.

King Asa is another person God fought for though his military physical might was significantly less than that of his opponent. Unlike his father Abijah and grandfather Rehoboam, Asa "- -did what was pleasing and good in the sight of the Lord his God" (2 Chron 14:2). Therefore, God fought his battle when he was attacked by an Ethiopian named Zerah whose army significantly outnumbered his own. Asa cried to God for help (2 Chron. 14: 11, NLT) and God helped him to defeat the Ethiopians and to carry away a vast amount of their treasures" (2 Chron. 14:12–13, NLT).

Unfortunately, Asa did not finish well. He later relied more on human being than God by entering an alliance with Benhadad king of Syria to fight against Israel. When an attempt was made by Hanani, the seer, to correct him for negating God's assistance, he imprisoned Hanani and became an oppressor of many people. He was smitten by leg disease which killed him. (2 Chron 16). You will not end this year with sickness, IJN. Have you reformed your life to please God in all things? Are you relying on Him persistently in all your battles of life (physical, spiritual, financial, marital, health wise, business, academic, etc.?). Do so and you shall be victorious, IJN. **Prayer: Father, in all my battles of life help me to rely totally on You for victories IJN**

Tuesday October 8, 2019
Topic: YOU SHALL END THE YEAR SAFELY

Scriptures: "Once we were safe on shore, we learned that we were on the island of Malta." (Acts 28:1, NLT).

Praise the Lord. Today is October 8th and is day #281 in year 2019. The number of days remaining to end this year is 84. By God's grace, you will enjoy divine safety in all your trips this season, and you will see the end of this year and beyond, safe and sound in the mighty name of Jesus.

Paul began his 2000 miles to Rome at Caesarea. It was one of his most important and problem-laden trips. Along the way he suffered many hardships including hunger, rejection of views, dangerous storms, series of legal interrogations, shipwrecks, etc.

God had promised safe passage to Paul and his co-travelers (Acts27: 23-25) and in spite of the challenging conditions on the way God ensured nothing harmed them. As indicated in today's opening scripture they "were safe on shore" arriving in Malta near Rome. Even the poisonous viper that bit Paul on arrival was unable to harm him (Acts 28:3). Paul continued to witness to others, even as a shipwrecked prisoner and the gospel was spreading like wildfire.

The journey of year 2019 we started in January will soon come to an end safely on the shore of December 31, IJN. It does not matter what hardships you have encountered along the way, as we are in the third quarter of the year, I pray for you that, regarding this year "- -the glory of this latter house shall be greater than of the former" (Hag 2:9). The Almighty God will still load you daily with more benefits that will make you forget all the hardships you have encountered thus far, IJN.

Prayer: Father thank You for my journey so far this year, please let me end the year safely with no harm or hurt, IJN.

Wednesday October 9, 2019
Topic: REDEEMER IS RISEN

Scriptures: "And, behold, there was a great earthquake: for the angel of the Lord descended from heaven, and came and rolled back the stone from the door, and sat upon it." (Matthew 28:2).

Praise the Lord. Today is October 9th and is day #282 in year 2019. The number of days remaining to end this year is 83. By God's grace, any evil stone placed over your destiny shall be rolled away, and you will see the end of this year and beyond, safe and sound in the mighty name of Jesus.

Hallelujah! Jesus Christ the Redeemer is risen, just as He promised (Jn 2:18-22). The resurrection of the Lord Jesus Christ was first noticed by 2 women who came at dawn to see the tomb in which Jesus was buried (Matt 28:1). An angel (not earthquake) rolled back the stone covering the tomb, as indicated in today's scripture. The stone was not rolled back so that Jesus could get out but so that others could get in and see that Jesus had risen from the dead as he promised.

Clothed in raiment, white as snow and countenance like lightning, the angel that sat on the rolled back stone was so terrifying to the keepers of the tomb that they shook "and became as dead men" (Matt 28:4). The angel said to the women "Fear not ye" - - "He is not here: for he is risen, as he said" - - - "go quickly and tell his disciples that he is risen from the dead- -"(Matt 28:5-8).

Lessons to be reminded of and/or learn from incidence at the tomb and resurrection of Jesus Christ include the following: (1) because Jesus resurrected, believers in Him will also resurrect (2) 'stones' of limitations including: eternal death, sorrows, shame, sickness, poverty etc. are rolled away from the life of believers in Jesus (3) the reality of the resurrection brings joy not fear, therefore any time you are afraid, remember the empty tomb, (4) believers are to spread the good news about Jesus' resurrection (5) the power of resurrection is available to the believer to fulfill destiny; therefore, with Jesus nothing shall be impossible for the believer.

Prayer: Father, remove all limitations from my life, give me all round victory and the grace to reign with You in eternity, IJN.

Thursday October 10, 2019
Topic: BOUNTIFUL BLESSINGS

Scriptures: "Blessed shalt thou be in the city, and blessed shalt thou be in the field" (Deuteronomy 28:3).

Praise the Lord. Today is October 10th and is day #283 in year 2019. The number of days remaining to end this year is 82. By God's grace, you will be soaked in divine blessings anytime anywhere, and you will see the end of this year and beyond, safe and sound in the mighty name of Jesus.

As the Israelites were getting closer and closer to entering the promised land, Moses was constantly reminding them the need for them to be obedient to the commandments of God as given through Moses. Deuteronomy chapter 28 contains 68 verses in which two words stand out - blessings and curses. The first 14 verses describe the specific blessings that will "come to and overtake" those that will hear diligently the voice of God and observe and do all his commandments. The remaining 54 verses describe the various curses that shall come to and overtake transgressors of the law (that is the disobedient). Note that the verses devoted to the curses for the disobedient are more than quadruple those verses of blessings for the obedient to the law. It behooves the believer to strife to be obedient to God and His servants.

Today's opening scripture is the beginning of the enumeration of the blessings that will come to the obedient. He or she shall be blessed in the city and blessed in the field. Essentially, this scripture is saying the believers who hear the Lord and obey Him shall be blessed anywhere they go any time. That will be your portion, IJN. God can pour out His blessings on His obedient followers anywhere, any time because He owns the heavens and the earth (1 Chron. 29:11, Psalm 24:1). Not only does God have plenty of blessings, His blessings " maketh rich, and he addeth no sorrow with it" (Pro. 10:22b). Go for God's boundless and bountiful blessings that can follow you everywhere.

Action: How many blessings have you received from God this year 2019? Try to document them into categories. It will surprise you what the Lord has done!

Prayer: Father, circumcise my ears to hear and obey You, obey Your commandments and be blessed bountifully, IJN.

Friday October 11, 2019
Topic: READY FOR THE NEW JERUSALEM?

Scriptures: "In all, there were 284 Levites in the holy city" (Nehemiah 11:18).

Praise the Lord. Today is October 11th and is day #284 in year 2019. The number of days remaining to end this year is 81. By God's grace, you will see the end of this year and beyond, safe and sound in the mighty name of Jesus.

For many reasons Jerusalem has always been very important in God's agenda. Known also as Zion, Jerusalem is the "- -city of God, his holy mountain--"(Ps. 48:1-2). God says He is jealous of Jerusalem and Zion (Zech. 1:14), He placed it in "center of nations" (Ezek 5:5, NLT), and calls it "my resting" in Ps. 132:14. Jesus preached, healed, arrested and tried in Jerusalem. Concerning Jerusalem God said, "I have graven thee upon the palms of my hands; thy walls are continually before me" (Isa. 49:16).

After the broken walls of Jerusalem were rebuilt under the leadership and supervision of Nehemiah, the city was not fully inhabited (perhaps for fear of attack) and therefore was weak and despicable. Nehemiah next task was to bring people into it. Detailed strategies adopted to do this are spelt out in Nehemiah chapter 11. Among people recruited and listed that dwelt in the holy city of Jerusalem were families of Judah and Benjamin, (Neh. 11: 3-9), mighty men of valour (Neh. 11:14), priests and the 284 Levites mentioned in today's opening scripture. Although the Levites were cursed based on the original curse imposed by Jacob on his son Levi, (Gen. 49: 5-7) they became the priestly tribe and residents of the cities of refuge by God's grace and due to their loyalty to God (Exodus 32:26–29).

As believers and followers of Christ we share common factor of restoration with the Levites in that Jesus Christ exchanged His righteousness for our sins on the cross (2 Cor. 5:21) thereby enabling us to become a nation of priests unto Him (1 Peter 2:9; Rev 1:6). All of us who commit to be on the Lord's side (accepting Jesus as our Savior), like the Levites, will dwell in the Holy City (new Jerusalem) (Rev. 21). We are commanded to pray for Jerusalem and to love her so that we can prosper (Psalm 122:6). Beloved, give your life to Jesus Christ so that you can be ready for the new Jerusalem. *Prayer: Father prepare me to be ready for "the holy city, the new Jerusalem" described in Rev 21, IJN.*

Saturday October 12, 2019
Topic: SHAKE OFF THE SNAKE

Scriptures: "But Paul shook off the snake into the fire and was unharmed" (Acts 28:5)

Praise the Lord. Today is October 12th and is day #285 in year 2019. The number of days remaining to end this year is 80. By God's grace, you shall be unharmed throughout this season, and you will see the end of this year and beyond, safe and sound in the mighty name of Jesus.

Satan manifested as a serpent (or snake) when he first attacked man in the garden of Eden (Gen 3). The serpent, described as, "more cunning than any beast of the field" deceived Adam and Eve to eat the forbidden fruit (Gen 3: 13-15). God cursed the serpent saying, "- I will put enmity Between you and the woman, And between your seed and her Seed; He shall bruise your head, And you shall bruise His heel." (Gen 3: 15). Any snake (physical or spiritual attempting to attack you shall have its head cut off, IJN.

Scarcely has Paul arrived at the shore of Malta after a long, hazardously dangerous and stormy journey than he was attacked by a poisonous snake (Acts 28: 1-2). Paul was laying firewood on the fire set up to keep him warm as it was cold and raining. The snake jumped out of the fire and bit him on the hand. Paul shook off the snake into the fire and was unharmed. The people saw the snake hanging on Paul and waited long expecting him to suddenly drop dead. However, what they saw was that he wasn't harmed. They then changed their minds from calling Paul a murderer to deciding he was a god (Acts 28:3-6). In this season, every evil expectation of people about you shall be disappointed and converted for your advancement, IJN.

Child of God let us continue to serve God faithfully and depend on Him completely for protection. He has promised that "nothing shall by any means hurt you" (Lk. 10:19) and that "No weapon that is formed against you shall prosper" (Isa. 54:17). Connect with and stay connected to and be committed to Jesus Christ and He will shake off the storms and the snakes from your life, IJN.

Prayer: Father as you did for Paul, shake off and destroy by fire all physical and spiritual storms and snakes from my life, IJN.

Sunday October 13, 2019
Topic: WHEN GOD IS SILENT

Scriptures: "And when Saul enquired of the Lord, the Lord answered him, neither by dreams, nor by Urim, nor by prophets." (1 Samuel 28:6)

Praise the Lord. Today is October 13th and is day #286 in year 2019. The number of days remaining to end this year is 79. By God's grace, your requests shall not go unanswered by the Lord, and you will see the end of this year and beyond, safe and sound in the mighty name of Jesus.

Although God has promised to answer when we call on Him (Jer. 33:3), sins can often be a blocker from hearing from God: "But your iniquities have separated between you and your God, and your sins have hid his face from you, that he will not hear" (Isa 59: 1-2). This aforementioned scripture describes what happened to Saul when he desperately wanted to get direction from God. I pray that the Almighty God will not be silent to your requests and that He will answer you positively and expressly, IJN.

The Philistines prepared and gathered at Shunem to attack the Israelites who had pitched at Gilboa (1 Sam 28:4). When Saul saw the host of the Philistines "he was afraid, and his heart greatly trembled" (v.5). As indicated in today's opening scripture Saul's desire to enquire about the war from God by dream, or Urim or by prophets yielded no desired result. This was because Sauls's disobedience to God had robbed him of the Spirit of God (1 Sam 16:15). Also he has lost the services of priests and prophets who he had slain.

Instead of repenting of his sins of disobedience and shedding of innocent blood, Saul, out of frustration went to Endor to consult with a woman with familiar spirit to bring up Samuel who has been dead (1 Sam 28:7-14). Sins not immediately dealt with can breed more sins, "And when sin is allowed to grow, it gives birth to death" (James 1:15, NLT). Samuel appeared to Saul and reproached him for his misconduct and then prophesied that Saul and his sons would die the following day (1 Sam. 28:15-19). Lessons: When it appears that God is silent to your prayer, (1) don't give up, (2) search for sins to confess and repent of, (3) keep praying & fasting (1 Thes. 5:17, Mk 9:29), (4) don't consult palm readers, familiar spirit, unbelievers, etc. Keep trusting God and pray more. **Prayer: Father, destroy anything that will hinder answers to my prayers and please deliver me from the "spirit of Endor", IJN.**

Monday October 14, 2019
Topic: PARTAKING IN GOD'S PRIVILEDGES

Scriptures: "The Lord shall cause thine enemies that rise up against thee to be smitten before thy face: they shall come out against thee one way, and flee before thee seven ways" (Deuteronomy 28:7)

Praise the Lord. Today is October 14th and is day #287 in year 2019. The number of days remaining to end this year is 78. By God's grace, all your enemies shall flee before you, and you will see the end of this year and beyond, safe and sound in the mighty name of Jesus.

One of the privileges of a bona fide believer in Jesus Christ is overcoming his/her enemies. The enemies of the believers are numerous and are of various kinds and calibers – spiritual, physical, principalities, powers etc. The modus operandi of the enemy is also highly diversified. However, as today's scripture implies all enemies of the child of God (irrespective of number or types) are subject to defeat and/or destruction. In addition, God has promised that "No weapon formed against you shall prosper, And every tongue which rises against you in judgment You shall condemn. - - -"(Isaiah 54:17).

What must the believer do to appropriate this privilege of divine protection? The answer, as given by the word of God through Moses is to, "-- hearken diligently unto the voice of the Lord thy God, to observe and to do all his commandments-"(Deut. 28:1). May we all live a life of obedience and holiness so that, "--When the enemy shall come in like a flood, the Spirit of the Lord shall lift up a standard against him (Isaiah 59:19).

Prayer: Father, as a partaker of Your privileges please fight all my battles and let me overcome all my enemies

Tuesday October 15, 2019
Topic: SINGING TO THE SAVIOR

Scriptures: "The number of them along with their brothers, who were trained in singing to the Lord, all who were skillful, was 288." (1 Chronicles 25:7)

Praise the Lord. Today is October 15th and is day #288 in year 2019. The number of days remaining to end this year is 77. By God's grace, your name shall be included in the the Choir of heaven who will praise the Lord forever, and you will see the end of this year and beyond, safe and sound in the mighty name of Jesus.

Singing songs and making music to the Savior, the Lord of lords and the King of kings is an important aspect of practicing the Christian faith. This is a sharp contrast to the Islamic faith where many regard music as haram (forbidden), and singing is very rare in Mosque practices. The Bible is full of musicians, songs and singing (Gen 4:21, Exo 15:1-18, Judges 11:34.,1 Sam.18:6–7, (Deut. 32:1–43, Matt. 9:23; 26:30, Mk 14:26, Lk 5:25, Eph. 5:19, etc.)

David is described as "the sweet psalmist of Israel" (2 Sam. 23:1) and he is credited with writing about half of the 150 songs recorded in Psalms, along with some in the historical books. He was the official musician in Saul's court (1 Sam.16:14–23). David's son, Solomon wrote 2 Psalms and 1005 other songs (1 Kgs 4:32) and the book of Song of Solomon. Although David was not permitted to build God's Temple, before he died, he made detailed arrangement for how the Temple would be built and how Temple services would be conducted. Singing to God was a strong component of David's plan and as indicated in today's opening scripture the choir he set up consisted of 288 skillful Levites who were well trained in singing to the LORD.

The purposes of singing unto to the LORD are many and include 3 major ones of (a) praising God (Ps. 150, 1 Cor.10:31), (b) praying to God (Ps. 3-8, James 5:13) and (c) proclaiming God's word (Eph. 5:19). Singing to the LORD can attract many benefits to the singer including (i) victory over the enemy (2 Chron. 20: 21-24), (ii) longevity of life (Ps 104:33), (iii) attraction of God's presence (2 Chron. 5: 1-14).

Prayer: Father fill my mouth with songs of praise, thanksgiving and victory, IJN

Wednesday October 16, 2019
Topic: REASON TO REJOICE

Scriptures: "And as they went to tell His disciples, behold, Jesus met them, saying, Rejoice!" So they came and held Him by the feet and worshiped Him." (Matthew 28:9)

Praise the Lord. Today is October 16th and is day #289 in year 2019. The number of days remaining to end this year is 76. By God's grace, you will you will have multiple reasons to rejoice this season, and you will see the end of this year and beyond, safe and sound in the mighty name of Jesus.

The word "rejoice" is used some 187 times in the Bible (NKJV), 42 of which occur in the New Testament. According to Matthew's account of the Gospel, "Rejoice" (or 'All Hail') was the first word spoken by Jesus after His resurrection. The occasion was when He appeared to the women who had gone to His tomb to seek Him and were told by an angel to go tell the disciples about His resurrection (Matt. 28:1-7).

Before Jesus appeared to these women on their way to telling the disciples about Jesus' resurrection as instructed, their joy was mixed with fear (v. 8). The fear disappeared after they had an encounter with Jesus.

As indicated in today's opening scripture, when Jesus met the women and said, "Rejoice" they held him by the feet and worshiped Him. They were no longer "ear witnesses" alone, they have also become "eyewitnesses" of the risen Christ. In addition, they touched him as they held Him by the feet and worshiped Him. The women could rejoice because fear was gone, hope came alive and they were encouraged and emboldened to carry the message of Jesus' resurrection to the disciples.

If you have Jesus as your LORD, you have reason to rejoice for the Bible says, "- - Christ in you, the hope of glory" (Col. 1:27). Because He lives, you shall live (2 Cor. 13:4). Invite His presence into your life and situations for "in His presence is fullness of joy" (Ps. 16:11). Obey the command "Rejoice always" (1 Thess. 5:18) and cultivate that attitude.

Prayer: Father, let me experience ceaseless joy by reason of Jesus that lives in me, IJN

Thursday October 17, 2019
Topic: TRIBULATION TIMES

Scriptures: "From the time that the daily worship is banished from the Temple and the obscene desecration is set up in its place, there will be 1,290 days "Blessed are those who patiently make it through the 1,335 days" (Daniel 12:11-12, MSG)

Praise the Lord. Today is October 17th and is day #290 in year 2019. The number of days remaining to end this year is 75. By God's grace, you will see the end of this year and beyond, safe and sound in the mighty name of Jesus.

Daniel's continued vision about the wonders of the end time is the main focus of chapter 12 of his book. He received information about a time of trouble never seen before, resurrection of the dead, some to everlasting life and some to shame and contempt, etc. (Dan 12: 1-3). Included in his vision also was a question posed by one of 2 people he saw: "How long shall it be to end of these wonders?". The answer (in part) provided to this and other questions is what we have in today's opening scripture above.

The numbers 1290 days, 1335 days and the 1260 days mentioned in Revelation 11:3 has generated considerable discussions and opinions in the context of the seven-year tribulation period. In this regards a summary of timeline and sequence of events as some people see it is as follow:

• Sometime after the rapture, the Antichrist enters a treaty with Israel marking the beginning of the seven-year tribulation.

• At the midpoint of the tribulation (1,260 days or 3.5 years later, the Antichrist breaks the treaty, desecrates the temple, and begins to persecute the Jews.

• At the end of the tribulation (1,260 days after the desecration of the temple, Jesus Christ returns to earth and defeats the forces of the Antichrist.

• During the next 30 days (leading up to 1,290 days after the desecration of the temple), Israel is rebuilt and the earth is restored.

• During the next 45 days (leading up to 1,335 days after the desecration of the temple), the Gentile nations are judged for their treatment of Israel.

While there has been much speculations about the numbers above, the obvious point is that the time of persecution has a definite end because God is in control of it and He will be victorious over evil. You too shall be victorious over your enemies. ***Prayer: Father; please deliver me from tribulation, now and at the end of time, IJN.***

Friday October 18, 2019
Topic: REACTING TO REPROOFS

Scriptures: "He, that being often reproved hardeneth his neck, shall suddenly be destroyed, and that without remedy" (Proverbs 29:1).

Praise the Lord. Today is October 18th and is day #291 in year 2019. The number of days remaining to end this year is 74. By God's grace, you will receive and prosper from constructive criticism, and you will see the end of this year and beyond, safe and sound in the mighty name of Jesus.

Simply put, to reprove is to criticize with the intention to correct. Reproof is an expression of censure or rebuke. Reproof may also entail discipline. For reproof to produce the expected beneficial result, the parties involved (the one reproving and the one been reproved) must have the right attitude. The key element of that attitude is love. The Bible declares, "For whom the Lord loveth he chasteneth,- " (Heb. 12:6). Therefore, rebuking must be done with love and received with love.

As indicated in today's opening scripture wrong attitude of detesting and rejecting reproof can lead to destruction beyond remedy. Destruction will not be our portion, IJN. First and foremost, every believer must exercise self-reproof or self-discipline by deliberately avoiding sins and repenting of those sins committed in order to avoid God's reproof (Rev. 3:19). Then we must tell and train those in our circle of influence (children, spouses, friends, ministry members, etc.) to do the same. In this regard, children tend to pose a greater challenge in and should be handled with greater prayer, care and counseling and use of the scripture (Pro. 3: 11-12; 6:23; 13:24, 22:15, 23:13; 29:17, Eph. 6:4, Heb. 12:5-11).

In general, appropriate reproof can be done using the tools of (a) Name of Jesus (Phil. 2: 8-9, Lk. 1:37), (b) prayer (1 Thes. 5:17, Matt. 7:7), (c) the word of God (2 Tim. 3:16),

(d) Counseling and Love (Heb. 12:6, Rev. 3:19) etc. Some of the benefits of reproof done and received with right attitude include (1) life instead of death (Pro 6:23; (2) driving foolishness away (Pro 22:12), (3) peaceful fruits of righteousness (Heb. 12:11), (4) wisdom and knowledge (Pro 29:15, 12:1).

Prayer: Father, whether I am the object or subject of reproof, give me the grace to derive blessings from it rather than destruction, IJN.

Saturday October 19, 2019
Topic: RIGHTEOUS VERSUS WICKED RULER

Scriptures: "When the righteous are in authority, the people rejoice; But when a wicked man rules, the people groan." (Proverbs 29:2, NKJV)

Praise the Lord. Today is October 19th and is day #292 in year 2019. The number of days remaining to end this year is 73. By God's grace, you shall not partake in the sorrows emanating from the activities of any wicked man ruling over you, and you will you will see the end of this year and beyond, safe and sound in the mighty name of Jesus.

Sadly, it is very rare to find righteous leaders any more especially in the political arena. Greed, ungodliness, power drunkenness, corruption, lack of compassion for the poor, insensitivity, ineptitude, nepotism, racial prejudice, etc. are some of the factors that characterize the reign of the wicked. On the contrary, the righteous are expected to exhibit godliness, passionate in doing what is right, compassionate and caring for the poor, eschewing evil, etc. While the menaces of the wicked tend to create hardship for the ruled, the good will and programs of the righteous should make room for people's wellbeing, progress and peaceful existence.

As indicated in today's opening scripture, people will rejoice or mourn depending on whether their ruler is righteous or wicked. Majority of the kings who ruled in ancient Israel and Judah were wicked exposing their people to untold hardship. King Ahab who ruled Israel for 22 years has been rated as about the worst king of his time in 1 Kings 16:30. On the contrary, Asa was a good ruler of Judah for 41years. His reign was marked by revival in the worship of the LORD, removal of paganism and evil activities, safety and reduced crime and by military peace. Although Asa wavered in his faith and trust in God towards the end of his life the Bible says "Asa did that which was good and right in the eyes of the LORD his God (1 Chron 14:2)

As a follower of Christ, you have important roles to play in any system you find yourself. These roles include living a godly life as example of righteousness (1 Tim 4:12-16) and being a shining light for uprightness (Matt 5:16). Additionally, and perhaps more importantly, the believers can significantly influence what goes on the system by engaging in effective intercessory prayer for those in authority in that system (1Tim 2:2, Jer.1: 5-10). **Prayer: Father, please give us righteous leaders that we Your people may rejoice, IJN**

Sunday October 20, 2019
Topic: GIVING GLORY TO GOD

Scriptures: "The voice of the Lord is upon the waters: the God of glory thundereth: the Lord is upon many waters" (Psalm 29: 3)

Praise the Lord. Today is October 20th and is day #293 in year 2019. The number of days remaining to end this year is 72. By God's grace, you will greatly glorify the God of glory this season, and you will see the end of this year and beyond, safe and sound in the mighty name of Jesus.

With respect to God, the word glory in the Old Testament connotes greatness of splendor. In the New Testament, the word "glory" means dignity, honor, praise and worship. In summary, giving glory to God can mean to acknowledge His greatness and give Him honor by praising and worshiping Him, primarily because He, and He alone, deserves to be praised, honored and worshiped.

Psalm 29 from which today's scripture has come admonishes that glory be given to God. Who are the people to give this glory to God? David said the "mighty" (Ps 29:2). Does this include you? Yes, especially if you are a born-again child of God. The Bible says you are the son (or daughter) of God (John1 :12), God is mindful of you, He has crowned you with glory and honor and has given you dominion over all His works (Ps. 8: 4-6). Hallelujah! Furthermore, God has magnified you, sets His heart upon you and even visits you every morning (Job 7:17-18) Remember, the word of God in Pro. 23:7. So you must count yourself privileged to be among the people asked to give glory to God.

We are to give glory to God for many reasons including (1) He is the God of Glory, (Ps. 29:3 & 1 Chron. 29: 11), (2) Glory is due to His name (1 Chron 16: 29, Ps. 29:2, Ps. 115:1a, 1 Chron 16: 29), (3) He said He will not share His glory (Isa. 42:8), (4) For all the wonderful works of God in our lives, the lives others and in the world in general etc. (2 Peter 3:5). Before there was anything; light, plant, etc., there was water (Gen 1:1-2)

Today's opening scripture says the voice of the Lord is upon the waters and the LORD is upon many waters. As you think and encounter waters in (drinking, cooking, washing, etc.) may God speak words of peace, prosperity, healing. victory etc.) into your life, IJN. *Action / Prayer: Think of what the Lord has done for you in the 293 days so far of year 2019 and give Him glory*

Monday October 21, 2019
Topic: RESTORATION

Scriptures: "Thus saith the Lord of hosts, the God of Israel, unto all that are carried away captives, whom I have caused to be carried away from Jerusalem unto Babylon;" (Jeremiah 29:4)

Praise the Lord. Today is October 21st and is day #294 in year 2019. The number of days remaining to end this year is 71. By God's grace, you shall not be carried away into captivity, and you will see the end of this year and beyond, safe and sound in the mighty name of Jesus.

As indicated in today's opening scripture, God caused some Israelites to be carried away into captivity in Babylon. Why? Because of their disobedience to God's commandments and their deep involvement in paganism, idolatry and witchcraft. Furthermore, they ignored all of the warnings that God sent to them through His prophets. While in captivity God sent a message through Jeremiah to the captives, that they should move ahead with their lives - Build houses, and dwell in them; plant gardens, and eat the fruit of them, get married and increase in number, pray unto the Lord for their captors, etc. (see Jer. 29:4-23). God also promised saying "- - after seventy years be accomplished at Babylon I will visit you, and perform my good word toward you, in causing you to return to this place" (Jer. 29:10).

God kept His promise such that after the 70 years Israel began to return (read Ezra chp.1). The books of Ezra and Nehemiah tell the full story of the restoration of the Jewish nation after the Babylonian Captivity. The first return occurred in 536 BC (Ezra chaps. 1-6), the second in 457, BC (Ezra chps. 7-10), and the third return in 444 BC (Neh. chaps. 1-13).

Lessons: Have you suffered any displacement, or lost something (job, money, friendship, marriage, etc.), don't let your life grind to a halt during troubled times. Seek the face of God and trust Him the more, encourage yourself, make necessary adjustments and keep moving. God can turn your adversary to an advantage. It was in captivity that Esther became the Queen of the land. Another lesson to learn is to pray for those in authority, even if they are evil (1 Tim 2:1-2). The LORD commands it, ours is to obey it.

Prayer: Father restore unto me everything I have lost and deliver me from spiritual and other forms of captivity IJN

Tuesday October 22, 2019
Topic: GOD OF COVENANTS

Scriptures: "I have led you forty years in the wilderness. Your clothes have not worn out on you, and your sandals have not worn off your feet." (Deuteronomy 29:5)

Praise the Lord. Today is October 22nd and is day #295 in year 2019. The number of days remaining to end this year is 70. By God's grace, your life and all that you have shall be preserved by the Lord, and you will see the end of this year and beyond, safe and sound in the mighty name of Jesus.

God is a covenant maker and covenant keeper. He made a covenant with Israel at Horeb or Mt Sinai in which Israel would be His treasured possession as a kingdom of priests and a holy nation so long Israel would obey His laws and do everything He said. Israel agreed (Exo 19 &20).

At Moab, just before entering the promised land, the Mt Sinai covenant (centered on the 10 commandments) was renewed and expanded to include the descendants of Israel (Deut. 29). Moses reminded them of God's faithfulness in preserving, protecting and providing for them as illustrated in today's opening scripture above. Moses then exhorted them to be faithful to this renewed covenant as they were preparing to enter the promised land (29:9).

God has led you 295 days so far this year and you are only 70 days away from entering the 'promised land' of year 2020. You are alive, hopefully, you are not wearing rags, you are not walking about shoeless, you are not in the street begging for bread. Moreover, if you are a believer your feet are being shod with the preparation of the Gospel of peace" (Eph. 6:15). That is, "God's word is a lamp unto your feet, and a light unto your path" (Ps. 119:105). That is why you have not slipped neither have you taken the step of death. Count up your blessings and shout Hallelujah.

Prayer: Oh God that keeps covenants preserve me and all that pertains to me from all evils and keep me to the end to reign with you in eternity, IJN

Wednesday October 23, 2019
Topic: DEALING WITH GENERATIONAL SINS

Scriptures: "For our fathers have trespassed, and done that which was evil in the eyes of the Lord our God, and have forsaken him, and have turned away their faces from the habitation of the Lord, and turned their backs." (2 Chronicles 29:6)

Praise the Lord. Today is October 23rd and is day #296 in year 2019. The number of days remaining to end this year is 69. By God's grace, you will not turn away from the Lord forever, and you will see the end of this year and beyond, safe and sound in the mighty name of Jesus.

As far as God is concerned, sins not repented of must be punished no matter how long ago or how recent they were committed (Rom 3:23; Ezek. 18:4). Many people, cities or nations today may be suffering from the effect of sins committed by their ancestors since God said "- -am a jealous God, visiting the iniquity of the fathers upon the children unto the third and fourth generation of them that hate me" (Exo 5:20).

Hezekiah became king of Judah at age 25 and ruled for 29 years (Chron 29). The Bible says he "- did what was right in the eyes of the Lord, - "(v 2). I pray all of us will emulate him in this regard, IJN. One of the right and early things Hezekiah did was he recognized the sins of his ancestors (see today's opening scripture above) and took appropriate steps to deal with them. He said, "Now it is in mine heart to make a covenant with the Lord God of Israel, that his fierce wrath might be turned from us" (v.10). Hezekiah also embarked on several reform projects. For example, he assembled and exhorted the priests and Levites to sanctify themselves and cleanse the temple, (v. 12-17).

Are there stubborn, persistent, intractable and pass-down problems tormenting you and your family? Examples may include sickness, bareness, untimely death, inability to get or hold a job, etc. Any of these may be linked to sins committed (ignorantly or otherwise) by yourself or your ancestors. Examples: shedding of innocent blood, enslavement, idolatry, polygamy, cheating, adultery, homosexuality, land grabbing, forsaking God, etc. In Jesus name intercede in prayer of confession and repentance for yourself, your ancestors, your cities, nations, etc. God said He will hear, answer, forgive and heal the land (2 Chron 7:14).
Prayer: Father, I repent of any personal and ancestral generational sins, please visit my foundation with your mercy and forgive every sin, IJN

Thursday October 24, 2019
Topic: PRAYING FOR PEACE

Scriptures: "And seek the peace of the city whither I have caused you to be carried away captives, and pray unto the LORD for it: for in the peace thereof shall ye have peace" (Jeremiah 29:7)

Praise the Lord. Today is October 24th and is day #297 in year 2019. The number of days remaining to end this year is 68. By God's grace, there will be peace in your place of habitation as you pray to the Prince of peace to bring peace to that place, and you will see the end of this year and beyond, safe and sound in the mighty name of Jesus.

Although God caused the Israelites to be carried away in captivity to Babylon (due largely to their sins of idolatry and disobedience), He was still very interested in their welfare and restoration. In this regard, Jeremiah (directed by God) sent a letter to the captives in Babylon containing specific instruction as to activities God wanted the captives to continue to do even in captivity (Jer. 29:5-7). Among the long "to do list" is praying for the peace of the city of their captivity for, as God said in today's opening scripture "- - in the peace thereof shall ye have peace". In other words, "peace begets peace" and for the captives to be at peace there must be peace in their city of dwelling. Therefore, the captives were mandated to seek peace of the city and to pray unto the LORD for it.

In the present world peace has become a scarce commodity. Since the World War II, there have been over 250 major wars with countless number of casualties. There are over 35 major conflicts going on in the world today. Factors such as poverty, terrorism, conflicts, armed robberies, diseases etc. are on the increase thereby compounding the problem of lack of peace.

The answer to the world peace is in Jesus Christ who is the Prince of Peace (Isa. 9:6). He is the one who can give peace like no one else in John 14:27. The peace Jesus Christ gives surpasses all understanding and guards the hearts and minds against all evils (Phil. 4:7). Anyone who will have Christ-like peace must know Him as his/her Lord and Savior. This condition is well captured in a Church's billboard that said:

NO CHRIST, NO PEACE. KNOW CHRIST, KNOW PEACE. *Action/Prayer: Pray for the peace of the community or nation you are located in; and pray: Father, wherever I am and whatever I am going through, let Your peace surround me, IJN.*

Friday October 25, 2019
Topic: COUNFOUNDED ENEMIES

Scriptures: "A hungry person dreams of eating but wakes up still hungry. A thirsty person dreams of drinking but is still faint from thirst when morning comes. So, it will be with your enemies, with those who attack Mount Zion" (Isaiah 29:8)

Praise the Lord. Today is October 25th and is day #298 in year 2019. The number of days remaining to end this year is 67. By God's grace, uneasiness and lack of satisfaction shall plaque your enemies, and you will see the end of this year and beyond, safe and sound in the mighty name of Jesus.

Available information indicates that Mount Zion in the Hebrew Bible initially meant the City of David (2 Sam. 5:7, 1 Chron.11:5), but its meaning has shifted, and it is now used as the name of ancient Jerusalem's Western Hill. Mount Zion is also referred to as City of God (Ps. 87:2–3; 76:2). In general, Mount Zion can connote the people of God (Ps. 78:68).

Today's opening scripture alludes to the divine security available for Jerusalem. The enemies that attack her hoping to plunder her and prosper from so doing shall have their expectation dashed as they shall fail woefully and go empty handed. Concerning Mount Zion, the Bible declares it "- -cannot be removed, but abideth forever" (Ps. 125:1). Furthermore, the Bible declares, "As birds flying, so will the Lord of hosts defend Jerusalem; defending also he will deliver it; and passing over he will preserve it" (Isa. 31:5).

Believers who put their trust in God shall be like Mount Zion whose enemies shall be confounded. Therefore, all enemies' attacks on such believers shall be futile because they are God's Jerusalem and "As the mountains are round about Jerusalem, so the Lord is round about his people - -" (Ps. 125:2). Your enemies shall flee before you in seven ways, in the mighty name of Jesus.

Prayer: Father please confound all my enemies and let all their attacks on my household be futile, IJN.

Saturday October 26, 2019
Topic: GIVING WILLINGLY TO GOD

Scriptures: "Then the people rejoiced, for that they offered willingly, because with perfect heart they offered willingly to the Lord: and David the king also rejoiced with great joy" (1 Chronicles 29:9).

Praise the Lord. Today is October 26th and is day #299 in year 2019. The number of days remaining to end this year is 66. By God's grace, you will always be a willing giver to the Lord, and you will see the end of this year and beyond, safe and sound in the mighty name of Jesus.

God is a giver and we can learn many lessons from His style of giving. Let me just discuss 3 of these lessons (1) God's giving is based on love. John 3:16 says because of love God gave to the world His only Son (Jesus Christ). Is your giving to God based on love for Him? Giving must be part and parcel of any genuine love. (2) God is generous in His giving. Not only did God give the world His only Son, He has also "- - given unto us all things that pertain unto life and godliness - -" (2 Pet. 1:3). Furthermore, every good and perfect gift comes from God (James 1:17). (3) God gave willingly. For example, no one coerced Him to surrender and sacrifice His Son for the redemption of sinners. Similarly, all other gifts to man were given willingly.

Following God's style of giving can be very beneficial. Giving willingly to God attracts special reward that money cannot quantify. This reward is joy and the principle is well illustrated in today's opening scripture above. After he himself has given willingly and bountifully many precious things towards building the House of God (1 Chron 29:1-4), David encouraged the congregation to do the same (1 Chron. 29:5). The people responded and "- - offered willingly" (v. 6). In return God responded to David's and the peoples' willing offering by giving them joy in proportionality to the level of their giving. The people 'rejoiced' while David 'rejoiced with great joy'. What type of joy do you want from God - no joy? small joy? great joy? What you give and how you give it will determine what you get. God loves a cheerful giver (2 Cor. 9:7).

Prayer: Father, everything I have comes from You, give me the grace to give to You bountifully and willingly, IJN.

Sunday October 27, 2019
Topic: DELIVERANCE FROM DEATH

Scriptures: "The Jews who were in Susa gathered also on the fourteenth day of the month of Adar and they killed 300 men in Susa, but they laid no hands on the plunder." (Esther 9:15, ESV)

Praise the Lord. Today is October 27th and is day #300 in year 2019. The number of days remaining to end this year is 65. By God's grace, you will not be killed or plundered this season, and you will see the end of this year and beyond, safe and sound in the mighty name of Jesus.

One of the promises of God to His faithful followers is divine deliverance from death. In some instances, not only will God deliver His own from death, He can even turn the tide of death against the enemies of His people, this is what the LORD meant in Isa. 49:25-26 when He said "- -Even the captives of the mighty shall be taken away, and the prey of the terrible shall be delivered. Biblical examples of people for whom God miraculously turned the tide of death against their enemies include Shadrach, Meshach, and Abednego; Daniel; Elijah and the exiled Jews in Persia (Dan 3: 20-27; 6: 16-24; 2 Kings 1: 1-11; Est 9: 1-25).

Although the word, God or LORD, is not specifically written anywhere in the book of Esther, the divine acts of a sovereign God can be seen all over the pages of this book. It was God that made Esther, a Jewess orphan maid, to receive favor and grace leading to her becoming the Queen of the land (Esther 2 & 3). In her new status as Queen she was able to convince the king to save the lives of her people - the Jews. The Jews were already on death row due to evil plot of Haman, the enemy of Mordecai who was Esther's uncle. Haman's plot to get Mordecai and all the Jews killed backfired and Haman ended up hung in the gallows he prepared for Mordecai (Est 4 to 7). Mordecai was honored and promoted to be second in command to the king, and all the Jews were freed by a new decree (Est.8).

On the day the Jews were scheduled for execution (13th of the twelfth month), it was their enemies that were killed in mass because the tide of death has been turned against them. On the following day, the Jew also killed 300 men in Susa as indicated in today's opening scripture (Es. 9). As year 2019 is coming to an end your life shall not come an end, IJN. **Prayer: Father, turn the tide against any enemy planning to harm or kill me IJN.**

Monday October 28, 2019
Topic: REMOVING BARENESS REPROACHES

Scriptures: "And when Rachel saw that she bare Jacob no children, Rachel envied her sister; and said unto Jacob, Give me children, or else I die." (Genesis 30:1)

Praise the Lord. Today is October 28th and is day #301 in year 2019. The number of days remaining to end this year is 64. By God's grace, no form of bareness (spiritual, financial, biological, etc.) shall be your portion, and you will see the end of this year and beyond, safe and sound in the mighty name of Jesus.

According to God's foundational agenda and plan, no human being is to be barren (Gen.1:28; Exo 23:26, Deut.7:14). The principle is still the same today, bareness is a reproach and can be removed with the help of God. Out of the 8 cases of barrenness in the Bible the only one that did not end up with child/children was David's wife, Michal. She remained barren for life because she "touched God's anointed" by despising David while he was passionately worshipping the Almighty God (2 Sam 6).

Jacob's journey into marriage began at a well at Haran where he first saw Rachel. Eventually, Jacob loved Rachel so much that he " - served seven years for Rachel; and they seemed unto him but a few days, --" (Gen 29:20). Jacob ended up marrying Leah and Rachel for an additional 7 years of service since he was told tradition of the land forbade giving out the younger sister into marriage before the first born.

As typical of any polygamous relationships, problems (unhealthy rivalry, envy, hatred, etc.) began to multiply in Jacob's household. Leah had children, but Rachel was barren (Gen. 29: 30-35). Out of frustration, Rachel made the statement in today's opening scripture. Note that sometimes bareness may be generational, possibly due to a curse. Each of the 3 great patriarchs (Abraham, Isaac and Jacob) had a wife who had difficulty in conceiving children. Generational bareness in your family is here by broken permanently, IJN.

Rachel did not give up. As she continued to pray, "- -God remembered Rachel, and God hearkened to her, and opened her womb. And she conceived, and bare a son; and said, God hath taken away my reproach:" (Gen. 30:22-23). Rachel became the mother of 2 sons - Joseph and Benjamin (Gen. 35:24). **Prayer: *Father, please remove all marital reproaches including that of barrenness, IJN.***

Tuesday October 29, 2019
Topic: HEALING FROM THE HEALER

Scriptures: "O Lord my God, I cried unto thee, and thou hast healed me." (Psalm 30:2)

Praise the Lord. Today is October 29th and is day #302 in year 2019. The number of days remaining to end this year is 63. By God's grace, you will enjoy all round divine healing this season, and you will see the end of this year and beyond, safe and sound in the mighty name of Jesus.

Sickness is a disease, illness or malady that causes some discomfort such as pain. Since Adam and Eve sinned at the beginning of creation, sin and sickness have afflicted humanity. Today, there are so many types of sicknesses, some physical and some spiritual. If we broaden the definition above the types of sickness will increase and may include spiritual, financial, marital, business, poverty, etc. Satan is the ultimate source of all sicknesses.

The good news is that the loving God sent His son Jesus Christ into the world to redeem sinners from the penalty of sins and to destroy all the works of devil which include sickness. The Bible says, "- - For this purpose the Son of God was manifested, that he might destroy the works of the devil" (1 John 3:8). The work of the devil includes propagation and imposition of sickness.

Jesus is the ultimate healer of all sicknesses. The Bible says at the name of Jesus every knee should bow (Phil. 2:9-11). Jehovah Rapha, one of the names of Jesus, illustrates very well His ability to heal. Jehovah Rapha can be translated "I am the Lord your Healer" (Exo 15:26). When Jesus died at the Cross, he had not only taken all our sins, he took along the results of our sins which include sickness (Col. 2:14; Isa 53: 4-5, Matt 8:17).

In today's opening scripture the Psalmist (possibly David) provides us with a clue of how we may deal with sickness. He said he cried to the LORD his God and He healed him. Are you suffering from any sickness? Cry to God in the name of Jesus, repent of any known sins, ask for mercy and God's healing power, plead the blood of Jesus on yourself, and claim the wonderful promises of God to heal (Pro 4:20; Matt 8:17; 1 Pet 2:4; Matt 14:14). The healer will heal you, and you shall be free from sickness, IJN. **Prayer: *Jehovah Rapha, please heal me from sins, sicknesses and sorrows, IJN***

Wednesday October 30, 2019
Topic: COMPASSION THAT TURNS CAPTIVITY

Scriptures: "That then the Lord thy God will turn thy captivity, and have compassion upon thee, and will return and gather thee from all the nations, whither the Lord thy God hath scattered thee" (Deuteronomy 30:3).

Praise the Lord. Today is October 30th and is day #303 in year 2019. The number of days remaining to end this year is 62. By God's grace and compassion, you have entered an era of freedom from captivity, and you will see the end of this year and beyond, safe and sound in the mighty name of Jesus.

One important attribute of God that believers cannot survive without is that God is "- full of compassion" (Ps. 78:38; 86:15; 111:4; 112:40). No wonder the Bible declares, "- -his compassions fail not" (Lam. 3:22). Furthermore, the prerogative on whom to show compassion rests solely on God. (Rom. 9:15).

In today's opening scripture, there are 3 promises God made to the Jews provided they display obedience to Him as spelt out in Deuteronomy 27, 28 and 29. Two of these promises (turning their captivity and gathering them from all nations to which they have been scattered) are driven by (or contingent on) the third and central promise which is 'have compassion upon thee'. In this season I pray God will manifest His compassion to you, IJN.

The unfailing compassion of God is life transforming. Not only can it turn captivity and cause scattered people to be gathered, it can be a platform for manifesting all kinds of miracles such as healing the sick (Matt 14:14), opening blind eyes (Matt 20:34), cleansing the leper (Mk. 1: 40-42), multiplying limited food resources to surplus to feed multitudes (Matt 15: 32-39), debts written off (Matt 18: 23-27), etc.

God's tank of compassion is always full and inexhaustible. He is not a respecter of persons; what he did for the Jews, He can do for you and much more. By His compassion He can save your soul and do other miracles in your life. Call on Him NOW.

Prayer: Father, by Your compassion please transform my life, turn my captivity and fill my mouth with laughter and my tongue with singing, IJN.

Thursday October 31, 2019
Topic: COUNTDOWN TO "THE DAY OF THE LORD"

Scriptures: "And the sword shall come upon Egypt, and great pain shall be in Ethiopia, when the slain shall fall in Egypt, and they shall take away her multitude, and her foundations shall be broken down." (Ezekiel 30:4).

Praise the Lord. Today is October 31st and is day #304 in year 2019. The number of days remaining to end this year is 61. By God's grace, your foundation shall not be broken, neither will you fall into the hand of the enemy, and you will see the end of this year and beyond, safe and sound in the mighty name of Jesus.

The word of the Lord came to Ezekiel in which he was asked to prophesy against Egypt and its allies to foretell their destruction and great sorrow mainly because of their pride and idolatry (Ezek. Chps 28-30: 1-3). The imminent day is described as "the day of the Lord" in which God would manifest Himself as the God of vengeance.

One lesson we can learn about Ezekiel's prophesy against Egypt relates to the phrase "the day of the Lord". With respect to Egypt the scope of this phrase is limited to the diminishing of Egyptian power by the Babylonians. In a broader context "the day of the Lord" describes the Lord's final judgment of the world at the end of human history (Dr. Jeremiah). The "day of the Lord" is used some 20 times in the Bible (Isa. 2:12; 13:6, 9). One thought and believe is that the day of the Lord will be an instantaneous event when Christ returns to earth to redeem His faithful believers and send unbelievers to eternal damnation. Various descriptions of the day of the Lord are given in the Bible in Joel 3:14, Joel. 1:15, 2 Pet 3:4; 1 Thes. 5:1. Joel 2:1 and Zech. 14:1 tells us what our attitude should be.

The countdown to the day of the Lord has begun. Nobody knows when the last day will be, but it is imminent. Are you ready to meet Jesus Christ? You can be ready and avoid going to eternal damnation by giving your life to Jesus Christ and accepting Him as your Lord and Savior. This is how to avoid a punishment worse than that of Egypt described in today's opening scripture. **Prayer: *Lord Jesus, on the day of he Lord let me not be found wanting, let me be ready to reign with You, IJN***

Friday November 1, 2019
Topic: WALKING AWAY FROM WEEPING

Scriptures: "For his anger endureth but a moment; in his favour is life: weeping may endure for a night, but joy cometh in the morning" (Psalm 30:5).

Praise the Lord. Today is November 1st and is day #305 in year 2019. The number of days remaining to end this year is 60. By God's grace, you shall not weep any more, joy will permeate your life, and you will see the end of this year and beyond, safe and sound in the mighty name of Jesus.

Welcome to the first day of November. Psalm 30, from which today's opening scripture comes, is the first Psalm to be labeled as a Song and a Psalm. The difference between a song and a psalm was that a psalm was sung upon musical instruments, a song with the voice. Apparently, psalm 30 was sung both ways during the occasion of David's dedication of his house.

There are 3 important attributes of God worth noting in today's opening scripture:

#1. God's anger endureth but a moment. The Bible says God is slow to anger (Neh. 9:17, Ps. 103:8, 145:8, Joel2:13, Jonah 4:2, Nah. 1:3). Whenever we offend God and He is angry with us, the sooner we repent, the sooner his anger is turned away and he is willing to be at peace with us (Isa 54: 7-8). If God marks iniquity none of us can stand (Ps. 130:3).

#2: In His favour is life. God's favor connotes His lovingkindness which is actually greater than life (Ps. 63:3). God's has no pleasure in the death but in the life of a sinner who will repent (Ezek 18:32; 33:11).

#3: Weeping may endure for a night but joy cometh in the morning. The Bible says there is time for everything (Eccl. 3:1). If God's anger does not persist and His favor is not removed or diminished, weeping cannot last long. Are you facing any tough time or hardship now? Just trust God and cry for His favor regarding the situation. Be encouraged, that situation will soon give way to something better, IJN. Like the widow in Nain you can walk away from weeping , IJN (Luke 7: 11-16)

Prayer: Father, favor me to live a life of abundance devoid of sorrow and weeping, IJN

Saturday November 2, 2019
Topic: CIRCUMCISION OF THE HEART

Scriptures: "And the Lord thy God will circumcise thine heart, and the heart of thy seed, to love the Lord thy God with all thine heart, and with all thy soul, that thou mayest live". (Deuteronomy 30:6).

Praise the Lord. Today is November 2nd and is day #306 in year 2019. The number of days remaining to end this year is 59. By God's grace, your love for the Lord and people will wax stronger and you will live and not die, and you will see the end of this year and beyond, safe and sound in the mighty name of Jesus.

In physical sense circumcision means, for male, the removal of the prepuce, and for female, the removal of the clitoris, prepuce or labia, possibly for religious rite in both cases. Spiritually, circumcision means to purify. Circumcision is first mentioned in the Bible when God made a covenant with Abraham and told him to memorialize the covenant with the token of circumcising every male person of his household (Gen 17: 10-25). The ordinance of circumcision was an outward physical sign of one's willingness to obey God and be one of His chosen people.

God who is omniscient and knows the end from the beginning allowed the use of circumcision in the Old Covenant as a symbol of what must happen to a person's heart under the New Covenant, which is where circumcision was aimed from its inception. Circumcision of the heart mentioned in today's scripture refers to having a pure heart, separated unto God. God says He will circumcise the heart of His people for 2 major purposes: (1) that they can love Him with all their heart, and with all their soul, and (2) that they may live. Earlier in the book of Deuteronomy, God also said the people themselves were to do the circumcision of their own heart so that they will be "- -no more stiffnecked" (Deut. 10:16). The 2 scriptures (Dt. 10:16 & 30:6) support each other, thus lending credence to the efficacy of spiritual circumcision. In this process the sinner must cooperate with God's plan to get their hearts spiritually circumcised through repentance of sins and acceptance by faith of the salvation offered by Jesus Christ (Col.2:10-11).

Spiritually circumcised heart has been changed from stony heart to heart of flesh (Ezek 11:19; 36:26) and is ready for God's kingdom. Without Christ your heart will remain uncircumcised. Receive Jesus Christ as your Savior today and get your heart circumcised

Prayer: Father, circumcise my entire body for Your use, IJN.

Sunday November 3, 2019
Topic: CANCELLATION OF CURSES

Scriptures: And the Lord thy God will put all these curses upon thine enemies, and on them that hate thee, which persecuted thee." (Deuteronomy 30:7).

Praise the Lord. Today is November 3nd and is day #307 in year 2019. The number of days remaining to end this year is 58. By God's grace, all your enemies shall be cursed by the Lord, and you will see the end of this year and beyond, safe and sound in the mighty name of Jesus.

A curse is an evil invoked on someone. Curses may originate from various sources such as Satan, self, somebody else or from God. No matter the source, all curses have causes for the Bible says "- -the curse causeless shall not come". (Pro. 26:2). One of the most common causes of curses is disobedience. For example, the long list of curses in Deuteronomy 28: 16-68 are contingent on disobedience just like the blessings enumerated in verses 1 to 14 of the same chapter depend on obedience.

Disobedience to God is a sin and a major breeding ground for sins is the uncircumcised heart which the Bible says is desperately wicked (Jer. 17:9, James 1:14-15). As indicated earlier sins attract curses. All curses no matter their sources can be removed by God. One-way God can remove curses is to circumcise the wicked heart of the accursed person. This spiritual circumcision of the heart is what God promised to do to the Israelites and their descendants, including believers like us (Deut. 30:6).

Not only can God remove curses from those He has circumcised, He can transfer the curses to their enemies as indicated in today's opening scripture. Are you a victim of curses, generational or otherwise? cry to God to forgive and terminate the sins that may be magnetizing curses to you.

Prayer: Father, deliver me from disobedience and let all curses be cancelled from my life IJN.

Monday November 4, 2019
Topic: PURSUING TO PREVAIL

Scriptures: "And David enquired at the Lord, saying, Shall I pursue after this troop? shall I overtake them? And he answered him, Pursue: for thou shalt surely overtake them, and without fail recover all." (2 Samuel 30:8).

Praise the Lord. Today is November 4th and is day #308 in year 2019. The number of days remaining to end this year is 57. By God's grace, whatever you pursue this season you will overtake victoriously, and you will see the end of this year and beyond, safe and sound in the mighty name of Jesus.

Concerning David, it can be said that "Many are the afflictions of the righteous: but the Lord delivereth him out of them all" (Ps. 34:19). One of David's afflictions was the attack by the Amalekites on his household and the city Ziklag to which David had run to escape death pursuit by Saul (2 Sam 27: 1-4). Upon arrival in Ziklag David and his army found out that the Amalekites had invaded the city, burned it down and carried all their people and property away including David's 2 wives. All the people wept until they could weep no more. David was in great danger and distress as all his followers threatened to stone him (2 Sam 30: 1-6). David encouraged himself in the Lord (v.6) and enquired from the LORD as indicated in today's opening scripture. As promised by the Lord, David pursued his enemies and recovered all (2 Samuel 30:8).

There are many lessons to learn from this story, but time permits me to mention only three: #1 It is advisable to enquire from God for every decision (engage prayer, word of God, appropriate counseling and other Godly ideas). David did not enquire from God before escaping to Ziklag, enemy's territory. No wonder he lied again there and suffered rejection and captivity of his family and other people. #2. Most of the time crying and complaining do not solve problems. While others were sobbing and engaging in pity party, David encouraged himself in the Lord and got clear revelation of what to do to move forward and find solution. Weep not, Look unto God for help for every problem you face. #3. If you are a believer, there is a "priest" in your life. Bring him or her into your problems as David brought Abiather into his situation and got divine direction. ***Prayer: Father, let me recover everything I have lost; and prevail in all areas of my life IJN***

Tuesday November 5, 2019
Topic: PROSPERING FOR GOD'S PLEASURE

Scriptures: "Then the Lord your God will make you most prosperous in all the work of your hands and in the fruit of your womb, the young of your livestock and the crops of your land. The Lord will again delight in you and make you prosperous, just as he delighted in your ancestors" (Deuteronomy 30:9, NIV).

Praise the Lord. Today is November 5th and is day #309 in year 2019. The number of days remaining to end this year is 56. By God's grace, the Lord will delight in you and you shall be fruitful and prosperous, and you will see the end of this year and beyond, safe and sound in the mighty name of Jesus.

In terms of prosperity, God has wonderful promises and plans for His people. For example, God said His people will prosper and be in health, even as their souls prosper (3 John v.2); that whatsoever His people do will prosper (Psalm 1: 1, 3); that His people will not lack any good thing (Ps. 23:1, 84:11-12, Phil 4:19); that the righteous shall flourish (Ps. 92:12-15), etc.

In general, obedience is usually one of the required conditions for accessing God's promises of prosperity. The importance of obedience to prosperity is well illustrated in the fact that today's opening scripture above is sandwiched between 2 verses that require the people to obey the voice of the Lord and follow all his commands (Deut. 30: 8, 10). Thus, anyone who wants to prosper and retain the prosperity must obey the voice of the Lord God of prosperity. Furthermore, the prosperity God gives must be used in ways to delight and please Him. You shall be blessed to be a blessing, IJN.

How may your prosperity delight the Lord? Here are a few suggestions: Use your talents, time and treasures to win souls, find needs in your place of worship that you can help to meet, such as financial support for building project, the Choir, lawn care, scholarship for needy students, help feed the poor, support mission work, etc. God will delight in you, IJN.

Prayer: Father, proper me and let me be pleasing unto You, IJN

Wednesday November 6, 2019
Topic: BRINGING FORTH GOOD FRUIT

Scriptures: "And now also the axe is laid unto the root of the trees: therefore every tree which bringeth not forth good fruit is hewn down, and cast into the fire". (Matthew 3:10).

Praise the Lord. Today is November 6th and is day #310 in year 2019. The number of days remaining to end this year is 55. By God's grace, all your undertakings shall manifest fruitfulness, and you will see the end of this year and beyond, safe and sound in the mighty name of Jesus.

John the Baptist was a forerunner of the Messiah who was preoccupied with preparing people for the coming of Jesus Christ. He preached and baptized people in the wilderness saying, Repent ye: for the kingdom of heaven is at hand"(John 3:2). His message is still relevant today and every believer is commanded to preach it (Mk. 15: 16-17)

Among those that came to John to be baptized were the Pharisees and the Sadducees. However, John perceived their motive for coming was not for true repentance as they have even queried John's mission at some point (John 1:24-29). Therefore, John immediately launched his assault on the them calling them "brood of vipers" (Matt. 3:7). Basically, he associated them with death and, with Satan who through a snake deceived Eve (Gen 3:1, 2 Cor 11:3). Furthermore, John challenged them to bear fruits in keeping with repentance (v.9). He pointed out to them the consequence of not bearing fruit which is as indicated in today's opening scripture. Addressing the same issue pertaining to fruit bearing Jesus Christ declares, "Every branch in me that beareth not fruit he taketh away: and every branch that beareth fruit, he purgeth it, that it may bring forth more fruit (John 15:2).

After genuine repentance and salvation, followers of Jesus Christ are expected to bring forth good fruit in terms of manifesting Christ-like virtues and winning souls for the kingdom. You must be careful to examine your own life, making sure that you truly belong to Christ and bear fruit. If you don't, the axe is laid at the root of your tree.

Prayer: Father, please deliver me from the spirit of Pharisees and Sadducees and let me bring forth good fruit, IJN.

Thursday November 7, 2019
Topic: AVOIDING LAZINESS

Scriptures: "For we hear that there are some which walk among you disorderly, working not at all, but are busybodies." (2 Thessalonians 3:11)

Praise the Lord. Today is November 7th and is day #311 in year 2019. The number of days remaining to end this year is 54. By God's grace, you will not walk disorderly and you shall not be jobless; you will see the end of this year and beyond, safe and sound in the mighty name of Jesus.

Laziness is a common temptation that must be avoided. The Bible is full of many scriptures that condemn laziness. Few examples are: "Despite their desires, the lazy will come to ruin, for their hands refuse to work" (Pro. 21:25); " Work hard and become a leader; be lazy and become a slave" (Pro. 12:24, NLT); (Pro 20:4).

To illustrate that lazy people have no place in the kingdom of heaven, Jesus told a story in which 3 servants were given 5, 2 and 1 talent(s) respectively. The ones with 5 and 2 traded and double their amounts while the one with 1 buried his 1 talent. When the master returned for accountability, he praised the servants who doubled their initial amounts but condemned the servant who buried his 1 talent (Matt 25: 14- 29). The master ordered that the lazy unprofitable servant "be thrown into outer darkness,.." (Matt 25:30).

As pointed out in today's opening scripture it is abnormal not to work (idle or lazy) acting as a busybody instead. Then, in the verses that follow, Paul said "We command such people and urge them in the name of the Lord Jesus Christ to settle down and work to earn their own living. As for the rest of you, dear brothers and sisters, never get tired of doing good" (2 Thes. 3:12-13).

There should be no room for laziness (spiritual and secular) in the life of a Christian. Both God and Jesus were always working (John 5:17). We must follow their examples and their commands in terms of attitude to work. It is a sin to break the command to "labour and do all thy work" (Ex 20:9). Jesus told a parable indicating we are to occupy till He comes (Lk. 19:11-27). We are asked to always abound in good works (1 Cor. 15:58). **Prayer: *Father, deliver us from the spirit of laziness; please provide jobs for the unemployed and let all of us work for You as well as for our sustenance, IJN***

Friday November 8, 2019
Topic: REWARDING FOR RIGHTEOUSNESS

Scriptures: "And now it is true that I am thy near kinsman: howbeit there is a kinsman nearer than I " (Ruth 3:12)

Praise the Lord. Today is November 8th and is day #312 in year 2019. The number of days remaining to end this year is 53. By God's grace, Jesus Christ shall be your closest kinsman, and you will see the end of this year and beyond, safe and sound in the mighty name of Jesus.

Righteousness can be defined as the state of being just or rightful. Whether in the secular or in the spiritual things, doing right will always attract rewards. Sometimes ago a security guard in an African country (whose monthly salary was $100) found $10,000 (mistakenly dropped by a customer on the bank premises) and returned the money to the bank. The bank traced and delivered the lost money to the rightful owner. The security guard received national attention and was honored by rewards of over $15,000. May you live rightfully to attract rewards not only from humans but also from God.

Ruth was a Moabite widow whose life story portrays righteous living, faithfulness, kindness, integrity, and total dependence on God. As a result of famine, Elimelech, Naomi his wife and their two sons left Bethlehem (known as "house of Bread" ironically) to search for bread in the pagan nation of Moab (Ruth 1: 1-6). Unfortunately, Elimelech and his 2 sons who had since gotten married to 2 Moabite ladies died in the foreign land. This left 3 widows in Elimelech's household. Any death covenant on your household is cancelled, IJN.

Naomi decided to return to Bethlehem after learning that the famine there was over. Ruth and Orphah wanted to go with her in Ruth 1:16. Without any hesitation Orphah returned to her people. In Bethlehem, Ruth remained with Noami, serving her and caring for her from the proceed of working very hard, gleaning grains. Naomi introduced Ruth to Boaz, one of her kinsmen who was very wealthy. Ruth worked for Boaz and he was impressed by her hard work and kindness. By divine appointment Boaz ended up marrying Ruth (Ruth 3-4). God rewarded Ruth and, with Boaz they had a son called Obed. Therefore, they became ancestors of David and Jesus (Matt 1:5). What a glorious reward for Ruth! **Prayer: *Father, give me the grace to do right in Your sight and be a recipient of Your exceeding reward, IJN.***

Saturday November 9, 2019
Topic: HANDLING HATRED

Scriptures: "Marvel not, my brethren, if the world hate you" *(1 John 3:13)*

Praise the Lord. Today is November 9th and is day #313 in year 2019. The number of days remaining to end this year is 52. By God's grace, those that hate you will turn around to hail and honor you, and you will see the end of this year and beyond, safe and sound in the mighty name of Jesus.

The world is full of hatred. Terrorist groups such as Boko Haram, Al-Qaeda, ISIS, Taliban, Hezbollah, Ku Klux Klan, Hamas, Al-shabaab are motivated by hatred tendencies. In year 2015 one in five (or 20%) of victims of hate crimes in U.S were attacked because of their religious orientation.

Hatred has been one of man's age long intractable problems. The first recorded incidence of hatred in the Bible is that of Cain who hated his brother Abel and killed him. Cain killed Abel because God accepted Abel's superior offering and rejected that of Cain which was inferior (Gen 4: 1-16). Other incidences of hatred in the Bible include: (a) Joseph's brothers hated him because of the love of the father for him (Gen 37:4), (b) Esau hated Jacob for taking the father's blessings that traditionally should have been Esau's, (Gen 27:41), etc.

Why is there so much hatred for followers of Christ? The reasons are many and include (1) fulfillment of God's word (Matt 24:9); (2) the world hated Jesus and God so they likewise hate their followers (Jn 15:18; Matt 10:22, 24:9); (3) believers are light amidst unbelievers (darkness), and darkness always hates the light. (Jn 3: 19-21, Matt 5:14-15); (4) people hate the truth (Gal 4:16, Amos 5:10, Jn 17:17) (5) believers' moral and obedience to God exposes the laxity of unbelievers which may provoke jealous anger. Believers must learn to manage hatred to their advantage and for God's glory by:

(1) expecting and preparing for persecution (II Tim. 3:12 NKJV); (2) rejoicing if/when hated for Christ's sake (Matt 5:10-12); (3) forgiving and returning love for hatred (1 Thes. 5:15, 1 Pet 3:9); (4) avoiding unnecessary conflict (Matt. 5:9; Rom. 12:18; 14:19); (5) endeavoring to live peaceably with all men (Rm 12: 18).

Prayer: Father, give me the grace I need for total victory over any manifestation of hatred.

Sunday November 10, 2019
Topic: STAYING STEADFAST IN THE SAVIOR

Scriptures: "For we are made partakers of Christ, if we hold the beginning of our confidence stedfast unto the end" (Hebrew 3:14).

Praise the Lord. Today is November 10th and is day #314 in year 2019. The number of days remaining to end this year is 51. By God's grace, you will remain diligently devoted unto the Lord till the end, and you will see the end of this year and beyond, safe and sound in the mighty name of Jesus.

Passion, persistence and persevering are among the critical determinants of whether and how well most games of life can be finished, winning. Jesus Christ had optimal disposition about these factors and was able to finish his mission to the world successfully, declaring "It is finished" (John 19:30). Now, Jesus Christ "- - is set down at the right hand of the throne of God" (Heb 12:2).

One of our privileges as believers and followers of Jesus Christ is that, as joint heirs with Him, we shall one day, sit with Him on His throne (Matt 19:28). That is part of being "partakers of Christ" as mentioned in today's opening scripture. For that to happen we must remain steadfast with the Lord to the end. Jesus Christ declares, "- -he that shall endure unto the end, the same shall be saved" (Matt 24:13). You will end 2019 well, IJN.

Don't let anything derail your journey to the Kingdom of God where Jesus has gone to prepare a mansion for you (John 14:1-3). Trials and troubles are part of the afflictions of life from which we have assurance of deliverance as believers (Psalm 34:19). Often, theses afflictions serve as platform for promotion of the believer after deliverance. The Bible says if we suffer with Jesus, we will also be glorified with Him (Rm 8:17). Furthermore, the sufferings of this present time are not worthy to be compared with the glory which shall be revealed in us (Rm. 8:18).

To be steadfast with the Lord, let us love and serve Him passionately, pray persistently, persevere in studying the word, witnessing to unbelievers and fellowshipping regularly with other believers, etc.

Prayer: Father, thank You for saving me, please let me remain steadfast in You so that I will finish well and reign with You, IJN.

Monday November 11, 2019
Topic: ELIMINATION OF THE ENEMY

Scriptures: "The Lord hath taken away thy judgments, he hath cast out thine enemy: the king of Israel, even the Lord, is in the midst of thee: thou shalt not see evil any more" (Zephaniah 3:15)

Praise the Lord. Today is November 11th and is day #315 in year 2019. The number of days remaining to end this year is 50. By God's grace, all your enemies are cast out and you will not see evil any more, and you will see the end of this year and beyond, safe and sound in the mighty name of Jesus.

We must all be grateful to God that His greatest benefit to man is that of love-based forgiveness. The Psalmist said if God marks iniquities nobody can stand, all will be dead (Psalm 130:3). In the earlier chapters of the book of Zephaniah the prophet identified the sins of Judah to include idolatry (1:4-6); complacency (1:12); corrupt leaders (3:3-4); injustice (3:1, 5). Are not all these the order of the day in our society today?

In today's opening scripture the prophet indicates that Judah's sins as mentioned above have now been taken away and that God is amid her. It is for this reason that the verse proceeding today's opening scripture says "Sing, O daughter of Zion; shout, O Israel; be glad and rejoice with all the heart, O daughter of Jerusalem" (Zeph. 3:14). Note that Zion, Israel, and Jerusalem are essentially the same as used in this verse. These people are to sing, shout, be glad and rejoice in adoration of God because the LORD has pardoned and commuted Israel's sentence.

Lessons from today's opening scripture: (1) True Christians (and anyone who will repent of his/her sins and accept Jesus as LORD) are forgiven and their judgments taken away, (2) shouting and singing of praise to God is comely and beneficial in enticing God's presence (2 Sam 6:15; Isa. 12:6), frightening the enemy (1 Sam 4:5-8), and provoking victory (2 Chron 20: 21-27), etc. (3) As believers and followers of Jesus Christ, God is in our midst (Heb. 13:5, Matt 18:20), (4) Believers and followers of Jesus Christ don't have to fear the enemy for the LORD has overcome him; we too have been given the power to overcome him (Mk 16:17). All your enemies shall be eliminated because of God's presence with you. ***Prayer: Father, with Your presence and power in my life cast out my enemies and let me not see evil again, IJN.***

Tuesday November 12, 2019
Topic: ENTERING LIFE EVERLASTING

Scriptures: "For God so loved the world, that he gave his only begotten Son, that whosoever believeth in him should not perish, but have everlasting life." (John 3:16).

Praise the Lord. Today is November 12th and is day #316 in year 2019. The number of days remaining to end this year is 49. By God's grace, you will not perish given your faith and believe in Jesus Christ, and you will see the end of this year and beyond, safe and sound in the mighty name of Jesus.

Salvation is the ticket that one needs to enter eternal life, an era called everlasting life where there will be no countdown any more. Salvation is the deliverance from the power of sin and its effects which ultimately is death. From today's opening scripture we know that there are 4 personalities that must be actively involved in order for salvation and everlasting life to manifest for an individual. The four personalities are (a) God, the Father, (b) His Son, Jesus Christ, (c) Holy Spirit, and (d) the sinner who needs salvation.

God, the Father because of love and grace is the originator or salvation. He gave His only son to redeem sinners (Jn 6:44, Eph. 2:8). Jesus Christ the son, full of grace and in obedience to His father, sacrificed his life on the cross to pay the penalty for sins (John 1: 14, Eph. 5:2, Heb 9:22). Jesus Christ is also the mediator and the conduit for salvation. No one can come to the Father except through Him (1 Tim 2:5). The Holy Spirit plays a convincing role (John 16: 8-11) and leads sinners to Christ (Rom 8:14). The sinner must repent of his/her sins, asks for forgiveness, believe in Jesus and accept by faith the salvation He offers (Rom 3:23, Ezek 18:4, Rom. 10: 9-10, Jn 1:12).

Have you gotten your ticket for everlasting life in the Kingdom of God? Apply and get it today by accepting Jesus Christ as your Lord and Savior and start your journey of life everlasting.

Prayer: Father, thank You for my salvation through Jesus Christ your Son; please remove from my life anything that will block my way to everlasting life with You, IJN

Wednesday November 13, 2019
Topic: FREEDOM FROM FIERY FURNACE

Scriptures: "If it be so, our God whom we serve is able to deliver us from the burning fiery furnace, and he will deliver us out of thine hand, O king" (Daniel 3:17)

Praise the Lord. Today is November 13th and is day #317 in year 2019. The number of days remaining to end this year is 48. By God's grace, your unrelenting enemies shall be consumed by fire, and you will see the end of this year and beyond, safe and sound in the mighty name of Jesus.

Today's opening scripture is a confession of the confidence, trust and faith that 3 Hebrew boys, Shadrach, Meshach, and Abednego, had in their God in terms of His ability to set them free from the fiery furnace of king Nebuchadnezzar. The trio had refused to worship the gods of Nebuchadnezzar and to bow down to his golden image as he has decreed (Dan 3: 9-12). They refused because the decree was against the commandments of God (Exo 20:23, Deut. 5:7, Lev. 26:). At the king's command, the fire was heated 7 times stronger and the 3 boys thrown into the furnace for disobeying the king's decree (Dan 3: 19-21).

Immediately, the boys landed in the fire, God sent His Son to join them to "buffer" them from been burnt. Instead of the 3 Hebrew boys, it was the hefty men that dragged them into the fire that were consumed by the heat of the furnace (v. 22). King Nebuchadnezzar was the first to notice the presence of the fourth person walking alongside the 3 boys. He was amazed and praised the God of the boys, proclaiming that no one could deliver like that God (vs. 24-28). The king then made a decree that any one that "speak anything amiss against the God of Shadrach, Meshach, and Abednego, shall be cut in pieces, and their houses shall be made a dunghill" (Dan 3:29). "The king then promoted Shadrach, Meshach, and Abednego, in the province of Babylon" (v.30)

Jesus Christ is the "buffer" you need to deliver you from the various "fiery furnaces" of life (Isa. 43: 1-3). Have you given your life to Him? If not do so today and avoid the unquenchable hell fire which shall be worse than Nebuchadnezzar's fiery furnace (Rev. 21:8).

Prayer: Father, deliver me and let my enemies be the ones to be consumed by any form of fiery furnace they have set for me, IJN

Thursday November 14, 2019
Topic: LIBERATION OF LOT

Scriptures: "When Abram heard that his nephew Lot had been captured, he mobilized the 318 trained men who had been born into his household. Then he pursued Kedorlaomer's army until he caught up with them at Dan" (Genesis 14:14).

Praise the Lord. Today is November 14th and is day #318 in year 2019. The number of days remaining to end this year is 47. By God's grace, you will not lose any member of your family to captors, and you will see the end of this year and beyond, safe and sound in the mighty name of Jesus.

Although Lot lost his father (Haran) when he was young, he had good care and good role models in his grandfather Terah and his uncle Abraham who raised him. Regrettably, Lot did not emulate his ancestors' sense of purpose and commitment to God. When Abram left Ur of the Chaldeans for Canan at God's instruction, Lot went with him (Gen 12: 1-4). As Lot followed Abram about, they both had large flocks and herds that the land space became too small to hold them together in the same spot. To avoid further quarrelling that had ensued between Abram and Lot's herdsmen, Abram suggested they should separate from one another. Lot quickly chose the best part of the land for himself and his flocks. After Lot left, God gave Abram unlimited expanse of land (Gen 13). Lot's short-sightedness and greedy desires for the best of everything led him into sinful and ungodly culture in Gen 14.

As noted in today's opening scripture, Abram, with only 318 trained men, chased Kedorlaomer's army (of 4 nations) and caught up with them. With God's help he recovered Lot, his family and his possessions (Gen 14:18-20).

Some of the lessons we can learn from the liberation of Lot include (a): Avoid Lot's pitfalls (greed, lack of respect for the elder, drunkenness, incest, indecisiveness, being unequally yoked with unbelievers, etc. (b) There is forgiveness with God given that Lot was still described as "just" (1 Pet. 2:7-8); (c) Be courageous and trust God like Abram who faced large and powerful army to rescue Lot (d) Be adequately prepared like Abram trained his 318 men for potential tasks/conflicts (e) Honor God with your tithes. **Prayer: Father, keep me and all mine liberated from and protected against satanic attackers and oppressors, IJN.**

Friday November 15, 2019
Topic: ENEMIES OF THE CROSS

Scriptures: "Whose end is destruction, whose God is their belly, and whose glory is in their shame, who mind earthly things.)" (Philippians 3:19

Praise the Lord. Today is November 15th and is day #319 in year 2019. The number of days remaining to end this year is 46. By God's grace, nothing, including your belly shall displace the Lord in your life, and you will see the end of this year and beyond, safe and sound in the mighty name of Jesus.

The Cross is most likely the most popular and most familiar of all Christian symbols. There is hardly any Christian home that one will not find symbols of the Cross. Just look around, we find them on T-shirts, steeples, buildings, books, brochures, Bibles, worn around necks, everywhere. Even many people ignorantly carry in their body tattoos of the Cross against the injunction of the Bible in Lev.19:28, NIV.

There is no doubt that many users of the Cross do not know its significance. The Cross symbolizes the crucifixion and resurrection of Jesus Christ by whom we are reconciled to God (Col 1:20). The Cross is the "identity card" of Jesus Christ the Son of God. Invariably, the Cross is also the I.D. card of followers (disciples) of Jesus Christ because He says we should carry it daily and follow Him (Luke 9:23 and 14:27). It was on the Cross that Jesus Christ, because of love, paid for us the penalty for sins (which is death, Rm 3:23). By this Jesus saved us from eternal death and gave us eternal life. Thus, the Cross means life rather than death; love rather than hatred; and joy rather than sorrow. Essentially, the Cross is the power of God for the believer.

Those who do not believe in Jesus Christ and walk in His ways are described as "enemies of the cross--" (Phil 3:18-19). The end of such people is destruction according to today's opening scripture. Apostle Paul further characterizes enemies of God as people whose god is their appetite, whose glory is in their shame and who set their mind on earthly things (Phil 3:19). If you have not given your life to Jesus Christ or you are hypocritical about it, serving your appetite instead of God, you are towing a dangerous path of being the enemy of the Cross. Change your way and cry to God for the grace to accept him and serve Him.

Prayer: Father, give me the grace to serve You faithfully and don't let me be crushed by the Cross, IJN

Saturday November 16, 2019
Topic: FELLOWSHIPPING WITH THE FATHER

Scriptures: "Behold, I stand at the door, and knock: if any man hear my voice, and open the door, I will come in to him, and will sup with him, and he with me." (Revelation 3:20)

Praise the Lord. Today is November 16th and is day #320 in year 2019. The number of days remaining to end this year is 45. By God's grace, you will open your heart to Jesus to come in and fellowship with you this season, and you will see the end of this year and beyond, safe and sound in the mighty name of Jesus.

One of the reasons why God created man is so He can fellowship with man. That is why God was constantly visiting Adam in the garden of Eden in the cool of the day (Gen 3:8). God's desire to fellowship with man is also evident in His statements such as, "Come now, and let us reason together" (Isa. 1:8), "- I will never leave thee, nor forsake thee" (Heb. 13:5), "Come unto me, all ye that labour and are heavy laden, and I will give you rest" (Matt 11:28).

God who chastises whom He loves (Heb. 12:6) may fellowship with His people purposely to make the crooked way straight (Isa 42:16). In today's scripture the Almighty God talks about the Church at Laodicean. Some of the weaknesses of this church known to God include (a) Lukewarm nature in that they are neither cold or hot (Rev. 3:15-16; (b) ignorance and self-deceit, for they say they are rich whereas they are wretched and poor (Rev.3:17), (c) they have kept Jesus locked out of the Church. It is for the purpose of correcting these anomalies God says he "- -stands at the door, and knock - - "(Rev 3:20).

The problems of the Laodicean Church as enumerated above as well as many other problems are rampant today, not only in Churches, but also in many nations, communities and in individual lives. Are you lukewarm with respect to serving God? have you done self-analysis of yourself? Are you maximizing your potential? Jesus Christ wants to fellowship with you. His stands at the door, knocking. The one who is the Door that you should be knocking at (John 10: 7,9, Matt. 7:7) has graciously reversed the role and is knocking at your door. Open to Him and He will come and dine with you. He will make the crooked ways straight and bring you many other blessings such as joy, peace, prosperity, etc. IJN. ***Prayer: Father, please give me the grace to enjoy constant fellowship with You, IJN***

Sunday November 17, 2019
Topic: FINDING DIVINE FAVOR

Scriptures: "And I will give this people favour in the sight of the Egyptians: and it shall come to pass, that, when ye go, ye shall not go empty." (Exodus 3:21)

Praise the Lord. Today is November 17th and is day #321 in year 2019. The number of days remaining to end this year is 44. By God's grace, you will not go out or come in empty this season because of the Lord's favor on you, and you will see the end of this year and beyond, safe and sound in the mighty name of Jesus.

Welcome to the seventeenth day of this month. One of the significant things recorded in the Bible that happened on the seventeenth day of the month is that the ark rested on the mountains of Ararat (Gen. 8:4). I decree to you that today the Lord shall give you rest from wandering thoughts, sickness, anxiety, poverty, and all forms of troubles, IJN.

Favor can be defined as "something done or granted out of goodwill rather than from justice or remuneration; a kind act". It is the favor of God that can make a man stand out and be outstanding. We see the display of God's favor throughout the Bible. For example, Noah found favor (Gen 6:8) and himself and his entire household were preserved in the ark and saved from the same flood that destroyed the rest of the world. Joseph found favor and got promoted from the prison to the palace (Gen. 39 & 41).

In today's opening scripture God promised that Israel would not go out of Egypt empty because of the favor that He would give them before the Egyptians. We see the fulfillment of this promise in Exodus chapter 12 when Pharaoh had no choice but to let the people of God go as the Bible declares in Exo 12:35-38.

Beloved, if you are looking for favor, accept Jesus as your Lord and Savior and remain connected with Him for the Bible declares, " For whoso findeth me findeth life, and shall obtain favour of the Lord " (Pro. 8:35) **Prayer: Father, endow me with Your favor and let me not go empty; let me be full of Your blessings, joy, peace, love, etc. IJN.**

Monday November 18, 2019
Topic: FIGHTING WITHOUT FEARING

Scriptures: "Ye shall not fear them: for the LORD your God he shall fight for you" (Deuteronomy 3:22)

Praise the Lord. Today is November 18th and is day #322 in year 2019. The number of days remaining to end this year is 43. By God's grace, you will not have any reason to fear in this season, and you will see the end of this year and beyond, safe and sound in the mighty name of Jesus.

During their journey to the promised land, the Israelites faced many enemies. It seemed the closer they got the more severe the attacks. However, as long as they remained obedient to God, He fought for them faithfully and ensured all their enemies were destroyed. When God fought for them, they had nothing to fear. Prominent among the last attackers of the Israelites prior to entering the promised land were two kings and their armies. King Sihon of the Amorites refused to let Moses and the Israelites pass through his land. Instead, Sihon and his army fought them. God delivered Sihon and his people to the Israelites and they destroyed them completely and carried all their livestock (Deut. 2: 30-37).

It was as if king Og of Bashan was waiting to fight against the Israelites. No sooner did Israel arrive at Bashan, that king Og and his army came to battle with the people of God. Again, God delivered Og and his army to the Israelites and they utterly destroyed them, took all their possessions and settled some of their people on their land before crossing over Jordan to the promised land. (Deut. 3: 1-20).

The words in today's opening scripture were spoken by God unto Joshua who has been ordained to take the Israelites to the promised land instead of Moses. God promised him that as he has witnessed the destruction of the 2 kings (Sihon and Og) and their armies so will He do to any kingdoms that would withstand him in their process of taking the land.

Prayer: Father, fight all my battles for me so I can finish well at the expected destinations; don't let me end at "the top of Pisgah", IJN.

Tuesday November 19, 2019
Topic: COMPASSION AND MERCY OF CHRIST

Scriptures: "They are new every morning: great is thy faithfulness." (Lamentations 3:23)

Praise the Lord. Today is November 19th and is day #323 in year 2019. The number of days remaining to end this year is 42. By God's grace, the faithfulness of the Lord shall ensure abundant supply of His mercies and compassion to you every morning this season, and you will see the end of this year and beyond, safe and sound in the mighty name of Jesus.

The word "They" in today's opening scripture refers to "mercies and compassion" of God mentioned in Lamentation 3:22 which states "It is of the Lord's mercies that we are not consumed, because his compassions fail not". Mercy and compassion are among the benefits that the Lord loads us with every day (Psalm 68:19). Mercy is not receiving the punishment or death that one deserves to receive based on guilt. Compassion is a feeling of deep sympathy and sorrow for another who is stricken by misfortune, accompanied by a strong desire to alleviate the suffering.

The LORD is full of both mercy and compassion (Ps. 119:64; Ps. 145:8). The prerogative as to who to show mercy and/or compassion to lies with the LORD. Hence the Bible declares "For he saith to Moses, I will have mercy on whom I will have mercy, and I will have compassion on whom I will have compassion" (Rom 9:15).

Mercy and compassion of the LORD can do great things in the life of a believer aside from their roles in salvation. David enjoyed great deliverance due to God's mercy (Ps. 18:50). Mercy of the LORD can bring healing as it did for the blind Bartimaeus (Mk. 10: 46 -52), the two blind men (Matt. 9:27-30), Mercy of God can terminate barrenness as it did in the life of Zacharias and Elizabeth (Lk 1: 7, 57-58). Cry to God now for His mercies and compassion. ***Prayer: Father, as the year 2019 is coming to an end shower me with more of Your mercies and compassions, IJN***

Wednesday November 20, 2019
Topic: SURMOUNTING "SENNACHERIB'S" SIEGE

Scriptures: "So there was gathered much people together, who stopped all the fountains, and the brook that ran through the midst of the land, saying, Why should the kings of Assyria come, and find much water?" (2 Chronicles 32:4)

Praise the Lord. Today is November 20th and is day #324 in year 2019. The number of days remaining to end this year is 41. By God's grace, you will not be under any siege this season, and you will see the end of this year and beyond, safe and sound in the mighty name of Jesus.

Simply put a siege is an attack with an intension to destroy the victim. King Sennacherib (KS) of Assyria was a proud and an ungodly king who invaded Judah under king Hezekiah. KS laid siege to the fortified towns, giving orders for his army to break through their walls. He terrorized the Israelites and mocked their God claiming He could not deliver them from his hand. He sent letters to people of Judah to threaten them and discourage them from listening to Hezekiah their king (2 Chron. 9-19).

Unlike Sennacherib, King Hezekiah was a Godly king who had personal and growing relationships with God and developed a powerful prayer life. Concerning him the Bible declares "Hezekiah trusted in the Lord, the God of Israel. - -He remained faithful to the Lord in everything, and he carefully obeyed all the commands the Lord had given Moses. So, -- - Hezekiah was successful in everything he did" (2 Kgs 18:5-7).

Today's opening scripture alludes to part of Hezekiah's efforts to foil Sennacherib's siege against Judah. In addition to cutting of water supply to the invaders, Hezekiah prepared his people militarily and encouraged them to be strong and know that they had a God who could help them fight the battle. More importantly, "- -King Hezekiah and the prophet Isaiah son of Amoz cried out in prayer to God in heaven" (2 Chron 32:20). God answered their prayer, and in 2 Chron 32:21 delivered them. The LORD that helped Hezekiah surmount Sennacherib's siege shall help to disgrace and destroy every Sennacherib's siege over you, IJN.

Prayer: Father, let all forms of siege in my life (physical, spiritual, etc. be over, IJN

Thursday November 21, 2019
Topic: SACRIFICE FOR SIN

Scriptures: "For God presented Jesus as the sacrifice for sin. People are made right with God when they believe that Jesus sacrificed his life, shedding his blood. This sacrifice shows that God was being fair when he held back and did not punish those who sinned in times past" (Romans 3:25)

Praise the Lord. Today is November 21st and is day #325 in year 2019. The number of days remaining to end this year is 40. By God's grace, your thanksgiving to Jesus for the sacrifice for sin He made will count upwards continuously, and you will see the end of this year and beyond, safe and sound in the mighty name of Jesus.

One common problem of all human beings is sin, for the Bible says, "All have sinned and fall short of the glory of God" (Rom 3:23). The penalty for sins is death (Rom 6:23, Ezek 18:4). In the Old Testament sacrifices or offerings called "sin offering" (Lev. 4; 5:1–13; 6:24–30; 8:14–17; 16:3–22) and "trespass offering"(Lev. 5:14–19; 6:1–7; 7:1–6) were made to atone for sins. Both types of sins usually called for blood sacrifice to be made with specific instructions in order for atonement to take place.

The sacrifices in the Old Testament pointed forward to the perfect and final sacrifice of Jesus Christ. As indicated in today's opening scripture, God presented Jesus Christ as the sacrifice for human sins. Thus, Christ's atoning death on the cross is the only needed sacrifice for sin, offered once for all (Heb.10:1–10). All a sinner must do to be made right with God and avoid death penalty for his/her sins is to repent and believe that Jesus sacrificed his life for the sins of man. That is, Jesus Christ is the sacrifice for man's sins.

Salvation means being saved (or freed) from sins and from its consequences with ultimate end in hell. Jesus Christ is the only one qualified and authorized by God to pay the price of salvation for any one (Acts 4:12). Jesus tells us who He is in John. 14:6. Accepts His salvation today and avoid spending eternity in hell (Matt 25: 46; Rev 20:15). Just confess your sins, ask him to forgive you and save you and come into your heart to be your Lord (Rom 10: 9-11, Jn. 1:12). ***Prayer: Father, thank You for sacrificing Your Son Jesus Christ for sinners, please let many who are yet to believe in Him be drawn to the Cross for salvation in Jesus mighty name.***

Friday November 22, 2019
Topic: SACRIFICE FOR SIN

Scriptures: "And the messengers returned to Jacob, saying, We came to thy brother Esau, and also he cometh to meet thee, and four hundred men with him." (Genesis 32:6)

Praise the Lord. Today is November 22nd and is day #326 in year 2019. The number of days remaining to end this year is 39. By God's grace, you will see the end of this year and beyond, safe and sound in the mighty name of Jesus.

Beware that not everyone will be happy to see you prosper, sometimes not even close relatives and friends. No wonder the Bible says, "And a man's foes shall be they of his own household" (Matt 10:36). An example is Jacob who served his uncle Laban for about 20 years (Gen. 31:41). Though Laban unfairly changed his wage 10 times (Gen. 31:7,41), Jacob continued to serve Laban faithfully.

God blessed and rewarded Jacob such that his flock became bigger and more beautiful than Laban's. Jealousy filled the heart of Laban's sons in Gen 31:1. Even Laban himself began to display negative attitude toward Jacob.

The LORD told Jacob, "Return unto the land of thy fathers, and to thy kindred; and I will be with thee" (Gen 31:3). Jacob obeyed and on the way the angels of God met him and Jacob said "This is God's host: and he called the name of that place Mahanaim" (Gen. 32:2). After the encounter with angelic hosts Jacob sent his messengers with gifts to Essau to announce his intention to meet with him hoping to find grace in his sight (Deut. 32:3-5). Today's opening scripture describes the report the messengers brought back to Jacob from Essau. Jacob was fearful of the reunion with Essau given he had jilted Essau by stealing the family blessing from him (Gen. 25:29-34 & 27:18 -42). As God would have it the reunion and reconciliation went smoothly (Gen. 33): "And Esau ran to meet him, and embraced him, and fell on his neck, and kissed him: and they wept" (Gen 33:4).

Learn from Jacob and be proactive in reconciling with anyone who is at loggerhead with you. If you are not born again you are an enemy who is at loggerheads with God. Jesus Christ can reconcile you with God if you accept Him as your Lord and Savior (Rom 5:10). **Prayer: Father, let my ways please You and let everyone, including my enemies be at peace with me, IJN. (Pro 16:7)**

Saturday November 23, 2019
Topic: GOD IS GOOD, LET US DO GOOD

Scriptures: "Withhold not good from them to whom it is due, when it is in the power of thine hand to do it" (Proverbs 3:27)

Praise the Lord. Today is November 23rd and is day #327 in year 2019. The number of days remaining to end this year is 38. By God's grace, you will be empowered to do more good for the needy this season, and you will see the end of this year and beyond, safe and sound in the mighty name of Jesus.

The phrase "God is good" is mentioned at least 2 times in KJV, and 7 times in the Message version of the Bible. My father in the Lord said that God is not a talkative and so when he says something more than once it means it is very important. The Bible says "- - -Jesus went about doing good- -" (Acts 10:38). The same Jesus washed the feet of His disciples and told them "For I have given you an example, that ye should do as I have done to you" (John 13:15).

Every human being has the potential to do good because we carry "Godly genes" in our body given that God made us in His own image. If the Lord Jesus Christ did good work you too, can do good work. Moreover, the Bible declares, "- -we are his workmanship, created in Christ Jesus unto good works, which God hath before ordained that we should walk in them" (Eph. 2:10). Good work is part of the purpose you were created.

Today's opening scripture admonishes us not to hold back on doing good for which we are created. Look around round you, there is somebody who can use an act of goodness from you. The person may be a fellow Christian (Gal 6:10) or a poor person (Pro 19:17) or anybody. Just be a "good Samaritan". Remember doing good amounts to sowing mercy and as the Bible says, "Blessed are the merciful: for they shall obtain mercy" (Matt 5:7). You shall be blessed, IJN.

Prayer: Father please increase my capacity to do good in Your name

Sunday November 24, 2019
Topic: WAY OF THE WISDOM

Scriptures: "I will instruct thee and teach thee in the way which thou shalt go: I will guide thee with mine eye (Proverbs 32:8)

Praise the Lord. Today is November 24th and is day #328 in year 2019. The number of days remaining to end this year is 37. By God's grace, you will receive divine direction in all you do this season, and you will see the end of this year and beyond, safe and sound, IJN.

The Bible says Jesus Christ is the wisdom of God (1 Cor. 1:24). Therefore, we can say the way of the LORD is the way of Wisdom. If you have God as your instructor or teacher you have gotten it made because unlike human beings God is omniscient, i.e. has unlimited knowledge, (1 Jn 3:20). Jesus, described as a "teacher come from God" (Jn 3: 2) made teaching an important aspect of His earthly ministry (Mk. 12:25, Jn 7:14, 28; 8:10, 18:20). He promised His disciples that, "the Comforter, which is the Holy Ghost, -- shall teach you all things, and bring all things to your remembrance - -" (Jn 14:26).

God's teaching techniques are diverse and divine. He can teach by long distance using an invisible medium like the Holy Spirit (as in Jn 14:26) or He can do the teaching synchronously (directly Himself 'face to face' or 'mouth to mouth') as He promised Moses when He was sending him to Pharaoh (Exo 4:10-12, Num 12:8). God can teach properly and persistently (Isa. 28:26, Jer. 32:33, ESV). He is the best Instructor/Teacher!

In today's opening scripture as well as in Micah 4:2, God says He can teach you and be your 'divine GPS or Navigator' in the journeys of life. With His eye alone God can see ahead of you and know where death traps (that you should avoid) or divine treasures are laid up for you to access (Ps. 37:23). If you are a business person (everyone is) God can teach you how to profit (Isa. 48:17). God can teach all your children to have great peace (Isa. 54:13). Most importantly, God can teach you to find the "perfect way" - that is Jesus Christ who is the Way, the Truth and the Life (John 14:6).

Prayer: Father, please order my steps to walk in Your Way and in Your Word, IJN.

Monday November 25, 2019
Topic: MOSES' PLEA FOR MERCY

Scriptures: "And the LORD said unto Moses, I have seen this people, and, behold, it is a stiff-necked people" (Exodus 32:9)

Praise the Lord. Today is November 25th and is day #329 in year 2019. The number of days remaining to end this year is 36. By God's grace, you will be a delight to the Lord, and you will see the end of this year and beyond, safe and sound, IJN.

Though Moses was the meekest person in the world, he was mighty and wielded so much influence before God. On several occasions Moses was able to plead for mercy to convince God to reverse a negative plan He intended to mete out for sinful acts of violation of His law by the people under Moses. No wonder Jesus Christ (the epitome of meekness) said the meek are blessed and they shall inherit the earth (Matt 5:5). This connotes power and influence!

While Moses was on Mt Sinai receiving the 10 commandments (Decalogue) from God, the Israelites became impatient and requested Aaron to make them 'gods' which he did. This sparked off God's anger. Today's opening scripture above was God's initial reaction to the disappointing disobedience of the Israelites whom God loved so much. God told Moses, " - - let me alone, that my wrath may wax hot against them, and that I may consume them -" (Exo 32:10). Moses pleaded with God on behalf of the people (Exo 32: 11-13) and, "the Lord repented of the evil which he thought to do unto his people" (v. 14).

Just like Jesus interceded, and is still interceding, for sinners (1 Tim 2:5), Moses averted the destruction of the Israelites by interceding for them before God. Believers are expected to be intercessors that God is looking for (Ezek. 22:30). Any time true intercession takes place and God answers, everybody gains, including God. Intercede for your family, friends, colleagues, your community, your nation, etc. You shall be a positive change agent, IJN.

Prayer: Father, have mercy on me and my family and break every generational curse and evil agenda from all sources, IJN.

Tuesday November 26, 2019
Topic: DECREASE TO INCREASE

Scriptures: "He must increase, but I must decrease" (John 3:30)

Praise the Lord. Today is November 26th and is day #330 in year 2019. The number of days remaining to end this year is 35. By God's grace, the work of God in your hands shall increase greatly, and you will see the end of this year and beyond, safe and sound, IJN.

Long before Jesus Christ was born many prophecies were given concerning Him. For example, at least 2 passages in the Old Testaments pointed to the fact that a messenger would be sent to prepare the way for the coming of the Lord (Isa 40:3; Mal 3:1). When John the Baptist came to the scene, he confirmed that He was that messenger: "John replied in the words of Isaiah the prophet, 'I am the voice of one calling in the wilderness, "Make straight the way for the Lord." (John 1:23). John the Baptist, the greatest of Prophets (Matt. 11:9-11) fulfilled his purpose (Matt 11:10, Mk. 1:1-3). I decree that whatever you were sent in to the world to do shall be accomplished, IJN.

One day both Jesus and John the Baptist (together with their respective disciples) were in Judea baptizing believers. The disciples of John saw the crowd that was coming to Jesus, so they came to John and quipped, "Rabbi, the man you met on the other side of the Jordan River, the one you identified as the Messiah, is also baptizing people. And everybody is going to him instead of coming to us" (Jn 3:26, NLT). John explained to them that no one can receive anything unless God gives it from heaven (Jn 3: 27). He then reminded them that, as he had told them before, he was not the Messiah, but he was just sent there to prepare the way for Jesus Christ. He told them that he was filled with joy about Jesus' success. John then made the profound statement that we have in today's opening scripture that Jesus must increase, and he must decrease.

As a believer wherever you find yourself, you are a messenger sent there to prepare the way for Jesus Christ. Are you promoting your own agenda at the expense of the one who made it possible for you to be there? If you decrease so that Jesus can increase, He will increase you.

Prayer: Father give me the grace to do everything necessary for You to increase, IJN.

Wednesday November 27, 2019
Topic: REJOICING OF THE RIGHTEOUS

Scriptures: "Rejoice in the LORD, O ye righteous: for praise is comely for the upright.," (Psalm 33:1)

Praise the Lord. Today is November 27th and is day #331 in year 2019. The number of days remaining to end this year is 34. By God's grace, you will joyfully render praises to the Lord this season, and you will see the end of this year and beyond, safe and sound, IJN.

The righteous is somebody who is upright and in right standing with God according to God's standard. It is a status that only born-again Christians can attain from the moment they are redeemed by Jesus Christ whom they have accepted by faith as their Lord and Savior (Rom. 3:22). The opening scripture for today says such righteous one is to rejoice in the LORD, and that it is appropriate for the upright to praise God.

If you continue with the reading of Psalm 33, you will get a clue as to how the righteous is to rejoice. Essentially, this include singing new song with musical instrument (v.2-3). Furthermore, the righteous is admonished to rejoice and praise God for many reasons including (i) the word of God (v.3, 6), (ii) the works of God (v. 7, 10, 11), (iii) the ways of God (v. 5, 13), (iv) waiting on the Lord (trusting Him), etc. The Bible elsewhere says the righteous should rejoice because they are blessed (Ps. 5:12), and when they cry God hears and delivers them from all their troubles (Ps. 34: 17, 19).

The rejoicing of the righteous has some notable characteristics including (a) it is always (Phil 4:4, Pro 8:30); (b) it is for evermore (1 Thess. 5:16, Isa 61:7; 65:18); (c) takes place anywhere habitable in the earth (Pro 8:31), (d) abundantly (Phil. 1:26), etc.

The unrighteous or those who still belong to Satan are not qualified to partake in the kind of rejoicing that is the entitlement of the righteous. The wicked's so called 'rejoicing' (if any) is transient and will lead him/her to hell. It's not worth it. Receive Jesus Christ as your Lord and Savior today and start experiencing the right rejoicing that will take you to heaven for everlasting rejoicing. Amen

Prayer: Father, separate me totally from sorrow and let me rejoice always in the LORD for evermore, IJN.

Thursday November 28, 2019
Topic: PRAYER OF PROTECTION

Scriptures: "O LORD, be gracious unto us; we have waited for thee: be thou their arm every morning, our salvation also in the time of trouble" (Isaiah 33:2, KJV)

Praise the Lord. Today is November 28th and is day #332 in year 2019. The number of days remaining to end this year is 33. By God's grace, you will continue to wait for the Lord and He will save you from every trouble. You will see the end of this year and beyond, safe and sound, IJN.

Prayer is one of the most potent weapons God has given His children for living a victorious life. Other weapons of warfare for disciples of Jesus include Faith, Holiness, Gifts of the Holy Spirit, Joy, etc. Jesus demonstrated the importance of prayer during His earthly ministry as he devoted considerable amount of time and efforts into praying, privately and publicly. Examples: praying at His baptism (Luke 3:21), regular time of withdrawal from the crowds (Luke 5:16) before choosing the Twelve (Luke 6:12), in the Garden of Gethsemane (Matt.26:36-56), on the Cross (Luke 23:34,46, Matt 27:46, Mark 15:34), etc. Since He ascended to heaven Jesus has not stopped praying for those that have come to God (Heb 7:25).

The Bible commands believers to "pray without ceasing" (1 Thes. 5:17). Also, Jesus Christ told his followers, "Watch ye therefore, and pray always" (Lk. 21:36) and Ephesians 6:18 declares "Praying always with all prayer and supplication--". Today's opening scripture is the prayer of the righteous remnant Israeli captives who were waiting for God to deliver them from the Assyrian oppressors.

If you have accepted Jesus Christ as your Lord and Savior, you have become the righteous remnant of Jesus Christ in this generation and you too can pray to Him for protection. In the remaining 33 days of year 2019 and beyond the LORD will preserve you from all evils, IJN.

Action/Prayer: Read Isaiah 33:2 in various versions of the Bible and use this scripture to pray daily for protection for yourself and your family for the rest of year 2019 as you are directed by the Holy Spirit. Have a blessed and delightful day, IJN.

Friday November 29, 2019
Topic: CALLING UNTO JESUS CHRIST

Scriptures: Call unto me, and I will answer thee, and show thee great and mighty things, which thou knowest not." (Jeremiah 33:3, KJV)

Praise the Lord. Today is November 29th and is day #333 in year 2019. The number of days remaining to end this year is 32. By God's grace, all your prayers shall receive speedy and favorable response, and you will see the end of this year and beyond, safe and sound, IJN.

Have you ever made a phone call and did not get an answer? Unanswered phone calls may be due to many reasons such as: technical problems with the line, no one to answer, busy line, refusal to answer, etc. Sometimes such unanswered calls can be very frustrating and disappointing. Unlike human to human calls, calls placed to the LORD will usually always receive an answer except on one condition- when sin is involved (Isa. 59:1-2).

The LORD's call line is never busy or dead due to the faithfulness of God who never slumber nor sleep (Ps. 121:45). Sometimes the LORD, who is omniscient can even answer a call before it is placed. No wonder He declares, "And it shall come to pass, that before they call, I will answer; and while they are yet speaking, I will hear" (Isa 65:24). May God always answer your calls henceforth, IJN.

In today's opening scripture, the LORD assured Jeremiah, who was then in the prison, that he had only to call unto Him and He would answer. God has given us (believers) the same privilege to call unto Him by prayer, praise, His word, etc. For this reason, the Bible declares, "The Lord is nigh unto all them that call upon him, to all that call upon him in truth" (Ps. 145:18). See also Isaiah 58:9, Matthew 7:7.

Calling on Jesus Christ /God can bring numerous breakthrough benefits including Salvation (Acts 2:21; Rom. 10:13; cf. Joel 2:32), healing, as in Blind Bartimaeus (Mk 10:46-52), blessings, as in Jabez (1 Chron. 4:10), etc. Call on Jesus Christ today for your own breakthrough. You shall have testimonies, IJN

Action/Prayer: Search and find out the different names of the LORD / GOD /Jesus Christ and used each one to pray. e.g. Jehovah Jireh (The LORD, Provider) please supply all my needs, IJN.

Saturday November 30, 2019
Topic: CHARACTER OF JESUS CHRIST

Scriptures: "For the word of the Lord is right; and all his works are done in truth" (Psalm 33:4).

Praise the Lord. Today is November 30th and is day #334 in year 2019. The number of days remaining to end this year is 31. By God's grace, the word of the Lord will settle you, and you will see the end of this year and beyond, safe and sound, IJN.

One way to understand the character of a person is by studying that person's words and works. Knowing the words and works of Jesus can be beneficial in many ways particularly in guiding us as His followers how to live like Him, in Eph 5:1-2, ESV.

According to John 21:25 the works of the LORD alone are so much that if they were to be written even the world itself could not contain the books that should be written. However, we thank the LORD for the grace that we have to know Jesus Christ (The Word, John 1:1) and to have access to the Bible, source from which we can learn a lot about the character of Jesus Christ.

The first part of today's opening scripture says the word of the LORD is right. Jesus Christ, the Word of the LORD is true and trustworthy (Jn 17:17). As the Word, He is divine, holy, perfect, sovereign, necessary, eternal, etc. The following key terms describe (in brief) the word and character of the LORD worthy of our emulation: (a) Inspired = breathed out by, and proceeding from God (3:16-17, Matt 4:4), (b), Inerrant = without error, perfect (Matt 5:48, Rom 3:4, Ps. 119:160), (c) Important (Heb 4:12, Jn. 6:63), (d) Infallible= incapable of error, incorruptible (2 Pet 1:19-21, Ps. 19:7), (e) Invincible = incapable of being defeated, sovereign (Ps. 62:11, Jn 10:29, Joshua 1:5).

As the opening scripture for today also indicates, the works of God are done in truth. The Lord's works are manifold and made in wisdom (Ps. 104:24 and they are miraculous (Deut.11:3, Jn 6:2, Acts 10:38). Furthermore, the LORD'S works are wonderful and full of wonders (Ps. 40:5, 78:4, Acts 2:11). In addition, all the works of the LORD are done with perfection (Deut. 32:4, Phil 1:6, Gen 1:31). A major driving force behind the works of the LORD is love and compassion (Jn 5:20, Matt 14:14, Mk. 1:41). May your words be right and your works be truth and both be driven by love and compassion in all you do, IJN.***Prayer: Father, let my words and works emulate Your's and portray Your attributes, IJN.***

Sunday December 1, 2019
Topic: THE WISE VERSUS THE FOOL

Scriptures: The wise shall inherit glory: but shame shall be the promotion of fools." (Proverb 3:35).

Praise the Lord. Today is December 1st and is day #335 in year 2019. The number of days remaining to end this year is 30. By God's grace, your wisdom and glory will increase this season, and you will see the end of this year and beyond, safe and sound, IJN.

Welcome to the first day of the last month of year 2019. Just in 30 days this year will end and we shall be promoted into a new year 2020 in Jesus mighty name. The Bible says, "Better is the end of a thing than the beginning thereof: - - " (Eccl 7:8). I decree that all the remaining 30 days of year 2019 shall be better for you than all the previous days of your life added together in Jesus name.

There are many differences between the wise and the fool. The biggest and most important of these differences is that the wise knows and believes that there is God (Ps. 111:10, Pro 9:10,) whereas the fool says there is no God (Ps. 14:1, 53:1). Whatever you believe or do is like a seed that is planted and, as the Bible says, "- - whatsoever a man soweth, that shall he also reap" (Gal. 6:7). I pray you have sown or will sow wise seed so that you can harvest glory and honor, IJN.

In today's opening scripture we see that the harvest of the wise is glory or honor while that of the fool is shame. Anybody who rejects God is a fool and the Bible says such a person will perish. Thus, in addition to shame, the fool will ultimately perish while the wise will be given power by God to prosper: "For the preaching of the cross is to them that perish foolishness; but unto us which are saved it is the power of God (1 Cor 1:18).

Why be a fool and perish when you can be wise and prosper by simply giving your life to Jesus Christ who died on the cross for sinners? Be wise and receive Jesus Christ today.

Prayer: Father, let nothing tamper with my glory. Please let the fools find Wisdom, IJN.

Monday December 2, 2019
Topic: WORD CREATED THE WORLD

Scriptures: "By the word of the Lord were the heavens made; and all the host of them by the breath of his mouth." (Psalm 33:6).

Praise the Lord. Today is December 2nd and is day #336 in year 2019. The number of days remaining to end this year is 29. By God's grace, the power in the word of the Lord will lift higher this season, and you will see the end of this year and beyond, safe and sound, IJN.

According to the record of creation heaven is the first created thing by God in the Bible: "In the beginning God created the heaven and the earth" (Gen 1:1). Heaven is spiritual while the earth is physical. That is why everything in the world has spiritual origin before physical manifestation can occur. In other words, nothing can happen without God's notice to whom belongs absolute power. Evil occurrences in your life are cursed to the root, IJN.

Today's opening scripture should open our eyes to the power of God's word by which everything - the heavens, the earth and all that are within them - were created. The word of God is spirit and life (John 6:63) and is full of power (Heb. 4:12). Profit from them, IJN.

The Lord who created us in His own image has also put His powerful word in our mouth: "Death and life are in the power of the tongue: and they that love it shall eat the fruit thereof" (Pro 18:22). The word of God is one of the weapons of warfare at our disposal as disciples of Jesus Christ (2 Cor 10:4-5). Furthermore, the Bible declares, "You will also declare a thing, And it will be established for you; So, light will shine on your ways" (Job 22:28). As the redeemed of the Lord your words shall make you shine for Jesus!

Your words carry power as a child of the most High God. You must use them wisely and learn to bridle your tongue (James 1:26). Examples: use God's word to praise Him, pray to Him to win souls for Him, to reverse bad situations in your life, to "call those things which do not exist as though they did" (Rom. 4:17, NKJV), etc. You are wired to be creative, go for it, IJN.

Prayer: Father, anytime I open my mouth, fill it with words of praise, power, promotion, productivity, progress, healing, deliverance, grace, glory - -, IJN.

Tuesday December 3, 2019
Topic: JUDAH'S BLESSINGS FROM MOSES AND JACOB

Scriptures: "And this is the blessing of Judah: and he said, Hear, Lord, the voice of Judah, and bring him unto his people: let his hands be sufficient for him; and be thou an help to him from his enemies" (Deuteronomy 33:7).

Praise the Lord. Today is December 3rd and is day #337 in year 2019. The number of days remaining to end this year is 28. By God's grace, you will receive the Lord's help to defeat all your enemies, and you will see the end of this year and beyond, safe and sound, IJN.

Judah is one of the, the 12 sons of Jacob, born to him as the fourth son by Leah, Jacob's first wife. Overjoyed of bearing Jacob another son, she named this fourth son Judah, meaning "praise" (Gen 29:35). Although Judah was reckless in his relationship with Tamar (Gen 38:29-30), he did some notable good things that made him stand out among his brethren. These include (a) He offered to substitute his life for Benjamin's his half-brother (Gen 43:8-9) thereby pointing to what his descendant Jesus would do for all people. (b) He acted as an intercessor for his brothers before Joseph (Gen 44:14-18).

Judah, like his other brothers, received double blessings - by Jacob (Gen 49) and by Moses (Deut. 33). Moses' blessing for Judah is as indicated in today's opening scripture above. Jacob's blessing for Judah was detailed in Gen 49:8-10.

One unique part of Jacob's blessing to Judah is that he was granted the birthright privileges of the first born; the leadership of Jacob's family would come through Judah's seed, as would the promised Messiah of Abraham's covenant (Gen 49:8-12). It is noteworthy that both Davidic's lines of kings (1 Chron 2:1-15; 3: 1-24) and Jesus Christ's ancestors traced their descent from Judah (Mt. 1:2-3; Lk. 3:33). If you are a believer in Jesus Christ, you have a stake in Judah's blessings because you are a joint heir with Jesus who is a descent of Judah. Shout Hallelujah and claim your blessings in prayer

Prayer: Father give me double blessings like Judah and much more: let my hands be sufficient for me; and be my Helper against my enemies; let me be head and not tail, hear my voice O God, bring me to my people and bless my family from generation to generation, IJN

Wednesday December 4, 2019
Topic: WARNING THE WICKED

Scriptures: "When I say unto the wicked, O wicked man, thou shalt surely die; if thou dost not speak to warn the wicked from his way, that wicked man shall die in his iniquity; but his blood will I require at thine hand- - " (Ezekiel 33:8).

Praise the Lord. Today is December 4th and is day #338 in year 2019. The number of days remaining to end this year is 27. By God's grace, no one's blood shall be required at your hand, and you will see the end of this year and beyond, safe and sound, IJN.

God does not want any person to perish (Ezek 18:23). Therefore, He says all should come to repentance (2 Pet 3:9) and be saved, ready for heaven. All must come to repentance because all have sinned (Rom 3:23). The penalty for not repenting from committed sins is death (Ezek. 18:4, Rm 6:23). Have you repented of your sins? Call on Jesus Christ today to forgive you your sins, save your soul and write your name in the book of life.

The wicked is anyone who fails to repent of his/her sins for such people are enemies of God. The wicked belongs to Satan and will go to hell if they die without repenting of their sins (Ps. 1:16, 9:16). Furthermore, the Bible says woe belongs to the wicked (Isa 3:11), they are cut off in darkness (1 Sam 2:9), they are swept away (1 Sam 12:25) etc.

God's warning is not limited to the wicked alone as regards his/her salvation. As today's opening scripture indicates, if the righteous has the opportunity but fails to witness to the wicked, the righteous will be held responsible for the spiritual death of that wicked person. The same warning is repeated in Ezek. 3:18 meaning witnessing is a serious issue. It is my prayer that no one's blood will be required at our hands

Prayer: Father, give me the grace to take my calling as a witness and a watchman more seriously, IJN.

Thursday December 5, 2019
Topic: GREATNESS AND GOODNESS OF GOD

Scriptures: "For he spake, and it was done; he commanded, and it stood fast" (Psalm 33:9).

Praise the Lord. Today is December 5th and is day #339 in year 2019. The number of days remaining to end this year is 26. By God's grace, every promise of the Lord concerning you shall materialize, and you will see the end of this year and beyond, safe and sound, IJN.

One manifestation of God's greatness is in terms of the wonders of His works and the potency of His words. God's creation of the heaven and the earth in Genesis Chapter one, was by decrees. As indicated in today's opening scripture whatever God spoke to happen concerning everything was done immediately without any delay. Not only are God's decrees done instantly, they stand fast and remain immutable forever.

In Jesus name and by the authority of the word of God in Job 22:28, I decree that everything God has said about you shall manifest without further delay. For example, I decree that you shall call upon the name of the LORD and be save (Ps. 18:4, Acts 2:22, Rm 10:13); you shall not die but live (Ps. 118:17); it shall be well with you (Isa 3:10); no weapon fashioned against you shall prosper (Isa 54:17): you shall be fruitful and multiply (Gen 1:28); you and yours shall be blessed according to Deuteronomy 28:1-14) etc.

Prayer: O great and good God, let every one of your promises about me be Yea and Amen, IJN

Friday December 6, 2019
Topic: DAILY GLADNESS

Scriptures: "This is the day which the LORD hath made; we will rejoice and be glad in it" (Psalm 118:24).

Praise the Lord. Today is December 6th and is day #340 in year 2019. The number of days remaining to end this year is 25. By God's grace, joy and gladness shall characterize your life henceforth, and you will see the end of this year and beyond, safe and sound, IJN.

The Bible says "Rejoice in the Lord always: and again, I say, Rejoice" (Phil. 4:4). For the believer in Jesus Christ rejoicing should be a constant daily affair for the word of God declares "Rejoice evermore" (1Thes 5:16). Believers and followers of Jesus Christ will rejoice in the Lord forever because there will be no sorrow in heaven where we will be with Jesus to enjoy the joy that is set before Him (Heb. 12:2, Rev. 21:4). By contrast, unbelievers who are not redeemed by the blood of Jesus are the ones that will be in hell where they weep and gnash their teeth perpetually (Luke 13:28). That will not be your portion, IJN.

In yesterday's ministration we talked a little bit about decreeing. What the psalmist says in today's opening scripture amounts to decreeing. God is the maker of everyday because He is the Ancient of days (Dan 7:9). I decree that in the remaining 25 days of this year we shall rejoice daily and experience great gladness in the mighty name of Jesus. Jesus is the reason for the season. You have reason to rejoice and be glad if you know Jesus.

Prayer: Father fill me with joy and gladness all the days of my life, IJN.

Saturday December 7, 2019
Topic: PRAISING GOD PERPETUALLY

Scriptures: "I will bless the LORD at all times: his praise shall continually be in my mouth. " (Psalm 34:1).

Praise the Lord. Today is December 7th and is day #341 in year 2019. The number of days remaining to end this year is 24. By God's grace, you will sing a new song of praise perpetually, and you will see the end of this year and beyond, safe and sound, IJN.

One definition of praise says: "the offering of grateful homage in words or song, as an act of worship: a hymn of praise to God.". The primary reason God created, called and chose us as believers is that we "should shew forth the praises of Him..." (1 Pet. 2:9). In 1 Thessalonians 5:18, the Bible says the will of God is that we give thanks to Him always.

David knew praise is important to God and he made up his mind to be passionate about praising and worshipping the Almighty in this regard. In today's opening scripture we can see David's deliberate determination to bless and praise God perpetually. David declares, "While I live will I praise the LORD: I will sing praises unto my God while I have any being" (Psalm 146:2).

Let us learn from David and accord praises to God not only because God asks for it but because praising God has many advantages including (a) allows God to forgive us readily (Ps 51) (b) it provokes increased blessings from God (Ps. 67:5-7) (c) it causes our enemies to be defeated (2 Chron 20: 22-23), it causes us to be set free from imprisonment (Acts 16:25-34).

Action/Prayer: As 2019 is coming to an end, let your praise unto God count upward and watch Him proper you, protect you against your enemies, provide all your needs IJN

Sunday December 8, 2019
Topic: DEFILEMENT IS A DESTROYER

Scriptures: "And when Shechem the son of Hamor the Hivite, prince of the country, saw her, he took her, and lay with her, and defiled her". (Genesis 34:2).

Praise the Lord. Today is December 8th and is day #342 in year 2019. The number of days remaining to end this year is 23. By God's grace, you will not defile anyone nor be defiled by anyone, you will see the end of this year and beyond, safe and sound, IJN.

Defilement means to debase or make foul, dirty, or unclean; Defilement can lead to spiritual, physical, emotional and other forms of destruction. In particular, the defilement of human life, the house of God, and the sabbath are serious sins to God often punishable by death (e.g. Exo 31:14).

The first instance of human defilement mentioned in the Bible is the case of Dinah, the daughter of Jacob and Leah who Shechem defiled as indicated in today's opening scripture. After Jacob reconciled with Essau, he bought a parcel of land in Shalem, one of the cities of Schechem to settle his family. The prince of that land named Schechem saw Dinah during one of her outings and defiled (or raped) her. Schechem requested his father Hamor to get Dinah for him as wife that he loved her. In actual fact Schechem simply lusted after Dinah thereby violating God's injunction against premarital sex (Heb 13:4).

Hamor and Schechem and their people negotiated with Jacob and his family to exchange their children in marriage beginning with Dinah and Schechem. Jacob's sons who were seriously upset at Schechem's action, deceitfully consented to the agreement only on the condition that all the men of Schechem would succumb to be circumcised. They agreed and were all circumcised in one day. On the third day when all the circumcised men of Schechem were sore, the 2 sons of Jacob, Simeon and Levi, Dinah's brethren took their swords and slew all the males in that city including Hamor and Schechem. They then took their sister Dinah spoiled the city of their wealth and people (Gen.34: 24-30). Defilement is a destroyer of destinies. Don't let anyone destroy your's. Avoid premarital sex, which is the most prevalent form of defilement. *Prayer: Father, help me to remain undefiled and indestructible for you, IJN.*

Monday December 9, 2019
Topic: MAGNIFYING THE MAJESTY

Scriptures: "O magnify the LORD with me, and let us exalt his name together." (Psalm 34:3).

Praise the Lord. Today is December 9th and is day #343 in year 2019. The number of days remaining to end this year is 22. By God's grace, you will be in the company of testifiers who have been mightily blessed by the Lord, and you will see the end of this year and beyond, safe and sound, IJN.

The Bible says "Great is the LORD, and greatly to be praised- - "(Psalm 48:2). Referring to God, a song writer says, "- - Everything written about You is great - - ". The word of God is great, His work is great, His wisdom is great, etc. In today's opening scripture, the Psalmist extends an open invitation to like-minded believers as him to magnify the LORD and exalt His name with Him.

Since God is mindful of man and even magnified him (Job 7:17) it makes sense that believers should magnify God in appreciation of Him. It is a privilege for the believer to be called upon to magnify God because He can magnify Himself (Ezek 38:23).

Ways to magnify the LORD include songs of praise and thanksgiving (Ps 69:30), speaking in tongues (Acts 10:46), calling Him all His names such as The Majesty, The Highest, Almighty, etc.

When Mary was told she was the favored one to be the mother of Jesus she joyously declared, "My soul doth magnify the Lord" (Lk 1:46). Do you want to be favored by God and receive miracles that can reverse impossibility in your life? Then magnify the Majesty in an unusual way to provoke Him to bless you in an unusual way

Prayer: Father, let everything within me and about me magnify Your Majesty, IJN.

Tuesday December 10, 2019
Topic: FAITH DISPELS FEARS

Scriptures: "I sought the LORD, and he heard me, and delivered me from all my fears." (Psalm 34:4).

Praise the Lord. Today is December 10th and is day #344 in year 2019. The number of days remaining to end this year is 21. By God's grace, you shall be bold as a lion and delivered from the torment of fear and you will see the end of this year and beyond, safe and sound, IJN.

Fear can be the best or the worst enemy of man depending on the type of fear under consideration. There are 2 major types of fear - (a) the reverential fear of God which is good and (b) devil-induced fear which is bad. Fear type (a) is described variously as wisdom of God (Job 28:28), the beginning of wisdom (Ps. 110:10, Pro 9:10) the instruction of wisdom (Pro 15:33) or the beginning of knowledge (Pro 1:7). Fear type (b) or devil-induced fear is described as a having torment (1 Jn 4:18). Devil-induced fear can mar or truncate a person's destiny as it did for Eve and Adam.

A born-again Christian should no longer be a victim of fear as he or she has been, by faith, delivered from the demonic bondage of fear. Bible scholars indicate that there are about 365 'fear not' phrases in the Bible. Instead of fear, the believer should love God and people, exercise his/her faith in God and prayerfully trust Him to take him/her victoriously through the situation involving fear.

Prayer: Father, because of my faith in You I shall not fear anything or anyone because I have You as my ally, IJN

Wednesday December 11, 2019
Topic: GOD'S SECOND CHANCE

Scriptures: "And the Lord descended in the cloud, and stood with him there, and proclaimed the name of the Lord" (Exodus 34:5).

Praise the Lord. Today is December 11th and is day #345 in year 2019. The number of days remaining to end this year is 20. By God's grace, the Lord will visit you this season to give you another chance to be blessed, and you will see the end of this year and beyond, safe and sound, IJN.

After Moses broke the first set of 2 tables of the 10 commandments (due to the idolatry sins of the Israelites) God lovingly gave the Israelites another chance to have the commandments. God said to Moses, "Hew thee two tables of stone like unto the first: and I will write upon these tables the words that were in the first tables, which thou brakest" (Exo. 34: 1). If there is any blessing that has eluded you this year, I decree that God will give you another chance to possess your bona fide blessing, IJN.

God invited Moses to the top of mount Sinai where He appeared to him as indicated in today's opening scripture. God reminded Moses who He is and His nature. Moses worshipped God and requested Him to go to the promised land with them (vs. 6-9).

The Lord promised to renew the covenant, work miracles among the people and drive out the enemies (vs. 10-11). Furthermore, God gave Moses many rules that should be written down to be passed on to the Israelites in terms of how they should relate to Him as God and how to live safely among themselves.

Moses spent 40 days and 40 nights on the mount with God and wrote down all the laws as directed. He then returned to the Israelites shinning (Exo 34: 11-34). If you want to shine, learn from Moses and spend time with God in prayer, praise, worshipping and studying His word.

Prayer: Father, please restore all my missed blessings and go with me into year 2018; please drive away all enemies from my way, IJN

Thursday December 12, 2019
Topic: POOR MAN'S ANSWER TO PRAYER

Scriptures: "This poor man cried, and the LORD heard him, and saved him out of all his troubles (Psalm 34:6)

Praise the Lord. Today is December 12th and is day #346 in year 2019. The number of days remaining to end this year is 19. By God's grace, you will not be in any trouble, and you will see the end of this year and beyond, safe and sound, IJN.

There are different types and levels of poverty. Majority of people are familiar with financial poverty because they are either in that category or they know somebody who is. Almost every country of the world has "a poverty line" which is an average income level below which all people whose annual income fall are described as "poor".

One type of poverty that is less known, which nonetheless characterizes majority of people, is "spiritual poverty". This refers to people who literarily are "beggars in spirit" and hungry and yearning for God, The poor in spirit are the first group of people Jesus Christ described as "blessed" in His beatitude address (Matt 5:3)

In today's opening scripture David described himself as poor (most obviously in spirit) and boldly said he cried and the LORD heard him and saved him out of all his troubles. David who was king was not talking of temporal poverty but spiritual poverty. David's testimony should be an encouragement to many believers who are poor in spirit; they stand to get answers to their prayer whenever they cry to God. The LORD who saved David from all the troubles of Saul, Goliath, Archish, Absalom, the Philistines, etc. will save you from all forms of troubled IJN.

Prayer: Father, with respect to poverty, turn my captivity and save me from all troubles in the market place of life, IJN

Friday December 13, 2019
Topic: CHRIST-LIKE CHARACTER

Scriptures: "Keeping mercy for thousands, forgiving iniquity and transgression and sin, and that will by no means clear the guilty; visiting the iniquity of the fathers upon the children, and upon the children's children, unto the third and to the fourth generation" (Exodus 34:7).

Praise the Lord. Today is December 13th and is day #347 in year 2019. The number of days remaining to end this year is 18. By God's grace, the mercy of the Lord shall be multiplied to you forever, and you will see the end of this year and beyond, safe and sound, IJN.

God has high expectations about His children in terms of how we live and behave. Believers' characters are supposed to be Christ-like. That is why the Bible declares, "Let this mind be in you, which was also in Christ Jesus:" (Phil 2:5).

God has wonderful ways of letting His followers know what He expects of us. One of such ways is by telling us who He is and His modus operandi. An example is when Moses was summoned to mount Sinai to receive the 10 commandments for the second time. God gave a long introduction of Himself to Moses part of which is included in today's opening scripture "And the LORD passed by before him, and proclaimed, The LORD, The LORD God, merciful and gracious, longsuffering, and abundant in goodness and truth, Keeping mercy for thousands, forgiving iniquity and transgression and sin, and that will by no means clear the guilt- -" (Exo 34:6-7).

What God is saying indirectly in this long introduction amounts to the words of the Psalmist "- -Ye are gods; and all of you are children of the most High." (Ps.82:6). Thus, the laws Moses was given have important roles to play in helping believers live like the LORD, displaying characters such as being merciful, gracious, longsuffering, abundant in goodness and truth, forgiving iniquity, etc. The more you prayerfully obey the commandments of the LORD the more you will conform to His will and ways.

Prayer: Father transform me from glory to glory till I become like You, IJN

Saturday December 14, 2019
Topic: GOD IS TRUSTWORTHY AND GOOD

Scriptures: "O taste and see that the LORD is good: blessed is the man that trusteth in him." (Psalm 34:8).

Praise the Lord. Today is December 14th and is day #348 in year 2019. The number of days remaining to end this year is 17. By God's grace, you will become a reference point regarding trusting the Lord and receiving His goodness and blessings, and you will see the end of this year and beyond, safe and sound, IJN.

In all ramifications the LORD is Good. The LORD is infinitely and immutably good in Himself and to others. All the divine Persons in the Godhead (Father, Son and the Spirit) are good. The Father is the source of all good and perfect gifts including salvation (James 1:17), the Son is the good Shepherd anointed to do good things (Acts 10:38) and the Spirit is the Comforter that teaches us all things and works good things in our heart including the conviction to become sons and daughter of God (1 Cor 2:13, Rom 8:14).

The phrase "the LORD is good" is repeated 7 times in the Bible (KJV), the first time being in Psalm 34:8 as in the opening scripture above. The Bible says the LORD is good to all, particularly all that wait for Him (Ps. 145:9, Lam 3:25). The goodness of the LORD is pervasive in the believer's life. For example, in the 348 days so far this year, we can count up on numerous daily benefits from God such as sleeping and waking up, eating and drinking, provisions, protection, healings, etc.

The Bible declares, "Being confident of this very thing, that he which hath begun a good work in you will perform it until the day of Jesus Christ" (Phil. 1:6). The good LORD is more than able to continue to infuse goodness into your life to ensure you finish the remaining 17 days of this year with joy. Just continue to trust Him and praise Him for being an infinitely good and trustworthy God. Since God made you in His own image the seed of goodness and trustworthiness are in you. If you water and nourish them, you will add value to your life and glorify God, your maker.

Prayer: Father, please let Your goodness and mercy follow me all the days of my life, IJN

Sunday December 15, 2019
Topic: ANOINTING FOR SUCCESS IN ASSIGNMENT

Scriptures: "And Joshua the son of Nun was full of the spirit of wisdom; for Moses had laid his hands upon him: and the children of Israel hearkened unto him, and did as the LORD commanded Moses" (Deuteronomy 34:9).

Praise the Lord. Today is December 15th and is day #349 in year 2019. The number of days remaining to end this year is 16. By God's grace, you will be anointed and filled with the wisdom of the Lord, and you will see the end of this year and beyond, safe and sound, IJN.

Anointing refers to the sanctifying power of God through the Holy Spirit. Anointing is a critical requirement for successful achievement in any assignment. The great success of Jesus Christ in His earthly assignment was because of anointing (Act 10: 38). King David was anointed (1 Sam 16: 1-13) and he turned out to be about the best king of Israel despite opposition.

Anointing can be ceremonial (as David's) or non-ceremonial. Whoever God chooses to use for special assignment He anoints. Anointing can be transferred in at least 3 ways: (a) by Conduction (e.g. laying on of hand by the anointed on the one to be anointed), (b) by convention (e.g. as in Acts 19:12 where anointing for healing transferred from Paul's body through handkerchiefs or aprons to heal the sick), (c) by radiation through divine waves

After God chose Joshua to succeed Moses in leading the Israelites to the promised land, God told Moses to lay his hands on Joshua and put some of his honor on Joshua (Num 27:12-23). Thereafter, Joshua was filled with the spirit of wisdom as indicated in today's opening scripture. Furthermore, Joshua's assignment became easier in that the Israelites obeyed Him and did whatever he told them readily.

Do you want anointing for successful achievement in your marriage, ministry, job, academics, career, business, etc.? Connect with God the Father, Jesus Christ His Son and with the Holy Spirit and you shall achieve your destiny, IJN

Prayer: Father, anointing me afresh for successful achievement in all areas, IJN

Monday December 16, 2019
Topic: COUNTING AND COMMITTING TO CHRIST

Scriptures: "He collected 1,365 pieces of silver on behalf of these firstborn sons of Israel (each piece weighing the same as the sanctuary shekel)." (Number 3:50, NLT).

Praise the Lord. Today is December 16th and is day #350 in year 2019. The number of days remaining to end this year is 15. By God's grace, you shall be chosen and favored by the Lord, and you will see the end of this year and beyond, safe and sound, IJN.

The entire Bible is the inspired word of God and every aspect of it is important (Heb. 4:12, Ps. 119:89). God chose the Levites over the first born of Israel and said they shall be His (Num 3:11-12). Furthermore, God assigned the Levites to minster to Aaron and be the ones in charge of the sanctuary work (Num 3:5-10).

This preferential treatment of the Levites is most likely due to the fact that the Levites were the only ones that declared to be on the LORD's side when Moses asked that question after he returned from mount Sinai and found Israel worshipping the golden calf (Exo. 32:26-29). If you honor the LORD, He will honor you (1 Sam 2:30)

God commanded Moses to number the Levites as well as the first born of Israel who were one month old and older according to their family. The number for the Levites came to be 22,000 and the first born of Israel were 22, 273 (Num 3:39, 43, MSG). God then told Moses, "Redeem the 273 firstborn Israelites who exceed the number of Levites by collecting five shekels for each one, using the Sanctuary shekel (the shekel weighing twenty gerahs). Give that money to Aaron and his sons for the redemption of the excess number of Israelites."

As indicated in today's opening scripture the total redemption money collected by Moses and given to Aaron was 1365 pieces of silver. From this it is obvious that the collection of money (including tithes, offering, etc.) for doing God's work and for supporting those doing such work is Biblical and God-ordained). Those who are now raising qualms against such collections are victims of ignorance, envy and jealousy. May God have mercy on them, IJN

Action/Prayer: Why don't you count all members of your family, ministry, business, etc.; dedicate the list to God and pray that none shall be missing, IJN (Num 31:48, MSG)

Tuesday December 17, 2019
Topic: WHEN GOD FIGHTS YOUR FIGHTS

Scriptures: "Plead my cause, O LORD, with them that strive with me: fight against them that fight against me (Psalm 35:1).

Praise the Lord. Today is December 17th and is day #351 in year 2019. The number of days remaining to end this year is 14. By God's grace, the Lord will fight against all your enemies, and you will see the end of this year and beyond, safe and sound, IJN.

King David is credited as the author of Psalm 35. Many Bible scholars think the Psalm must have been written when Saul persistently persecuted David and when he was the scorn and derision of many detractors. David knew the LORD as the best advocate who has never lost any case (1 John 2:1) as well as a man of war that never loses a war (Exo 15:3). Hence as in today's opening scripture and the remaining verses of the Psalm, David cried to the LORD to handle his fights.

The battles of life are diverse, numerous and could be overwhelming without divine assistance. These battles may be visible/physical or invisible/spiritual, internal or external, legal, marital, financial, academic, health-related, etc. The good news for a true child of God is that the LORD can fight all of them for you and you don't have to fear.

When the LORD fights your fights, the outcomes are wonderful and could include the following:

You will have peace (Ex. 14:14).
You will prosper (2 Chron 20:25).
You will be safe (Pro 21:31).
Your enemy will flee 7 ways (Dt 28:7).
You will not see your enemies anymore (Ex. 14:13).
You will have great victory (2 Sam 23:9).

If you serve God faithfully, He will fight all your fights and you shall be victorious, IJN.

Prayer: Father help me fight all life's battles including the good fight of faith and to make it to your kingdom, IJN

Wednesday December 18, 2019
Topic: REWARDING OBEDIENCE LIKE THE RECHABITES

Scriptures: "Go unto the house of the Rechabites, and speak unto them, and bring them into the house of the LORD, into one of the chambers, and give them wine to drink" (Jeremiah 35:2)

Praise the Lord. Today is December 18th and is day #352 in year 2019. The number of days remaining to end this year is 13. By God's grace, you will live an obedient life, and you will see the end of this year and beyond, safe and sound, IJN.

God places a very high premium on obedience. He said to the Israelites He would prefer and treasure them above all people if they would obey His voice and keep His covenant (Ex. 19:5). In addition, obedience to God attracts blessings while disobedience attracts curses (Dt 11:27-28).

There is no doubt that the LORD has sense of humor. When He wanted to give the people of Judah a refresher course on necessity for obedience, He instructed Prophets Jeremiah to invite the Rechabites to a wine "party" in one of the chambers in the Temple. The Rechabites lived very simple and frugal life in tents instead of houses and abstained from anything such as vineyard products they thought could pollute or kill them (1 Chron 2:55)

When the Rechabites came to Jeremiah and He served them wine they refused vehemently saying "- -We will drink no wine: for Jonadab the son of Rechab our father commanded us, saying, Ye shall drink no wine, neither ye, nor your sons forever. ----" (Jer. 35:6-8).

In contrast to the abhorrence of the Jews' disobedience, God commended the faithful obedience of the Rechabites to their earthly father and pronounced a blessing on their lineage, saying "Jonadab the son of Rechab shall not want a man to stand before me forever" (Jer. 35:19). Learn from the Rechabites; obey God your heavenly father and your earthly and spiritual fathers and you shall be blessed abundantly, IJN.

Prayer: Father, give me the grace to obey You 100 % so that I will receive rewards akin to that of the Rechabites, IJN.

Thursday December 19, 2019
Topic: BETHEL: A PLACE OF BLESSINGS

Scriptures: "And let us arise, and go up to Bethel; and I will make there an altar unto God, who answered me in the day of my distress, and was with me in the way which I went" (Genesis 35:3)

Praise the Lord. Today is December 19th and is day #353 in year 2019. The number of days remaining to end this year is 12. By God's grace, you will gravitate towards places of having encounter with the Lord and receiving His blessings this season, and you will see the end of this year and beyond, safe and sound, IJN.

Bethel has historical and spiritual significance in the life of the believer. Bethel was one of the first places in the Bible where the Hebrew people met with God. The most famous of these encounters was Jacob's dream of a stairway to heaven, with angels ascending and descending on it. God stood above the ladder and promised to bless and protect Jacob and his descendants. Jacob called the place 'the house of God' and 'the gate of heaven'. Jacob made a vow to God and promised to pay tithe on all God would give him (Gen. 28:10–22).

Shortly after Jacob met and reconciled with Esau, his brother, God spoke to him to go to Bethel and make an altar to God (Gen 35:1). As indicated in today's opening scripture Jacob obeyed God's instruction and went to Bethel with his family. They put away all strange gods and came clean to meet God, giving thanks to Him. God blessed them the more (Gen. 35:9).

From January 1 to this day, 353 days God has blessed us in many ways. Count up your blessings and take a trip to 'Bethel' to build an altar of thanksgiving to God. When Jacob did so God put terror on all his enemies (Gen 35:5). Bethel is a place of many blessings including promotion, productivity, protection and many other wonderful promises from God.

Prayer: Father, thank You for the blessings so far this year; for the remaining days of year 2019, as I prepare to go into year 2020, multiply the blessings of Bethel into my life and family, IJN.

Friday December 20, 2019
Topic: CONFOUNDING DEADLY CONTENDERS

Scriptures: "Let them be confounded and put to shame that seek after my soul: let them be turned back and brought to confusion that devise my hurt. (Psalm 35:4).

Praise the Lord. Today is December 20th and is day #354 in year 2019. The number of days remaining to end this year is 11. By God's grace, all evil workers seeking after your soul shall be confounded and shamed, and you will see the end of this year and beyond, safe and sound, IJN.

In His word the Holy LORD says, "--Vengeance is mine; I will repay- -" (Rom. 12:19). Hence in today's opening scripture we see David, when under deadly attack and persecution, he turned to the LORD for help asking Him to confound, confuse, put to shame and turn back those who sought his soul and were determined to hurt him.

Are you facing persecution or attacks from adversaries? Are there conspirators contending against you to frustrate your efforts. Are destiny destroyers attempting to hurt you or kill you? Don't fear, remain firm and fervent in the Lord and cry to Him for help to defend and protect you as He did for David.

Prayer Points:
1. Father, thank You for 354 days of protection and other blessings so far this year
2. Father, let the expectations and desires of my enemies concerning me fail, IJN.
3. Father, let all the evil agenda of my adversaries become advantage for my advancement.
4. **Pray according to today's opening scripture**
5. **Add your own prayer**

Saturday December 21, 2019
Topic: SHIELDED BY THE SAVIOR

Scriptures: "And they journeyed: and the terror of God was upon the cities that were round about them, and they did not pursue after the sons of Jacob" (Genesis 35:5).

Praise the Lord. Today is December 21st and is day #355 in year 2019. The number of days remaining to end this year is 10. By God's grace, the terror of God will be upon your detractors, and you will see the end of this year and beyond, safe and sound, IJN.

Hearing and obeying God's voice is important in the journey of faith. The Bible declares, "And thine ears shall hear a word behind thee, saying, This is the way, walk ye in it, when ye turn to the right hand, and when ye turn to the left." (Isa. 30:21). May the LORD give you clear direction in this season in the mighty name of Jesus.

Troubles were imminent for Jacob and his family in the city of Schemem where his sons had killed all the males in the area because the prince of Schechem had defiled Dinah, Jacob's daughter (Gen 34). For safety reasons and most specially to build an altar unto Him, God spoke to Jacob to move from Schechem to Bethel (Gen 35:1).

Jacob prepared his family for the move. He told them to put away strange gods, clean up themselves and change their clothes (Gen 35:2-4). Jacob's family obeyed and as indicated in today's opening scripture, they enjoyed divine protection during their journey and reached their destination safely. The Schechemites who would have attacked Jacob and his family in retaliation were preoccupied with terror from God such that they could not tamper with them. Your journeys in the remaining 10 days of year 2019 and in the upcoming years shall be safe and without the knowledge of your enemies. IJN.

Prayer: Father, please shield me and my family against all attacks. Let all our enemies hear great and terrifying noises that will scare them away from us such that we shall enjoy divine protection, IJN.

Saturday December 22, 2019
Topic: ACCOMPLISHING YOUR MISSION

Scriptures: "So Jacob came to Luz, which is in the land of Canaan, that is, Bethel, he and all the people that were with him." (Genesis 35:6).

Praise the Lord. Today is December 22nd and is day #356 in year 2019. The number of days remaining to end this year is 9. By God's grace, your journey through year 2019 will take you and all people with you safely to your destination on December 31st, and you will see and begin the new year 2020 joyfully, IJN.

There are many undertakings that don't get accomplished because God is not involved at all or He was involved at the beginning and along the way, due to little success, pride or other forms of sin sets in to push God out. That will not be your portion, IJN. Total obedience and dependence on God as well as holiness are basic ingredients for success in any endeavor embarked upon by the believer.

When God told Abram to leave his home town for a place yet unknown but to be revealed to him, he obeyed without argument (Gen 12:1-4). Similarly, God spoke to Jacob to leave Schechem for Bethel to live there and build an altar to God. Jacob consented readily without hesitation (Gen. 35:1-4). Not only did Jacob obey God's command to go to Bethel, he did something quite instructive and worthy of emulation. He said to his household and others with him, "- -Put away the strange gods that are among you, and be clean, and change your garments: And let us arise, and go up to Bethel- - "(vv2-3). Knowing that God required holiness from His followers (1 Pet 1-15-16, Matt 5:48), Jacob determined not to harbor sin in his household nor go with sin to do God's assignment in his new place of settlement. What a wise man!

What has God called you to do? Give your life to Jesus Christ? Serve Him?, Win souls?, Lead or plant Churches?, Cast our demons?, Set the captive free?, Heal the sick?, Be a light in the world?, Live long?, Pursue a career?, Forgive?, Do good?, Help build a Church?, etc. Pray about your assigned duties. Depend on God, trust Him totally and live holy in order to accomplish your mission. You shall fulfill your destiny, IJN.

Prayer: Father, help me to successfully accomplish all that You have ordained me to do in year 2017 and beyond, IJN

Monday December 23, 2019
Topic: GOD'S FAITHFULNESS IS GREAT

Scriptures: "Thou drewest near in the day that I called upon thee: thou saidst, Fear not." (Lamentation 3:57).

Praise the Lord. Today is December 23rd and is day #357 in year 2019. The number of days remaining to end this year is 8. By God's grace, the presence of the Lord shall be with you throughout this season, and you will see the end of this year and beyond, safe and sound, IJN.

The prophet writer of the book of Lamentation enumerates his own severe trials but points out his trust in the faithfulness of God and encourages others to do the same (Lam 3:1-22). No matter what you have been through in the 357 days so far this year you have reasons to give thanks to God for, "It is of the LORD'S mercies that we are not consumed, because his compassions fail not. They are new every morning: great is thy faithfulness." (Lam, 3:22-23). If trees can have hope (Job 14:7), how much more you that is made in the image of God.

In the remaining 8 days of this year determine to draw near to God and, according to his promise and as indicated in today's opening scripture, He will draw near to you (James. 4:8). When God is near to you, there no need for you to fear anything but God.

Prayer: Father, because of Your great faithfulness I have confidence that I will end this year gloriously, IJN

Tuesday December 24, 2019
Topic: EVIL OUTCOMES AWAIT MY ENEMIES

Scriptures: "Let destruction come upon him at unawares; and let his net that he hath hid catch himself: into that very destruction let him fall" (Psalm 35:8).

Praise the Lord. Today is December 24th and is day #358 in year 2019. The number of days remaining to end this year is 7. By God's grace, your enemy is the one (not you) that will fall into the trap he/she has set for you, you will see the end of this year and beyond, safe and sound, IJN.

This day is a special day in its own way as it leaves us with only 7 days (perfect number) before year 2020 rolls in. In accordance with the word of God, I decree that the Almighty God shall perfect everything concerning us in the remaining days of 2019 and beyond, IJN (Ps. 138:8).

Psalm 35 is believed to be written by David regarding his persecution by Saul. David prayed for his own personal safety and decrees woes to his enemies as reflected in today's opening scripture. In a way David pray a "back to the sender" type off prayer in this scripture. This is consistent with the word of God that says, "Whoso diggeth a pit shall fall therein: and he that rolleth a stone, it will return upon him" (Pro. 26:27). One of the ways God fights for those that belong to him is to cause their enemies to turn their weapons against themselves (1 Chron 20) and/or feed them with their own flesh and make them drink their own blood (Isa. 49:26). Your enemies are in for troubles!

For God to shield you and turn the destructive plans of your enemy against him/her you must belong to God (give your life to Jesus Christ) and remain connected with Him, praise and pray to Him regularly, and live obedient and holy life. You shall end year 2019 miraculously well, IJN

Prayer: Father, let every enemy that has pursued me this year repent or perish with this year. Please let Your special blessings accompany me into year 2020 and please stay with me throughout that year, IJN.

Wednesday December 25, 2019
Topic: CHRIST IS REASON FOR CHRISTMAS

Scriptures: "And God appeared unto Jacob again, when he came out of Padanaram, and blessed him" (Genesis 35:9).

Praise the Lord. Today is December 25th and is day #359 in year 2019. The number of days remaining to end this year is 6. By God's grace, you will enjoy the Lord appearances and His blessings this season, and you will see the end of this year and beyond, safe and sound, IJN.

Today is Christmas Day, the most important day in the life of all believing Christians as this day is the anniversary birthday of Jesus Christ the Savior of the world. Without Christ, there will be no salvation and no Christmas. Jesus Christ is the reason for the season! The Bible has but one message: God's plan to bring salvation to the world through Jesus Christ.

Today's opening scriptures points to the fact that Jacob, the patriarch, is one of the early people that profited from the pre-incarnate appearance of Jesus Christ. After Jacob stole the birthright of his brother Esau and cheated his uncle Laban, he got to a point when he realized he needed a deliverer. He cried to God for deliverance and God answered him according to His promise (Gen 32: 9-11; Lk 11:9). Based on his quest for deliverance, Jacob was given the opportunity to wrestle with Jesus Christ who blessed him as Jacob requested (Gen. 32: 24-29).

On this birthday anniversary of Jesus Christ, you too can be blessed with deliverance from unrepented sin and its resulting death penalty. Jesus said, he is "- - come to seek and to save that which was lost". If you confess your sins to Him today and ask for forgiveness, He will bless you with salvation as He has promised (John 3:16,18).

Action/Prayer: Like the 3 wise men, let us praise and worship God for the birth of Jesus Christ. Thank Jesus Christ for coming into this world to save sinners like you.

Thursday December 26, 2019
Topic: OMNISCIENT GOD

Scriptures: "Thou hast seen all their vengeance and all their imaginations against me." (Lamentations 3:60)

Praise the Lord. Today is December 26th and is day #360 in year 2019. The number of days remaining to end this year is 5. By God's grace, the imaginations and evil plans of your enemies concerning you shall be disappointed, and you will see the end of this year and beyond, safe and sound, IJN.

One important attribute of God is that He is omniscient meaning that He knows all things. Unlike humans, God does not need to learn anything neither does He forget anything. The Bible says, "- -he is before all things, and by him all things consist" (Col. 1:17). Concerning Jeremiah, God Himself declares, "Before I formed thee in the belly, I knew thee- - "(Jer. 1:5). The omniscience of God is a big advantage for those that belong to Him in so many ways. For instance, God's omniscience makes it possible for Him to be able to answer our prayer before we call (Isa. 65:24). Using His attribute of omniscience, God ensured Elijah's need for water and food were adequately met by a bird and a widow while many were dying of hunger in the land (1 Kgs 17:1-16).

Divine protection against the enemies is another important benefit derivable from God's omniscience attribute. A case in point is when the king of Syria was planning on his bedchamber to attack Israel at specific locations. All his plans were divinely revealed to prophet Elisha which he passed on secretly to Israel (2 Kgs 6:8-14)

In today's opening scripture the prophet writer said the vengeance and imaginations of his enemies were not hidden from God. Obviously, this prophet writer knew that God had said, "Vengeance is mine; I will repay- - ". (Rom. 12:19). Consequently, the prophet prayed to God to render a recompence to his enemies (Lam 3:64-66).

In the battles of life if the Omniscient God is your ally you will always be victorious.

Prayer: Father, please reveal and return to senders all the evil plans of my enemies against me and my family, IJN

Friday December 27, 2019
Topic: BE GOD'S 'BEZALEEL'

Scriptures: "Then wrought Bezaleel and Aholiab, and every wise hearted man, in whom the LORD put wisdom and understanding to know how to work all manner of work for the service of the sanctuary, according to all that the LORD had commanded". (Exodus 36:1)

Praise the Lord. Today is December 27th and is day #361 in year 2019. The number of days remaining to end this year is 4. By God's grace, you will be equipped with wisdom and understanding to enhance your success this season, and you will see the end of this year and beyond, safe and sound, IJN.

Working for God attracts emolument which no human being can match. God has promised to bless all those that serve Him (Ex. 23:25; Heb. 11:6). God has work for everyone who is willing to do His will (Mt. 20:1-7, Ex 35:10-21). A key ingredient needed to do God's work is wisdom which God "- -gives liberally to all men- -"(James 1:5).

As indicated in today's opening scripture, a man called Bezaleel is an example of someone who got wisdom liberally from God to coordinate the building of the Tabernacle. Concerning Bezaleel, Moses said, "- - See, the LORD hath called by name Bezaleel the son of Uri, the son of Hur, of the tribe of Judah; And he hath filled him with the spirit of God, in wisdom, in understanding, and in knowledge, and in all manner of workmanship; And to devise curious works, to work in gold, and in silver, and in brass, And in the cutting of stones, to set them, and in carving of wood, to make any manner of cunning work. ", (Ex. 35:30-33).

You too can be a Bezaleel that God can use to build His sanctuary beginning with your body which is the Temple of the Holy Ghost (1 Cor. 6:19) and including His Church (Mt. 16:18). If you lack that wisdom just ask God; He is generous and will give you liberally, IJN.

Prayer: Father, please give me wisdom and all that I need to be a partaker in building Your Church as well as my life, my family, my career, my ministry etc. for Your glory, IJN.

Saturday December 28, 2019
Topic: SHORT-LIVED GLORY

Scriptures: "Jehoahaz was twenty and three years old when he began to reign, and he reigned three months in Jerusalem". (2 Chron. 36:2)

Praise the Lord. Today is December 28th and is day #362 in year 2019. The number of days remaining to end this year is 3. By God's grace, your glory and honor shall be prolonged, and you will see the end of this year and beyond, safe and sound, IJN.

Josiah was a godly King of Israel. He began to rule when he was 8 years old and he ruled in Jerusalem for 31 years. He devoted considerable amount of efforts for religious reform and motivated his people to serve the LORD. It is said of him that, "- -he did that which was right in the sight of the LORD, and walked in the ways of David his father, and declined neither to the right hand, nor to the left" (2 Chron 34:2). He honored God and God honored him with long reign.

Several Kings that came to the throne after Josiah ruled only for very short period largely because they were wicked and ungodly. Notable among these short-lived kings was Jehoahaz son of Josiah who reigned only for 3 months as noted in today's opening scripture. Jehoahaz was dethroned by the king of Egypt. Jehoahaz's brother who was substituted for him also did not last on the throne because he failed to serve God (vs. 3-4).

The best way to avoid demotion and/or dethronement in your current or subsequent positions is to honor God while you are on the 'throne'. Serve God with your time and treasure, pay your tithes and offering, witness to others and live holy. God will ensure your security and promotion, and no one shall be able to dethrone you, IJN.

Prayer: Father, let my glory be long-lived not short-lived, IJN.

Sunday December 29, 2019
Topic: GIVING DILIGENTLY TO GOD

Scriptures: "And they received of Moses all the offering, which the children of Israel had brought for the work of the service of the sanctuary, to make it withal. And they brought yet unto him free offerings every morning". (Exodus 36:3).

Praise the Lord. Today is December 29th and is day #363 in year 2019. The number of days remaining to end this year is 2. By God's grace, you will give offerings freely and willingly to advance the Lord's work, and you will see the end of this year and beyond, safe and sound, IJN.

Giving offering to God is a covenant command that comes with a promise to receive in return (Lk 6:38, Mal 3:10-12, Acts 20:35). It should be done by faith, in obedience and with a grateful heart to God in appreciation of what He has already done and possibly in anticipation of what we expect Him to do.

We need to revisit the zeal with which Christians of old gave offerings to God and emulate them so that we can optimize our blessings. Abraham gave (in his heart) his son to God and God suspended the natural old age limitation to child birth so that Abraham could have the promised son and uncountable descendants.

In the congregation he led, Moses, at God's command, asked for offering to build the sanctuary only one time (Ex 35: 4-9), but the children of Israel willingly obeyed and brought offerings to Moses EVERY MORNING as indicated in today's opening scripture.

The diligent giving attitude of offerings by Moses' congregation is instructive and worthy of emulation. As we head toward year 2020 consider increasing your portfolio of daily gifts to God (e.g. prayer, praise, witnessing, money, service. etc.,). Remember, you can never out give God.

Prayer: Father let the zeal of Your house consume me (Ps. 69:9) to provoke me to give generously unto You, IJN

Monday December 30, 2019
Topic: CHRIST YOUR CONFIDENCE?

Scriptures: "Then the Rabshakeh said to them, "Say now to Hezekiah, 'Thus says the great king, the king of Assyria: "What confidence is this in which you trust?" (Isiah36:4, NKJV).

Praise the Lord. Today is December 30th and is day #364 in year 2019. The number of days remaining to end this year is 1. By God's grace, you will put your confidence and trust in the Lord, and you will see the end of this year and beyond, safe and sound, IJN.

The word confidence means full trust. Who you put your confidence in can mar or make you. When Christ is your confidence, you've gotten it made for you stand to gain many blessings. Example of these blessings include: (a) safety and deliverance form persecutors (Ps.7:1, Pro 3:26, Ps. 18:2, 30, Ps. 21:8), (b) you get great reward (Heb 10:35), (c) you do not suffer condemnation (1 John 3:21), (d) you receive God's mercy that makes you immoveable (Ps. 21:7, 32:10), (e) you get divine help (Ps. 28:7), (f) you are never put to shame (Ps. 31:1), etc.

There is a sharp difference between king Hezekiah of Judah and king Sennacherib of Assyria. The latter was ungodly and a terrorist who put his confidence in military strength and past victories. King Hezekiah, on the other hand, "did that which was right in the sight of the Lord", --, He trusted in the Lord God of Israel" --And the Lord was with him; and he prospered whithersoever he went forth- -" (2 Kgs 18:3-7).

When Sennacherib was planning to invade Hezekiah's territory, he sent Rabshakeh (his chief military staff) to ridicule and reproach Hezekiah, asserting that his confidence in the LORD could not safe him from been conquered and made to pay tribute (Isa 36: 4-7). When Hezekiah took the threat and reproach to God in prayer God arose to defend him and people of Judah by sending an angel to kill 185, 000 Assyrians invaders. Sennacherib returned home in shame and was killed by 2 of his sons while he was worshipping in the house of Nisroch his god (Isa. 37)

As year 2019 comes to an end and we prepare to transition into 2020, step up your confidence in Jesus Christ and He will defend you and you shall not suffer persecution, terrorism, defeat, ridicule or reproach, IJN.

Prayer: Father, arise for me and let no one question my confidence in You or ask me "Where is your God?" IJN

Tuesday December 31, 2019
Topic: WALKING WITH GOD

Scriptures: "Thus all the days of Enoch were 365 years. Enoch walked with God, and he was not, for God took him" (Genesis 5:23-24, ESV).

Praise the Lord. Today is December 31st and is day #365 in year 2019. The number of days remaining to end this year is 0. By God's grace, we have come to the end of year 2019. Glory be to the Almighty God, the Alpha and Omega who has enabled us to start and end year 2019 alive! May year 2020 be more glorious, IJN.

Hallelujah, we have come to the last day of year 2019. Glory be to God for 365 days of life full of uncountable daily benefits. (Ps. 68:19). While the number of days in year 2019 has now counted down to zero, our blessings, if counted one by one, will count upward to an astronomically innumerable level. God made all these possible and should be praised immensely!

On this last day of year 2019 and as we look forward to year 2020, let us take a brief look at Enoch's life style and learn some lessons. His lifespan here on earth was 'a year of years' - that is 365 days, each day representing a year. By today's standard, that is a long life. God will satisfy you with long life, IJN (Ps. 91:16). What did Enoch do with each day? He walked with God according to today's opening scripture. By walking with God we can infer that Enoch was instructed in things of God, was fixedly purposed and determined to live for God, was holy, perfect, obedient, very intimate with God, worked for God, outstanding among his peers, led his family to serve God, sought the will of God in all his decisions, etc.

God rewarded Enoch for walking with and pleasing Him by translating him such that he should not see death (Heb 11:5, Gen 5:24). God is also calling us to walk with Him or before Him as He told Abraham to do (Gen 17:1). Emulate Enoch and be translated before or during the rapture.

Action / Prayer: As part of your resolution for 2020, prayerfully determine to walk with God each of the 365 days of year 2020 and beyond, IJN

STUDY NOTES

www.ingramcontent.com/pod-product-compliance
Lightning Source LLC
Chambersburg PA
CBHW071232290426
44108CB00013B/1389